PETER BRADLEY was a Labour MP between 1997 and 2005. More recently, he co-founded and directed Speakers' Corner Trust, a charity which promotes freedom of expression, open debate and active citizenship in the UK and developing democracies. He has written, usually on politics, for a wide range of publications, including *The Times*, the *Guardian*, the *Independent*, the *New Statesman* and the *New European*.

The
Last
Train

1. My father with his parents, shortly before his emigration
to the UK in 1939.

The
Last
Train

A Family History of
the Final Solution

PETER BRADLEY

**Harper
North**

HarperNorth
Windmill Green,
Mount Street,
Manchester, M2 3NX

A division of
HarperCollins*Publishers*
1 London Bridge Street
London SE1 9GF

www.harpercollins.co.uk

HarperCollins*Publishers*
1st Floor, Watermarque Building, Ringsend Road
Dublin 4, Ireland

First published by HarperNorth in 2022

1 3 5 7 9 10 8 6 4 2

A catalogue record for this book is
available from the British Library

HB ISBN: 978-0-00-847497-3
TPB ISBN: 978-0-00-847552-9

Printed and bound in the UK using 100%
renewable electricity at CPI Group (UK) Ltd

MIX
Paper from
responsible sources
FSC™ C007454

This book is produced from independently certified FSC™ paper
to ensure responsible forest management.

For more information visit: www.harpercollins.co.uk/green

For my parents, who did not speak of these things,
for my grandparents who could not,
for our children who must,
for you.

CONTENTS

PART FOUR – RESETTLEMENT IN THE WEST

PART FIVE – RESETTLEMENT IN THE EAST

AFTERWORDS

A NOTE TO READERS

This book celebrates my family, and very many like it. But it is also a tragedy in five parts, each exploring a different stage in the evolution of an ancient and enduring hatred, and its impact on their lives.

Though I have sought to provide a broader historical context for my family's story, what is known of it inevitably shapes what I have written. But what happened to my forebears in Germany and in Latvia happened for the same reasons and in the same way to millions of others throughout Europe, across the centuries and in living memory.

There are sections in which I have felt the inclusion of my own observations are justified, and, in the Afterwords, I have added reflections on what I have learned and hope to impart. But I have carefully avoided making personal assumptions about events in which, to my great good fortune, I was not involved. Particularly in the chapters about Latvia, I have relied heavily on the testimony of those who were. Their voices should be heard.

I do not claim that this is a scholarly work. Indeed, I am indebted for much of what I have discovered to the learned historians whose works are referenced. Though I have tried to avoid them, the fault for any errors and misinterpretations is mine. But it is also the case that much about my subject remains unknown and perhaps unknowable. In particular, the study of the Holocaust in Latvia is still in its early stages and there are often widely diverging accounts, among witnesses and historians alike, of what happened and why.

With these provisos, I hope that this book contributes to an important field of learning and to a still more important debate about what we believe, how we came to believe it, and what our beliefs can make us do.

A growing number of scholars and organisations, including the International Holocaust Remembrance Alliance (IHRA), have, partly as a defence against pedantry, adopted 'antisemitism' as their preferred spelling of the term to which I refer throughout as 'anti-Semitism'. I do so only because that is the form most familiar to me and because, ultimately, jewhatred is Jew-hatred however it's spelled. For the same reason, though the term 'anti-Semitism' is nineteenth century in origin, I have applied it to all historical variants of the same prejudice.

In most instances, I have referred to German placenames with, where appropriate, the native form in brackets. Where there are better-known English alternatives, for example, Nuremberg (for Nürnberg), Munich (for München) and Vienna (for Wien), I have used them. I have retained the spelling of the American publications from which I have quoted.

PROLOGUE

A young man, 24 years of age, is sitting on a park bench in the sunshine. Except for something of a Mohican haircut, there's little about him that would attract your attention. Just an ordinary young man.

He's writing a letter home. It's a cheerful letter, though written in the stilted English of someone who's learned the language in the classroom but never spoken it colloquially.

He's writing to his parents 'of what kind my deepest impressions were in the first few days I spent in this country'.

He's fascinated by the English. 'I cannot find at all that English people are stiff or formal,' he writes. 'People are very polite, the most used phrases are "thank you so much" and "I'm sorry".'

He observes approvingly that the police are 'very obliging' and the people so honest that 'a newsagent can leave his bookstall and everyone who wants a newspaper lays his fee upon the table'.

He's amazed that young women smoke publicly in the street and 'go only in their bathing suits in some parks' and to see 'menfolk pushing prams or carrying bags'.

He's particularly impressed that grown men are not embarrassed to fly their kites or sail their model boats in the park. The English, he notes, love sport and animals and talking about the weather.

He ends by assuring his parents that the best way to learn English is through conversation: 'you easily can enter into one with any stranger sitting besides you on the seat or in the bus'. 'When you come here,' he writes, 'you will soon learn this language.'

1

But they never came.

The last time he saw them was as he boarded the train west for the Channel coast at Frankfurt South station on 10 May 1939. The train they took in November 1941 carried them to their deaths in the east.

On 26 March 1942 his mother, along with two aunts and two uncles, were made to strip naked and then machine-gunned into a ditch near Riga. His father Sally, a proud German patriot who'd served his country in the First World War, was last seen towards the end of 1943, a slave labourer on the Latvian railway. The memorial stone he shares with his wife Bertha and sister Meta in Bamberg's Jewish cemetery records that they were 'Aus der Heimat vertrieben': driven from their homeland and that Sally 'im Osten umgekommen': perished in the east.

The young man was one of the very few granted a temporary British visa on the eve of war and released from the concentration camp at Buchenwald, where he'd acquired his haircut. He had wanted to emigrate to the United States but the Americans were not interested in Jewish refugees – unless their name was Einstein.

The British classified the young man, along with thousands of other refugees who wanted only to enlist and fight the Nazis, as an 'enemy alien' and shipped him off to an internment camp in Canada. He sailed on the MV *Ettrick*, just 24 hours after the *Arandora Star*, carrying a similar human cargo, was torpedoed and sunk by a U-boat.

In 1942, the young man was finally allowed to join the British Army. Even then, when the troop train that crossed Canada to the eastern seaboard stopped to take on coal on American soil, armed US National Guards surrounded the carriages to ensure that none of the eager recruits went AWOL in the land of the free.

During the war the young man married a girl he knew from Frankfurt and when he came back from the army he got a job and they raised a family.

He lived a long and quiet life in middle England, worked hard, did well by his children. He never complained. He was never bitter. He bore no ill will.

He died in 2004, on the sixty-fifth anniversary of the day he fled his homeland, as a refugee, for the country he cherished and served as a free man.

I only know much of what I've written because he wrote down his family history, neither in anger nor for pity, but just so his children would know.[1]

INTRODUCTION

It is perhaps unusual to be haunted by something you yourself have written. But an image I conjured many years ago in the article that forms the Prologue to this book has tugged at my sleeve ever since, insisting that I had begun unfinished business.

It was the image of two trains, heading in opposite directions. One carried my father, Fred Bradley, west to a new life; the other bore my grandparents, Sally (Salamon) and Bertha Brandes, to the east, where they were lost.

Over the years, I could sense the resolution forming, unbidden but undeniable, that one day I should follow the route my grandparents had been compelled to take.

I had no detailed plan, no greater ambition. Had the path of Sonderzug Da 32, the 'special train' which 'evacuated' 1,000 Jews from Nuremburg to Riga, been easily discoverable, I might have made my journey and left it at that.

But it was not. There are no reliable records to be found and, in any event, where eighty years ago there had been railway tracks, now, for long stretches, there are none. So the route I eventually travelled could only be approximate and symbolic.

And in the end, my journey was of a different kind. When I set out in search of a rail route, I had not anticipated that the quest would lead me from one subject to another, from a single source to many others: to family documents, to libraries and archives, to histories, memoirs and testimony, to the accounts of similar journeys made by similar, haunted grandchildren.

Every question I asked led me back to my family – to my father who had been saved and to my grandparents who had not.

And always behind the urge to know what happened to them, lay a more profound, more insistent question: why? What awful accumulation of ideas and events had led my grandparents to that train?

How had Sally and Bertha's friends and neighbours come to ostracise them, boycott their business, force them from their home, plunder their property, abuse them in the street, rejoice as they were marched to the station?

Why did they put Sally and Bertha on that train?

Had they simply been bewitched by an ideology that at that time and in that place proved impossible to resist? Or had the Nazis harnessed a force with a deeper, and, perhaps, more enduring and universal appeal?

These questions and the answers I sought became the route I followed and the journey I made.

I did not originally intend to write a book, partly out of respect for my father's and my grandparents' privacy, and partly because it sometimes seems there has been so much remembrance that one more family's cannot really be required.

But I have also been driven by a powerful, external stimulus: what I have written is as much about the future as it is about the past.

My view of the world has changed over the last few years. The UK's decision to leave the European Union in June 2016 was deeply disillusioning for me. Whatever its bureaucratic faults and democratic deficiencies, the EU has brought nations and peoples closer together and, after centuries of bloodletting, helped to underwrite peace in Europe for three generations. That Britons could reject that legacy, preferring instead an outdated and misguided nationalism and a crude and ungenerous xenophobia, was profoundly unsettling to me, as it was to so many others.

The outcome of the US general election just five months later was a shock of equal magnitude. As the polls closed on the eastern seaboard, I tuned in to the BBC to hear the pollsters and the pundits confidently predicting that Hillary Clinton was about to become the first female President. I drifted into sleep, relieved and reassured.

I woke some time before dawn to find that the world had turned on its head. I switched off the radio in dismay and disbelief. In the darkness and the silence, as I sought the refuge of dreams, I was visited by an unexpected and most unwelcome thought: for the first time in my life, the world may not be the safe place for people like me, and for others, that I had always taken it to be. The years since have provided little comfort.

We are living in times of great turbulence and uncertainty, when, once again, simple solutions to complex problems appear so alluring to so many. All over Europe, in the US, in Russia and elsewhere, populist parties and authoritarian leaders – nationalist, isolationist, anti-immigrant and often both racist and anti-Semitic – are gaining ground. The politics of unreason are growing in appeal; democracy, it seems, is no longer inviolable.

Perhaps we have entered an inevitable historical cycle of doubt and uncertainty from which our democratic principles will emerge reinforced and reasserted. I hope that history will show that I have overreacted. Certainly, I don't feel at imminent risk. But at what point in my grandparents' lives did they realise that their world had irreversibly changed and that they were in jeopardy? And at what point did they know that it was too late to save themselves?

Against such a background, I have sought to understand and, perhaps, to explain why and how my family's story is relevant to what we think we know about our own history, and to the beliefs – the truths, the half-truths and the falsehoods – that shape our lives and those of others today.

For what we don't see and don't know, as much as what we do, determines the choices we make. We need to know our history, and ourselves, better.

* * *

What is it, here in Britain, that we might not see?

We believe, with some justification, that ours is a civilised and generous society, for centuries a place of enlightenment and sanctuary. We are proud that, unlike other European countries, we do not have an anti-Semitic tradition to speak of. In the Middle Ages, the Inquisition in Spain and Portugal converted Jews at the point of a sword and then burned them at the stake for good measure. There was no such persecution here.

Perhaps we do not see that this was because centuries earlier, in 1290, England had been the first European country to expel its Jews. France followed and, 200 years later, so did Spain, Portugal and a multitude of other kingdoms and principalities. There were no Jews in England when Shakespeare imagined the iconic, Jew-defining Shylock. There were no Jews in England for 366 years.

And perhaps we do not know that it was in this country, in Norwich in 1144, that the deathless, murderous calumny that the Jewish faith demands the ritual sacrifice of Christian children first emerged. The Blood Libel was made in Britain.

Of course, that was all a long time ago. But consider our more recent history. When we stand before the Kindertransport monument outside London's Liverpool Street station, we contemplate the weak, defenceless victims of European barbarism (or, rather, the ones who look most like us). The children are waiting, with sad, respectful resignation, for deliverance. We celebrate the humanity and compassion of the country that saved them.

But there is an absence here. We do not see the anguished parents they left behind. Because the parents were not permitted to accompany their children to freedom; they had to give up their sons and daughters and face their futures in Nazi Europe. That was the price they were asked to pay for their children's salvation. They are not represented in that poignant sculpture because they were not there.

It's right that we take pride in the saving of the children. But perhaps we do not see the limits, the rugged edges, of our compassion. There are known histories but, as the Black Lives Matter movement and the recent reassessment of 'empire' have reminded us, there are other histories – other people's histories – too.

My father didn't reach this country on the Kindertransport. He was a young man, almost 24, when he arrived in London in May 1939, after five months in Buchenwald. But, like the children in the sculpture, he had parted from his parents on a railway platform in central Europe. He knew he would not see them again.

He had seen it coming; his parents had not. They were assimilated Jews, German patriots, solidly middle class, upstanding citizens. His father was a First World War veteran. They thought they would outlive the Nazis. By the time they understood they could not, it was too late: they were trapped. No country would take the elderly and useless: their lives had no value.

Adolf Hitler told the Reichstag in January 1939: 'it is a shameful spectacle to see how the whole democratic world is oozing sympathy for the poor tormented Jewish people, but remains hard-hearted and obdurate when it comes to helping them'.[1]

The rest is history.

Except that it isn't. Because in living memory, the US and the UK and other tolerant, civilised democracies have turned a blind eye to genocide in Europe, Africa and Asia and are today closing their borders to desperate refugees from brutal conflicts.

And because the Holocaust did not destroy anti-Semitism.

My family's story is about those who were let in and those who were kept out; about the saved and the lost. I want to tell how it came to be that, after centuries of life in Germany – of poverty and prosperity; of anonymity and distinction; of segregation and public service – only seven members of my parents' families survived the twelve years of Nazi rule, while at least forty perished in the Holocaust and perhaps as many fled abroad.

As we thread our uncertain way through a larger history, I hope that how and why I came to know and now tell that story will help in some way to account for the absent, to restore their lost voices and, by illuminating the choices we have made in the past, to draw into a sharper contrast those that face us today.

My article, those many years ago, had one more, concluding paragraph: 'And to mark this special day to commemorate the Holocaust that swept away our family and six million others – Jews, gypsies, black people, Slavs, the disabled, homosexuals, liberals, Jehovah's Witnesses, people like you and me – and to mark the genocides that have followed since, I set out the bare bones of it, lest we forget.'

It is to clothe those naked bones that I have written this book.

And because other trains may wait in other stations.

Part One

ORIGINS

'Then answered all the people, and said,
His blood be on us, and on our children.'

Matthew 27:25, King James Version

1

FINDING MY FATHER

As I grew up, it was always said that I took after my mother's family. But, as each year passes, I see more and more of my father peering back at me from the bathroom mirror.

We weren't close. My mother was always the dominant force in our family affairs, or at least in mine. My father was never so content, or self-absorbed, as when securely anchored to his favourite armchair behind the breakwater of his daily newspaper. His hobbies and interests were solitary – stamp collecting, photography, trains – though every year until he was 79 he brought his skis down from the loft, packed a ruck-sack and set off by rail for the high Swiss Alps. There, for a blissful fortnight, he met up with old friends from another place and time, flirted innocently with the chalet girls and hurtled down steep, white slopes.

My father was different. He never played football with me in the garden. He never took me to cricket matches. It seems uncharacteristic but I do recall him lining up for the hundred yards dash at a school sports day. The other fathers towered over him. They seemed so athletic, so handsome, so heroic. He ran as fast as he could but he was no match for these Englishmen.

Our family was different. My sister Anne and I sensed it but didn't know how or why. When we were small, our parents often spoke German to each other at table but stopped when we began to pick out words and phrases we weren't supposed to understand. They didn't explain why they spoke this foreign language; nor did they encourage us to learn it. They didn't want us to be different.

Then one day, prying as inquisitive children do, I came upon a document in a desk drawer that suggested that our father had not been born with our family name. Fred Bradley had been Fritz Brandes. He had been someone else. He had had another life. For an impressionable young boy, a voracious consumer of myths and legends, this discovery was exhilarating as well as unsettling. But for many more years it remained a source of mystery: what did it mean, for our father, for us, for me? There were no answers, not least because we did not know the questions to ask.

But this sense of 'difference' had a profound effect on me from a very early age. It has, I believe, influenced almost everything I have done over the last sixty years – for better and for worse. It has made me sometimes envy the certainties and self-confidence of others. But it has also emboldened and enlightened me. It has taught me always to question and often to reject the complacency of received opinion and the inequity of the status quo. It has helped me make right decisions; it has led me into error.

Throughout my life – at school, at work, even as a Member of Parliament – I have never been able to resolve whether I am part of the establishment looking out, or an outsider looking in. No matter how much at times I've wanted to fit in, I've never really felt that I do. At critical moments, and not always wisely, I have made it a point of principle not to. As I say, this sense of difference has been both a strength and a weakness, a blessing and a curse.

My father did want to fit in. He did not want to be different. He did not ask to be blessed, cursed, or chosen. In 1933, at the age of 18, he was an intelligent, industrious only child of loving and relatively well-off parents in the beautiful Bavarian city of Bamberg. A promising, probably prosperous life lay before him. He should have had the opportunities I – and most of his school friends – had.

But he was Jewish.

He was a German Jew. That was the mystery. That was the difference. That was the problem.

From 1933 onwards, the world closed in on him until, in the wake of the terrible events of Kristallnacht in November 1938, his father was sent to Dachau and he to Buchenwald. It was there that he learned, as a matter of life or death, never to stand out in a crowd.

And in 1933, in Frankfurt, my mother was a vivacious young girl of 15, creative, sporty and popular with her classmates, until many of them stopped talking to her. For she was Jewish too.

My mother escaped Germany in 1936. My father was one of the last German Jews to emigrate, just four months before his country of refuge declared war on the country of his birth. By then, many of his generation – cousins, Jewish friends and acquaintances – had left for the USA, for Britain, for Shanghai, for the Philippines, South Africa, Latin America; for any continent, any country, any place that would take them. Most of the older generation – his parents, his uncles and aunts – stayed behind, too committed to their Fatherland, too confident in the service they had rendered it, too set in their ways to uproot, and too blind to the consequences of remaining.

My father was for the rest of his life unstintingly grateful for the safe home Britain had given him. He understood and appreciated the value of the rights and freedoms that so many who have not had to live without them now take for granted.

But as a young refugee in London, though he met with great kindness, he also routinely encountered prejudice, because he was twice different: a German and a Jew. With more cause than most, he wanted to fight the Nazis. Instead, he was interned as an enemy alien, first in a camp on the Isle of Man and then far away in Canada. And when he was finally allowed to join the British army in 1942, he was sent not to Europe to confront the enemy, but to India to defend the empire. There, thousands of miles from anywhere he could call home, he learned that he would never see his parents again.

After all my father had endured, perhaps it's no surprise that he wanted to live an anonymous, unremarkable, quintessentially English life. But despite the dark memories, the distance and the years, he remained fondly nostalgic about his childhood in Bamberg. He cherished the friendships he made there, especially with those who had not ostracised him when the Nazis came to power. He restored contact with many of them after the war and attended annual school reunions until late in life. He rarely spoke about the hardships or the injuries of the Nazi years, but he remembered every kindness.

My father did not identify as a Jew, certainly in my lifetime. He had grown up in a Jewish household, albeit a liberal and assimilationist one. His father Sally was a model modern German Jew: as a German, he was a veteran and a staunch patriot; as a Jew, he dutifully served on the community's committees and chaired Bamberg's celebrated synagogue choir, in which he sang solos in a magnificent *basso profundo*. His mother Bertha was less observant by inclination but compliant by nature. As my father noted in the brief family history he wrote in later life: 'although we ate no pork, the household was no longer kosher in the accepted sense; we observed the Passover laws, the High Holidays, fasted on Yom Kippur, lighted candles on Chanukkah, and my father went regularly to synagogue on Friday nights and Saturdays'.[1]

When my father emigrated, he took his Lederhosen with him. As far as I know, he never wore them again. But they remained an important memento of a lost innocence – so much so that, writing home from India in 1945, he referred to them as 'a holy relic' and instructed my mother: 'please make no attempt to clean them. This is sacrilege!'[2] He kept them for the rest of his life; I have them still.

He also brought with him his Tallit and his Torah, his prayer shawl and holy book.[3] These I was more surprised to find in a small trunk, which, until my mother's death in 2010, had remained hidden in the dark recesses of a cupboard under the stairs. Inside rested cherished fragments of earlier lives: with his holy books and his regimental insignia were gathered in neat, chronological bundles the 700 letters he and my mother had daily exchanged when he was in India. There too, each stamped by the censor's swastika, were the thirty-five that had reached him from his parents between the time of his emigration and the eve of their deportation.

I don't know whether or how often he revisited the memories he had reverently preserved in that modest wooden trunk. But he did not, perhaps could not, abandon them.

* * *

My father contended with his past. He did not deny it, but he allowed it little purchase on the present. Though he had preserved the artefacts of his religious affiliation, what happened during the Nazi years had destroyed what little faith he had had.

My grandfather had been both a Jew and a German – or a German and a Jew. My father was an assimilationist first and last. For him, racial identity had condemned the Jews of Europe to a fate from which the Jewish faith could not, and the Jewish God did not, save them. The covenant was broken beyond repair. If his parents had had to die because they were Jews, my father wanted no more of Judaism; he simply wanted to live as an Englishman. So the fracture of his faith led him also to repudiate the idea of a Jewish race: in his view, those who did not believe in a Jewish God could no more be Jews than an atheist can be a Christian. As he wrote: 'My definition of a Jew is a person who professes the Jewish faith and practices observance of its ordinances to a greater or lesser extent. As regards a Jewish "race", this is without scientific foundation. In an age of greater religious tolerance, it was substituted by those miserable peddlers of hate, the anti-Semites, to keep in being an entity they could vent their pathological spleen on and hold responsible for all the ills of society.'

This rejection of Jewish identity had taken deep root. For many Jews, Nazism had made an unanswerable case for Zionism as a national liberation movement and for the creation of a Jewish homeland as the best and perhaps only hope for what remained of world Jewry. My father was not a Zionist, though always a steadfast supporter of Israel. Even as the case for the Jewish state was being made and won as the ghastly evidence of the death camps emerged, his often-strident antipathy to Zionism and Zionists peppers the letters he wrote my mother from India. In his history, he wrote: 'That the concept of race has been taken on board by the Zionists (though they strenuously object to being called racists) is not to their credit. The Jews are the Chosen People – chosen for what: discrimination, ostracism, persecution, the Holocaust?'

Over time, this antagonism diminished. In the mid-1990s, he wrote to a fellow Bamberger: 'I am no longer an anti-Zionist, but a non-Zionist; I wish them the best of luck, but do not identify myself with them.'[4]

My father's views were only in part a response to the traumatic history through which he had lived. They were also the product of a scientific mind and a humanist instinct. Nonetheless, despite my own commitment to rationalism, they were a point of difference between us.

I was raised far less of a religious Jew than even he was. I knew nothing of the Torah or the Talmud, never saw the inside of a synagogue, never observed the Sabbath, knew neither Hebrew nor Yiddish, never openly identified as a Jew.[5]

But I felt that if our family history had taught us anything, it was that we had not been granted the right to decide for ourselves who we were – or who we are.[6] My grandfather was born a Prussian and lived as a patriotic German. But he died an alien Jew, robbed of his home, far from his Fatherland. Our identities and our fates are too often determined by those who have the power to tell us what we are and to treat us as they may. We live our lives on licence – not just the Jews but many minorities.

We are sometimes on the inside, often on the outside, sometimes both at once. My father wanted to bury 'the difference' deep in the earth where it would gradually degrade and dissolve. I believed that there would always be those determined to seek it out and dig it up. For, wherever they have lived, Jews have always prayed and sometimes imagined that they were at last here to stay. But rarely have they been in any place long.

To understand why, we must take two steps back, first to medieval Europe and then 1,000 years earlier still.

2

THE ARCHITECTURE
OF ANTI-SEMITISM

My father loved Bamberg. Little more than a year after the end of war, at a time when he would have been acutely aware of the fate of his parents, he wrote to the Mayor, Luitpold Weegmann, 'in spite of everything, I shall never forget my Bamberg'.[1]

In the 1930s, the people of his home town were no different to the people of towns and cities throughout Germany and far beyond. There were certainly those who despised and resisted Adolf Hitler. Weegmann, who had been in office before the Nazis came to power, was one of them. My father recounted admiringly that: 'he got the sack because he had called Julius Streicher a "Schleimscheisser" [slimy shit] ... in front of a newspaper vendor who tried to sell him *Der Stürmer*'.[2] The Mayor was perhaps fortunate to have lost only his job.

There were the friends and acquaintances whose private compassion and small, symbolic acts of kindness remained forever in my father's grateful memory. He called them 'the light in the darkness' of those days.

But there were also those about whom my father had less to say; those who were ready to do their Jewish neighbours harm, who heaped insults and indignities on them, who connived in and benefited from their misfortunes. There were those who set fire to their synagogue, ransacked their property, assaulted them. There were the ones who meticulously planned their deportation and those who joined the Gestapo or the SS and played their part in the Final Solution.

And there were the many more, the majority, who were at best indifferent to the fate of their former school friends, workmates and fellow citizens.

My father had faith in humanity. He wanted the good he sought to outweigh the evil he had found. But how could it have been that, for so many years and with such barbarous consequences, the bad had so completely overwhelmed the good?

How did Nazi ideology find such fertile ground for so all-consuming a hatred of the Jews? How could an irrational prejudice against a tiny minority of Germany's population – the preoccupation of just a handful of political activists in the 1920s – have transformed the whole of Europe into a charnel house within two short decades?

National Socialism was born of the dreadful congruity of many factors: the ignominy of Germany's defeat in the First World War; the humiliation misguidedly meted out to it by the victors at Versailles; the collapse of its post-war economy; the fear of Bolshevism; and the frailty of the democratic institutions of the Weimar Republic. Hitler promised to sweep all these disasters aside and to restore to Germans the virtues for which they yearned: order, prosperity and pride. He was going to make Germany great again.

For the Nazi ideologues, political, economic and even military strength could not, on their own, establish Germany's supremacy. They had first to bend the will of the German people to the imagining and then the fulfilment of their national destiny. But if Germans were to be convinced that they were indeed an invincible master race, they had first to be freed from the indignities of the recent past.

The means of absolution were simple: defeat was evidence not of weakness but of treachery; Germany could only have been brought low by the betrayal of an enemy within – and that would never be allowed to happen again. In a banner emblazoned on every front page, *Der Stürmer* proclaimed, 'Die Juden sind unser Unglück!' ('The Jews are our misfortune!') Germany would triumph only when the Jews were utterly and irrevocably vanquished.

But the Nazis did not begin with a blank canvas. Not even *Der Stürmer*'s slogan was original.[3] Anti-Semitism was deeply rooted in

German – or, rather, Christian – culture. The Nazis did little to the Jews that others had not done to them over the previous 1,500 years, from sun-baked Andalusia to the snow-bound Pale of Settlement and everywhere between.

In 2001, three years before my father died, my wife Annie and I accompanied him and my mother on a final pilgrimage to the places in Germany in which they had grown up.

In Bamberg's beautiful thirteenth-century cathedral he pointed out with proprietorial pride the historic ornaments with which he was so familiar. Here the sculpted tombs of popes, monarchs and Holy Roman Emperors, here the ancient relics, here the wonderful wood-carvings above the altars. There, on its plinth, the enigmatic Bamberger Reiter, the 'Bamberg Horseman', thought variously to represent kings, emperors and even the Messiah of the Book of Revelation. For Claus von Stauffenberg, the aristocratic army officer who tried to blow up Hitler, he was a symbol of resistance; for the Nazis, the ideal of racial purity.

But my father didn't guide us to what have become for me the most significant of all the cathedral's adornments. It was another 18 years before, standing outside in the Cathedral Square, I gazed up at the two elegant statues that flank the grand, Romanesque Fürstenportal, the Princes' Gate.[4] To the left, *Ecclesia*, the Christian Church, stands majestic and serene, consecrated by a noble crown; to the right, *Synagoga*, the Jewish synagogue, bowed, bare-headed and blindfolded, leans upon a broken staff. The tablets of the Jewish law are slipping from her left hand.

For all the beauty of both figures, equal in grace, this medieval depiction of the divergence of the Old and New Testaments had another purpose. It also proclaimed the unmistakable, unalterable conviction that Christianity had triumphed over Judaism for all time and that Christians had established their hegemony over Jews in the here-and-now. The sculpted relief of the Last Judgement in the Tympanum above the great door points the moral: to the left, above *Ecclesia*, the beatific believers lift their eyes to their Saviour; to the right, the gurning damned, conspicuous among them a money-lender, are dragged to hell by a grimacing demon. On the column beneath *Syngoga*, for good measure, a devil is gouging out the eyes of a Jew already, like her, blind to the hope of salvation.

The statues and the relationship between them were of the greatest significance in thirteenth-century Europe. In Bamberg, they framed the cathedral's ceremonial entrance for both bishops and princes, and they faced out onto the public realm of the great square, broadcasting their indivisible theological and political doctrine in incorruptible stone.

They were no less prominent in other great medieval cathedrals, notably at Strasbourg and Reims. For the church buildings of the Middle Ages were not just symbols of spiritual and temporal power; they were also monumental public billboards. The good Christians of these cities would have had little difficulty interpreting their message.

Nor did my father point out the altogether coarser imagery inside the cathedral, the two caricatures of Jewish men daubed onto the otherwise plain high-vaulted ceiling above the nave.[5] It's quite likely that he was unaware of their existence. The ceiling is so high, the cartoons so randomly placed and so indistinguishable, that, if you noticed them at all, you would assume they were patches of damp or discoloured plaster. I only found them through the magnifying lens of my camera. But

2. Bamberg Cathedral's great Fürstenportal.

22

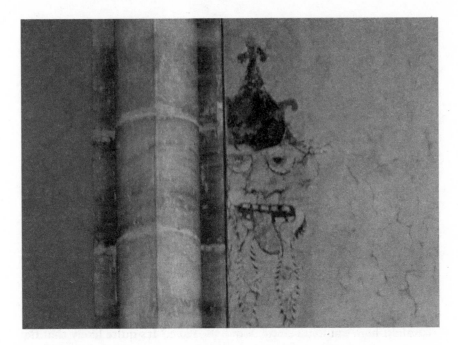

3. A Jew, identified by his pointed hat, glares down malevolently on the Christian congregation in Bamberg Cathedral.

there they are: through heavy-lidded, starting eyes, the Jews stare down malevolently on the Christians below, their noses protruding, their teeth exposed, their tongues lolling and drooling from their open mouths.

Many centuries ago, while the scaffolding allowed, someone with the barest artistic skill was authorised, or otherwise thought it necessary, to place these grotesques on the ceiling of this grand and dignified cathedral. There they have remained.[6]

The contrast between the rough depictions of these brazen Jewish intruders in the house of God and the sculpted beauty of the sorrowful *Synagoga* outside could not be starker. Nor could its meaning be clearer: *Synagoga* reassures us that so long as Judaism accepts its supersession and its subjugation, it has an acknowledged place in the Christian scheme. But the grotesques warn that in the everyday world, Jews, especially those who cling obstinately to their discredited faith, are to be feared and reviled.

The caricature of the repulsive, degenerate Jew became a standard feature in the sacred art of the Middle Ages and of anti-Jewish propaganda in every age thereafter. As Simon Schama has pointed out, the attribution to Jews of bestial, sub-human qualities was not a twentieth-century invention: 'The ugliness of their physiognomy was the unmistakable sign of their moral filthiness. They became in the Christian imagination a species of beast, given to beastly habits: hence the appearance on the sculptural decoration of German cathedrals and churches ... of the Judensau – Jew-Sow – Jews sucking from the teats of a sow and opening their mouths wide to ingest its excrement.'[7]

And as the once serene depictions of *Ecclesia* and *Synagoga* absorbed the coarser, uglier character of the Bamberg graffiti, their message became less allegorical and more menacing. In the carving of a fourteenth-century choir stall in Erfurt Cathedral, a resolute *Ecclesia*, protected by a shield embossed with Christian symbols, is nobly mounted on a prancing steed. She is poised to drive her lance into the throat of a defenceless *Synagoga* who, with eyes tight shut, straddles a sow. This very public art speaks not just of the defeat of a religion, but also of the necessary punishment of a people.[8]

3

ARTICLES OF FAITH

How many times down the centuries and with what awful consequences had the calumnies against the Jews been repeated and recycled
– that they are Christ-killers, child-murderers and the poisoners of
wells; that they are alien, duplicitous and decadent; that they are usurers
and profiteers; that they are communists, cowards and conspirators;
that they are vermin – before Joseph Goebbels concluded that: 'if you
tell a lie big enough and keep repeating it, people will eventually come
to believe it'.

Of how many giants of the European tradition, Christian saints and
secular heroes alike, has an often outspoken and sometimes violent
hatred of the Jews been overlooked, excused or forgiven?

For all their antagonisms and divergences, one objective unites the
religious, intellectual and political movements that have most significantly shaped European history. All have predicated their own
fulfilment on the disappearance of the Jews: Christianity through persecution and conversion; the Enlightenment through atheism and
assimilation; Marxism by ideology and absorption; Nazism by extermination.

Anti-Semitism is not an aberration. It does not strike like debris from
deep space. It is an infection in the body of our culture. Without this
understanding, it is doubtful that we will be able either properly to
diagnose the symptoms as they mutate and reassert themselves, or to
develop and apply effective remedies against them.

25

We need to begin with the ideas and events that forged our European culture, for they explain why the cathedrals at Bamberg, Strasbourg, Reims and Erfurt were decorated as they were and, ultimately, provide the cumulative historical context for what happened in the twentieth century.

Perhaps they also explain why, just twenty years after traumatised British soldiers had liberated Belsen, boys at my school, rubbing their noses and whining nasally, could appropriate 'Jew' as a casual term of abuse for anyone who failed to share his crisps at break, or was considered in some other way mean, greedy or undependable. Perhaps they should be forgiven. I still have *The Pocket Oxford Dictionary*, presented to me along with the Bible when I entered the school – my passports to truth and virtue. It's before me now: venerable, much-thumbed, swathed in Sellotape. Authoritatively and unapologetically, it defines 'Jew' as '1. n. Person of Hebrew race; (fig., hist.) unscrupulous usurer or bargainer. 2. V.t. (colloq.) Cheat, overreach'.[1]

Uniquely as a term of abuse, 'Jew' requires no derogatory adjective. It's why, in part at least, I never refer to myself as a Jew, always as Jew*ish*.[2] Perhaps it's also why, more nobly and certainly more defiantly, David Baddiel, comedian, author, screenwriter and more, describes himself in his Twitter profile simply as 'Jew'.

And perhaps these ingrained ideas, these articles of faith, explain why, another half-century later, age-old anti-Semitic tropes have returned to currency in mainstream politics in the United States, across continental Europe, and in the UK.

As Simon Schama points out, the seeds of the timeless hatred of the Jews were planted in the Christian Bible. It is in John's Gospel that Jesus himself accuses the particularly pious Jewish Pharisees of willing his death: 'Ye are of your father the devil, and the lusts of your father ye will do. He was a murderer from the beginning, and abode not in the truth, because there is no truth in him. When he speaketh a lie, he speaketh of his own: for he is a liar, and the father of it.'[3]

It is St Paul who, in his letter to the Thessalonians, memorably indicts the Jews as Christ-slayers who have 'both killed the Lord Jesus, and their own prophets' and warns that 'they please not God, and are contrary to all men … for the wrath is come upon them to the uttermost'.[4]

In the fourth century, as the early Church strove to assert itself over the Synagogue, these teachings were of central importance and the literature long established. In the mid-second century, Justin Martyr's *Dialogue with Tryphon*, echoing Paul, cast the Jews as dissolute Christkillers, rejected by God. Fifty years later, Tertullian's *Adversus Iudaeos* argued that, with Judaism now obsolescent, the old laws, the ones falling from Synagoga's hand, had been superseded and the Christians had succeeded the Jews as God's chosen people.

At the end of the fourth century, the great theologian St Augustine of Hippo, meditating in his *Confessions* on the recalcitrance of the Jews, confided to his God: 'How hateful to me are the enemies of your Scripture! How I wish that you would slay them with your two-edged sword, so that there should be none to oppose your word!'

Augustine did not, however, advocate the literal slaying of the Jews, for as he continued, 'gladly would I have them die to themselves and live to you!'[5] He believed that God had a purpose for them. He argued that the Old Testament should be venerated for its prophecies of the Messiah and that, while it was certain that the Jews had murdered Jesus, their crime had been committed through the blindness of their faith rather than the unalterable wickedness of their souls. For Augustine, as for Justin and Tertullian, the preservation of the Jews, albeit in dejected servitude, remained an essential part of God's plan: in the fullness of time, their conversion would at last presage the end of days. That is the doctrine immortalised in Bamberg Cathedral's Fürstenportal.

Modern theologians are divided on whether St Augustine was a fomenter of hatred or, if not exactly a friend, ultimately a defender of the Jews. But there can be little doubt about the teaching of other early Church fathers. For Gregory, Bishop of Nyssa, the Jews were the embodiment of all that was ugly and evil: 'murderers of the Lord, assassins of the prophets, rebels and detesters of God, they outrage the Law, resist grace, repudiate the faith of their fathers. Companions of the devil, race of vipers, informers, calumniators, darkeners of the mind, pharisaic leaven, Sanhedrin of demons, accursed, detested, lapidators, enemies of all that is beautiful.' That is the dogma crudely scrawled above the nave of Bamberg Cathedral.

For much of the next 1,500 years, Christians wavered between the two schools of thought, neither of which was good news for the Jews. More often than not, Gregory's prevailed.

His contemporary, the ascetic, 'golden-mouthed' John Chrysostom, taught that: 'brothel and theatre, the synagogue is also a cave of pirates and the lair of wild beasts ... Living for their belly, mouths forever gaping, the Jews behave no better than hogs and goats in their lewd grossness.'[6] In Antioch in 387, he preached a series of eight sermons that established a template for the long tradition of Christian anti-Semitism. Writing shortly after Hitler's ascent to power, James Parkes, doughty champion of Christian–Jewish understanding, wrote that: 'in these discourses there is no sneer too mean, no gibe too bitter for him to fling at the Jewish people. No text is too remote to be able to be twisted to their confusion, no argument is too casuistical, no blasphemy too startling for him to employ.'[7]

Yet in his day and for centuries thereafter, John's sermons were regarded as neither excessive nor unorthodox. On the contrary, Parkes describes them as: 'the most complete monument of the public expression of the Christian attitude to the Jews in the century of the victory of the Church'. A decade after he had delivered them, John was appointed Archbishop of Constantinople, the city at the heart of the new Christian Roman Empire.

Indeed, his authority derived from temporal as well as spiritual powers. In 325, the first Christian Roman Emperor, Constantine, enjoined the bishops at the Council of Nicaea, 'let us therefore have nothing in common with the Jews who are our enemies, let us studiously avoid all contact with their evil way ... for how can they entertain right views on any point having compassed the death of the Lord'.[8]

A generation later, the pagan Emperor Julian relieved Jews of a heavy burden of taxation and promised to restore and resettle Jerusalem at his own expense once he had liberated it from the Persians. But his death in the campaign of 363 left his pledge unfulfilled and, though they could not know it, Julian had been the Jews' last hope. It was the adoption of Christianity as the official religion of the Roman Empire that sealed their fate.

Successive emperors, while often offering protection against the worst excesses of Christian zealots, were clear that Jews should be regarded as second-class citizens. Under Theodosius they were forbidden to own Christian slaves or marry Christians; they could not build new synagogues; they were barred from public service. After the Council of Chalcedon in 452, Gratian decreed that there could be no further debate about the ascendancy of the Church for: 'he who leaves anything to his private judgment after the decision of so many bishops is truly a profanator and a desecrator'.

A hundred years later, Justinian, the great codifier of Roman Law, decreed that Jews could not bear witness against Christians and, in 553, banned the *Mishnah*: 'for it is not included among the Holy Books, nor was it handed down from above by the prophets, but it is an invention of men in their chatter, exclusively of earthly origin and having in it nothing of the divine'.[9]

John and Gregory, the abominators of the Jews, had triumphed. And 1,500 years later, it is difficult to overstate the influence on Christian theology of these venerable saints, to this day revered in the Catholic, Anglican and Orthodox Churches. John Chrysostom's sermons remain in print.

By the end of the nineteenth century, according to my father's Bamberg friend Herbert Loebl, 'no less than 114 Popes and 96 Church Councils ... passed decrees against them [the Jews] which turned them into pariahs, derided, degraded, disenfranchised and often disinherited'.[10]

The Reformation, the great overturning of Catholic orthodoxy, brought little relief. The Protestant founding fathers were the Jew-baiters in chief. John Calvin wrote that: 'their rotten and unbending stiffneckedness deserves that they be oppressed unendingly and without measure or end and that they die in their misery without the pity of anyone'.[11]

His Judeophobia was eclipsed by that of Martin Luther, the radical theologian who transformed Christian practice but left ancient anti-Semitism intact and augmented. He could think of no worse a denunciation of the Catholic Church than to label it 'the Devil's Synagogue', and his advice to the princes on how to deal with 'this damned, rejected race of Jews' explains why Julius Streicher regarded *On the Jews and their Lies* as the most satisfyingly anti-Semitic treatise ever written:

> First, their synagogues should be set on fire, and whatever does not burn up should be covered or spread over with dirt so that no one may ever be able to see a cinder or stone of it ... Secondly, their homes should likewise be broken down and destroyed ... in order that they may realise that they are not masters in our land ... Thirdly, they should be deprived of their prayer-books and Talmuds in which such idolatry, lies, cursing, and blasphemy are taught. Fourthly, their rabbis must be forbidden under threat of death to teach any more ... Fifthly, passport and traveling privileges should be absolutely forbidden to the Jews ... You ought not, you cannot protect them, unless in the eyes of God you want to share all their abomination ...

On and on runs Luther's diatribe in language of the greatest violence and in phrases that foreshadow those of Treitschke and Streicher:

> Such a desperate, thoroughly evil, poisonous, and devilish lot are these Jews, who for these 1,400 years have been and still are our plague, our pestilence, and our misfortune ... they are venomous, bitter, vindictive, tricky serpents, assassins, and children of the devil, who sting and work harm stealthily wherever they cannot do it openly ... next to the devil, a Christian has no more bitter and galling foe than a Jew. There is no other to whom we accord as many benefactions and from whom we suffer as much as we do from these base children of the devil, this brood of vipers.[12]

On this point if no other, Protestants and Catholics could agree: in Europe, the oppression of the Jews would continue unabated.

Indeed, in Bamberg, new public art reinforced the old message. In 1715, an imposing sculpture was installed in the civic heart of the city, before the town hall on the Obere Brücke (Upper Bridge) across the Regnitz.[13] Beneath the agonised figure of the crucified Christ and flanked by the apostles Luke and Mark, Matthew recalls from his Gospel the moment at which Pilate yields to the Jewish mob and Christ's fate is sealed: 'But they cried out the more, saying, Let him be crucified.'[14]

Why this verse above all others? Half a millennium and a Reformation had passed since the creation of the elegant, instructive sculptures of the great cathedral. Perhaps the Prince Bishops believed that, for the avoidance of doubt, they should issue a public reminder that nothing had changed in the way good Christians should regard bad Jews. There should be no backsliding, no reconciliation, no let-up.

If the Reformation had signalled little change, the Enlightenment, with its emphasis on reason, freedom of conscience and universal values, promised a radical reappraisal of the rights and status of Jews in secular society.

Certainly, the seeds of Jewish enfranchisement were sown in the humanist, anti-clerical philosophies of the eighteenth century, and the French Revolution brought in the first harvest. But the revolt against religious dogma applied to Judaism as well as Christianity and, of still greater significance, the rejection of Christian intolerance was contaminated by a new, more material set of complaints against the Jews. These were based not so much on Jewish religious beliefs and practices, as on the malign economic and political influence enlightenment thinkers, both radical and reactionary, attributed to Jews in the new industrial, capitalist society.

Those who wonder why today's progressive thinkers still labour over the 'Jewish question', or how campaigners for equality can still harbour racist thoughts and theories, might study the writings of some of the towering figures of the Enlightenment. The influence of those great prophets stills resonates today, in our cultural values, in our political thinking, in our democratic institutions – for better, but also for worse. For, in paving the way for Jewish equality in the nineteenth century, they also established the basis for a phenomenon that only found its name in 1879: 'anti-Semitism'.

Voltaire, evangelist for tolerance and arguably the most influential polemicist of the age, was an uncompromising anti-Semite.[15] He loathed Christianity, which he regarded as a subversive 'Jewish-imposed belief'. But he believed that Christians, because they were essentially Europeans, could throw off their religious superstitions and recover their classical inheritance. By contrast, the Jews were irredeemably alien: they could never free themselves from the racial corruption of their Asiatic origins, nor from their obstinate commitment to a primitive religion inimical to the liberating values of the age.

He wrote in 1751 that: '[the Jewish nation] dares spread an irreconcilable hatred against all nations; it revolts against all its masters. Always superstitious, always avid of the well-being enjoyed by others, always barbarous, crawling in misfortune, and insolent in prosperity.'[16] For Voltaire this is a well-worn theme: 'One does not find a single generous action in the annals of the Hebrew people. They knew neither hospitality, liberality nor clemency. Their supreme happiness is to practice usury upon foreigners ... Their glory was to put to fire and sword the little towns which they seized. They murdered old men and children. They spared only the young women. They murdered their masters when they were slaves; they knew no mercy when they were conquerors; they are the enemies of the human race.'[17]

And, addressing himself directly to Jews, he threatened in the language of the Christian zealots he so abhorred: 'You have surpassed all nations in impertinent fables, in bad conduct, and in barbarism. You deserve to be punished, for this is your destiny.'[18]

Other leading thinkers were less hostile. Montesquieu argued that were Jews granted full civil rights, as they should be, their new status would inevitably lead them to a better-integrated form of Judaism. Jean-Jacques Rousseau expressed his admiration for the Jews precisely because, despite their age-old tribulations, they had maintained their own identity. But he also issued the prophetic warning that, precisely because of the endurance of their culture and community, Jews would remain 'forever strangers among other men' and, therefore, at risk within their host nations:

> To prevent his people from melting away among foreign peoples, he [Moses] gave them customs and usages incompatible with those of the other nations ... That is how this peculiar nation, so often subjugated, so often dispersed and apparently destroyed, but always fanatical in devotion to its Law, has nevertheless maintained itself down to the present day, scattered among but never intermingled with the rest; and that is why its customs, laws and rites subsist, and will endure to the end of time, in spite of the hatred and persecution of the rest of the human race.[19]

There were others who called for an end to discrimination. In Germany, four years after Pope Pius VI had issued an Edict that consolidated and augmented the anti-Jewish statutes of previous popes, Gotthold Lessing's play *Nathan the Wise* outspokenly and uniquely portrayed the Jew as noble and virtuous and issued a plea for religious tolerance.[20] For these reasons, it was banned by the Church and only performed in 1783, four years after its publication and two years after Lessing's death.[21]

But even in the newly secular France, few political progressives could entirely overcome their resentment of Jewish identity and many openly doubted that Jews were deserving of the privileges the Revolution conferred on others. In short, as Rousseau had anticipated, if Jews wanted their share of the new rights and freedoms, they would simply have to stop being Jews. In the National Assembly, the Count of Clermont-Tonnerre demanded: 'Everything must be refused to the Jews as a Nation in the sense of a corporate body and everything granted to the Jews as individuals ... They must make up neither a political body nor an order within the State; they must individually be citizens.'[22]

Nowhere could the cause of Jewish emancipation be taken up without political opposition – and, for that matter, civil unrest. While

Voltaire was inveighing against the Jews in France, the English Parliament introduced the Jewish Naturalisation Bill, which actually proposed to grant a limited form of citizenship to settled Jews who chose not to convert to Christianity. But the so-called 'Jew Bill', enacted in May 1753, lasted but six months. Such was the public outcry, incited and exploited by the Tory opposition to the Whig government, that it was repealed in December.

Though this was the age of rational enquiry, opponents of the bill found their inspiration in medieval canards about the blasphemous primitivism of Judaic ritual and the pestilential depravity of Jewish people. These they merged with more up-to-date conspiracy theories about the Hebrews' control of money and politics and their plans to convert churches to synagogues and Christians to Jews.

A generation later English Conservative thinkers closely identified Jews not only with the hated French revolutionaries but also with the harbingers of a new, pernicious economic order, just as in the twentieth century Jews were associated simultaneously with Soviet Bolsheviks and global capitalists. In his *Reflections on the Revolution in France*, Edmund Burke wrote in 1790 of: 'Jew brokers contending with each other who could best remedy with fraudulent circulation and depreciated paper the wretchedness and ruin brought on their country by their degenerate councils'.[23]

For Burke, non-Christians represented an existential threat to his conception of a Protestant, Anglican England, and Jews offered a particular corruption: their loyalty was suspect; through their liberalism they threatened the established order; as traders in paper money, they undermined the value of land and the traditional social hierarchy it represented.

Yet Burke's fiercest critics were no more sympathetic to the Jews. Like Voltaire, the radical Tom Paine in *The Age of Reason* abjures Judaism as the precursor to the Christianity he reviled and in *The Rights of Man* he identifies Jews with the chicanery, self-interest and degeneracy of the aristocrats he despised.

For reactionaries and radicals alike, the Jew, 'the other', had little or no place in the ideal society.

Some forty years later, a year after the passing of the first great Reform Act of 1832, William Cobbett, supporter though he was, believed that those who professed the Jewish faith, because of 'their mockery of Jesus; their hardness of heart: their shedding of innocent blood', were rightly excluded from the new franchise and, for that matter, condemned forever to wander stateless and scorned: 'They should, in no country on earth (as long as they adhered to their blasphemy), have any immunities, any privileges, and possessions in house, land or water, any civil or political rights; that they should, everywhere, be deemed aliens; and always at the absolute disposal of the sovereign power of the state, as completely as any inanimate substance, thrown on the land by the wind or the waves.'[24]

There could be no more succinct a summary of the experience of the Jews of Europe over the previous millennium and in the century to come.

4

A SMALL CITY
IN GERMANY

Spread out beneath its great, problematic cathedral, Bamberg is a city of around seventy-five thousand souls in the Upper Franconia region of northern Bavaria, some forty miles north of Nuremberg. It first came to prominence early in the eleventh century when Heinrich, Duke of Bavaria, on becoming King of Germany and then Holy Roman Emperor, made it the seat of both episcopal and imperial power. Built on seven hills, each dominated by a church, today it's a beautifully preserved medieval city. It's not hard to see why my father loved it.

It's likely that there were Jews living in Bamberg at or shortly after its founding. Adolf Eckstein, its long-serving rabbi in the years between emancipation and extinction, opened his history of the city's Jewish community with the telling observation that this 'possibility [is] all the more likely when we consider that at the end of the century, the Crusaders were persecuting them'.[1]

The Romans' destruction of the Second Temple and sack of Jerusalem in 70 CE had propelled Jews from the Holy Land east into Syria, Mesopotamia and Persia and north into northern Africa, Italy and Spain. It's likely that some reached the Rhineland with the Roman legions over the next 200 years and administrative documents show that a Jewish community was well established in Cologne from the early fourth century.

A second wave reached Germany in the second half of the eleventh century. In December 1066, a Muslim mob had slaughtered almost the

36

entire Jewish community of Granada and, in the years that followed, the newly dominant fundamentalist Berber dynasties obliterated the broadly tolerable accommodation between Muslims and Jews that had existed in Andalusia for 300 years. Many Jews fled further north.

Though their statelessness was their greatest misfortune, the growing network of Jewish traders that spread throughout the Diaspora became a valuable asset to be courted. In the ninth century, the Bishops of Augsburg, Regensburg and Salzburg encouraged Jewish merchants to settle in their cities. In 1084, after fire had ravaged the Jewish quarter in Mainz, Bishop Rüdiger invited the survivors to settle in Speyer 'to increase the lustre of the city a thousandfold'.[2]

But, within a dozen years of the Jews' welcome as an adornment to the economic and cultural life of southern Germany, the Christian soldiers of the First Crusade were seeking them out for slaughter.

In 1095, whipped into a religious frenzy by Pope Urban II's call for a Crusade to liberate Jerusalem from the Saracens, mobs turned first on infidels closer to home. Godfrey of Bouillon, crying vengeance for the murder of Christ, unleashed his troops on the Jewish communities in their path as they advanced across Europe towards the Holy Land.

In May 1096, a force recruited by Count Emicho of Leiningen gathered at Speyer. The bishop resisted his attack on the city's Jewish community. The Archbishop of Mainz also sought to protect his city's Jews, but 700 perished when his palace was overrun and the Jewish quarter was razed to the ground. A further 800 were massacred in Worms. Throughout the Rhineland, Jews were offered the choice of death or conversion. Many killed their children and took their own lives. In all, some 5,000 died at their own hands or on the swords of the Crusaders. In Bamberg, as elsewhere, those who survived the mob were forcibly baptised.

In the following year, despite the opposition of Pope Clement III but with the support of Bishop Rupert of Bamberg, Emperor Heinrich IV allowed the converts to readopt their faith and in 1103 granted protection to all Jews in his lands. The pendulum of Jewish life in Germany, swaying with irresistible regularity between protection and persecution, had been established. But already by 1140, Peter Abelard could write of the Jews that 'no people has ever suffered the like for the sake of their God'.[3]

In Bamberg, a small Jewish community established itself along a Judengaße (Jews' Alley), to the east of the cathedral precinct. It must have flourished, because in the epic account of his mid-twelfth-century travels through Europe, north Africa and the near East, Benjamin of Tudela describes Bamberg as one of several German cities that 'contain many rich and learned Jews'.[4]

But neither the status nor the safety of the Jews was assured anywhere in Christendom, as the Church sought constantly to assert its power over every aspect of the lives of non-believers. The third Lateran Council of 1179 prohibited Jews and Muslims from employing Christian servants. Echoing the old Justinian code, it also decreed that in a court of law the testimony of a Christian was always to be preferred to that of a Jew.

The fourth Lateran Council in 1215, the year of Magna Carta, marked a defining moment in Christian–Jewish relations.[5] Its edicts were designed to penalise, exploit, stigmatise and subordinate Jews at every turn. Canon 68 required Jews and Muslims to wear distinguishing clothing, ostensibly to prevent accidental sexual relationships with Christians but of course also marking them out for insult and assault. It also forbad Jews from appearing in public during Holy Week so as to avoid offending good Christians. Canon 69 denied Jews access to public office to ensure that they could never occupy positions of authority over Christians. Canon 70 authorised the bishops to use force to prevent baptised Jews from returning to Judaism.

Now Jews were in every way – spiritually, legally and economically – cast out. Ten years later, they were classified as common criminals, the killing of whom was not construed as a crime. In 1275 Jewish men were barred from bearing arms, a prohibition designed to render them at once emasculated and defenceless.[6]

The Lateran Council had also excluded Jews from most trades and professions. Denied a proper income and crippled by discriminatory taxes, most lived in poverty. Critically, the Third Lateran Council of 1179 had also proscribed Christians from charging interest on loans.

Though the Torah forbids it, some Jews resorted to money-lending at interest, entrapped by contemptuous Christians into one of the few occupations left open to them. Thus the lethal, enduring image of the Jew as usurer and predatory capitalist was born.

By now, to the ancient charges – that the Jews were Christ murderers and disowned by God – a deadly third had been added, namely that at Passover they kidnapped and butchered Christian children, using their blood in the preparation of unleavened Matzos. This notorious Blood Libel, still in circulation today, sparked murderous persecution all over Europe. It had originated in England in 1144 with the discovery of a boy's body in a shallow grave outside Norwich. The local Jews were accused of his murder and, in the years that followed, Thomas of Monmouth, a monk at the cathedral, embellished the story with accounts of ritual torture and worldwide conspiracy. Pogroms followed in Norwich in 1150; in Lincoln in 1255, 90 Jews were arrested and 18 executed.[7]

Despite proclamations against them by both pope and emperor, these blood libels and allegations of desecrations of the Christian Host gathered momentum in southern Germany. On 20 April 1298, a German knight named Rindfleisch, claiming divine inspiration, led a mob in the massacre of 21 Jews in the small Franconian town of Röttingen.

Over the next six months, up to 20,000 Jews were slaughtered in 146 towns and villages across central and southern Germany and Austria, 5,000 of them in Franconia.[8] On 12 July, 135 were butchered in Bamberg and twelve days later almost the entire Jewish community of Würzburg was put to death. On 1 August, the Jews of Nuremberg were overwhelmed. Finally, on 24 August, on his coronation as Holy Roman Emperor, the Habsburg Albrecht I issued an edict against further outrages.

But, as Simon Schama has observed: 'most ominously for the Jews, there were almost no sections of the German population – peasants, burghers and knights – who were not part of these armies of Judeophobic mass killing'.[9]

The peace was fragile. Barely forty years later, in 1336, Johann Zimberlin, an inn-keeper and self-proclaimed prophet, led a marauding gang of Judenschläger ('Jew slayers'), on a murderous campaign across Franconia and Alsace.[10] The Bishop of Strasbourg intervened when the mob began to threaten Christians, though not before they had murdered around 1,500 Jews, much of whose property he had been happy to expropriate.

In 1348, as the Black Death swept through Europe, the Jews were accused of poisoning the wells and rivers. Despite the attempts of the pope and the emperor to protect them, they were massacred in 350 towns, in 210 of which not one was left alive.[11] Other than confessions under torture, evidence was rarely presented; indeed, Jews were routinely slaughtered before the plague had actually arrived. In one such case, in February 1349, almost the entire Jewish community of Strasbourg was paraded through jeering crowds to a great pyre on which, according to the chroniclers, up to 2,000 were incinerated over the course of six days.

In Bamberg, Jews burned down their own houses and perished in the flames in defiance of the mob. Their synagogue, which had served the community for perhaps 200 years, was seized by the Prince Bishop and eventually converted into a Christian church.

There were those among the lords and bishops, and in other strata of German society, who sought to protect the Jews out of moral or religious scruple. There were material reasons too: for the powerful, they represented a coveted material asset.

The Jews of Bavaria were in effect the property of the emperor. In 1342, Emperor Ludwig the Bavarian had introduced a Goldene Opferpfennig, literally 'a golden sacrifice penny', a direct poll tax on every Jew over the age of 12. But the emperors also derived a considerable income by subcontracting to the feudal lords the lucrative right to protect the Jews in their domains. The mob attacked them partly out of religious zealotry and partly for the plunder. The bishops and princes offered them protection for the same reasons.

According to Herbert Loebl, the Jews of Bamberg were at various times subject to a Trade Tax; a Goose Tax; a Horse Tax; a New Year Tax; a Death Tax; a Removal Tax (to compensate the ruler for the loss of other revenues when a Jew left the city); a Cathedral Hill Tax (which was otherwise out of bounds to Jews); a Body Duty, due when a Jew (or sheep or cattle) passed a customs post; an Interregnum Tax to cover the period between the death of one protector and the assumption of another; and a War Tax on Jewish refugees fleeing to Bamberg from the countryside during the Thirty Years' War.[12]

In 1422, when the Franconian princes expelled the Jews from their territories, the Prince Bishop of Bamberg found a way to profit by ejecting them from their homes and communal institutions at the bottom of Cathedral Hill and awarding their properties to his courtiers. The dispossessed Jews were resettled on an island in the River Regnitz, then the site of a prison and an open public toilet. Here, they started again, built a synagogue, a Mikveh and a school and awaited the next eviction.[13] It was not long coming. In 1442, they were again expelled from Bamberg, returning on the payment of crippling levies.

Long before the age of mass communication, campaigns of violence against Jews were a trans-continental phenomenon, often incited by itinerant friars. In 1451 St John Capistrano, the 'Scourge of the Jews', preached against them in Bamberg's Cathedral Square. A painting in Bamberg's Historisches Museum, attributed to Sebald Bopp, depicts wealthy Christians confining their fripperies to a 'bonfire of the vanities' as a recalcitrant Jew, identifiable by his pointed hat, is dragged towards the pulpit.

In 1475, fifteen members of the tiny Jewish community of Trento in northern Italy were burned at the stake, having confessed under torture to the ritual murder of a two-year-old Christian boy.[14] As the hue and cry spread north, Jewish communities throughout Germany once again came under attack. In 1478, Bamberg's Jews were compelled to attend the sermons of the Dominican Friar Peter Schwarz, himself said to have been a Jewish convert. When they refused baptism, they were again expelled.

They were permitted to return in 1499, largely because the Prince Bishop found forgoing the tax revenue they represented too painful. Henceforward, the very threat of expulsion could prove extremely profitable. In 1515, 1565, 1585 and 1593, the Jews were allowed to remain in Bamberg only on payment of ever-increasing amounts of protection money.

Jews were under threat of expulsion not just from little city states in southern Germany. England had been the first major country in Christendom to eject its Jews en masse when Edward I issued an Edict of Expulsion in 1290. It was only revoked by Oliver Cromwell, 366 years later, in the face of stubborn opposition.[15] In 1306, the Jews were evicted from France, readmitted in 1315 and expelled again in 1394. In 1492, they were banished from Vienna and in the same year Ferdinand and Isabella cast them out of Spain. Ferdinand II did likewise in the Kingdom of Naples and King Manuel I threw them out of Portugal in 1497. Each expulsion was the culmination of a sustained campaign of terror – conducted in Spain and Portugal by the Inquisition – and, of course, extortion.

The pattern had been established. Nowhere in Europe could Jews live in undisturbed peace, and never on equal terms with Christians.

It is now, in the late fifteenth century, that my family makes its first appearance.

Part Two

THE FAMILY
AS HISTORY

'I am a stranger. I am a Jewess.
You might have thought I was wicked.'

George Eliot, *Daniel Deronda*

5

LIVES ON LICENCE

Against this background of intermittent but inevitable persecution and extortionate but unreliable protection, my family carved out such lives as jeopardy allowed. Some achieved wealth and distinction; others endured poverty and hardship. Some were poets, scientists and intellectuals; some were high officials, bankers or merchants; most were humble artisans, shopkeepers and village rabbis. Theirs is the story of German Jewry through bad times and less bad times.

Though Bamberg's Jewish community was constrained in so many ways, it was never restricted to the segregated quarters into which Jews were crammed in many larger European cities. Over five centuries, until the 1930s, sixteen generations of my mother's family, the Zunzes, lived in Frankfurt. For 350 of those years, almost from its inception in the second half of the fifteenth century to its dissolution at the beginning of the nineteenth, they were confined to its ghetto.

A small and relatively well-integrated community of Jews had lived in Frankfurt since the middle of the twelfth century. But in 1349, in the wake of the Black Death, a mob torched the houses of its 10 families, in the process burning down the Bartholomäus church around which they were clustered. Those who survived fled the city. In due course they returned and a period of renewed calm prevailed.

In 1460, however, protests about the contaminating proximity of Jews to the rebuilt church led the city council to decree that they should be expelled to a purpose-built settlement outside the city walls, in effect, Europe's first 'ghetto'. For though that baleful designation derives from the few sequestered streets to which Venice restricted its Jews in 1516, Frankfurt's gated, guarded Judengaße preceded it by half a century.

When it was completed in 1462, the Judengaße housed some sixty members of eleven families. Within twenty years or so, Pesach, patriarch of the Zunz family, with his wife Ogy, their son Michel and his wife Hindle, had left the small, walled town of Zons near Cologne in the Lower Rhineland to join them.[1]

While the year in which they entered the ghetto is not recorded, it's known that the house in which they took up residence, the Haus zum Affen ('House of the Monkeys'), was built in 1478.[2] By then, Zons must have become a particularly hostile environment for Jews. Three years earlier, Emperor Frederick III had garrisoned his army there as he sought to break the siege of nearby Neuss by Charles the Bold, Duke of Burgundy. Despite its restrictions, Pesach and his family must have regarded the narrow, heavily policed Judengaße as a safer haven than a small town full of rapacious mercenaries.

Their beginnings in Frankfurt were not auspicious. Two years after Pesach died in 1488, he was effectively excommunicated by Rabbi Gomprecht, the ghetto's community leader, for having defied his authority. The nature of the offence and why it took the rabbi two years to pronounce his judgement over a dead man are intriguing, but unknown.

There's more. His widow Ogy then married a man called Aberle but drowned in a well in 1499. The death was treated as suicide, a terrible sin for Jews and Christians alike. The court, anticipating that, to avoid the scandal, Michel would seek to make off with his mother's corpse, ordered that it be handed over to the public executioner, hanged, quartered, burned and, as was the practice of the day, either cast in a barrel into the River Main or buried under the gallows. The burial register simply records that the body was interred according to the requirements of the law.[3]

What followed makes the unexplained circumstances of Ogy's death more suspicious still. For the widowed Aberle then married Ogy's granddaughter, Fegelchen, thus becoming his stepson's son-in-law.

Fegelchen, having wed her step-grandfather, was now her father's step-mother.[4] It is perhaps too late to unpick the tangled strands of this ancient web.

Though he glosses over these events, the bones of the Zunz family's fortunes up until the end of the nineteenth century are recorded in Alexander Dietz's monumental history of the 625 Jewish families of Frankfurt, published in 1907.[5]

According to Dietz, the Zunzes were, in equal measure, a pious and prosperous family. Pesach and Ogy's great grandson Michel, who died in 1585, is described as 'very wealthy' and 'the wise leader of the community'; his son Löb was 'a man of the holy scriptures' and 'a jewel of his time'. So it goes, generation by generation: a subsequent Michel was 'one who always walked the way of righteousness', Moses was 'praised as modest and pious, who always set his eyes against evil', Herzl was 'the honourable and the noble'; his son 'the respected' Amschel was 'ready for any good deed', while another, Simon, 'served God with all his soul'.

But while many in the family made a good living, largely in textiles and banking, there were also those who lived from hand to mouth and a few who converted to Christianity to escape the poverty of the ghetto. Some of the better-off also met with misfortune. Dietz recounts the unhappy experience of Michael Alexander Zunz, who had a significant banking business in Amsterdam, Hamburg, Vienna, Metz and Nancy. But when, in 1717, the firm of Samuel and Meyer Levy, which had advanced him 60,000 Gulden, went bankrupt, its creditors had Zunz imprisoned in a Viennese jail for 18 weeks while they tried to recover their losses from him.[6]

There were other delinquents. For much of the sixteenth and seventeenth centuries, the Zunzes were known as zur Sonne after their home at Sun House (and at other times, von Zons and Zuntz). One of them, Michael zur Sonne, seems, literally, to have sullied the family's reputation for, as I was surprised to discover from an audio commentary at the Ghetto Museum in Frankfurt, in 1690 the town inspectors issued him with a stern reprimand: 'a great deal of rubbish has accumulated at both the front and the back of his property and, with all due respect, he fails to keep a clean house'. Whether he mended his ways has not been established.

The practice of deriving family titles from the buildings in which the Jews of the ghetto lived gives rise to a legend, in our family if not in theirs, that the Rothschilds owe their name to a house (of the red shield) sold to them by the Zunzes. Even if our role in the birth of a dynasty is apocryphal – and I hope it isn't – the ties between the two families were close. There were several intermarriages and members of three generations of the Zuntz branch lived in the house owned by the Rothschilds at Judengaße 148. There they administered the many charities the banking family established to support 'the poor Jews of the city', as well as a foundation of their own.[7]

The last in that line, Karl Klonimus Zuntz, volunteered for the German army at the outbreak of the First World War and was wounded, disabled and decorated. A little over twenty years later, he, his wife and their three children were deported to the death camps. His is the suitcase, abandoned at Auschwitz, and discovered there by chance 20 years later by Peter Zuntz, that is commemorated in Maries Lehmann-Brune's *Der Koffer des Karl Zuntz* ('The Suitcase of Karl Zuntz').[8]

Constrained though life may have been, the Jews felt their ghetto offered them some kind of protection. But it could not be guaranteed. On the afternoon of 22 August 1614, a baker named Vincenz Fettmilch entered the Judengaße at the head of a mob. While the women and children fled to the Jewish cemetery, the men set up barricades and armed themselves as best they could. They resisted for several hours but were in the end overwhelmed. Some 1,380 Jews, herded into the graveyard, feared the worst. Next day, however, they were ordered to leave Frankfurt.

As they were marched out of the ghetto, the cry went up, 'the Judengaße is ours', and townsfolk poured in to plunder what they could and destroy what they chose. Jewish books were impaled on pikes and burned on bonfires; the synagogue and school were laid waste; houses were demolished.

The emperor was so outraged that 'his Jews' had been assaulted that Fettmilch and his lieutenants were arrested and put to torture. Löb

Zunz, the man of holy scriptures, and his brother Herz were called as community leaders to testify at their trial. The defendants were convicted and sentenced to a gruesome public execution. On 28 February 1616, by proclamation, all Frankfurt's shops were closed and a huge crowd gathered in the horse market, the Roßmarkt. After the sentence was read out, two fingers on Fettmilch's right hand were cut off before his head was severed from his neck by a sword. It was mounted on the bridge over the Main while his corpse was quartered and hanged from a gallows. The grateful Jews were paraded back into their ghetto behind a military band and the gates were once more locked behind them.

It was from the stifling grip of the ghetto that two of the more remarkable of what became my paternal grandmother Bertha Herzstein's family emerged to live their eventful lives. They were remarkable not least because, for Jews of their day, they were exceptional.

Samson Salomon, Samson of Baiersdorf, achieved eminence as chancellor in the court of the local princeling. His sister-in-law, Glückel von Hameln, was a scholar, businesswoman and mother of 13.[9] If these were not accomplishments enough, her seven volumes of memoirs have come to be regarded as one of the most revealing accounts of the life not only of a Jewish woman, but of any woman of her times.

The records of the Herzstein family begin in 1602. According to the family tree compiled by my great grandfather, Heinrich Herzstein, Juda Selke came from Vienna to Fürth in 1640. It's more likely that he was one of a number of Jews who arrived there in 1670 after Leopold I, Holy Roman Emperor and Archduke of Austria, bowing to public pressure, expelled the entire Viennese Jewish community 'for the glory of God'.

In any event, Juda Selke's descendants did not stray far from a handful of Upper Franconian towns and villages close to Bamberg, principally Baiersdorf and later Bayreuth, for almost 300 years. When they left it was not by choice.

Juda's family made its mark. His son Samson Salomon, born around 1640, achieved success and celebrity in one of the few high offices open to Jews in the seventeenth century. The rulers of the myriad German principalities, as well as extorting heavy taxes from 'their' Jewish community, often looked to Jews to provide financial counsel. Several served as Hoffaktor, or 'Court Jew', the position to which Samson was appointed by Christian Ernst, Margrave of Brandenburg-Bayreuth.

The office bestowed rare privileges, which Dr Abraham Schweizer, in his study *The Jewish Community at Baiersdorf*, describes 200 years later with poignant pride:

> Margrave Christian Ernst had appointed as his court agent a highly respected, intelligent Jew of Baiersdorf, Samson Salamon, who rendered valuable services also to other powerful personages. The Margrave issued this court Jew with an official court agent's charter for his proof of identity when required. Such a court agent's charter was a splendid document. Written on parchment, each page decorated with beautiful ornamental borders, bound in red velvet, tied with black and yellow silk ribbons, with a pendant official seal of 15 cm diameter and cast in a copper casket, it bore the prince's signature in his own hand and measured 38 x 27 cm. The bearer of such letters patent was entitled to the special protection of authorities everywhere, which had to afford him assistance in various ways. He also had the right to bear arms and, together with his family and servants, was exempt from payment of all the fiscal imposts on the Jews. The granting of such court agents' letters patent constituted a high honour. Samson accordingly enjoyed great prestige and far-reaching influence at the Margrave's court; both immeasurably benefited his oppressed fellow Jews.[10]

As Dr Schweizer suggests, Samson was prepared both to exercise his influence and extend his charity in the service of his community. In 1695, he persuaded the Margrave to grant the Jews in his domain freedom of trade. He also prevailed on him to reject a petition from the Huguenots of nearby Erlangen for the expulsion of the town's 30 Jewish families so that they could expropriate their houses.

But the privileges of the Hoffaktor were beset by perils, for ministers with the ear of the prince were routinely exposed to the jealousies and jockeying of political rivals. If they were Jewish, the resentment could prove fatal.

Samson's near contemporary, Joseph Süß Oppenheimer, provides a gruesome example. Court Jew to Duke Karl Alexander of Württemberg, he was the target of a particularly venomous campaign. The Duke protected him, but when he died Oppenheimer was arrested and tried on trumped-up charges of embezzlement, debauchery and, of all things, supporting Catholicism. When he refused to convert to Christianity, he was hanged in a metal cage, especially constructed for the purpose, and his corpse put on public display. Two centuries later, Joseph Goebbels commissioned *Jud Süß*, a cinematic blockbuster, 'based' on Oppenheimer's life and reputedly watched by 20 million Germans. So virulent was its anti-Semitism that its director, Veit Harlan, was convicted after the war of crimes against humanity.

Happily, however, Samson was a survivor. When he died in 1712, he was given pride of place in Baiersdorf's Jewish cemetery. The inscription on his tombstone credits this 'father to the poor and oppressed' with the building of a hospital as well as the synagogue and describes him as 'great and distinguished in his works … he stood by his fellow religionists in danger and in need, a man of piety and benevolence all his days'.

He was joined two years later by his wife Rebekka, likewise remembered for her charity for 'she provided for the community a well of fresh water, every month distributed corn and bread to the poor' and arranged dowries for the daughters of poor Jewish families.

Their sons, Veit and Salamon, followed Samson both as Court Jews and as benefactors of their community. Though it's not clear what tribulations they suffered or what fate befell them, Dr Schweizer records that 'fortune … did not always smile on them; their good deeds were ill rewarded with ingratitude'.

Glückel von Hameln's unending quest for advantageous marriages for her many children led to her encounter with Samson.

Her life began in relative comfort in Hamburg and ended modestly in Metz. In her time, she knew prosperity and some distinction but always uncertainty and sometimes jeopardy. In her memoirs, she dispassionately describes the expulsion of Ashkenazi Jews from Hamburg in 1648 and the gauntlet they were obliged to run in seeking refuge in nearby Altona:[11]

> They lived there for a time and through the efforts of prominent men of the Community obtained permits to trade in the town. Each was valid for one month … It was a very hard life especially for the poor and needy, who risked going without a pass; if they were caught they were imprisoned. This meant ransoming them and called for much expense and trouble before they were released. In the mornings, as soon as the men came from the synagogue, they went to town, returning to Altona towards evening when the gates were closed. When they passed through the gates their lives were in continual peril from attacks by sailors, soldiers and all sorts of hooligans. Each woman thanked God when her husband returned home safely.[12]

Such dangers had to be accepted by Jews as part of everyday life. As Glückel piously observes time and again: 'if we are sometimes punished, it is because of our own misdeeds. We must accept all with love … If the Holy One, blessed be He, bestows sorrows and troubles, this portion must be accepted for good.'[13]

Such faith and forbearance were both learned and necessary. So was a sense of humour. For a brief period in the mid-1660s, it seemed that deliverance was at last at hand for the Jews. Word of a new Messiah, Sabbatai Zevi, spread like wildfire throughout the Diaspora. Glückel's in-laws were among the many who gathered stores in preparation for the long-awaited migration to the Holy Land. But all was in vain: the prophet proved false. As Glückel observed: 'we were like a woman in travail, a woman on the labour-stool who, after great labour and sore pains, expects to rejoice in the birth of a child, but finds it is nothing but wind'.[14]

Dr Schweizer, commending her 'profound wisdom and deep piety', describes her as 'one of the most outstanding woman personalities of seventeenth century Germany'. That may well be the case. But had Glückel not written her autobiography, it's unlikely that anyone else would have troubled to celebrate the life of a woman of her day, especially a Jewish woman.

Betrothed at 12 and married at 14 to Chaim, a merchant and banker, Glückel was wealthy and well connected to the extent that, in 1674, Frederick, the future King of Prussia, and Maurice, Prince of Nassau, attended the wedding of her eldest daughter Zipporah. This distinction made her very happy for, as she records, 'for a hundred years, no Jew had had such a high honour'.[15] For Glückel and other Jews of her class – as for the admiring Dr Schweizer 200 years later – prestige within the Jewish community was important. But its warm glow was far surpassed by the notice and acceptance of Gentiles, especially those of high birth.

The memoirs Glückel wrote as a distraction after the premature death of the husband she adored reveal her as scrupulous and humane.[16] Though she enjoyed the trappings and prestige of her wealth (at least until her second husband lost it), she understood that the fortunes of Jews were always uncertain. She was charitable within her community but, above all, dedicated to the welfare of her family.

Her many travels on business and match-making led her to Bamberg. She was warned not to tarry as 'great hatred for the Jews ruled' in the city.[17] These fears were not exaggerated. In 1669, food shortages had led to renewed attacks on Bamberg's Jews and in 1683 they were only able to avoid another expulsion by the payment of a substantial bribe. Now, in 1699, a fresh economic crisis triggered another pogrom against Jewish merchants, who were falsely accused of hoarding grain. On 29 April, a mob ransacked a Jew's house but were met by an unexpected response when the owner bombarded the rioters with the plums he had stored in his attic. Fearing they had been shot, they retreated in disarray and the fabled victory was celebrated in Bamberg's Jewish community for centuries thereafter.[18]

Despite the disturbances, the wedding of Glückel's son Zanvill to the daughter of Moses Bamberg took place as planned and it was during the festivities that the marriage between her son Moses and Samson

Salamon's daughter, mysteriously identified in the family tree only as 'N.N.', was broached.

The engagement was soon announced, the terms of the marriage contract agreed and the date for the wedding set. But then a double disaster struck. First, Samson decided that his house was not big enough to host the wedding and that another must be built. Then, like Joseph Süß Oppenheimer, he was forced to contend with the assaults of a rival at court. Glückel describes them in terms recalling the biblical story of Esther that would have been particularly meaningful for Jews:

> The Margrave had taken a new counsellor who was a Haman against Samson Baiersdorf and wished to destroy him. In truth he was in a critical position; all his possessions were in the Margrave's hands, and he did not know which way to turn. This was the reason he did not celebrate the marriage within the agreed time. But the Holy One saw the great good that came from his house, the hospitality to rich and poor alike, all he did for the Jews of the whole land – he supported the whole dukedom – and the good that he would do in the future. So God turned the evil of this Haman to good, so that the evil one fell lower and Samson Baiersdorf from day to day rose higher and higher. It is impossible to describe in what honour and trust he, a Jew, is held by the Margrave. May God grant that this exalted position remain his till the coming of the Messiah.[19]

A year later, in 1700, the wedding took place 'with all the splendour in the world'.[20] But, now 54, Glückel was finding the stresses and exertions of business increasingly difficult to bear. She fretted about the prospect of bankruptcy 'so that those who trusted me should be losers through me, thus disgracing me, my children and my sainted husband who lay under the sod' and worried that she might forgo the chance of 'living respected and rich in my old age'.[21]

Having refused many suitors in the eleven years of her widowhood, she finally agreed to marry Hirsch Levy, a widower and 'a fine, upstanding Jew, very learned in Talmud, possessed of great wealth and a magnificent household'.[22] But she had premonitions that all would not go well. Before they were married, Hirsch sent her an expensive gold chain: 'I thought in my deepmost heart, "God grant that the end may be as fine as the beginning." But, my Lord and Master, the golden chain, unfortunately, became rope and iron fetters.'[23]

Hirsch, though by all accounts an honourable businessman and a respected figure in his community, lost his fortune and hers two years later and died in 1712. Reluctant to become a burden on her children, Glückel lived for a while in straitened circumstances. At length she agreed to move in with one of her daughters, ending her days in stoic reflection: 'There are many people who are very keen on making money and are never satisfied so that much evil comes of it … One must know that there is moderation in all things, and learn how to conduct oneself.'[24]

Dr Schweizer ends where he began, concluding with satisfaction that 'these are the sentiments of a noble, modest Jewish woman who, deeply rooted in the spirit of her age, stood out through her unusual intellect'.

It may be tempting, three centuries later, to mock Glückel's preoccupation with wealth and status. But that would take too little account of the unenviable position Jews occupied in the society of her times and of their desperate yearning for the social acceptance and material security routinely denied them. That Glückel had both the talent and the strength of character to overcome the disabilities of religion and gender – and that she did so while remaining unapologetically committed to her faith, family and community – was surely the remarkable achievement of an exceptional woman.

The worldly success of Glückel and Samson set them apart from the large majority of their fellow Jews, including the Zunzes in the Frankfurt ghetto. As Ruth Gay observes: 'If one imagines an observer visiting a German ghetto in the fourteenth century and returning in the eighteenth, that visitor would have found few changes. The handful of Jews who escaped to the wider world, notably the court Jews who flourished in the seventeenth and eighteenth centuries, were such spectacular exceptions that they only underscore the unvarying life they had left behind.'[25]

In its earliest days, Frankfurt's Judengaße had provided a relatively benign environment for its inhabitants. Pesach's son Michel moved to Die Kanne, a handsome building with a 12-metre frontage on the eastern side of the street, with views of gardens and open fields to the rear. He and his neighbours had all they needed to sustain their religious and community life: a synagogue, a ritual bath, a community building, two taverns, a dancehall and a hospital, all within easy reach.

But they had almost no rights. They were barred from practising any craft or acquiring any land or property outside the ghetto. Most were limited to shopkeeping or, inevitably, to pawnbroking and money-lending. Nor could there be any doubt that the ghetto was a prison: its three gates were guarded at all times and locked at night, and throughout Sundays and holy days. No Jew was permitted under any circumstance to live outside its walls and they were only allowed beyond them in exceptional circumstances, with official permission. When Jews did venture into the city, they were obliged to wear a yellow circle on their coats and, for good measure, a distinctive hat for men and a blue veil for women, all of which attracted mockery and missiles.

Nevertheless, the relative security of the ghetto continued to attract Jews from other towns and villages. But because its size could not be increased, as the community grew, existing buildings had to be subdivided or extended upwards and outwards across a single street no more than 13 feet wide and a quarter of a mile long.

Pesach's grandson Herz, a horse trader, had moved around 1520 to his mother-in-law's house, Haus an der Pforte, by the ghetto's northern gate. Ten years later he moved again to the house's former stables where he lived with five other families in what had become the Haus zur Sonne. In 1573, his son Michel divided Haus an der Pforte into three dwellings. Later they were themselves subdivided into eight at the front and three more in the rear. By the end of the sixteenth century, the ghetto's population had swelled to 2,200.

This was the ghetto to which Frankfurt's Jews had triumphantly returned after Fettmilch's incursion. But grateful as they were for the emperor's continuing protection, it was accompanied by a new set of prohibitions. The number of families allowed to live there was now limited to 530; no building could be taller than three storeys; no rear-facing wall could have windows overlooking Christian properties; no more than twelve marriages could take place in a calendar year and no couple could marry before the groom had reached the age of 25 and the bride 18.

Yet still the ghetto continued to expand and, as it did, the over-crowding increased and living conditions deteriorated. When much of it was destroyed by fire in 1711, 3,024 people in 505 households sharing 203 houses were crammed into the space originally occupied by 60 families. The ghetto had become not only one of Germany's largest Jewish communities, but also one of Europe's most densely populated and unwholesome quarters.

Even as the Age of Reason dawned, no restriction on Jewish life was evidently too tyrannous, no humiliation too mean, for the Frankfurt authorities to conceive and impose. In 1715, lest Jewish women offend good Christian folk, a new dress code was introduced which, inter alia, required that 'without any shyness or deception or any attempt to evade it', they forswear velvet and silk, other than 'a little cap in only one colour'; likewise their Sabbath clothing should be of one colour only and limited in cost; jewellery other than a wedding ring was also forbidden.[26]

So close were the buildings that little air and almost no light penetrated the Judengaße. There was little sanitation and no space for exercise or relaxation. But the city council saw no reason to concern itself with the wellbeing of Jews. When, in 1769, the community petitioned to be allowed to take the air in an open space called Glacis, permission was refused. The City Council minuted its disgust at the 'boundless arrogance of this race, which always strives to set itself up as equal to the Christian citizens'.

Small wonder that one visitor to the ghetto at the end of the eighteenth century found its inhabitants in poor health: 'Most of the people among the Frankfurter Jews, even those who are in the blooming years of their life, look like the walking dead. It would not be necessary to compel them to wear their short black cloaks and their collars to distinguish them from the others. Their deathly pale appearance sets them apart from all the other inhabitants in the most depressing way.'[27]

The ghetto was devastated by fire three times, in 1711, again in 1721 and finally in 1796, under the bombardment of Napoleon's army. On the first two occasions, it was rebuilt and the Jews were forced to return. But the third conflagration, which, for the third time, consumed almost all the Zunz family homes, led to its eventual dissolution. In 1811, Karl von Dalberg, the Grand Duke of Frankfurt and the French-appointed Governor of the Rhine Federation, issued his 'Highest Regulation, for the equality of civil right of the Jewish Municipality', granting Jews rights as citizens and allowing them to take up residence in the city itself.[28]

The journalist, satirist and political commentator Ludwig Börne wrote that: 'after many hundreds of years, the walls were shattered and the captive beasts slipped rejoicing through the breaches to breathe in the free, fresh air'.[29]

His tone was sardonic. The Jews, though liberated from their ghetto, had to pay 440,000 Gulden for their new privileges. When these were withdrawn after the defeat of the French at Waterloo in 1815, the down payment proved non-refundable.

6

THE AGE OF REASON AND UNREASON

I had a beautiful homeland.
The oak trees grew
So tall there and the violets nodded gently on the breeze.
It was a dream.

It kissed me in German and spoke in German
(You cannot imagine
How good it sounded) the words: 'I love you'.
It was a dream.

Heinrich Heine, In Exile[1]

The Enlightenment and the Revolution offered Jews new hope of freedom and equality, or something approximating them. But there was a price to pay: to become more French or English or German, they would have become less Jewish. In these circumstances, what were Jews to do?

Some, like my mother's forebear Leopold Zunz, believed that modern Jews could build bridges with reform-minded free-thinkers.[2] In 1818, with Edward Gans and Moses Moser, he founded the Verein für Cultur und Wissenschaft der Juden (the Association for Jewish Science and Culture), which sought 'through culture and education to bring the Jews into harmonious relations with the age and the nations in which they live'.

Others sought to escape discrimination by converting to Christianity. One such was Heinrich Heine, the great Romantic poet and radical with whom my family cherishes its, albeit tenuous, connection.[3] He had been an early collaborator with Zunz and a supporter of the Wissenschaft movement. But he came to believe that the deadweight of old Judaic orthodoxies and the parochialism of the ghetto were inimical to the Enlightenment values he espoused. He concluded that entrance to mainstream German cultural life demanded the renunciation of his religious roots. By 1825, he had embraced baptism as 'the ticket of admission into European culture'.[4]

But ceasing to be 'one of them' could not make him 'one of us'. Only six months later, he wrote to Moser: 'I am now hated by Christian and Jew alike. I much regret that I have had myself baptised; I don't perceive that things have gone better for me. On the contrary, I have since had nothing but misfortune.'[5] In 1831, he left Germany for Paris where he lived in exile until his death in 1856.

Others came to a similar realisation: even in the most enlightened circles, a Jew might be admired for his talents but never entirely accepted for his origins. As Hannah Arendt observed, these 'exception Jews' had effectively traded the status of pariah for that of parvenu. Heine's friend Ludwig Börne wrote that 'some reproach me with being a Jew, some praise me because of it, some pardon me for it, but all think of it'.[6] The year before he died in 1836, he reflected: 'Jew, Jew, that is the last red cent in the miserable bank of their wit. But after all this, I wish that I could have my three louis d'or back, those with which I honoured the pastor for my Christianity. I have been baptised now for eighteen years and it doesn't help me. Three louis d'or for a little place in the German madhouse. It was pure waste!'

At the beginning of the nineteenth century, as the Jews emerged from the Frankfurt ghetto, they could see before them, at least on the far horizon, rights and freedoms of which they had only dreamed. But progress towards them was faltering and it was compromised.

Between 1802 and 1806, as Bamberg's administration passed from the Prince Bishops to the new Kingdom of Bavaria, a period of irresolute liberalisation had begun. In 1804, though Jews were still paying the civic authorities 2 florins 52½ kreuzer in protection money and 9 kreuzer in Goose Tax per quarter, they were at last admitted to the city's schools and in the following year allowed to bear arms, albeit as army conscripts.[7] In 1808, the Jewish poll tax was abolished and in 1809 the Religions Edict classified the Jews as a religious society, though not a faith community. Then, on 10 June 1813, the Judenedict, 'concerning the circumstances of members of the Jewish faith in the Kingdom of Bavaria', awarded them the status of citizens of Bavaria and finally abolished the protection regime. For the first time in 700 years, Jews were allowed to own land and join the craft guilds.

But that did not mean that they had been granted equality. While the Judenedict conferred duties of citizenship, they were not matched by rights. Indeed, they brought with them particularly repressive ordinances. Not least among them was the Matrikel Gesetz, a registration law that, replicating earlier restrictions, limited the right of settlement in Bamberg to no more than sixty-nine Jewish families. Those excluded from the list were obliged to leave the city.

Only when the holder of a permit died or relocated could another take his or her place. Eldest sons had effectively to wait on the death of their fathers before they could settle, marry and raise a family in their own community. Younger sons had little choice but to convert or leave. In the three decades that followed, some 11,000 Bavarian Jews emigrated, including around half of the younger generation. Levi Strauss from Buttenheim, a village just outside Bamberg, was one of them.[8]

Jews had also to adopt 'German' names. The first to do so in Bavaria, on 21 February 1814, was the banker Josef Samuel Heßlein, whose (presumed) descendant Artur lodged with my grandparents before he emigrated to Brazil in 1939. Ironically, by then the Nazis had required Jews to adopt 'Jewish' middle names so that the process of assimilation begun in the nineteenth century could be undone in the twentieth.

But just as the cause of Jewish equality had accompanied Napoleon's victories across Europe, so it fell back in the wake of his defeats. As the French armies retreated, conservative nationalists began to assert themselves, encouraged by and, in turn, inciting often violent popular outbursts against the Jews.

In August 1819, mobs crying 'Hep! Hep! Jude verreck!' ('Death to the Jews!') took to the streets first in Würzburg and then in Frankfurt and other towns and cities throughout Germany in protest against what they regarded as the growing presumption and overweening influence of the Jews.[9] The Bavarian government appeased them by slowing the process of reform. This sensible step, it explained to its disappointed Jewish citizens, had been taken to protect their interests, for without it the violence against them would surely have intensified.

Anti-Jewish sentiment was by no means limited to the mob. In 1837, the *Bamberger Tagblatt* inveighed against local Jews who, it claimed, had monopolised the city's renowned hop trade, proclaiming that they were 'detrimental to the Christian inhabitants ... for the dirty and ignorant Jew does not consider anything sacred, and knows no other music than the sound of money, mortgage certificates, and haggling'.[10]

Though the Bavarian Diet of 1831 had called for Jewish emancipation, the government continued to drag its feet. In 1850, under pressure from the Catholic Church, the Privy Council rejected the Frankfurt Parliament's proposed amendment of the German Reich constitution calling for an end to religious bars to citizenship.

Nevertheless, even if the pace was often halting, progress was being made on a number of fronts. In 1849 the first Jew, Dr David Morgenstern, was elected to the Bavarian State Parliament. In the following year, Rabbi Samson Wolf Rosenfeld succeeded in establishing a Jewish cemetery in Bamberg, the first since 1487 when Jews were forced to bury their dead several miles from the city.[11] It is here, in the Siechenstraße cemetery, that my father laid the memorial to his parents and Aunt Meta. Four years later, in 1854, dignitaries from church and state attended the ceremonial reopening of Bamberg's rebuilt synagogue in Generalgaße.

But it took another decade before the Matrikel restrictions were abolished in 1861 and yet another before, on 6 April 1871, three months after the unification of Germany, a decree removed 'all remaining restrictions of civil and political rights derived from the difference in religious creed' and German Jews had at last been granted their emancipation.[12] Finally, in 1880, taxes levied exclusively on Jews were abolished.

This was a time of optimism, ambition and achievement for Jews throughout the new Germany. Economically, the transformation of their fortunes was dramatic. In mid-century, by some estimates, up to half Germany's Jews were beggars, not least because so many had been denied rights of residence. Within a generation, around 60 per cent could be described as middle class, the majority involved in some form of trade.[13]

In Bamberg, Jews founded businesses, many of which soon led their sectors in industry, trade and retail. Their children attended university and entered the professions. Many enthusiastically embraced the city's cultural life and several became prominent patrons of the arts. Others were among the city's leading philanthropists, founding charities promoting education, healthcare and the relief of the poor.[14]

In 1737, the number of Jewish families allowed to live in Bamberg had been limited to forty-eight and each had to pay the considerable sum of 2,000 thalers for the privilege. By 1880, the community had swelled to 1,270 (4.3 per cent of the city's population). By 1901, at 1,350, it was the largest it had ever been, or would be.

My great grandfather, David Adolph Zunz, was the very model of the new, liberated German Jew. He was prosperous, progressive in his politics and relaxed in his religion, voracious in his appetite for knowledge and novelty, outward-looking and confident in the society he would bequeath his children. His life in Frankfurt, from 1831 to 1910, encompassed the best years German Jews had ever experienced.

He left a singular testament. The diary he kept in 1847 and 1848 captures an adolescent's wide-eyed wonder as tumultuous events unfold around him. It encapsulates too the sense of optimism that young middle-class Jews would have felt as, freed from the ghetto, they looked to embrace the promise of a new, liberal order. But it also illustrates, with almost casual resignation, the suspicion and often violent hostility with which they were still widely regarded.

Adolph had attended The Philantropin, the famous Frankfurt Jewish school founded in 1804 by Mayer Amschel Rothschild 'for enlightenment and humanity' of Jews and non-Jews alike. My mother was a pupil there almost a century later.[15] At the age of 15 Adolph began his apprenticeship in the banking and lottery business run by his maternal uncle Joseph Trier. Twenty years later, he was running the city lottery. When Frankfurt was absorbed into Prussia in 1866, the business had to be wound up. Adolph then founded a credit bank, which he managed until he was almost seventy years old.

By then he was a member of 32 scientific and charitable societies, ranging from the learned Anthropological Society to the progressive Prison Society. He was also closely involved with the Language Society, which promoted Volapük, a universal language created in 1879 by Johann Martin Schleyer, a German priest who believed that he was acting on the instructions of God, revealed to him in a dream. Within 10 years, Volapük could claim a million speakers. Sadly, however, its leading advocates fell into presumably incomprehensible schisms and the fledgling lingua franca soon gave way to Esperanto.

Although he had not been able to pursue his scientific interests at university, in later life Adolph carried on a lively correspondence with his magnificently bearded cousins, Hugo, reputedly a friend of Marx and Engels, and Moritz Schiff, whose radical political activities had led both into exile and whose revolutionary scientific research subsequently won each great renown in their different fields.[16]

Adolph's diary offers a rare and sympathetic eyewitness account of the year of revolutions that threatened the established order throughout Europe.[17] Indeed, it was in Frankfurt's St Paul's church that Germany's first prototype Parliament met in March 1848 and where, in May, its first National Assembly sought to hammer out the constitution for a democratic, unified Germany.

The first part, covering July 1847 to March 1848, is chiefly concerned with the affairs of the Trier family business, Adolph's extensive social life and his enthusiastic observation of and participation in the modern excitements the city had to offer. There is so much to see and to celebrate: the construction of pavements and the renumbering of houses; the new omnibuses that will break the monopoly of profiteering and often drunken coachmen; the popular frenzy that gripped the city on

4. David Adolph Zunz, polymath and modern German Jew, in 1898.

the occasion of the Englishman Mr Green's balloon ascent from its showground.

Adolph is a modern Jew who takes a rather casual view of religious observance. On 20 September, he announces that 'today I tried to get through the Day of Atonement as best I could. I did not fast. All good things come in threes, and I have already fasted three times.'[18] Indeed, he is not by nature an abstainer and devotes much ink to the delicacies he devours at the soirées and in the salons of his friends and relatives.

However, the spring of 1848 brings a new focus and a change in tone. In France, King Louis-Philippe had been forced to abdicate and the Second Republic declared. The shockwaves spread rapidly for, on 4 March, Adolph notes that, emboldened by the 'unsettling news' from Paris, Frankfurt radicals had gathered at the Reithalle to petition the Senate for sweeping reform.[19]

But political upheaval could take an unpredictable turn, especially for Jews. Almost in passing, Adolph mentions that, despite the tumult, 'everything was peaceful; only outside Rothschild's house you could hear whistling and hissing'. Later that month, hostile crowds again surround the banker's house in the mistaken belief that the reactionary and recently deposed Austrian Chancellor Metternich is staying there, en route to exile in England. In April, when the German states go to war with Denmark over the future of Schleswig-Holstein, the mob is back again. The Jews, as ever in uncertain times, provided a ready target for public grievance.

Indeed, elsewhere the Jews did not escape so lightly. In Rotenburg an der Fulda, then home of the Brandes family, rioting was directed not at the political establishment but at the Jewish community. It was quelled by military intervention but only after three months of violent unrest.

For a week, Frankfurt's insurrectionists presented petitions demanding reform, demonstrated in the streets and threatened to storm the Römer, Frankfurt's ancient city hall. Looting broke out and troops were drafted in. After a week's deliberation, on 10 March, the Senate published its uncompromising response to the reformers' demands. The following day, Adolph records that 'apart from the freedom of the press and the amnesty already announced a week ago, there will be no further concessions'. The Senate had also, in familiar terms, declined to enfranchise the city's Jews: 'With regard to the Jewish community, the Senate said it had always done all it could for the Jews, but that suddenly to grant them emancipation would be too great and too hasty a step. The Senate would do all it could but it would take time.'

Adolph wryly observes that: 'attitudes towards the Jews have generally not been very favourable this week, particularly among the lower classes. Indeed, some of the troublemakers who had been arrested when they tried to storm the cathedral said they had been paid to do it by Jews agitating for emancipation.'

By 30 March, as delegates arrived to make the preparations for elections to a constituent national assembly, the mood was uncertain: 'Everywhere in the town, there is jubilation and shooting in the air. But it's doubtful whether our prospects justify this optimism. Share prices keep falling. The news from Schleswig-Holstein and Milan brings the threat of war.[20] In Germany, here and there, there's talk of a republic. As things stand, a state of anarchy is by no means impossible and is widely feared.'

The fear of an uprising seems especially justified when the family's own interests are threatened. Adolph records on 1 June that: 'The workers at the oilcloth factory at Griesheim got up something of a revolt and so on Monday evening we got eight or ten guns and sabres together and were only awaiting the arrival of Uncles Gustav and Meyer, who had been there all day, before setting off at once with the weapons and spending the night there. Luckily, however, the uncles brought reassuring news which rendered the expedition unnecessary.'

The workers had clearly been emboldened by expectations of an egalitarian future for: 'they said in their petition that Uncle had grown rich by their labour; they didn't know why they had to submit to such drudgery but not he since, after all, sooner or later everything would be shared out etc. etc.' In the end the workers were appeased, 'at least until next Saturday when pay day comes round again'. Adolph may have been a reformer, but he was no revolutionary.

Throughout the summer of 1848, the German states jockeyed for power, hereditary rulers sought to face down republicans and reformers, left competed with right and faction with faction. By September, Frankfurt was in uproar over Prussia's abandonment of the war with Denmark. As Prussian troops were sent in to quell the rioting, Adolph coolly observes, 'the last three pages were written behind barricades to the sound of musket fire'.

Here, tantalisingly, his diary ends. What Adolph did next is not known. But he lived a prosperous and fulfilling life. He was at the height of his powers when German Jews were finally emancipated in 1871 and was ideally placed to enjoy the golden age of German Jewry. His children were not so blessed.

The signs were always there, even when rights and opportunities for German Jews seemed so limitless. By the close of the century, as Heine had found at the beginning, Jewish attempts to assimilate were still being resisted, on the one side from religious Jews desperate to keep their faith and community alive, and on the other from many in mainstream German society who stubbornly, and sometimes violently, refused to acknowledge Jewish equality. Even in possession of equal rights, Jews were still not admitted to the higher reaches of the civil service, the diplomatic corps and the army, and were often excluded from professional associations and social clubs.

Ruth Gay cites the example of the banker Gerson von Bleichröder, financial consultant to the German government, personal adviser to Chancellor Bismarck and the first Jew to be ennobled without having first converted. His distinctions counted for little in polite society for: 'despite his own title and the lavish balls he gave in his Berlin house, attended by members of the court and the foreign diplomatic corps, neither Bleichröder nor his wife was ever welcomed into the world of the aristocracy. Even Bismarck seems to have regarded Bleichröder as a shameful secret.'[21]

The lives of two brothers, on my father's side, illustrate how, as the century progressed, it gradually became possible for Jews to make their way in German society. But they had first to surmount the many obstacles placed in their way.

Herz Samson Herz and his wife Rosalie settled at Kulmbacher Straße 7 in Bayreuth around 1815. Samson was an observant Jew, a devout lover of German literature and a friend of the novelist Jean Paul for whom he was 'my Samson'. Jakob, born in 1816, was the eldest of their six sons and five daughters. Julius, the seventh child, was born in 1825.[22]

After Samson had lost his fortune, his children grew up in poverty and hardship. Jakob, a gifted and diligent pupil, graduated from Bayreuth's grammar school in 1835 but it was only with the support of distant relatives that he was able to go on to study medicine at the University of Erlangen. He had to overcome other disabilities for, according to family legend, he fainted at the sight of his first cadaver.

Nevertheless, as his memorialist Dr Abraham Lewinsky reports, his scholarship and character 'gained the respect and esteem of his fellow students and teachers alike' and, in 1841, he was appointed an assistant in the Department of Surgery.[23] His reputation grew steadily as he published scholarly articles and joined learned societies in Germany and beyond, and, in 1847, he was promoted to the position of demonstrator.

But when he sought to become a salaried lecturer in 1854, his application was rejected, despite the support of several of his colleagues. According to Lewinsky, 'only his religion ... barred his advancement in his academic career. But for being a Jew, he would have had every chance of occupying the Chair of Surgery.' Jakob was advised to convert to Christianity but declined.

Even after 1861, when the Bavarian Diet permitted Jews to take up residence in Erlangen for the first time since 1711, the university was prepared to offer Jakob no more than an honorary professorship. Only when he threatened to leave was he finally appointed a full professor, the first Jew to achieve such status in a Bavarian university.[24]

Further distinctions followed. The king awarded him the Knight's Cross 1st Class of the Order of St Michael for his service to the wounded of the war of 1866 in which Prussia defeated Austria and its Bavarian allies. He was also offered the post of personal physician to Kaiser Wilhelm I, but again rebuffed, politely, the condition that he convert.

The following year, in recognition of the 'humanity, untiring zeal and noble selflessness' of his service to both university and town and, in particular, for his provision of healthcare to the poor, he became the first Jew to be made an honorary citizen of Erlangen.

Finally, in 1869, he was appointed Professor in Ordinary and, having three years previously joined the left-liberal Progressive Party, was elected to the Erlangen College of Municipal Authorities. Dr Lewinsky paints the portrait of a man at the height of his powers, equally at home in his Jewish faith and the wider German culture: 'Inspired by true love of his country he supported every patriotic enterprise. He loved his homeland, Bavaria, but the unification of Germany, too, was the fulfilment of one of his most ardent desires.'

In 1871, when he volunteered to take charge of a hospital train bringing wounded soldiers back from the Franco-Prussian war, his sense of patriotic duty got the better of his failing health. News of his death and tributes to him filled the pages of the *Erlanger Tagblatt* for several days. On 2 October, the paper lamented the loss of a 'dear brother, one of the Fatherland's most loyal sons and among the greatest benefactors of the poor and needy'.

Two days later, it declared that, despite the torrential rain, crowds flocked to 'the grandest funeral in Erlangen in living memory'. A local photographer exhibited a life-size portrait of the great man in his studio and sold copies to his admirers. As Andreas Jakob, head of the Erlangen City Archive, has wryly observed, 'had Herz been a Catholic, he'd have qualified for sainthood'.[25]

In 1875, a bronze statue, paid for by public subscription, was erected in the centre of Erlangen, the first of any Jew in Germany and a source of some pride for my father.[26] Sixty years later, it was torn down by the grandchildren of those who raised it.

5. The destruction of the Jakob Herz statue in Erlangen on 15 September 1933. Reproduced by kind permission of Stadtarchiv Erlangen, VI.N.b.271a or VI.N.b.271, Photographer: Wilhelm Panneck.

Jakob's brother Julius also achieved celebrity. Having emigrated to Vienna, he became a notable railway engineer and, in due course, a director of Austria's leading bank, the Creditanstalt für Handel und Gewerbe.[27] He was knighted in 1875 by Emperor Franz Joseph, taking the hereditary title Julius Herz Ritter von Hertenried, one of only a handful of Jews to achieve such distinction. His son Paul, a noted tennis player, married into the Ephrussi dynasty and made it into the pages of the *Semigotha*, the Austrian equivalent to *Burke's Peerage*.

At the dawn of the twentieth century, the Herz family's future must have seemed very promising. They could not have foreseen that *Semigotha* would a generation later provide invaluable intelligence for the Nazis who, for plunder as well as destruction, sought out the Jews who had presumed to join the European nobility.

In 1879, as Adolph Zunz and Julius Herz were enjoying the fruits of their newfound success and status, the first reference to 'anti-Semitism' made its appearance in a Jewish newspaper.[28] The neologism was coined by Wilhelm Marr, founder of the League of Anti-Semites. He argued that Jews and Germans were unalterably, irreconcilably and scientifically different on racial rather than simply religious or cultural grounds. He warned that the Jews' attempts at assimilation were simply a cover for their increasingly successful pursuit of power and that they had to be stopped before they completely overwhelmed what he called 'Germandom'.[29]

The following year, a petition of 250,000 signatures was presented to the German Chancellor, calling on him to limit Jews to subordinate ranks in public office and debar them from teaching Gentile children. They demanded too that he restrict the immigration of Jews fleeing pogroms and poverty in eastern Europe.

This new anti-Semitism had particular traction in Germany's universities. Ruth Gay describes how Jewish students sought to organise to defend themselves. In 1886, at the university in Breslau (now the Polish city of Wrocław), they formed a fencing society so that they could challenge those who insulted them. But, as she observes, 'its very existence

6. Kurt Loeb-Feis in First World War uniform, proudly, or perhaps
defiantly, displaying the duelling scars he won in 1912.

was problematic, for the gentile clubs at first questioned whether Jews
were even permissible as dueling partners'.[30]

Family albums feature sepia photographs of my maternal great uncle
Kurt, his already scarred face elaborately bandaged after some misad-
venture with a rapier at Heidelberg University. Whether he was a
member of one of these fraternities and had acquired at least some of
his injuries in defence of Jewish honour is unknown. I had assumed
that his exploits were evidence of his integration into the more rarefied
social circles of his university. Perhaps the opposite is the case.

*　*　*

Lower down the social scale, the prejudice was altogether cruder. In her otherwise joyful account of life in the small Jewish community in the Hessian village of Oberaula in the 1880s and 1890s, Johanna Harris-Brandes, a cousin of Sally's, recalled the failed attempt by the new village parson to integrate Jewish and Christian children in knitting and gym classes: 'The class combined into one loud chorus, with mocking voices they repeated stingingly again and again: "They stink, those Jews, they stink, they stink, those Jews, they stink." Silently Jenny and I, ten and twelve years old, left the schoolroom, and that was the first and last time that Jewish girls attended the knitting class.'[31] The boys' gym class fared no better. Before it had even begun, the teacher cried out, 'will every stinking Jew here clear the yard', and that was that.

Johanna lived an emblematic life. Born in 1879, one of twelve children, she grew up in a poor and relatively primitive rural Jewish community, left her teacher/rabbi father's ramshackle home in the country and moved to Frankfurt where she established a business, manufacturing orthopaedic corsets and bandages. There she married Leopold Harris, a trader in soya and the inventor of a flame-resistant paint.

Leopold was also a leading Social Democrat. Immediately after the First World War, he was elected Chairman of the Workers and Soldiers Council and, in April 1919, he was appointed President of Frankfurt's police force. But his tenure lasted little more than six months. Refusing to follow instructions from Berlin to expel Polish Jews from the city, he resigned his post in November. When the Nazis came to power, he was high on their hit list. He fled to Strasbourg in 1933 but died there the same year. Johanna escaped Nazi Germany at the very last moment, reaching London the day before war broke out.

In sixty short years, Johanna's life story charts the journey of Germany's Jews from the political and economic optimism of the late nineteenth century to the existential catastrophe of the early twentieth.

For the most part, the Brandes and Zunz families were town dwellers. We know about some of them – Glückel, Samson and the Herz brothers for example – because it is the business of memorialists to celebrate the few who stand out from the crowd. But what of the lives of the many who make up those crowds, those whose virtues and achievements, often in the most unpromising of circumstances, ought to be no less celebrated?

The Brandes family had lived in Rotenburg an der Fulda, a small country town near Kassel in what was then Prussia, since at least the middle of the eighteenth century. The Jewish cemetery that hugs the hill overlooking the town is full of them.

A Jewish community had been established in Rotenburg since the founding of the town at the beginning of the thirteenth century but was wiped out in the pogroms of 1348. It was fully 350 years before Jews returned, but by 1738 the community was sufficiently large and prosperous to establish a synagogue and, two years later, the cemetery. By the end of the eighteenth century, there were some 200 Jews in Rotenburg, among them what became the Brandes family.

The Jewish Museum at Rotenburg proudly displays a Schutzbrief of 1733, the letter of protection which, by the authority of the Landgrave of Hessen-Kassel, allowed Salomon Eleazer Abt to reside in the town. According to the registers of the time, he would have paid somewhere between three and six Gulden for the privilege, just one of the taxes and charges he had to render to the local and regional nobility and their agents.

Records show that Geisel, born there in 1767, married Binchen Hirsch Abt in 1792. It was he who, in compliance with the Napoleonic decree of 1808, adopted the family name Brandes.[32] According to Johanna, her great grandfather was 'much honored' and 'a Kabbalist and a great expert in the knowledge of the *Torah* and other wise books'.[33]

Geisel and Binchen's son, Salomon Levi Brandes, born in 1802, was a master nailsmith. Though his wife Gütschen thought him 'the most unpractical man in the whole world', his son Moses, Johanna's father, described him more sympathetically as 'only a simple man, unknown and leading a quiet life', but with a rare talent: 'He used to sit daily in front of our little house, weather permitting, forging and hammering his nails, and while he was so occupied he thought out the loveliest stories and fairytales imaginable. He hardly ever sat there alone, there was always a swarm of children around him ... who devotedly followed each word he uttered.'[34]

Johanna's memoirs, written in old age in New England, cast a flickering candlelight over the lives of everyday folk living a simple village life.[35] Though they were immune from neither poverty nor prejudice, joy is never far from hardship in the childhood she describes:

> Our room is beside our parents' bedroom, and a wretched little room it is. It contains our three beds, which two and three of us children share. It is just as well. Our winters are incredibly cold and our little house is very old. There are cracks in the walls and in winter the snow and rain manage to creep through them and through the badly shut window. We children huddle close together then, keeping warm and hearing the wind howling. But getting up in the morning on days like that is the most difficult thing in the world. You go downstairs; open the heavy back door and run (as fast as the ice covered ground permits it) down to the flowing brook to perform morning ablutions. In summer time this can be the greatest fun the world, but in winter the ice has to be hacked open first.[36]

The rites and rituals of life and death were the business of the whole community of some twenty-five families. Johanna describes how, at the circumcision of her mother's seventh son and youngest child, all the Jewish women crowd into her bedroom to witness his ceremonial bath, each tossing a coin into the water for the midwife. Everyone turns out to celebrate a wedding, and especially to gawp at the bride's trousseau as it's paraded through the village.

And at the heart of all things is family life, punctuated and regulated by an age-old religious observance:

> Now mother lit the Sabbath candles, she covered her eyes and said the blessing over them, thanking God for giving us the Sabbath. Then she settled comfortably in her chair, so tired from a heavy

week's work. We children stepped before her and she blessed each one of us, her hands resting on our hair ...

Father is blessing now, then he blesses bread and wine while the aroma of the delicious food can be smelled everywhere. Paula brought the steaming soup tureen on the table and father put his arm around Mama's shoulder ... Mother looks at us and smiles so happily at our healthy, clean children's[?] faces. Tears, real big tears, stream down her face, they are the tears of happiness and satisfaction.

In Oberaula and villages like it, even in the late nineteenth century, old superstitions were difficult to dislodge: 'There were still real witches in our village. People knew who they were and pointed them out, nobody liked to be friends with them, and of course, the most important thing of all, they were never allowed to come into a shed near the cattle, for they would give the cattle the "bad eye" and this meant no more milk from the cows, and disease for the oxen.'[37]

But change is coming, for 'there, leaning against the wall of the village inn, was the strangest object the village had ever seen, gaped at by its inhabitants ... We had just seen the first bicycle.'[38]

There are many examples of cooperation and even friendship between Jews and Gentiles in Oberaula. But there are also clear dividing lines, some crudely anti-Semitic, others based more on social distinctions. In a telling vignette, Johanna recalls an exchange between her father and the parson. Envious of the success of the little Jewish school, the parson, who doubled as the local school inspector, had suggested that it merge with the Christian school. Though Moses had eventually agreed to the ill-fated experiment with the knitting and gym classes, this was for him a step too far:

'Mr. Parson,' father replied, 'I have to admit it, we are lucky here to have a man as school inspector who has definitely progressive ideas. Of course I agree that we should try everything for a better understanding between the Jewish and the gentile population, but I also feel that we professional people should set an example first.'

'And how am I to understand that?' asked the parson with a slight edge to his voice.

'Let's take for example the new, Jewish doctor,' said father, 'who sits day and night over his books, an educated and cultured young man. You, Mr. Parson, are one of his neighbors too. Have you, or the Magistrate, or the Postmaster, ever cared to exchange a friendly word with him?'

'But why should I?' called the Parson out heatedly. 'This man as a Jew is naturally outside my circle of society, just as I could never contemplate social relationships with the village gendarme or similar people and least of all with a Jew.'[39]

Cordial relations between Jews and Gentiles were not impossible, but, in such a social hierarchy, they were problematic. Moses's enduring friendship with Herr Gutfreund, the senior teacher at the Christian school, had to remain a 'shameful secret'. In the evenings, the children would listen for the sound of a pebble thrown against their window: 'That was the "big" teacher, who loved to visit us in the evening and sit and talk to us, but it had to be kept a secret because the school inspector parson, who lived next door, was not supposed to find out. Yes, anti-Semitism, in spite of all seeming friendliness, is often deeply embedded in some hearts ...'[40]

Moses died in 1910. For fifty years, he had taught the Jewish children of the village and served, unpaid, much to his resentment, as its rabbi and cantor. He had lived in a universe no greater than the confines of his community, one in which everyone and everything was known, in which every family celebration and each misfortune was the concern of all. It was a world of hardship, superstition, simple beliefs and simpler pleasures. But it was rapidly contracting.

By the time her father had died and the inconsolable Gutfreund had shed his many tears, Johanna and most of her brothers and sisters had left Oberaula, some for the city, some for foreign lands. The youngest, Leo, was killed on the Russian front in November 1914.

But sleepy little Oberaula was not a good place for Jews. In the elections to the Reichstag on 6 November 1932, 78 per cent of its citizens voted for the Nazi Party, almost twice the average for the rest of Hesse-Nassau. The following year, 25 gravestones in the Jewish cemetery were defaced and, on 1 April 1934, the school to which Moses had dedicated his life's work was closed. On Kristallnacht in November 1938, the synagogue was destroyed and Leo's name erased from the village war memorial. In 1943, his widow, their daughter, son-in-law and two grandchildren were deported to the camps from which they did not return.

Part Three

THE LAST GENERATION

*'If there is a hierarchy of suffering, Israel is at its head;
if the persistence of the torment and the patience with
which it is borne is ennobling, then Jews are among
the high-born of every nation.'*

Leopold Zunz, *Synagogale Poesie des Mittelalters*[1]

7

FOUR FAMILIES

The focus falls now on people I have come to know through family albums and yellowed documents: my grandfather, my grandmother, great uncles and aunts who, in different circumstances, I might have embraced. I glimpse in their grainy photographs, in their Sunday outings and their family celebrations, in their artless smiles and awkward poses, little slices of their abbreviated lives; I sense their personalities. My family's careers no longer simply thread in and out of the great, impersonal sweep of history. As the past slows towards our present, and as events become larger and noisier and more clearly defined, history itself is made up of the lives of my grandparents and their generation, and I stand in the places where they stood.

For 1,000 years, Europe's Jews had been subject to an almost unrelieved cycle of forced conversion, segregation, extortion, assault and expulsion. Finally, the latter half of the nineteenth century ushered in a new age of equality and optimism. Few could foresee that this life, so long awaited, so joyously welcomed, so deeply cherished, would end so abruptly and so soon.

Perhaps Theodore Herzl did. As a journalist in Vienna, he had been alarmed by the popular appeal of Karl Lueger's crudely anti-Semitic mayoral campaigns.[1] As the *Neue Freie Presse* correspondent in Paris, his fears had been intensified by the virulence of the anti-Jewish sentiment unleashed by the Dreyfus trial. In 1896, a generation before the Nazis came to power and at the height of what seemed the golden age for

Germany's Jews, he published his seminal argument for a Jewish state. His case was founded on neither religious nor nationalistic grounds. The 'propelling force', he declared, was 'the misery of the Jews':[2]

> We have honestly endeavoured everywhere to merge ourselves in the social life of surrounding communities and to preserve the faith of our fathers. We are not permitted to do so. In vain we are loyal patriots, our loyalty in some places running to extremes; in vain do we make the same sacrifices of life and property as our fellow-citizens; in vain do we strive to increase the fame of our native land in science and art, or her wealth by trade and commerce. In countries where we have lived for centuries we are still cried down as strangers, and often by those whose ancestors were not yet domiciled in the land where Jews had already had experience of suffering. The majority may decide which the strangers are; for this, as indeed every point which arises in the relations between nations, is a question of might … If we could only be left in peace … But I think that we shall not be left in peace.[3]

Mine is the first generation of our family born outside Germany since records began, in the case of the Zunzes, over 500 years ago. Marriage outside the Jewish faith, or at least the Jewish community, was all but unheard of even in my parents' time. Two of my father's cousins set their hearts on marrying Gentiles. As we shall see, one succeeded by means of a cunning deception; the other, lacking ingenuity, failed with tragic consequences.

Yet none of my generation – neither my sister, nor my two cousins nor I – have married Jews. None of us even bear the name with which our fathers were born. But though our break with tradition seems conclusive, we do not disclaim our past.

The Bradleys are the progeny of four families: the Brandeses and Herzsteins on my father's side and the Zunzes and the Loeb-Feises on my mother's. They were fairly typical of their times in that their fortunes fluctuated largely according to the prevailing attitude to Jews and the constraints placed on them. In this, they were unexceptional German Jewish families.

My great grandfather Heinrich Herzstein lived a long and fruitful life, from 1837 to 1926, and enjoyed the best years Europe had to offer its Jews. My father remembers him as 'revered by the family, a true patriarch' and one who was not to be contradicted: 'when his mind began to wander, he told me that he went round the world in a Zeppelin in 1857; when I began to query this, Zeppelins not being invented until the turn of the century, I was hushed by some uncle in no uncertain terms'.

Heinrich was still doing his daily press-ups at the age of 84. But as a young man, when he felt the time had come, he consulted his cousin, the great Professor Herz, on whether it would be wise for him to marry since both his parents had died young. Jakob took one look at him and declared: 'Heinrich, Du bist pumperlg'sund. Du kannst ruhig heiraten' ('You're as fit as a fiddle, no reason why you shouldn't').[4] And so, having been rejected by her sister, Heinrich married Philippine Fleischmann, the daughter of a Bayreuth cattle trader, 18 years his junior.

Heinrich and Philippine prospered. He owned two businesses in Bayreuth: a wholesale supplier of tailors' materials and a draper's shop. Philippine died in 1919, according to my father's chronicle a victim of the great Spanish Flu epidemic. But the records of the Jewish cemetery state that she 'drowned in a state of mental confusion' and her death certificate confirms that she was a suicide. My father eventually confided that, having recovered from the flu, his grandmother had thrown herself into the Roter Main, which flows through Bayreuth. He did not elaborate on the reasons, if he knew them.

Overleaf is a photograph taken in 1928, two years after Heinrich's death. My father's uncles and aunts have gathered to celebrate his Bar Mitzvah. It's the last time they came together in such numbers. The photographer is clumsy: though my father musters an uncertain smile, peering between the shoulders of two uncles, the rest stare warily into the lens; Uncle Gustav nods his blurred head as the shutter clicks; light glints from Uncle Karl's spectacles; Uncle Richard has raised a cigar to his lips; Uncle Hugo has audaciously advanced to inspect the camera. The group poses uncomfortably in irregular ranks and at a curious angle, as if the ground is slowly subsiding beneath them. In some ways it was. Though the Nazi Party had won just 2.6 per cent of the popular vote in that year's elections, only two years later, with the German economy in ruins, it was the second largest party in the Reichstag. By 1932 it was the largest.

It's the sheer mundanity of that photograph that is so compelling: all those ordinary people, so complacent, so ignorant of the future. But that year of 1928 was the turning point, the beginning of the end for the Weimar democracy. Within fifteen years, none of the seventeen family members captured in that frozen moment remained in Germany: six had fled; eleven had been murdered.

These are the seven children of Heinrich and Philippine, the last of the German Herzsteins.

Karl, the eldest, was born in 1876. He and his wife Emma had two daughters. The first, Lotte, emigrated to the US with her husband

7. The Herzstein and Brandes families at my father's Bar Mitzvah in 1928, the last time they were all together. Back: Uncles Gustav and Ernst, Aunts Rosel and Martha, Sally; Middle: Aunts Else and Hannah, Uncles Siegfried and Max, Aunt Emma, Uncle Julius; Front: Uncle Karl, my father, Uncle Hugo, Cousin Gretel, Bertha, Uncle Richard.

Helmuth Hirsch and settled in Providence, Rhode Island. The other, Thesi, my father observed, 'lacked charm'. But she fell in love with a Gentile, Herbert Ehm from Elbing in East Prussia. When the family disapproved, the couple contrived to allow a hotel bill to fall into their parents' hands and were married forthwith. Herbert and Thesi survived the war. Karl and Emma did not.

Gustav, born in 1878, managed a textile mill near Bayreuth. He married Gretel Schühlein, a relative of Albert Einstein, through whom the family likes to boast – or, at least, I do – of its kinship with the great man. Their daughter Friedel married Albert Fleischmann, a dentist. Friedel and Albert emigrated first to Rome and, when Mussolini's regime ramped up its anti-Semitism, to the US where Gustav and Gretel were eventually able to join them by way of Guatemala.

Richard, born in 1879, practised as a barrister in Bayreuth and was arrested almost immediately the Nazis came to power. He was detained for only one day but that was time enough for him to read the writing on the wall of his police cell. On his release, he emigrated to Jerusalem with his wife Martha and daughter Anneliese. When he died, they moved on to the USA.

Ernst, born in 1881, was a civil engineer. Though a pacifist, he served at the front in the First World War, was twice wounded and awarded the Iron Cross. He did not marry. He did not outlive the Nazis.

Next came Rosa (known as Rosel), born in 1884. 'Outgoing and exuberant', according to my father, she married Hugo Rosenthal who took over Heinrich's retail business. A man of many interests including fishing and stamp collecting, he was admired and envied as the owner of the family's first wireless set. In the course of Kristallnacht, he attempted to escape the mob by skinning down a drainpipe, earning the sobriquet 'the cat burglar'. Rosel and Hugo died in Latvia.

Rosel and Hugo's daughter Erna fell in love with a Gentile barrister but, though 'very attractive and high-spirited', she lacked her cousin Thesi's inventiveness and the family was not prepared to allow another daughter to marry out. A match was arranged with Kurt Simon, a young man from Hugo's hometown of Kirchberg and, according to my father, 'a cad'. They settled in Brussels whence Kurt absconded to Chile, taking Hugo's stamp collection and what remained of Erna's dowry, but leaving his wife and daughter Jeanne to fend for themselves. Erna was hidden throughout the Nazi occupation of Belgium by Willy Rijgersberg, a Dutchman whom she subsequently married. Jeanne died in Auschwitz.

I remember Erna and Willy well. They lived in Brussels in an apartment on the Boulevard Lambermont, and we regularly visited them en route from our family holidays to the ferry port of Ostend. Erna was a flamboyant woman with a loud, expressive voice, to which the extravagant flailing of her arms added emphasis. Willy was calm, kind, understanding. I was fascinated by the guitar hanging from their living room wall. It, they, and Erna in particular, seemed so exotic. I knew little of the tragedies she had endured.

My father's mother, Bertha, born on 21 January 1886, was the second youngest of the children.

The youngest, Julius, was born in 1891. My father recalls him as an introvert and a hypochondriac. A bachelor, he worked for some time in a bank in Schweinfurt before retiring to live on his private income in his father's rather grand, four-square house at Bayreuth. Julius perished in Latvia.

Though Moses Brandes' life is the best documented, his parents Salomon and Gütschen had five more children, Binchen, David, Jeisel, Hirsch and Malchen.

Hirsch was a veteran of the Franco-Prussian war of 1870–1 and so staunch a patriot that he had a record of his service inscribed on his tombstone. It still proudly stands in the Jewish cemetery at Rotenburg. He and his wife Hannchen had four daughters and three sons, of whom Sally, my grandfather, was the youngest.[5]

Hirsch had a drapery business in the centre of Rotenburg, on the banks of the Fulda. In a photograph, taken in 1912, Hirsch and Sally flank a neat little line of children posing proudly at the entrance to the shop, which proudly boasts the 'largest stock of velvet, silk and lace fabrics'.[6] Two robust-looking women are framed in the window of the apartment above.

8. Hirsch Brandes with his son Sally and grandchildren Hermann, Kurt,
Lutz and Gretel outside his shop at Rotenburg.

Here is a roll-call of the last Brandeses of Rotenburg, the seven children of Hirsh and Hannchen.

Joseph, the eldest, fell from a ladder and died at the age of 18. Moses, known as Max and remembered by my father as a jovial and kindly man, took over his father's business and became chairman of Rotenburg's Jewish community, earning the nickname 'the Jewish Mayor'. He and his wife Johanna (Hannah) had four children, my father's photogenic cousins: Kurt emigrated to South Africa and was able to rescue his parents shortly before the outbreak of war; Hermann and Ludwig (known as Lutz) emigrated to the USA. Gretel, whose photographs reveal a lovely young woman with a square, open face, married Hans Goldschmidt, manager of the Tietz department store in Oberhausen. Neither Gretel, nor Hans, nor their daughter Margit, survived the Holocaust.

Sally's sisters, Meta and Paula, neither of whom married, travelled to America but returned and, in 1902, opened their own draper's and haberdashers' shop, Geschwister Brandes, Brandes Sisters, in Rengsdorf on the Rhine. When it was forced out of business in 1934, Meta and Paula were virtually penniless and, in 1936, Meta, also a partner in Sally's business, returned to Bamberg to live with him and Bertha. Neither Paula nor Meta survived the Nazis.

A third sister, Rosa, married Max Rosenthal, a cattle dealer from Meinerzhagen. She died of natural causes. Their son Walter emigrated to Palestine, their daughter Ilse to the UK. Max perished somewhere in Poland, either Sobibor or Belzec.

Jettchen, born in 1870, married Jacob Hecht and lived in Rengsdorf. Of their five children, Adolf emigrated to California and Erich to Chile; Artur came to the UK in 1933 and lived in Whitechapel. He was able to rescue his parents shortly before the outbreak of war and looked after them until they died. My father never forgot that Artur gave him half a crown when, newly arrived in London in 1939, he could not afford to repair his shoes. Artur's police internment record describes his occupa-

9. Paula, Max, Jettchen, Meta, Rosa and Sally Brandes.

tion as butcher, but when he died suddenly after the war he was selling ice cream from a van in Rickmansworth.

Jettchen and Jacob also had two daughters. Susi married a Gentile and, though divorced, survived the war hidden in a Catholic convent. She was the only member of the Brandes family left alive in Germany after the war. Gerda perished at Auschwitz.

My grandfather Sally, born on 4 January 1882, left school at the age of 14 to be apprenticed to a draper at Northeim in Westphalia. He married Bertha Herzstein in 1913 and they set up home together in Bamberg. Their only child Fritz, my father, was born on 13 May 1915.

They were all just everyday people.

When my maternal grandmother Helene's parents, Sigmund Loeb and Eugenie Feis, married, they merged their family names.[7] Both came from small towns along the WeinStraße, the wine-growing district of the Rheinpfaltz (the Palatinate). Various branches had vineyards in the wine-producing towns of Deidesheim, Wachenheim and Bad Dürkheim.

The Feises were a well-to-do family of winegrowers and traders with a wide range of interests. Simon, 1831–91, owned a grand house in Frankfurt, Im Trutz (literally, 'In Defiance'), with a fountain in the hall and an organ in the music room. The house was large enough to entertain the entire cast of the nearby Frankfurt Opera in after-show parties. Jacob, 1842–1900, emigrated to London where he ran a successful business importing gloves and feathers. He was also a distinguished Shakespeare scholar and translator of the works of Ruskin and Tennyson. His *Shakespeare and Montaigne*, published in 1884, remains in print.

Sigmund Loeb sold wine from his vineyards as far afield as America but died at the relatively young age of 45. His widow Eugenie, struggling to cope with six children, resorted to what appears at first sight a particularly cold-hearted solution. Though she could not have foretold it, her stratagem saved the lives of my mother, uncle and grandparents, and her own.

She arranged with Jacob and his wife Anna to adopt one of her children. They chose Marie who, in 1897 at the impressionable age of 14, found herself cut adrift from her family and transplanted to a foreign city and an alien culture. In due course, she married Walter Tuteur, a wealthy stockbroker from a German Jewish family who had settled in London. They lived very comfortably in Hampstead with their two daughters. I remember Great Aunt Marie as something of a *grande dame*, living out her old age in a hotel on Eaton Square in Belgravia.

Eugenie's sons both enlisted in the German army and died in the First World War. Oswald was, according to my uncle, 'a head-strong intellectual' who had studied medicine, became a medical researcher and married a fellow scientist. On the outbreak of war in 1914, he joined the Army Medical Service and, having claimed that he could ride in order to accelerate his commission, promptly fell off his horse at Metz and died of a fractured skull.

Kurt studied medicine at Heidelberg where he acquired his much-prized duelling scars. It is said that following an affair with a fellow officer's wife, he engineered a transfer to Turkey. He was involved in the construction of the Constantinople–Baghdad railway in Mesopotamia (now Iraq) when, in 1918, his camp was attacked by Arab guerrillas and he was shot in the head while tending to the wounded. He is buried in Mosul.

Adolph Zunz and his wife Hermine Hirsch had three children.

When their daughter Emma married Emil Nickelsberg in 1892, Adolph provided a dowry of 75,000 Marks, a substantial sum. But Emma was a modest and kindly woman and a model citizen, insisting during the First World War that she live on the meagre official rations to which the less well-off were limited. She and Emil had two children, Paul and Marta.

Karl Hermann, my maternal grandfather, married Sigmund and Eugenie Loeb's fourth daughter Helene.[8] He was 41, she 26. She had been married before, to a Dr Blum, who in mysterious circumstances shot himself in a wood shortly after their wedding in 1907. She kept his love letters for the rest of her long life.

Hermann and Helene had two children, my uncle Vernon and my mother Gertrude, known as Trude.[9] Vernon was born Werner Adolf

Zunz on 13 December 1911 in Offenbach where the family lived in a spacious apartment with a large verandah, albeit overlooking a factory yard.[10] Gertrude was born on 6 October 1918.

Hermann had been a relatively prosperous businessman. He owned a factory in Seligenstadt that made evening gowns sold to couture houses in the great cities. In 1910, he acquired a second in Offenbach but it failed, possibly when he was called up to the Landsturm (Home Guard) during the First World War.

After the war, the Seligenstadt business, now jointly owned with a partner, survived until the hyper-inflation of the 1920s turned Hermann's savings to dust. My uncle described the father he loved as 'a modest, honourable and kindly man', but 'in no way equipped to adapt himself to the changing, difficult times in which he lived'. He was squeezed out of the company, took to trying to sell items of haberdashery to local shops, and, when the coming of the Nazis made it virtually impossible for him to earn a living, was forced on occasion to resort to the soup kitchens to feed his family.

In 1931, the Zunzes moved to Frankfurt and, after attending Art School in Dresden, Werner studied architecture at the University of Darmstadt. But in 1936, as he was beginning to establish himself professionally, he received a letter from the Reichskulturkammer (the Reich Chamber of Culture), informing him that, as a Jew, he would be incapable of producing work in conformity with Aryan values and was henceforth barred from practice.[11]

He recognised that it was time to go. He left Germany in January 1936 with a 'J' stamped in his passport and 10 Reichmarks, around £1, the maximum emigrating Jews were allowed, in his pocket. My mother followed him later that year and their parents and grandmother joined them in 1939, a few months before war broke out. It was Aunt Marie's sponsorship that had saved them all.

Hermann's brother Wilhelm Albert, known as Albert, was the last remaining Zunz in Germany. He was a mechanical engineer who, according to my uncle, was always cheerful and optimistic despite the many hardships he endured. He had himself baptised in 1905 and served in the German army throughout the First World War. In 1920 he married Ida Stoll, a Gentile woman. They were both socialists and possibly members of the Communist Party. As such, they were obvious targets for the Nazis. Albert did not survive them.

10. Bertha and Sally Brandes with their assistant Else Engelhaupt and Lord, the dog, outside their first shop at Dominikanerstraße 1 in 1913.

8

THE END OF THE BEGINNING

My first night at Bamberg's Hotel Alt-Ringlein was restless. The room was cosy enough and the mattress soft. But the night was warm and drinkers from the Ambräusianum had spilled out onto Dominikanerstraße. There they kept up their beery banter and later their discordant choruses into the small hours. And when the last reveller had stumbled home and sleep had finally come, the Council's refuse trucks came rattling and wheezing down the narrow street to take away the debris of the night before in readiness for the night to come.

Here, at Dominikanerstraße 10, in a second-floor apartment above what was then the Mahr distillery and bar, the Brandes family had lived between 1915 and 1925. They had moved there just two years after Sally and Bertha had opened their first business a few doors down the street at Dominikanerstraße 1.

In one of the battered Brandes family albums that survived the war in the vaults of the A.E. Wassermann Bank, there is an old sepia photograph of that first shop. The fascia announces that these are the premises of S Brandes and a sign in the window advertises *Manufaktur: Kurz und Seidenwaren*, haberdashery and silks, with 'Reste nach Gewicht' ('remnants by weight') a speciality. Outside on the pavement stand the newly wed Sally and Bertha, he spruce and suited with a proprietorial watch-chain across his broad chest, she in a pale blouse and a long dark skirt, gazing rather wistfully, or perhaps short-sightedly, into the camera. The year is 1913. All is good.

* * *

93

Sally Brandes had married Bertha Herzstein on 24 October 1913. As was still the custom in many Jewish communities, the marriage was arranged. But it was a happy one. My father said that he never heard a cross word between his outgoing, gregarious father and his rather more reserved and private mother.

The newly-weds invested Bertha's dowry of 25,000 Marks, worth a not-insignificant £1,250 at the time, in their new shop and, on the strength of the first day's takings, and much to her alarm at his extravagance, Sally treated Bertha to champagne at the best hotel in Bamberg.

By the time their son Fritz was born two years later, Sally had been called up to the German army.[1] Being medically unfit for the trenches because of a hernia, he served on the staff of a POW camp at Landau in the Palatinate before being posted to Belgium to serve as a court martial interpreter. My father's first memory was of cheering crowds on Armistice Day. When his patriotic father returned home, he telegrammed from the Belgian border to announce that he was back 'on German soil'.

In 1920, Sally and Bertha were able to move their shop to premises at Lange Straße 16 in Bamberg's main shopping district. They were fortunate that, at a time when paper money had lost almost all its value, their capital had been invested in the business. They were thus able to withstand the rampant inflation and devaluation that wiped out the savings of much of the German middle classes, including those of Hermann Zunz.

Sally was successful in business, a leading member of the Bamberg lodge of the Oddfellows, chairman of the synagogue choir and an all-round pillar of the community. Half the family's friends were Jewish, half Gentile. The Brandeses were solidly, respectably middle class and certainly as German as they were Jewish.

In his family history, my father wrote that, but for the intervention of the Nazis, 'I would not have made the break (from Judaism in its widest sense) although I would have continued the trend towards less and less observance'. But his was a Jewish home: 'My paternal grandfather still wore his skullcap and presided over a strictly kosher household.

My parents were more liberal ... my father went regularly to synagogue on Friday nights and Saturdays. He was devout in his own selective way. My mother came from a less observant family but went along with my father's tradition with, I suspect, only slight motivation.'

Fritz attended primary school at seven and four years later entered the Neues Gymnasium (now the Franz Ludwig Gymnasium), a predominantly Roman Catholic grammar school. Sally wanted him to leave before he took his Abitur exams so that he could join the family business but Fritz mobilised his mother, teachers, classmates and friends and managed to stay on.[2]

However, life for Bamberg's Jews was not entirely serene. In 1919, amid the unrest that followed Germany's defeat, the city's police reported that 'anti-Semitic agitation is increasing everywhere in Northern Bavaria. It is not restricted to ... a relatively small circle of far right-wing individuals, but extends into all strata of the population.'[3]

In the February of that year, Bavaria's first prime minister, the Jewish Socialist Kurt Eisner, was fatally shot in the back by Anton Graf von Arco auf Valley, a monarchist, anti-Bolshevik, anti-Semite. In the mayhem that followed, Eisner's successor Johannes Hoffmann declared a People's State of Bavaria. His government was almost immediately forced to retreat to Bamberg by an alliance of communists and anarchists, which declared a rival Bavarian Soviet Republic. In May, the Freikorps, paramilitary groups of ultra-nationalist army veterans enlisted by the German government, extinguished Bavaria's brief but chaotic period of revolutionary independence. In August, the Bamberg Constitution established the Free State of Bavaria within the new Weimar Republic.

But the experience of the Schreckensherrschaft, the six-month 'rule of horror', had created a toxic popular loathing of the left, which the Nazis ruthlessly exploited in the coming decades.

At von Arco's trial, the state prosecutor remarked that 'if the whole German youth were imbued with such a glowing enthusiasm we could face the future with confidence'. Though sentenced to death, he served only four years of a commuted five-year sentence. He was, however, obliged to vacate his well-appointed cell in Landsberg Prison on the arrival of Adolf Hitler, the leader of the new Nationalsozialistische Deutsche Arbeiterpartei, the National Socialist German Workers Party, who had been jailed for his part in the Beerhall Putsch, his party's failed attempt to seize power in Munich. Hitler settled down to enjoy his newfound celebrity and, over the next nine months, to write *Mein Kampf.*

In 1926–7, the police began to record increasing numbers of assaults on Jews by 'members of radical right-wing organisations and uniformed mobs', many of them former Freikorps members who had flocked to the Nazi standard. In October 1926, the Bavarian government expelled twenty-six Jewish immigrant families from Bamberg on the grounds that they were Polish citizens.

Six months later, in April 1927, the newly launched Bamberg Nazi propaganda sheet *Die Flamme* published an article under the headline 'Bamberg Retail under Jewish Domination', targeting several of the city's Jewish shopkeepers, including Sally.

These were disturbing portents, but life was still good and the Brandes business continued to prosper. In 1933, it moved again, this time to larger premises on a prime site at Grüner Markt 4. The new shop opened on Tuesday 2 February, just two days after President Paul von Hindenburg had appointed Adolf Hitler German Chancellor.[4]

Friedrich Nietzsche wrote of Heinrich Heine that 'the highest conception of the lyric poet was given to me by Heinrich Heine. I seek in vain in all the realms of history for an equally sweet and passionate music. He possessed that divine malice without which I cannot imagine perfection ... One day it will be said that Heine and I have been by far the foremost artists of the German language.'[5]

While the Nazis revered Nietzsche – though he would most likely have abominated them – they considered Heine degenerate. His were among the books burned by a crowd of 40,000 students and others in Berlin's Opernplatz (now Bebelplatz) on 10 May 1933. Just as the Nuremberg Laws on Citizenship and Race were to plagiarise the Canons of the Fourth Lateran Council, so this outrage found centuries-old precedents. Some 700 years earlier, in June 1242, the public execu-

-tioner lit a bonfire of 10,000 manuscript copies of the Talmud in the Place de Grève in Paris. Around 300 years later, in 1553, the Talmud was again committed to the flames throughout the city states of Italy.

As the books burned in Berlin, the mob was exhorted by Joseph Goebbels: 'The era of extreme Jewish intellectualism is now at an end … The future German man will not just be a man of books, but a man of character … And thus you do well in this midnight hour to commit to the flames the evil spirit of the past.'[6]

Though it took two visits to Berlin for me to find it, the site of that infamous bonfire is now marked by a memorial. On it is engraved that famous and most prescient observation of Heine's, that: 'where they burn books, they end up burning people'.

This was only one of Heine's chilling prophecies. In 1834, a century before they were so precisely and painfully fulfilled, he wrote that:

Christianity – and this is its fairest merit – subdued to a certain extent the brutal warrior ardour of the Germans, but it could not entirely quench it; and when the cross, that restraining talisman, falls to pieces, then will break forth again the ferocity of the old combatants, the frantic Berserker rage whereof Northern poets have said and sung so much …

The thought precedes the deed as the lightning the thunder. German thunder is of true German character: it is not very nimble, but rumbles along somewhat slowly. But come it will, and when ye hear a crashing such as never before has been heard in the world's history, then know that at last the German thunderbolt has fallen … There will be played in Germany a drama compared to which the French Revolution will seem but an innocent idyll.[7]

A century later, in dreadful counterpoint, Hitler's favourite ideologue Alfred Rosenberg announced that the moderating influences of both Christianity and humanism had indeed been swept away. Now, he proclaimed, 'the actions of history and the future no longer signify class struggle or warfare between Church dogmas, but rather the conflict between blood and blood, race and race, people and people …'[8]

And he concluded, as the frantic Berserker rage was unleashed, 'in such a manner reason and understanding divorce themselves from race and nature'.[9]

Within weeks of their election in March 1933, the Nazis had set aside the fragile constitutional democracy of the Weimar Republic.[10] An Enabling Act of 24 March vested almost absolute power in the Chancellor, allowing him and his government to legislate by decree without recourse to Parliament, and they wasted no time in applying these new powers to the persecution of German Jews.

Over the next twelve years, the Nazis introduced some 2,000 laws, decrees and ordinances – an average of around one every two days – designed to degrade and dehumanise Jews in every conceivable way and to strip them of their rights, their property and, ultimately, their existence.

On 1 April, Aryan citizens were encouraged to boycott Jewish-run concerns and Jewish professionals. The *Bamberger Tagblatt* published a list of forty-nine businesses, including Sally's, along with twelve lawyers, seven doctors and two dentists with whom Gentiles were advised not to consort.

Throughout Germany, SA (Sturmabteilung) Storm Troopers daubed the Star of David and crude anti-Semitic slogans in yellow and black across the windows of Jewish shops and offices. Thugs in uniform stood menacingly at the doors to deter Gentile customers. Many Jews were abused or physically assaulted. Then came the burning of the books.

Sally tried to carry on as usual. A week after the boycott, he took out an advertisement in the paper that had encouraged his customers to desert him: 'Are you looking for new silk or woollen wear for this spring and summer? You'll find all you could want here.' At first sight, it seems his marketing campaign had the desired effect. In its annual review, the *Bamberger Jahrbuch* (Yearbook) of 1933 was glowing in its praise for his establishment: 'Grüner Markt has been enriched by the tastefully decorated windows of the newly arrived S Brandes shop specialising in woollen and silk fabrics ... Thanks to its courteous and professional service, S Brandes has secured a large number of customers.'[11]

But the Nazis were just getting into their stride. On 7 April the Law for the Restoration of the Professional Civil Service barred Jews from government service while the Law on the Admission to the Legal Profession effectively prevented young Jews from taking up the law.

On 24 April, the Law Against the Overcrowding of German Schools and Universities limited Jews to 1.5 per cent of new applications and required that they make up no more than 5 per cent of the total student body.

From 15 May 1933, Jews were no longer allowed to Germanise their names and on 14 July the Law for the Repeal of Naturalisation and Recognition of German Citizenship removed the right to German citizenship from anyone who had acquired it since the end of the First World War.

On 24 September the Farm Law forbade Jews from owning farms or working in agriculture and, from 4 October, the Editorial Law barred them from editing newspapers and removed them from membership of the Journalists Association.

Local authorities and a wide range of professional and voluntary associations were quick to apply their own prohibitions and indignities. As early as March 1933, the city of Cologne (Köln) barred Jews from municipal sports facilities and in April the German boxing association banned Jewish fighters. In Baden, that same month, the speaking of Yiddish in cattle markets was outlawed.

On 14 September 1933, in Erlangen, the City Council unanimously declared that the statue of Jakob Herz, paid for sixty years earlier by public subscription, represented a 'cultural disgrace which has offended the entire German people'. The following day, to the delight of the assembled townsfolk, it was hauled down and lowered into a wooden crate, where it lay like a corpse until, in 1944, it was melted down to fuel the Nazis' war effort. Herz's grave in Baiersdorf was also desecrated.[12] In Bayreuth, a street commemorating his brother Julius was renamed.[13]

In Bad Dürkheim, the bench commemorating the war-dead Kurt and Oswald Loeb-Feis in the woods overlooking the town was flung down the hillside.

In Bamberg, Robert Loebl, an Iron Cross veteran, received a curt note informing him that his membership of the German-Austrian Alpine Club, which he had joined in 1921, had 'lapsed' and, to avoid embarrassment, the boat presented to the local rowing club in memory of a Jewish officer killed in the First World War was sunk.[14]

Well intentioned though it surely was, the *Jahrbuch*'s puff piece for Sally's business did not tell the whole story. The rise of the Nazis had led to a fall in his sales and by the end of 1933 he was forced to reduce his staff from eight to six.[15] He tried to weather the storm and the following March declared in the local press that 'the largest and most well-known manufacturers in Germany are competing with my business to supply the latest and most beautiful Spring fabrics in wool and silk'. But there were other troubles to face.

Shortly after S Brandes had moved to Grüner Markt, the business was forced to change its name. A Georg Kübrich, who owned a shop opposite Sally's old premises on Lange Straße and displayed a vindictive, anti-Semitic streak, threatened to take Sally to court to enforce an obscure regulation requiring firms founded after a certain date to register their names in full. In 1934, S Brandes was obliged to become Sally Brandes – Specialising in Woollen and Silk Fabrics.[16]

Fritz would dearly have liked to pursue his love of science at university but didn't have the heart to disappoint his father a second time. In any event, it was by now out of the question for a Jew to attend university. So on 15 April 1935, a month after his school graduation, he took up an apprenticeship at Schwarzschild Ochs, a well-known drapery business in Frankfurt, to prepare for the eventual takeover of his father's business.

He lodged with the 'gentle, Orthodox yet tolerant' Grünebaums, who had been his father's landlords in 1911 when he had worked in Frankfurt. Despite the ever-tightening grip of the Nazis, Fritz enjoyed the relative freedom that the large Jewish community in Frankfurt could afford a young man. He was a scout leader in the Bund Deutsche Jüdische Jugend (BDJJ), the League of German Jewish Youth, through which he first met my mother, and joined the kayaking and skiing sections of a Jewish sports club. On a skiing trip to the Bavarian Alps, he began his lifelong love affair with photography, going without food to save for the Leica he bought in 1936.

But Nazi measures against the Jews were intensifying. In 1935 they were banned from military service and from acting on stage or screen. In September, a sign appeared outside the weekly market on Bamberg's Maxplatz, warning that 'Jews enter at their own risk'.

Then, on 15 September, the Nuremberg Laws formalised the Nazis' persecution purely on the basis of race. They stripped Jews of their German citizenship, their right to vote or to hold political office and, according to the third article, the Law for the Defence of German Blood and Honour, forbade marriage or sexual relations between them and Aryans.

The Nazis researched the genealogy of suspected Jews with extraordinary zeal. My uncle recalls in his Zunz family history that his friend Percy Imelmann discovered that his paternal grandmother had been Jewish only when his father was summarily dismissed from his post as chair of English Literature at Frankfurt University. The family emigrated to England.

When later the persecution of German Jews gave way to extermination, those categorised by the Nuremberg Laws as half-Jewish and those married to non-Jews were normally spared deportation, at least so long as their marriages lasted and the Gentile partner remained alive. But Herbert Loebl recounts a chilling story that illumines the complicity of the Catholic Church in Bamberg, as elsewhere (though not everywhere), in the Nazis' deadly assault on the Jews: 'The scion of a prominent Bamberg Jewish family was married to a non-Jewish wife. This woman was anxious that her son – brought up as a Catholic – should enter the priesthood. The Church authorities agreed on one condition: that the marriage be annulled. The consequences of such a step could not have been unknown to the Church. The woman agreed and thereby signed the death warrant of her former husband.'[17]

In reality, the Nuremberg Laws served only to confirm in statute what had been the de facto position of Germany's Jews since the day Hitler assumed power. As Hannah Arendt put it: 'they had been second-class citizens, to put it mildly, since January 30 1933; their almost complete separation from the rest of the population had been achieved in a matter of weeks or months – through terror but also through the more than ordinary connivance of those around them'.[18] She cites the testimony of Dr Benno Cohn, a Jewish community leader in pre-war Berlin, who recalled that 'there was a wall between Gentiles and Jews. I cannot remember speaking to a Christian during all my journeys over Germany.'[19]

The pace of persecution abated in 1936 as Germany played host to the winter and summer Olympics and the Nazis sought to conceal their rampant anti-Semitism from their honoured guests. Nonetheless, early in the year, Jews were barred from becoming tax consultants and vets and in October, after the games, from teaching in state schools.

In January and April 1938, new edicts prevented Jews from changing either their names or those of their businesses. In August, if their surnames were not included on a register of those considered identifiably Jewish, they were required to adopt Sara or Israel as middle names. As documents thereafter record, both German and British, my father became Fritz Israel Brandes.

A decree of 26 April required Jews to register all assets over the value of 5,000 Reichsmarks (c. £430 in January 1939). From July, Jewish physicians were allowed only to treat Jewish patients and from September Jews were altogether barred from the legal professions. From October, the passports of all Jews were invalidated unless they had a large red 'J' for Jude stamped in them.

No opportunity to exclude, deprive or humiliate eluded the lawmakers. In March 1938, Jews were forbidden to own private gardens, from July they were barred from health spas and after Kristallnacht on 9 November they were excluded from cinemas, opera houses and concert halls.

Sally's shop had remained at Grüner Markt 4 until 1937 when, under pressure from the Nazis, the landlord, a lawyer named Roessner, terminated the lease. Nothing daunted, Sally, the patriotic optimist, confident that he could outlast the Nazis and believing that ownership would allow him to control his own destiny, bought a new shop at Grüner Markt 15, opposite the old one. He acquired his premises on 1

January 1938. Ten months later, on 11 November, the day after
Kristallnacht, he was arrested and sent to Dachau.

Sally's old shop at Grüner Markt 4 is occupied today by the Bamberg
branch of a rather smart kitchen and tableware retailer, WMF. When I
visited in April 2019, I mentioned to the friendly manageress that my
grandfather had traded there before the war; she expressed polite interest before remarking that the store had, a year earlier, celebrated its
eightieth anniversary in the premises.

Perhaps, after I had left, she recognised the significance of what she
had told me.

Dr Martin Morgenroth, president of Bamberg's Jewish congregation
between 1930 and October 1938, kept a journal in those fateful years.[20]
It catalogues the frequent cultural events – lectures, talks, concerts –
that took place in the community. And it meticulously records the
several deaths, including a significant number of suicides, the few births
and the many emigrations that testify to the contraction of the community – at first gradual and then rapidly accelerating as the Nazi
repression intensified.

At the end of 1930, there had been 875 Jews in Bamberg, a little
more than 1 per cent of the city's population (though 10 per cent of its
doctors and 20 per cent of its lawyers). By May 1939, the month my
father emigrated, the community had shrunk to 418. At the end of the
war, there were just twelve Jews left in Bamberg, spared the Holocaust
because they were married to Aryans.

Dr Morgenroth would have been keenly aware of the risks he ran in
keeping his journal. His account is accordingly guarded and, for the
most part, dispassionate. But it provides the clearest evidence of the
Nazis' determination to make Jewish life intolerable.

Though he makes no mention of Hitler's ascent to the Chancellorship
on 30 January 1933, his entry for 15 March records that 'in the wake
of the take-over by the new regime, the following members of our
community were arrested on suspicion of political activities: Attorney
W Aron, Mr Rimple, manager of the Tietz department store, and Mrs
Fraustaedter'.

On 16 April he notes that while the others had been released, Willy Aron remained in detention. On the same day, he reports that two Jewish lawyers had lost their professional licences, barred by new regulations that prevented non-Aryans from practising unless they were established before 1914, had served on the front or lost a father or son in the war.

He also mentions that 'calm prevailed during the boycott of Jewish businesses on 31 March (*sic*). Most establishments closed voluntarily.' On 1 May, his entry reads: 'As of today all ritual slaughter in the German Reich is prohibited.'

On 15 May, he reports abruptly that 'Attorney Wilhelm Aron died suddenly at the concentration camp Dachau, near Munich, at the age of 27 … The official death certificate listed pneumonia as the cause of death. By the order of the criminal police, the coffin, sealed in Dachau, was not to be opened.'

In fact, Aron had been brutally beaten and had died of his injuries in the camp. To conceal them, his body had been doused in petrol and set alight and the remains placed in the sealed coffin for delivery to his parents. The cause of his death was officially given as 'heart failure'.

Aron's offence, apart from being Jewish and an outstanding young lawyer, was that he had been a defiantly anti-Nazi social democrat. He had also had the temerity to suggest that the Nazis themselves had been responsible for the burning of the Reichstag on 27 February 1933, for which they blamed the communists as a pretext for mass arrests.[21] My father knew him. They had been members of the same youth group.[22] Fifty years later in a letter to Herbert Loebl, he wrote: 'During my time at Buchenwald I met a fellow inmate who was a witness of Willy Aron's murder in Dachau: Willy had to sit at a table, hands on the table; at the slightest movement he was beaten across the back with a truncheon; this made him wet himself, for which he was "punished" with further blows until he was dead. Small wonder they posted SA sentries at the Jewish cemetery for six weeks after he had been buried there.'[23]

Though Dr Morgenroth's language is restrained and occasionally enigmatic, the community was clearly doing all it could to adapt to life under the Nazis. On 22 May, he refers to the founding of a Committee for Aid and Rehabilitation, 'the task: to aid in training and help in the adjustment to a new mental attitude'. On 15 June, he records that 'to minimise the terrible effect of the recent political upheaval, an optional third hour of religious instruction was initiated. A stronger awareness of Jewish values will act as a counterbalance to any feelings of inferiority.'

But this was not a straightforward task. Since 1904, the Ressource, a magnificent building on Hainstraße, had provided the Jewish community's principal cultural centre, equipped with a library, a theatre, a cinema and a space for religious and social celebrations. In the First World War it had served as a military hospital. But as early as 1934, its governing committee had been forced to sell the building for 40,000 Reich Marks to Ostmark-Selbsthilfe, a holding company, which, on 18 June 1934, passed it to the Gestapo. It served as their local headquarters until they set fire to it in 1945, presumably to prevent discovery of their records. Ironically, many were housed in the building's fire-proofed basement and fell into the hands of the occupying Americans.

On 11 December, Morgenroth records that the community had acquired the Weiße Taube (White Dove), an inn on Zinkenwörth, which could be used for educational and community purposes and so that 'Jewish travellers, deprived of accommodation at Aryan hotels, will now be able to stop in a place with a welcoming atmosphere'. A few years later, this last remaining Jewish institution in Bamberg became the marshalling point from which the city's Jews, my grandparents among them, would be marched to the railway station and their fate in the east.

By then, Sally and Bertha had lost their home. They had lived in a second-floor apartment at Herzog-Max Straße 16, opposite the synagogue, since 1924. In 1935, the leases of all Jews living in council-owned accommodation were cancelled. Sally and Bertha moved to a first-floor flat at Friedrichstraße 17 where they remained until, in September 1939, they were forced into the Judenhaus, the Jew house, at Hainstraße 4a.[24]

On 15 September 1935, Morgenroth describes the marking of the twenty-fifth anniversary of the opening of the synagogue of which

Bamberg's Jewish community was so proud. Many dignitaries from out of town attend but the mood of the speeches and the music alike is solemn, 'reflecting the aura of these troubled times'.[25]

'This', Dr Morgenroth reflected, 'was our last celebration as citizens of the German Reich.' On that day, the Reichstag unanimously adopted the Nuremberg Laws. Henceforth, 'a Jew cannot be a citizen of the Reich'.

On 10 August 1936, Morgenroth had noted that 'by ministerial ordinance, all religious instruction in Bavarian schools is suspended'. Thereafter, he confines himself to the cataloguing of the births, marriages, deaths, emigrations and occasional gatherings of a besieged community.

Dr Morgenroth made his final entry on 31 October 1938, just nine days before Kristallnacht overwhelmed Bamberg and every other Jewish community in Germany. Days later, his journal was confiscated.

The pressure had been building relentlessly and not only through oppressive legislation and its zealous enforcement. Overt and increasingly violent anti-Semitism was by now a feature of everyday life for Jews throughout the Reich.

In old age, Ernest Haas recalled how his family had been forced by the intensity of their neighbours' persecution to move from their home in Neumarkt to the larger town of Fürth, some thirty miles south of Bamberg: 'My new teacher was a violent Nazi who instigated the other kids to wait for me after school to fetch me and beat me up which now happened several times a week. Life for the whole family now became more and more difficult in Neumarkt. Several times a week SA used to march by our house singing "*Hängt die Juden! Stellt die Bonzen an die Wand!*" ("Hang the Jews! Shoot the capitalists!") or "*Wenn das Judenblut vom Messer spritzt!*" ("When Jewish blood splatters from the knife!").'[26]

If the family found relief in their new home it was temporary, for it was from Fürth that the Haases were deported on the same transport that carried the Brandeses and the Herzsteins to Riga.

But even as the noose tightened throughout the 1930s, German Jews clung desperately to the hope that the Nazis did not really mean what they were saying. John Katten, the son of Bamberg's Rabbi Max Katten, recalled his father's reluctance to accept the inevitable: 'My father was the spiritual leader of the Bamberg community and, even though the anti-Jewish decrees were getting worse, he did not want to leave. Even when all the Jewish children, including me, were thrown out of school and shops had signs saying "Don't sell to Jews" and "Boycott Jewish shops," he still thought it could not get any worse. "We can live with it." My father was very German. He had fought in the First World War and his family could trace their being in Germany back to 1646.'[27]

In the end, shortly after Kristallnacht and with the help of Joseph Hertz, the Chief Rabbi of the UK, Rabbi Katten and his family were able to emigrate to England. He officiated at my parents' wedding.

Numberless Jewish veterans were not so fortunate. They too had believed that their front-line service provided not only the proof of their love of country but surely also insurance against harm. But for the Nazis it meant very little. Even while the First World War was raging, anti-Semitic parliamentarians had mounted a campaign of insinuation that Jews were shirking their duty to the Fatherland. Others loudly claimed that Jewish capitalists were engaged in profiteering while Jewish revolutionaries were fomenting trouble behind the lines.

In fact, 100,000 Jews had served with the German forces, 80,000 at the front. Some 12,000 were killed and 35,000 were decorated, among whom seven Bambergers won the Iron Cross First Class. The rate of Jewish participation in the military, at 17.3 per cent, was almost identical to that of the general population.[28] But the familiar charge of Jewish duplicity, cowardice and betrayal was an essential element of the Nazis' account of Germany's defeat and a key theme of their propaganda effort. There was little that Jewish organisations could do to counter it.

Just as the bench commemorating the fallen brothers Kurt and Oswald was sent tumbling down the hill above Bad Dürkheim, so the sacrifices made by Jewish women during the war were erased from the record. I have a plain metal ring presented to my grandmother Helene Zunz, their sister, in grateful acknowledgement of the jewellery she donated to the war effort. Around its circumference is embossed '1914 Vaterlandsdank' – the thanks of the Fatherland.

I stand before the black granite stone my father had placed in Bamberg's Jewish cemetery on Siechenstraße to commemorate his father Sally, his mother Bertha and his aunt Meta, all 'driven from their homeland'. Now his own name has been added in the space he left below.

Immediately behind it stands a line of gravestones, some decorated by elaborate military carvings and engravings – a spiked helmet, a sword and scabbard, a regimental crest – each marking the grave of a Jewish soldier killed in the First World War: 208 had served; 125 had been decorated.

In the Taharahalle, the cemetery's hall of remembrance, a great stone memorial commemorates the thirty-nine local Jews who had fallen for the *Vaterland*. On the opposite wall, five long tablets list the 279 Jews of Bamberg who perished a generation later in the Holocaust. The family names of twenty-four of the war dead feature on those tablets. They would have been their brothers, fathers, husbands, sons.

Throughout the 1930s, the veterans' faith in their country's gratitude remained strong. In reality they had little alternative but to trust in it. In his account of those times Werner M. Loval, who, as Werner Loebl, had spent his boyhood years in Bamberg and attended the same school as my father, wrote: 'Until well into the 1930s, my father and his brothers considered themselves "loyal German citizens of the Jewish faith" and unequivocally looked on Bamberg as their home. The intensifying rise of anti-Semitism, they believed, was an irrational phase that, with time, would pass. They did not share the Zionist view that life for Jews in Christian Europe was hazardous and only a Jewish state could guarantee them a normal existence. Instead, like most German Jews, their reaction to anti-Semitism was, "It cannot last!"'[29]

Such optimism could not have survived Kristallnacht. But by then it would be too late for the vast majority of Jews left in Germany – and for the large numbers who had emigrated to the countries both east and west that were shortly to fall under Nazi dominion.

On 7 November 1938, a 17-year-old Polish Jew, Herschel Grynszpan, shot Ernst vom Rath, a diplomat, at the German embassy in Paris. In a postcard found on him when he was arrested, he had written to his parents, who were in the process of being expelled from Germany to Poland with other Jews of Polish origin: 'I could not do otherwise, may God forgive me, the heart bleeds when I hear of your tragedy and that of the 12,000 Jews. I must protest so that the whole world hears my protest, and that I will do. Forgive me.'

Perhaps rumours of a gay relationship between Grynszpan and vom Rath or suspicions that the diplomat had not been a good Nazi dissuaded Joseph Goebbels from holding a show trial. Grynszpan was instead sent to Sachsenhausen concentration camp and was not heard of again.

But vom Rath's death on 9 November served its purpose for the Nazis. Goebbels declared that 'the Führer has decided that … demonstrations should not be prepared or organised by the party, but insofar as they erupt spontaneously, they are not to be hampered'. This barely disguised incitement was enough to precipitate a night of unprecedented violence against Jewish communities throughout Germany and Austria (which had been annexed in March).

The date of 9 November is a fateful one in recent German history. It was the day on which the Kaiser abdicated in 1918 and on which, in 1989, the Berlin Wall fell. It was also the day of Hitler's abortive Beerhall *Putsch* in 1923 and, on that evening in 1938, Nazis the length and breadth of Germany gathered to celebrate its fifteenth anniversary. So, as Goebbels will have known, the mobs that were to wreak havoc throughout the night would already be assembled and doubtless emboldened by alcohol.

On the night of 9–10 November, an estimated 1,400 synagogues were damaged or destroyed, most by arson, some 7,000 Jewish businesses were vandalised and ransacked, and ninety-one Jews were killed. This was Kristallnacht, the night of the broken glass. The SA led the carnage.

In the following days, 35,000 Jewish men below the age of 60 were arrested and taken into 'protective custody', among them my father at Buchenwald and my grandfather at Dachau.

What happened in Bamberg is well documented because, as Karl Mistele recounts, the ringleaders were prosecuted after the war. The local Nazis were meeting in the Zentralsaal and the Luitpold Hall. Lorenz Zahneisen, Lord Mayor and Nazi party district leader, spoke at both gatherings, according to Mistele, 'calling on the Jews of Bamberg to disappear'. Warning that he could not guarantee the protection of the 'parasites', he declared that 'a single drop of German blood is worth more to us than the whole of world Jewry'.[30]

Outside, with the police ordered not to interfere, members of the Hitler Jugend, the Nazi youth wing, had begun daubing Jewish homes and businesses with anti-Semitic slogans. Those who had attended the meetings dispersed to local inns for more drink and, in one of them, Zahneisen received instructions from party headquarters in Bayreuth to 'attack'. He called SA and SS (Schutzstaffel) troopers into a separate room and relayed the order to ransack the synagogue on Herzog-Max Straße and the Weiße Taube on Zinkenwörth.

Just thirty years earlier, at its grand opening, the synagogue had been lauded by the *Bamberger Tagblatt* as 'an adornment of the whole city', which Zahneisen's predecessor, Dr Franz Michael Lutz, had pledged, as a special duty, to protect 'willingly and for all time'.[31] Now, crowbars were requisitioned from a local garage and used to demolish its main door. Petrol was poured inside and the building set alight. When the fire brigade arrived at 1.20 a.m., Zahneisen ordered the chief to stand aside, and when firefighters tried to enter the building, they were forcibly repelled by the mob. By 3.00 a.m., the flames had broken through the roof.

Thugs forced their way into Jewish homes and dragged out their occupants, beating and abusing them in the street. Among their victims was Siegmund Bauchwitz, a popular doctor until he had been barred from treating non-Jews. He was also a war veteran, holder of the Iron Cross First Class and commended by his Colonel as a selfless, fearless patriot and 'a dear, loyal comrade to us, without whom we could not imagine the Regiment'. On Kristallnacht, he was pulled from his bed and beaten to a pulp.[32] Another contingent trashed the furniture at the Weiße Taube.

Two Jewish women, Anna Engelmann and Grete Bing, terrified and in despair, committed suicide in Bamberg in the aftermath of that dreadful night, both on 14 November; a restaurateur, Herz, died of a heart attack.[33]

There is a street in Bamberg, then Sophien Straße but renamed in 1948 to commemorate the life and death of Willy Lessing, who lived there. He was a prominent business leader and the Chairman of the Assembly of Representatives of Bamberg's Jewish community. On hearing of the fire, he rushed to the synagogue to save the Torah scrolls. He was set upon by the mob but, though badly injured, managed to reach his home. A group of men, some in uniform, dragged him out, beat

11. Bamberg Synagogue on Kristallnacht. Reproduced by kind permission of the Stadtarchiv Bamberg.

him savagely and left him lying in the street. He died of his injuries some two months later, on 17 January 1939.

His friend Thomas Dehler wrote an epitaph that could serve for all the Bamberg Jews of his generation: 'Willy Lessing died because he loved his homeland too much. He was a man of the world with world-wide connections ... but he remained in Bamberg despite all threats and warnings. He could not imagine that the Bambergers, who owed him and his family so much, could ever deny them protection. And they killed him anyway.'[34]

On 10 November, orders reached the police from Berlin to detain all Jewish men at Bamberg's police station on Sand Straße. A total of 168 were arrested and, on the afternoon of the following day, 107 between the ages of 18 and 60 were dispatched by express train to the concentration camp at Dachau.[35]

A police report of 11 November, quoted by Mistele, states that: 'After the disclosure of the death of the diplomat vom Rath, murdered by a cowardly Jewish assassin, anti-Jewish demonstrations developed ... The rage of the agitated populace led to the complete destruction of the Jewish restaurant and youth hostel at the White Dove Inn ... [the synagogue] was completely destroyed by fire. During the night some Jews provoked the enraged masses by appearing on the streets. This led to the temporary detention of all Jewish males in Bamberg by the police. There were no instances of looting.'[36]

In fact, Kristallnacht had provided every opportunity for wholesale looting by both state and citizenry. As punishment for its complicity in vom Rath's assassination and the 'hostile attitude of Jewry against the German people', and, in a particularly sick twist, to compensate for the damage caused in the course of Kristallnacht, a fine of 1 billion Reichsmarks was imposed on the German Jewish community, to be paid by a levy of 20 per cent of the value of every Jew's assets.

In Bamberg, the stoutly built synagogue, though completely gutted, did not burn to the ground. In March 1939, on the orders of the Nazi Party, it was blown up and the 32,000 RM cost of its demolition was added to the Jewish community's indebtedness.[37] The ground on which it had stood became the property of the city.

In his memoir, Werner Loval recalls his and his sister's experience: 'The day after Kristallnacht we found out our whole world had changed and I was left reeling. Everything had happened at once. When Erika and I went to our respective schools the next morning, we were expelled and sent home ... But the worst blow by far was that by the time we got home, we found our father had been arrested. He was gone and we had no idea when he would return.'[38]

His father Sali was released after three weeks' detention, traumatised by his experience. Loval wrote that 'not long before he and his father had been pillars of the community and Bambergers respectfully lifted their hats when they passed him on the street. Now he was considered worse than scum and treated as such.'[39] When Sali died six years later in Ecuador, the family had no doubt that the trauma of Dachau had contributed to his death.

Kristallnacht followed a similar pattern in towns and cities all over Germany. My mother's cousin Paul Nickelsberg wrote of his terrifying experience in Offenbach:

Rich and poor homes were destroyed by deliberately planned vandalism. I saw half a dozen men led by a Stormtrooper swarm into the house of a neighbour over the street. A minute later, windows were smashed, beds broken, bedding and furniture thrown out of the second floor window. Our house would be next.

I sent the nurse Idada out with the children until things quietened down. But I decided to stay. Sus, our cook, stayed with me. Nearing her fifties, buxom but nimble, she deserves all credit for her courage.

But the bandits passed our house. Nothing happened. Only very few Jewish dwellings out of hundreds were spared. Mine was one of those few exceptions. The synagogue was set ablaze. There was a manhunt for Jews in the streets and arrests in their homes.[40]

He concluded: 'never forget 10 November 1938. No man's house is safe, neither life nor limb, neither church nor temple until the disgrace of that day has been wiped from the face of the earth.'

I'm sitting over a cup of Milchkaffee in the Neustadt Eckchen, a modest little café at the fork of am Kies and what used to be am Rasen, now Neustadtstrasse, in neat, orderly, unassuming Rotenburg an der Fulda.

This had been the draper's shop outside which the proud war veteran Hirsch Brandes, his son Sally and a line of little grandchildren had posed for the innocent sepia photograph of long ago. This was great uncle Max Brandes' shop – and above it, his extended family's home – until they were reduced to wreckage in November 1938.

The citizens of Rotenburg and of neighbouring Bebra and Kassel could not wait for Kristallnacht. The riots erupted in these little Hessian towns on 7 November, the day vom Rath was shot, and continued the next day and into Kristallnacht itself. Max, his wife Johanna and their son Ludwig fled on 8 November to Johanna's brother Siegfried Strauß in Krefeld.[41] The following day their home and shop were destroyed and their warehouse ransacked.

A few days later, the Rotenburg police demanded they return to clear the wreckage, which was causing offence to the local townspeople who had wrought it. Of the goods and personal possessions looted from the building, two quilts were returned, though the family no longer had beds on which to lay them.[42] They did, however, recover the family's silver cutlery, which they'd had the foresight to thrust into an oven as they fled. That's all they had left.

Earlier, Heinrich Nuhn, who, with his wife Inge, has dedicated thirty years to researching and conserving the history of Rotenburg's Jewish community in a wonderful little museum and on an extensive website, had shown me one of the museum's most prized exhibits: a silver teaspoon, donated by Max and Johanna's grandchildren from South Africa and the USA.

As I sip my coffee, I read the extraordinary account of that night and those to come, set out by Henny Rothschild in a letter to relatives in New York. It was written a year later as she and her family waited anxiously in the Hotel Zeeland in Vlissingen for their US entry visas.[43]

She describes how she and her husband had gone to bed at their home in Marktplatz on 7 November 'in the best of moods': 'Already at the stroke of midnight it all began at our home: the windows up to the dining room above were smashed in by means of fire department ladders; down below, on the ground floor, the bolted-down shutters were chopped to pieces by hatchets; cobblestones flew into our beds, from which we escaped at the last minute, only with great effort and distress. I never want to live through such a night again ... Not a single house [belonging to the Jews] was spared, not a single house was not broken into ...'

In the morning the police ordered the family to clear away the glass and other wreckage from outside their house as the townsfolk, in holiday mood, gawped appreciatively at the destruction.

Nuhn cites in a footnote to Henny's account the records of the Rotenburg-Altstadt church, written, it seems, at the war's end in 1945: 'The most terrible thing was the ransacking and total destruction of the synagogue in Brotgaße which the schoolchildren – under the leadership or at least the tacit approval of the teachers – carried out by throwing stones and through other violent actions. The big Torah scroll containing the holy texts of the Old Testament was dragged through the Steinweg; someone donned the rabbinical vestments in a show of mockery and scorn. The Jewish cemetery halfway up the Katzenkopf hill was ignominiously desecrated.'

The Rothschilds fled to relatives in Göttingen where the terror and destruction followed them and their menfolk were arrested by the Gestapo. There they received a letter from the Brandes family enclosing one from a neighbour advising, 'you don't need to come back again, you won't find anything left', along with a clipping from the *Rotenburger Tageblatt*, declaring 'Rotenburg ist Judenfrei' ('Rotenburg is free of Jews').

Then, on 21 November, like the Brandeses, they received the order to make good the damage to their property within a week or face the consequences. Returning to Rotenburg, Henny had to pay a carpenter to repair the destruction in which, a fortnight earlier, he had energetically participated: 'you can imagine all that was stolen during this operation. Plenty of people managed to stuff their pockets full; a lot of supposedly respectable citizens there were not too pious to keep from enriching themselves with Jewish belongings.'

After the war, one of those who had led the attacks, a teacher, gave his testimony to the district court at Kassel. He'd been woken in the small hours by an SA comrade and told to bring an axe but leave his uniform at home. He explained: 'I obeyed the order because, as a soldier in the First World War, that's what I learned to do.'

Working methodically in small groups, the SA first took the Jews into 'protective custody' so that they could go about their work undisturbed. After a few hours vandalising the homes of some of his Jewish neighbours, the teacher returned home, changed his clothes and set off to school to instruct his class. Two hours later, perhaps during his lunch break, he was back at work, throwing furniture out of the window of another of his fellow citizens. Then he returned to his teaching duties.[44]

As I look up from my reading, I see across the little square a group of middle-aged men passing the time of day over a beer they've bought from the stand by the river. Outside the café, a woman and two men in their mid-seventies enjoy their coffee in the warm spring sunshine.

It's a small town: the parents of these elderly folk would likely have known Max and Johanna and their children, Ludwig, Kurt, Hermann and Gretel. They may have shopped here. Perhaps they participated in the shocking events of that far-off November, perhaps not.

Another elderly lady neatly parks her mobility scooter at the front of the café, dismounts cautiously and enters, stepping over the Stolpersteine that commemorate the brief lives of Gretel and her daughter Margit who had lived, too briefly, in the flat above the shop.

In Baiersdorf, on Kristallnacht, the ancient synagogue that Samson Salomon and Glückel von Hameln had built and adorned was destroyed. Shortly thereafter, the town's last remaining Jewish family was expelled, first to Erlangen and then, when their attempts to emigrate were blocked, to the ghetto at Izbica in Poland, which served as a staging post for the death camps at Belzec and Sobibor.

On 23 November 1938, the *Erlanger Tagblatt*, which sixty years earlier had celebrated the city's great Jewish benefactor Jakob Herz as a 'dear brother', now exulted:

> With the removal of the Kohn family Baiersdorf has become practically free of Jews. So a problem of the last centuries has finally ended … The Star of David, which insolently shone above the local synagogue for four centuries, was taken down and the interior of the synagogue was destroyed. As the synagogue was partly damaged through this, this rather dilapidated building will be demolished. In a few years, where the synagogue and Jewish cemetery is now, it is intended to build a new school and to make sports fields for the training of our youth. Neither shall the name 'Judengaße' remind us any longer of what unfortunately once used to be, but shall never be again.[45]

Following Kristallnacht, no German Jew could have been under any illusion about the Nazis' intentions. There was a rush to secure passports and visas, but for most it was already too late.

9

THE BEGINNING
OF THE END

Now the *Entjudung der Wirtschaft*, the elimination of Jews from the German economy, was in full swing. Within days of Kristallnacht, Hermann Göring issued his Decree on the Exclusion of Jews from German Economic Life: all Jewish business activities were outlawed, all state contracts with Jewish-owned firms cancelled and all Jewish concerns compulsorily expropriated. As of 1 January 1939, all Jewish economic activity had to cease.

At the same time, Jews were excluded from the welfare system and those who were unemployed but deemed fit for work had to register for forced labour. As Werner and Erika Loebl had found, all Jewish pupils were expelled from German schools.

Sally Brandes was released from Dachau on 11 December, but only so that he could sign over the deeds in the forced sale of the business he and Bertha had built together. Five days after his release, he made it over to one Anton Stemmer, a Nazi Party member from Würzburg. The notice read: 'Transfer of business: Sally Brandes, Specialty Women's Fabrics. The above mentioned company is as of 15 December 1938 transferred to Toni Stemmer. Sale price 33,000 RM. Signed Sally Brandes, FriedrichStraße 17.'[1]

Stemmer signed a separate contract: 'Transfer of business: Anton Stemmer, Grüner Markt 17. [It was actually 15.] The above named company has been taken over as of 15 December 1938. The business will continue to trade without significant changes as a textile retail outlet. Anton Stemmer, born 3 March 1907 in Haßfurt; average employees 10; anticipated wages and salaries 9,000 RM; working capital 40,000 RM, accruing annual business tax 6,500 RM; former occupation managing director. Dated 17 February 1939. Signed Anton Fr. Stemmer.'

On 31 January 1939, the *Bamberger Tagblatt* reported that the Bamberg economy was 'free of Jews'.[2] On 28 February, Stemmer, nevertheless keen to trade on Sally's reputation, advertised his new shop as 'S. Brandes, now Toni Stemmer Grüner Markt 15. The shop of choice for silks, woollens and velvets.'[3]

Shortly after the war, Ludwig Berger, a Bamberg Council official, informed my father, perhaps with unwitting irony, that 'Bamberg was by and large spared air raid attacks. We were only bombed twice, in February 1945, but the Grüner Markt quarter was hardest hit. In short, your parents' shop no longer exists: it was flattened and is now no more than a building site. The then owner, Stemmer, was killed in the air raid.'[4]

In his post-war claim for compensation my father suggests that Sally actually received as little as 8,000 RM for his business and was only allowed to draw 300 RM a month for living expenses. In any event, the valuation of Sally's stock and premises had been derisory. My father estimated them at 60,000 RM.[5]

My father and his parents, aunts and uncles and my mother's parents and grandmother lived through all this. They endured their own gradual but relentless exclusion from economic, social and cultural life. They had to watch helplessly as Nazi propaganda, in politics and the press, in the classroom and in public places, infected the minds of those around them and legitimised first the boycotts and the insults, then the segregation, then the violence and the destruction.

Fritz had foreseen what Sally could not. He wrote that 'from the time of the Austrian Anschluß, I realised that I would not outlast the Nazis in Germany'. He had made such good progress at Schwarzschild Ochs that his employer waived the third year of his apprenticeship. But, when the firm was 'Aryanised', he was given notice that his employment was to be terminated as of 31 December 1938.

Kristallnacht brought that date forward. On 10 November, the company wrote him a glowing reference, commending him for his personal qualities as well as the skills he had developed in sales, accounting, stenography, typing and in English, Italian and German correspondence, but dismissing him forthwith: 'Because of the Aryanisation of our business, Mr Brandes leaves our service as of today with our best wishes for his future.'[6]

Next day, he was arrested. He wrote: 'I was arrested by the Gestapo. "Are you German?" "Yes." "Are you Jewish?" "Yes." "Come along." This was the beginning of 5 months in Buchenwald Concentration Camp. We were allowed to send a printed message to our next of kin: "I am sitting in here. I am well."'

As prisoner number 26339, he was confined to the *Pogromsonderlager* at Buchenwald.[7] This 'Pogrom Special Camp', surrounded by barbed wire, comprised five hastily assembled wooden blocks without ventilation, heating or sanitation. Into them a total of 9,845 Jews were crammed. A total of 252 of them died before the 'special' barracks were demolished in February 1939 following an outbreak of typhus. Fritz, now prisoner number 4273, was moved to Block 20 in the main camp.

12. The inventory of my father's possessions, confiscated on admission to Buchenwald.

An official form records that on admission to Buchenwald on 12 November, he had been obliged to give up his personal effects, namely his cap, shoes, socks, coat, jacket, trousers, pullover, keys, washbag, wristwatch and signet ring. He signed for their return exactly five months later when he was released at noon on 12 April 1939.

In the course of those five months, some 800 of the 10,000 prisoners at Buchenwald died of disease, malnutrition or at the hands of their captors.

My father wrote in his chronicle that 'the fact that I adopted instinctively the attitude of the hunted animal – eyes everywhere, be as inconspicuous as possible, never be the first, never be the last in any group – left me physically unscathed by the experience'.

Otherwise, he had little to say about Buchenwald. My mother's cousin Paul Nickelsberg's account of his time there is also sparing. But his description throws some light on what they both endured.

It was not until 12 November that the doorbell rang twice at the Nickelsberg home in Offenbach.[8] First came the postman delivering long-awaited affidavits from Paul's brother-in-law in the US in support of the family's immigration application. He was followed by a Gestapo officer who asked Paul to accompany him to police headquarters. There Paul found his business partner, also taken into 'protective custody'. The two men were bundled into a car and driven to a holding camp outside town. There they joined around 800 other prisoners and had their details recorded by Gestapo agents who searched them and pocketed the cash they were carrying.

The guards were a low type of bone-headed soldiery. They made us go through stupid Prussian drill, march on, left and right turns, lie down and roll around on the dusty floor. They made us sing – yes, we had to sing – and the last song was a sneering mockery of the Jews. They kept on with this practice till late in the evening. An elderly man died right there from a heart attack. Late at night we were given some bread and sausages and half a cup of tea. At midnight, we were loaded on trucks and taken to the railway station.

There a waiting mob insulted and assaulted them. On the train, they were allowed neither to talk nor sleep. At dawn they arrived at Weimar: 'State police took over. They lashed out at the closely packed crowd with their rifle butts, hit us over the head, drove us into trucks. After about an hour's drive they chased us through a wider gate. This was concentration camp Buchenwald.'

Paul relates what he experienced in Buchenwald with the greatest reluctance as 'it is not my purpose to arouse the readers' feeling with descriptions of atrocities'. Yet what he recounts is horrific enough.

On arrival, the thousands of new prisoners were lined up in a vast yard and thirty barbers in grey-and-blue-striped cotton uniforms sheared their hair.[9] The one who attended to Paul warned him to learn to speak without moving his lips and never to walk, always to run everywhere. They stood there until late at night. The food they were given was the first some had had for three days.

He continues:

At midnight we were driven into a shack made of flimsy board. There was no room for us to lie down. We stood or sat crammed closely together; some lay upon each other.

There was unrest, noise, disturbance from the beginning. Many could not stand their thirst any longer. In addition to the general excitement and anxiety, it produced fits of anguish and hysteria. They yelled and screamed and cursed each other and tried to get out. Suddenly some came down with diarrhea. They struggled to the exits to relieve themselves outside. The Capos – older prisoners who had been appointed guards – beat them back with cudgels.

Now hell broke loose with yells, howling, blows, curses. Many soiled themselves. The stench inside was sickening. Some managed to sneak out. The German guards picked them up, dragged them along, flogging them with horsewhips. Again and again, the guards came in, dragged someone out … You heard the heavy impact of the heavy leather on their bodies, the shrieks and whimpering of the poor, tortured victims through the night …

In the morning we were ordered out again. Many prisoners, poor, staggering wrecks, were unable to walk. They were covered in blood with gashes on their heads, chests and shoulders and with crazed, frenzied staring eyes. More turned pale, shaken with spasms of dysentery. We were ordered not to move from the spot where we stood. Some, in their distress, tried to get to the latrines. The commandant announced over the loudspeaker that if this did not stop, severe punishment would follow. About 20 were strapped to a block to receive 25 blows from a cane. I was too far away to witness this repulsive punishment but I could hear it.

Paul recounts how the weeks passed 'in dull, grey misery'. In late November, a chill rain started, turning the compound to thick and slippery mud. The inmates had no protection against the cold and damp, nor against disease. Every morning a dozen bodies were brought out. Prisoners who had been in the camp for years and had been put to work twelve hours a day in local quarries had given up all hope of release.

After a month, on 10 December, Paul's name was called over the loudspeaker.

Release came to you as a shock … Mechanically you pack your things and hasten to the door with unseeing eyes … With about 100 others, I got a shave, passed a medical checkup – the Nazis would not let anyone out with signs of mistreatment on his body – signed some declaration which I never read.

We had to listen to a speech: we were not allowed to talk to anyone about the camp and what we had seen in it; for any misdemeanor of any kind, any incident we might be involved in, we would be imprisoned again, for life – which, however, might not be too long – and our wives and children would also face concentration camp.

Paul returned to Offenbach. My father remained in Buchenwald.

> O Buchenwald, I cannot forget you,
> For you are my fate.
> He who has left you, he alone can measure
> How wonderful freedom is!
> O Buchenwald, we do not whine and wail,
> And whatever our fate,
> We will say yes to life,
> For the day will come when we are free!
>
> Fritz Löhner-Beda, *The Buchenwald Song*[10]

After the war the people of Weimar, city of Schiller, Goethe and Gropius, protested that they had no idea about what had been going on at Buchenwald for the last eight years.

The remains of the camp are just a 15-minute drive, up through the spindly beech and pine forests that crowd the side of the Ettersberg. In Weimar, a bright spring sun is shining. But when I leave the bus at Buchenwald, it's dismal and cold. The sky is leaden. The air is chilled.

Around the car park stand a group of yellow-plastered three-storey blocks, the last of the old SS barracks: quarters for the sadists, criminals and inadequates in smart black uniforms who imagined themselves heroic Teuton warriors. Nothing else at Buchenwald remains so intact.

To reach the camp itself, tourists like me must make their way down the Carachoweg. This is where the worst of the SS waited to ambush new prisoners as they arrived from the trucks and trains, beating them with rifle butts and truncheons as they fled, bloodied and frightened, into the hell of Buchenwald.

Some 280,000 Jews, gypsies, homosexuals, political dissidents, religious suspects and prisoners of war from more than fifty countries passed through the narrow iron gates. Beyond them, 56,000 died of exhaustion, disease or starvation, or from beatings, medical experiments and execution. Still more thousands ended in the gas chambers of Auschwitz and elsewhere, or on the death marches as Allied troops advanced from east and west in the winter of 1944–5.

The gates still bear the banal legend *'Jedem Das Seine'* ('To each his own'), the Nazis' subversion of the Roman principle of equality before the law. Behind them and the barbed wire and watch towers stretches the huge, barren muster ground, the Appelplatz. Beyond it stood the sixty-seven barrack blocks into each of which 2,000 prisoners could be crushed, piled high on flimsy bunks, without heating in winter or ventilation in summer. None of the blocks remain. They were demolished in the 1950s by the Soviets, who feared that the typhus that had regularly devastated the camp – and with which Nazi doctors had infected prisoners so that they could monitor its lethal progress – might be lying dormant in the wood and the mortar.

Now the site of each block is marked by a numbered slab; a pit filled with black copper slag outlines its footprint. I stand at my father's barrack, number 20. What more can I do? I take a black stone for remembrance. It's on the desk before me now.

But it's on the Appelplatz where Buchenwald seems bleakest, where the misery of the place feels least resistible. Here on the stony ground, the prisoners had to stand to be counted, abused and beaten for hours each morning and every night. On a chill day at the end of March, when I was there, it's an unforgiving place in which to stand for just 10 minutes. In deep winter, with the wind blasting across the open terrain and the rain or snow beating down on ill-clad, exhausted, dysentery-raddled prisoners for hours on end and day after day, it must have felt like the end of time.

As they stood, frozen to their own footprints, they will have seen the smoke curling from the crematorium to their left as the day's dead were dispatched. And there they would have been forced to watch the public executions. It's likely that my father witnessed the hanging of Peter Forster on 21 December 1938. A political prisoner, Forster had broken out of the camp in May and managed to cross the border into Czechoslovakia. There he applied for asylum and it was while he was awaiting a flight to Paris that the fearful Czech government had second thoughts and sent him back to the gallows at Buchenwald.[11]

And there was the gruelling forced labour to which the sick and starving were marched each day. In my father's time, the prisoners built the so-called Blood Road into Buchenwald along the three miles of an old track from the Weimar to Ramsla highway. If my father worked on that road or broke stones for it in the quarry outside the camp, he never mentioned it.

Now I understand a little better why my father did not speak of his five months in Buchenwald. Why would a free man wish to recall, and in recalling perhaps relive, the experience of that awful, degrading, terrifying captivity?

The people of Weimar – including those who had grown rich provisioning the camp and those who profited from its endless supply of forced labour – did not want to think about it either.

Years later, asked about his experiences in the camp, my father wrote: 'Apart from the mental anguish, the deaths I witnessed, the execution we all anticipated and the humiliation we had to endure, I was unharmed. But my conscious decision never to be the first or the last in any group helped. The blows fell on others.'[12]

But my father's life had irrevocably changed. He wrote later: 'When I returned to Bamberg after my release and saw the ruins of the synagogue, something inside me snapped: the Almighty, All-knowing, All-merciful, Righteous God of the Jewish faith does not square with the events of 1933–45 and indeed not with the majority of events in the history of Jewry and humanity as a whole. Should anybody be inquisitive enough to enquire into my antecedents: I am an agnostic of Jewish background, a lapsed Jew.'

Paul Nickelsberg's accounts of his time in Buchenwald and his experiences as a Jewish businessman from the moment the Nazis took power in 1933 to the time of his emigration in April 1939 are particularly valuable, not least because they fill gaps in my father's account of the ordeals he and my grandfather experienced.

My uncle Vernon described him as 'rather unworldly and academically inclined', an accomplished pianist, devoted to his bicycle and to nature photography. I met him perhaps once or twice when I was a small boy and remember him as humorous and kind, the exceptional sort of adult to whom children are instinctively drawn. I recall being fascinated that one of his fingers was missing and bewitched by his tales of how it had been shot off during the First World War – a story that may or may not have been true.

Paul ran Kramp & Co. of Offenbach, a long-established family business that printed the labels for some of Europe's leading perfume houses. As my uncle recalled, Paul and his wife Mathilde, known as Tilde (and to Paul as Till), lived modestly in a house alongside the factory, rattled at regular intervals by the trains passing by on the Frankfurt–Sachsenhausen line. Though he was thrifty, he was also very generous and provided invaluable support to his uncles Hermann and Albert in their times of need during the 1930s.

Paul had served in the German infantry during the First World War, suffering shrapnel wounds as well as malaria contracted in the Pripet Marshes on what is now the Belarus–Ukraine border. While recuperating, he hatched a cunning plan.

In a brief memoir he wrote, 'I remembered those sixteen months in the water-soaked, lice-infected trenches in Russia, with biting cold in winter and biting mosquitoes in summer and thought, "enough is enough".'[13] He applied for a posting as an interpreter, claiming that as well as French and English, he had 'some' Turkish.

Despite flunking his Turkish entry exam, he managed, 'through one of those freak accidents that happen only in war' – and on the basis that he knew the Turkish for 'good morning' – to get himself posted to Istanbul. There, through chutzpah and cunning, he contrived to sustain the subterfuge. However, his grasp of Turkish can never have been much more than rudimentary, for he recounts one particularly droll anecdote about the army's requisitioning of a piece of land, which required him to negotiate with an illiterate farmer the signing of a legal agreement that neither could read.

Paul was nothing if not resourceful. He was a survivor.

In a memoir entitled *Work and Strength*, Paul recalled the momentous day of 30 January 1933. 'Hitler had become Chancellor of the German Reich. From the early morning Stormtroopers marched through the streets; the Horst Wessel song sounded everywhere. I went to the office as usual. The girls had pale faces. Very little was spoken. But as we looked at each other, a question, too big for words, could be seen in everyone's eyes. I tried to answer it and said, "from now on begins a chapter of pathological history".'

Kramp & Co., owned by the Nickelsbergs since 1845, had recently celebrated its centenary. With a workforce of some 300 at its height, it was one of the largest employers in Offenbach. But, as Paul recalled, 'we were like a family ... nobody could have known who was the boss'. Indeed, many of the workers had been there for more than twenty years, some for forty or fifty.

Shortly after Hitler had entered the Chancellery, an order was issued that all factories were to suspend work and tune in to the Führer's first radio broadcast. Paul summoned the shop floor committee to pass on the news. One of them argued indignantly that the firm should disobey: 'Do you think that there is even one Nazi sympathiser here? If we should find one single rat, we will break his bones!'

Paul determined to do all in his power to protect his business and its workers for as long as he could. He delegated nothing, taking responsibility for all company decisions, negotiating directly with the Nazi authorities. 'So I stayed', he wrote, 'until they were prepared to use brutal force and physical compulsion.'

On 1 April 1933, Germans were instructed to boycott Jewish businesses:

Goebbels had ordered the Stormtroopers to picket every Jewish store. They scared customers away and booed at those who insisted on entering the premises, and took photographs of them. Black patches with yellow dots were painted on businesses owned by Jews. Cartoons with insulting inscriptions were daubed on their doors.

I was tense about what would happen to us that day. But nothing did. Only later that day, I noticed that somebody had painted a black stripe on the doorpost. A few hours later, the black stripe was bordered with gold-bronze edges at the top and bottom. Only one of our workers could have done this. No-one else would have had access to gold-bronze paint. 'Bear it with pride' was the clear meaning the man wanted to convey.

In November, having taken exception to some aspect of his private affairs, the Gestapo took Paul's partner into 'protective custody'. He was held in an old warehouse along with fifty others. Though some had been badly beaten and the guards were 'rude and inhumane', Paul observed wryly that 'systematic indignity had not yet been developed to perfection'.

As the Nazi depredations intensified throughout the 1930s, the rate of emigration increased, particularly among younger Jews. Several of Tilde's brothers and sisters had managed to get out. Ludwig had already emigrated to the US in 1930; in 1933, her sister Line, a strong Zionist, went to Palestine; in 1934 Karl left for the Philippines and Alice joined Ludwig in America.

The introduction of the Nuremberg Laws the following year was, for Paul, a turning point: 'Before, my reaction to the turmoil we had been thrown in had mainly consisted in bewilderment, had been prevalently emotional. Now, notwithstanding the bitterness and disgust I felt, I tried to face our problems more clearly and more real-istically ... I saw clearly that the conditions under which Jews in Germany had been put were bound to slowly suffocate their vital strength. There could be no more hope that oppression might have reached its worst.'

Paul was not a religious Jew. His family had been free-thinkers from his grandfather Adolph's days and his own parents had maintained that tradition. Though he had a natural sympathy with secular Jewish values, 'this ... had nothing to do with any rites or religious practice'. But for the Nazis, these distinctions were immaterial: 'My attitude did not change when the time came when I had to suffer for being a Jew. I was quite happy to be one. I had to face my fate and had to find the strength to do so like the many thousands with whom I shared it. Each one of us was tried to the very core of his strength. This was our common plight and solidarity.'

But though he recognised the danger, 'I did not yet feel prepared to go. I still had a job to do. There were many others whose turn would come first. There was the rest of my family … This was not the moment to give up or to lose courage.'

Paul relates how he was asked many times in later life why he did not leave earlier. He resented the implicit assumption that he and others like him were somehow blinded to their jeopardy by a determination to hang on to their wealth: 'I refuse to concede that the motives of men are merely rational considerations of utility. Instinct has always produced stronger motives than intellect. Call it instinct or idealism or lack of initiative; approve of it or condemn it but it is according to human nature not to give up easily what you consider your own, what you have built for years with your own hands and thoughts, not to give up without fighting for it, not to give up before you have lost the fight.'

In any case, disposing of the business was by no means a straightforward proposition. He and his partner had spent much of the 1930s recovering from the economic crises that followed one after the other between 1929 and 1932. By the time the company had returned to profitability in 1938, legal restrictions meant that the winding-up process would have produced very little benefit for them. They were caught in a trap.

In July 1937, Tilde's brother Ludwig was able to sponsor their brother Alfred's emigration to the United States. By then, conditions in Germany were becoming intolerable. Jews were barred from most places of entertainment, culture and sporting activity. Jewish business-people were subject to arbitrary arrest and sometimes months of interrogation. Even when they were released, they might find that, in their absence, their company had been requisitioned by Nazi officials.

Paul tried to encourage a non-Jewish business associate and close friend to take over the company. Hans was 'a typical Aryan, tall, blond with a chest full of war decorations, a good man to have around in those troubles'. But Hans saw neither pressing cause for concern nor immediate need to act:

His attitude was typical for most Aryans of the upper middle class. He disapproved of Nazism and hated it. He was a faithful friend and not afraid of taking a risk to help me. But as long as nothing happened to me as his personal friend, he closed his eyes to the disgraceful things which were happening to Jews all over the country. These things seemed very, very remote ... I tried to convince him that those things were very real and that the Nazis' crimes had grown to monstrous proportions. He may have felt that I was exaggerating in my excitement and under the influence of my personal feelings. He refused to believe that such things might happen to his close friend.

Though selling the company represented the only way to pay the huge levies imposed on Jews when they emigrated, Paul believed it would take all of two years to get it into the kind of shape that Hans would feel able to take over.

By 1938, he had become convinced that the Nazis were preparing to confiscate all Jewish businesses, and when in April they demanded that all Jews render an account of their assets his suspicions seemed justified. By now his workers were looking at him 'the way you look at a hopelessly sick man' and were expressing concern about their own futures. As Hans continued to prevaricate, Paul forced the issue. He found a family of local industrialists looking to establish a favoured son in business and Hans, fearing that he might lose his advantage, agreed at last to become a partner: 'On 30 October, at the banker's office, we signed away what generations before us and we ourselves had built and preserved. Four copies, four signatures. It was like a surrender. I felt a shame for what I had done.'

The transaction still required official approval. They were just in time. It was granted just days before, on 12 November in the wake of Kristallnacht, Göring set his 1 January deadline for the 'Aryanisation' of Jewish businesses.

With the transfer of the business in hand, Paul could focus his energies on getting out of Germany. But his way was not clear. Though Ludwig had promised to secure affidavits to allow the rest of the family to join him in the US, when Paul made his application to the American consulate in March, he was told that he would have to wait until at least November 1939.

Then he was arrested and sent to Buchenwald. Tilde was prepared to wait no longer. Her sister Selma had been able to emigrate to the Philippines and, with affidavits from relatives in both countries, Tilde applied to both the UK and the Philippines. In January they were given their passports with the requisite temporary entry visas.

It took another three months to secure an exit visa from the Gestapo. Every item they owned had to be registered and accounted for. Everything they were allowed to take with them was subject to a levy. When all the emigration and property taxes were rendered and all their transport costs paid, Paul was left with around 15 per cent of the derisory sum he had received for his century-old family business.

In those final months, Paul and Tilde had many poignant encounters with old friends and acquaintances. One evening, an elderly widow called. She had heard that Paul had 'been away' and summoned the courage to offer Tilde what help she could. Paul had supported the family during her son's illness. Now, Paul writes with typical generosity, 'that evening, the good woman paid back tenfold'.

On another occasion, the aunt of a former employee called. He had been the only apprentice with openly Nazi sympathies and had left to join the army in which he was being rapidly promoted. The aunt told Paul, 'Heinrich always thought a lot of you and he does so even more now. Something has changed in him. And he looks at the army in a different way now. He sees that you were right in many more things than he had been able to see before.' Whether Heinrich's political loyalties had changed and what became of him are unknown.

Marie had been a close friend of Tilde's. But when she joined the civil service she was strictly forbidden to have anything to do with Jews and was under constant surveillance by her superiors and by informers.

One day, Paul and Tilde caught sight of her on a tram but, as she was not alone, made no attempt to attract her attention. When they alighted, they heard steps behind them in the dark street and a whisper: 'Thank God I've seen you. Are you leaving? I have to say goodbye.'

Choked with tears, she could say no more: 'A few days later, she came to the house in the darkness. "I cannot tell you how I feel. Do not think that I am mean and low. I thought of you many, many times. It is easier for me now that I've seen you before you go. Go to a happier world." I have never seen anyone weep as she did. She calmed down a little, kissed Till and, in the doorway, with a last sudden urge, pressed and kissed my hands as she left.'

On 23 March 1939, Paul and Tilde saw Tilde's parents off at the station. They were bound for New York. Paul and Tilde had decided to make for the Philippines. Tilde's sister Erna, the only one of her siblings still in Germany, was to travel with them and their two young daughters. They were ready to go on 2 April: 'Two taxis waited in front of our house. Across the yard, the windows of the factory opened one by one. Faces appeared at the windows, more and more faces, waving hands, waving handkerchiefs – "goodbye, goodbye!" We got in the cars and drove to the airport … Waiting, then the increasing drone of the propellers. Taxiing. Take-off. This land down below was Germany. We were free!'

They landed at Croydon airport, in London's southern suburbs, and three days later embarked on the P&O liner SS *Ranchi*, which reached Manila on 15 May. Six months later, on 2 November, they left on the Dutch steamship *Klipfontein*, landing at Portland, Oregon, on 17 November. Soon they were reunited with Tilde's parents, her brother Alfred and sister Alice and husband Harold in a house Ludwig had rented for them in Allentown, Pennsylvania. Thus began their long lives in America.

At the time of his leaving, Paul wrote:

The German people are set on their course with a torn and sick heart. I wish and I will work for their defeat, complete uncompromising defeat. There is no other way. Otherwise all those who are dear to me would perish miserably and for hundreds of years there would be nothing left on earth for any man worth living for.

Yes, Germany is my homeland. She has shaped me as an individual. She has given me all I know, all the ideas that formed her own past. And I have given her the best I could give, many years of my life, four hard years fighting in the war, twenty hard years of working through defeat.

But what you love can die. Despite all this, Germany is dead.

Nevertheless, he went on:

But I will not forget Marie and Hans and Willi and Kate and Rasel and the Pauls and Idada and Sus and many others. And I know the German nation goes its course with a sick and torn heart. Not all of them are Nazis; not all are anti-Nazis; most are wavering; many are painfully divided in themselves and almost all – with very few exceptions – are bearing part of the responsibility, part of the guilt of omission which made things possible, a very small one maybe but it will weigh heavier and heavier on their shoulders as the years go on and for the sick heart there will be no relief.

In the US, Paul, once the owner of a business employing 300, started work all over again, this time as a labourer. At least he was free. At least he was alive.

Paul left behind in Germany his sister Marta and her son Walter. Their story is extraordinary too. After the death of her father, Marta's uncles proposed that she wed a partner in the family firm. Appalled at the prospect of a marriage of convenience to a man she regarded as 'a bad sort', she left Offenbach, working as a clerk in Spain and Italy before returning to Germany. In 1928 she took a job with Wilhelm Koring, the owner of a tax consultancy in Essen and a non-Jew. They married in 1931 and their son Walter was born two years later.

In 1936 the Nazis issued Wilhelm with an ultimatum: if he did not divorce his Jewish wife, he would be barred from his practice. Courageously, he refused and for five years the family had no regular income other than Marta's interest in Kramp and work surreptitiously undertaken for Wilhelm's old clients.

In 1941, with most young men conscripted to the army, Wilhelm was forced to take up a lowly management post in a nearby coalmine. But exhausted and embittered by the hardship and harassment he and his family had faced and by his hatred of the Nazis, he took to drink and, in August 1943, died of a heart attack.

Without the nominal protection of an 'Aryan' husband, Marta's and Walter's lives were now in jeopardy. In September 1944, Marta was arrested and, with other Jewish wives in mixed marriages, deported to the Hessisch Lichtenau labour camp at Kassel. There she was put to work as a cleaner in a chemicals factory.

There had been no warning of her arrest. As Walter wrote in a letter to me, 'I came home from playing one afternoon and found our apartment empty. The neighbours told me what had happened. You can imagine the absolute despair of an 11-year-old suddenly left quite alone and having to deal with whatever happened.'

Walter is generous in his praise of the people of Altendorf, the village outside Hattingen where the family lived. Though there were exceptions, many proved steadfast friends and, with his mother gone, sympathetic neighbours took him in. But when they fell foul of the Gestapo, Walter was sent to join his mother in the camp: 'This was not a fenced-in concentration camp and nobody was physically harmed except through lack of care and nutrition … Escape from the camp was not an option because the prisoners had no ration cards with which they could get food and no identity papers to present at the checkpoints which were everywhere. The big "J" stamped on the Jewish women's ID cards would get them caught immediately and sent back to the camp – or somewhere much worse.'

The prisoners lived through the intensive Allied bombing of Kassel during the last six months of the war until finally, on 4 April 1945, American troops entered the city unopposed. The following month, Walter and his mother were able to return to their home. They looked after each other for the rest of her long life. Walter still lives in Hattingen.

Part Four

RESETTLEMENT IN THE WEST

'The Jews, the first victims of Hitlerism, are now more than ever before despairing men and women even in the land of the free.'

Josiah Wedgwood MP, House of Commons,
22 August 1940

10

THE EMIGRATION TRAP

Paul, Tilde and my father were among the fortunate few. By the time they left Germany, most avenues of emigration had been sealed shut, if not by the Nazis then by the democracies to which the Jews of Germany and Austria looked for sanctuary, with mounting desperation. For, as Hitler caustically observed, though these countries liberally condemned Germany for the increasingly flagrant outrages it committed, they were determined to keep Jewish refugees from their own borders.

When the Nazis came to power, there had been some 523,000 Jews in Germany, less than 1 per cent of the population. Almost 40,000, many of them political activists, Johanna Brandes' husband Leopold Harris among them, fled in the first few months. Throughout the mid-1930s, annual emigration rates, though lower, were relatively constant. But as the oppression intensified in 1938, and particularly after Kristallnacht, more and more Jews sought to emigrate. Approximately 36,000 left Germany and Austria in 1938 and 77,000 in 1939.[1]

By the outbreak of war, some 282,000 Jews had left Germany and a further 117,000 had fled Austria. Of these, 95,000 made it to the USA, 75,000 to Central and South America, 70,000 to Britain, 60,000 to Palestine, and 18,000 to Shanghai.[2]

Another 150,000 migrated west to France, Belgium and the Netherlands, north to Denmark and Norway or east to Poland and Czechoslovakia. When Germany invaded those countries, they found themselves once more at the mercy of the Nazis and their collaborators.

In the early years, before the development of the 'Final Solution', the Nazis' systematic persecution of the Jews had twin aims: to pressure as many as possible into leaving Germany and to exploit the opportunity to expropriate their property. As we have seen, they required that emigrating Jews relinquish the ownership of their homes and businesses, levied an emigration tax on them and strictly limited the transfer of what meagre resources remained in their bank accounts. Those who managed to get away were often impoverished as well as traumatised.

By the end of 1939, there were still 200,000 Jews in Germany and a further 57,000 in Austria. Many had desperately tried to emigrate but by then they were caught in a bureaucratic trap: they could only leave if they gave up their assets to the Nazis, but applicants without assets could not secure entry to countries of sanctuary. In some cases, visas would be granted only to those who had booked passage on a ship; but they could not book passage without a visa.

Though the plight of German Jews was clearly desperate in 1938 and 1939, the USA and Britain did little either to increase the numbers they were prepared to take or to simplify the visa application process. Throughout the 1930s, the US immigration quota for Germany, non-Jews as well as Jews, stood at around 27,000 a year. But until 1938, because of the obstacles placed in the way of would-be immigrants, that quota, modest as it was, was never filled.

To obtain a visa from the US authorities, an applicant was required to present five copies of the application, two copies of his or her birth certificate, a quota number and the identity of two American citizens as sponsors. Each sponsor would have to complete and notarise six copies of an Affidavit of Support and Sponsorship and submit a certified copy of their most recent federal tax return, one affidavit from a bank regarding their accounts and another from a responsible person regarding other assets. The applicant had, in addition, to provide a Certificate of Good Conduct from the German police, together with duplicate copies of any police, prison, military or other government dossier on them. They had also to undergo physical examination at an American consulate. From September 1939, they were required to produce proof of permission to leave Germany and proof of passage. From September

1940, they had also to provide several good character references from disinterested parties.

Between 1933 and 1937, only 33,000 German Jews were granted entry to the US – some 100,000 fewer than the quotas allowed. As the Nazi persecution intensified in the following four years, just 124,000 were admitted.[3] The German annexation of Austria in March 1938 and the Czech Sudetenland in October that year brought millions more within the ambit of the quota system but the limits remained. By the end of June 1939, 309,000 German, Austrian and Czech Jews had applied for the 27,000 places.

The US's failure to admit Jewish refugees was not simply a matter of bureaucratic indifference. Heightened by their experience of the Depression, few Americans were prepared to welcome competition for their jobs from an influx of foreigners who, many believed, would not just undermine the American way of life but might, as fifth columnists, actually threaten it.

A strong strain of anti-Semitism made Jews particularly unwelcome.[4] Leading politicians were outspoken in their opposition to Jewish immigration and no doubt confident that they reflected public opinion: a poll conducted in 1938 found that 58 per cent of Americans thought that German Jews were at least partly responsible for their own misfortunes; another in 1942, as the Final Solution was being implemented, found that 44 per cent believed Jews had too much power and influence; two years later, 44 per cent thought that Jews represented a threat to their country.[5]

When, in July 1938, President Roosevelt convened the Evian Conference to discuss the refugee crisis, he was more intent on distracting attention from the US's failure to fill its quotas than on finding new ways to address a problem growing more pressing by the day.

The Conference was not designed to provide relief for persecuted Jews – far from it. Even before its proceedings opened, Britain and the US had agreed to coordinate resistance to increased immigration to each other's countries or to British Mandate Palestine.[6]

Nor were they seeking to offload their responsibilities. Roosevelt's invitation to the conference was accompanied by the reassurance that 'no country will be expected … to receive a greater number of immigrants than is permitted by existing legislation'.[7] Despite fine speeches, only the Dominican Republic and later Costa Rica offered to open their borders to significant Jewish immigration.

Canada admitted almost none.[8] The Australian delegate T.W. White, Minister for Trade and Customs, observed that 'as we have no real racial problem, we are not desirous of importing one'.[9]

Six months later, a Bill was introduced into the US Senate calling for the admission of 20,000 German refugee children. After months of wrangling it was defeated, not least on the grounds that any available resources should be earmarked for needy American-born children.

Britain's attitude to Jewish refugees was scarcely more compassionate. A fortnight after the Evian Conference, the *Observer*, falsely claiming that 'Britain now has more Jews than Germany ever had', concluded with breathtaking cynicism that Jews might be better off in Nazi Germany for, 'if a further accretion of, say, 100,000 of them come into the country, how could the danger be diverted of an anti-Jewish feeling here?'[10]

Indeed, at Evian, both the British and French delegations claimed that their countries were already fully populated. In Britain as in America, immigrants were regarded as undesirable competition for jobs; refugees were allowed in only if they undertook not to work without the permission of the Ministry of Labour.

There were two exceptions: for those Jews able to bring with them businesses that would provide employment for British citizens and for those prepared to enter domestic service. Even if it were granted, permission to remain in the UK was temporary and the costs of dependency were to be borne, not by the British taxpayer, but by the existing Anglo-Jewish community and its charities.[11]

Even when, after Kristallnacht, Britain relaxed its restrictions to provide urgent refuge for some 10,000 children, the majority of whom were Jewish, the Kindertransport scheme, so often presented as evidence of Britain's exemplary generosity, was hedged about with terms and conditions. The taxpayer was not be troubled: charities and private benefactors had to guarantee payment for each child's fare, care, education and eventual emigration from Britain. In return, the government agreed to grant the children travel visas on the basis that, when the 'crisis was over', they would return to their families. They could not be accompanied by their parents or guardians and the few infants included in the programme had to be looked after by other children on their transport. Of those who had escaped to Britain on the Kindertransport, 1,000 were subsequently interned as enemy aliens. Many of their parents, abandoned to their fates in Europe, perished under the Nazis.

Britain's response to the Anschluß in March 1938 had been to tighten visa requirements for refugee Austrian Jews. In May 1939, the government severely limited any further Jewish immigration into Palestine. With the declaration of war in September, it cancelled all existing visas held by Jews in Germany.

More shameful even than Evian was the conference that took place five years later in Bermuda, at a time when the Allies were well aware that the Nazis were committing genocide.

Low-level American and British delegations met on 19 April 1943 in response to growing public concern to discuss the general issue of wartime refugees. They chose Bermuda as a means of discouraging media attendance. The World Jewish Congress was not invited: the Jewish character of the Final Solution was not on the agenda. The conference had no outcome: the US maintained its strict immigration quotas; Britain, not wishing to inflame Arab opinion, continued to restrict access to Palestine; no Jews were saved.[12]

The sorry saga of the SS *St Louis* epitomises the attitude of those countries that could have done so much more to save German Jews from the fate that awaited them. It came to be known as the 'voyage of the damned'.

The *St Louis* set sail from Hamburg on 13 May 1939 with 937 passengers, the majority Jewish. Most had transit visas for Cuba where they planned to stay until allowed entry to the USA. But by the time they reached Havana a fortnight later, the Cuban government had bowed to pressure from right-wing newspapers and a 40,000-strong demonstration in the capital and cancelled their landing certificates. On 2 June, after a week of fruitless negotiation, President Bru ordered the *St Louis* to leave Cuban waters.

The ship then sought to dock in Florida but was turned away by the US Coast Guard. In Canada immigration officials advised ministers that, when it came to Jewish immigrants, 'none is too many' and the government agreed.[13] The German captain, Gustav Schröder, who had done all he could to find a safe haven for his passengers, had no option but to return to Europe.[14] The ship docked in Antwerp on 17 June. Britain took 288 refugees, and the rest were dispersed across Belgium, France and the Netherlands. Some 254 of them subsequently fell into the hands of the Nazis and were lost in the Holocaust.

On 27 May, the *St Louis*'s sister ship, the SS *Orinoco*, also bound for Cuba, sailed from Hamburg. Learning of the *St Louis*'s difficulties, it dropped anchor in the Bay of Biscay but, finding no country prepared to take its 200 Jewish refugees, had to return them to Nazi Germany. My father had booked passage on the *Orinoco*. Fortunately, by now he was already in the UK.

In October 1941, when the German government finally put a stop to emigration, there were 163,000 Jews left in Germany. In the four years that followed, almost all of them perished in the camps and ghettos, or gunned down by death squads, or in the gas chambers, or on the forced marches of the final months of the war.

As I drafted these passages in the course of Donald Trump's presidency, it became increasingly difficult to ignore the parallels between the kind of populism he unleashed in the US and that of pre-war Germany. There are distinctions as well as comparisons to be made. But it is worth noting that, in the 1930s, at the same time as the US was closing its borders to desperate refugees from Europe, it also 'repatriated' up to 2 million people of Mexican origin who were, according to populist opinion, competing for 'American' jobs and welfare. Many of them were actually American citizens.

As late as 1940, an 'America First Committee' was constituted to oppose US involvement in the war. Its spokesperson, the all-American aviator Charles Lindbergh, drawing on tropes that resonate as much with the present as the past, told a rally in Des Moines on 11 September 1941: 'Instead of agitating for war the Jewish groups in this country should be opposing it in every possible way, for they will be among the first to feel its consequences. Tolerance is a virtue that depends upon peace and strength. History shows that it cannot survive war and devastation. A few farsighted Jewish people realise this and stand opposed to intervention. But the majority still do not. Their greatest danger to this country lies in their large ownership and influence in our motion pictures, our press, our radio, and our government.'[15]

Nor should we overlook the parallels in their attitudes to immigrants, refugees and asylum-seekers between some in Brexit Britain and the little Englanders of the 1930s and 1940s. Even as the war ended and news of the horrors of the Nazi death camps filtered through to the British public, my father wrote to my mother: 'Over the BBC I heard a news item that the workers of a Birmingham factory were so "shocked" at Nazi atrocities that they adopted a resolution against the employment of German refugees! It took them ten years to get "shocked" and then they adopt resolutions against German anti-Fascists who suffered more in one day than they during six years of war ... Why the hell can't they say: "we are afraid of the German refugees' competition so don't give them jobs!" Would at least be straightforward!'[16]

If, in the immediate aftermath of the war, the immigration of refugees and displaced persons was regarded as a potentially serious economic challenge, the admission of the Jewish victims of Nazism was perceived as a problem of its own kind. Echoing the *Observer* of 1938, Cabinet minutes from 1945, with benign concern for Jewish welfare, warned that 'the admission of a further batch of refugees, many of whom would be Jews, might provoke strong reactions from certain sections of public opinion. There was a real risk of a wave of anti-Semitic feeling in this country.'[17]

Perhaps the government was right to be concerned. In October 1945, when there can have been no doubt about the scope and scale of the Nazi atrocities, my mother wrote to my father that 'in Hampstead they signed a petition that all Refugees should be sent back to Germany and Austria'.[18]

There was nothing new in this. When Jews fled to Britain to escape the murderous pogroms in Tsarist Russia at the end of the nineteenth century, they were received by some with generosity but by others with thinly disguised contempt. In 1892, the anti-immigration campaigner W.H. Wilkins, by no means a lone voice, speculated that Russian Jews were the architects of their own persecution: 'With an imperfect knowledge of the facts we are hardly in a position to judge of the action which the Russian government has seen fit to take against its Jewish subjects … It is said … that the system of usury and extortion practiced by many of the Russian Jews upon the peasantry has, in large measure, tended to bring about the present state of things.'[19]

In 1905, with little opposition, the House of Commons passed the Aliens Act, largely designed to stem the flow of Jewish immigrants from Russia and eastern Europe. A Conservative Publication Department pamphlet entitled *Chinese and Aliens* declared: 'The Unionist Government wants to keep these creatures out of Great Britain. They don't want to see the honest Britisher turned out by these scourings of European slums.'[20]

What has changed in our attitudes to refugees from persecution? A country that prides itself on its traditions of toleration and sanctuary voted in 2016 to 'take back control' of its borders, not least in order to keep out immigrants: no matter that they may be fleeing for their lives from countries they do not wish to leave; no matter what they may have to contribute to our culture, our economy and our common humanity; no matter our moral duty.

Now as then, those few asylum-seekers we admit must do the most menial work. They must not be allowed to compete for British jobs, neither should they rely for their welfare on the British taxpayer. The same newspapers warn us that our culture and values are under threat, that our schools and hospitals are being swamped and that our country is 'full up'. The same kind of second-rate politicians build their careers on unprincipled populism. The same parties of government equivocate in the face of public opinion.

In her analysis of Britain's immigration policy in the 1930s, Louise London concludes in plain terms that it 'was designed to keep out large numbers of European Jews – perhaps 10 times as many as it let in'.[21]

The collective memory is, however, different: 'The myth was born that Britain did all it could for the Jews between 1933 and 1945. This comfortable view has proved remarkably durable, and is still adduced to support claims that Britain has always admitted genuine refugees, and that the latest harsh measures against asylum seekers are merely designed to exclude bogus applicants.'[22]

The truth about Britain as a place of sanctuary for those fleeing for their lives in the 1930s ought not to be so comfortable: 'The Jews excluded from entry to the United Kingdom are not part of the British experience, because Britain never saw them ... Memories of the unsuccessful public campaign to persuade the government to rescue Jews from mass murder quickly faded.'[23]

11

WELCOME TO GREAT BRITAIN

My father got lucky. While he was in Buchenwald, an aid agency secured a visa allowing him to stay in the UK for two years. Some fifty years later, he wrote that 'to this day I don't know who brought this about'.[1]

In the month after his release on 12 April 1939, he faced constant harassment from the Gestapo to whom he had to report at regular intervals. But finally, on 10 May, he took leave of his parents on a platform at Frankfurt South railway station. He wrote later: 'I knew it was our last goodbye.'

As he boarded the train for Vlissingen, the guard advised him to choose another compartment, as 'this one is full of noisy Jews'. At the border crossing at Kaldenkirchen, an SS guard enquired with a sneer, 'Are you emigrating?' As the train rolled into Holland, my father later confided that he recited a line from Götz von Berlichingen, the rumbustious sixteenth-century Franconian knight and poet. In all likelihood, he repeated the phrase Goethe famously attributed to Götz, '*er kann mich im Arsche lecken*' ('he can lick my arse').[2]

My father became an accidental Englishman, distinguished by the police registration number 743200. He had originally intended to emigrate to America. But when he applied to the US consulate in Stuttgart in 1938, he was told that he would have to wait until at least September 1939. That, of course, turned out to be the month the Second World War began. He wrote: 'This situation was totally inflexible. The US authorities took absolutely no account of the events in Nazi Germany; if you did not qualify for entry, if your life was in danger, that was your hard luck. A rumour in Buchenwald that the Kristallnacht had induced the Americans to relent and to open their country to us proved groundless; after the original euphoria we were plunged into the deepest gloom.'

Two further experiences consolidated the distaste he sustained for what he sardonically referred to as 'God's Own Country' for the rest of his life. While he was interned in Canada, the British authorities, having at last accepted that the Jewish prisoners they had sent there posed no threat to national security, did their best to encourage the Americans to admit those who qualified for entry. But Washington resolutely refused to allow 'Axis Prisoners of War' to cross the border. In any event, would-be immigrants were required to show that they had paid their own passage across the Atlantic, something the internees deported from Britain were patently unable to do.[3]

Later, when the British decided to repatriate and release the internees, the train carrying my father to Canada's east coast halted on American territory to take on water and fuel. It was promptly surrounded by National Guard troopers determined that no one should slip through the golden door.[4] That was when my father decided that America was not for him.

Not that the British had welcomed him with open arms. Without a work permit and having left Germany with no more in his pocket than the 10 RM permitted by the Nazis, the equivalent of £1, he was all but destitute. He subsisted on the support of the Jewish Refugees Committee, which gave him occasional work as a doorman at its premises at Bloomsbury House, the former hotel on the corner of Gower Street and Bedford Avenue from which the Kindertransport was administered. He told the story of how he had had to decline the thoughtful invitation of a Quaker family to a much-needed Sunday lunch because he could not afford the tube fare from his lodgings in Stamford Hill. He never forgot that humiliation, nor the guilt he felt that the Quakers might have thought him ungrateful.

Later, in a letter to my mother, he recalled: 'At that time I had to live on 20s a week and all of it went for board and lodging. No money for mending boots, laundry etc. Six weeks before I went off on the Big

Adventure [internment] I got my job with Bloomsbury House back which brought me up to 32/6 and the first thing I did was to have my boots mended and half my laundry done.'[5]

When war broke out, he tried to join the army. In his wooden trunk, I found a faded copy of the *News Chronicle* of 28 October 1939, folded open at page 7. There, under the headline 'German Joins Big Rush of Volunteers – Wants to Fight His Oppressor', the paper reports:

> A fair-haired, bespectacled German, 24 years old, stood in a long queue of volunteers at a London recruiting office yesterday, waiting his turn to join the British army.
>
> He was one of thousands who besieged recruiting centres throughout the country in prompt response to the call for men between 22 and 35.
>
> The German produced his identity documents, bearing the endorsement: 'Refugee from Nazi Oppression'. He had been in England since last May, when he was released from a Nazi concentration camp.
>
> 'Now,' he said, 'I want to fight with the British and show the Nazis something!' His case will be specially considered by the military authorities.

The military authorities clearly doubted that this Jewish victim of Buchenwald had sufficient grounds to fight the Nazis; worse still, they thought he might turn out to be a German spy. They rejected what I take to be my father's attempt to enlist.

His was a common experience. With the outbreak of war, tribunals had been established to assess the threat posed by the 73,000 German and Austrian citizens living in Britain, most of them recent refugees. By February 1940, 569 had been interned as 'high risk' Category A (and perhaps as many were detained on the advice of MI5, along with seamen captured in British ports); a further 6,700 were classed as Category B and 'subject to restriction and supervision', while the remaining 66,000, including 55,000 mostly Jewish refugees, were considered 'no risk' and placed in Category C.

My father came up against a 'distinctly hostile' tribunal chairman and, like everyone else on the day, was classified as Category B.[6]

In May and June 1940, as the Nazis swept towards the Channel coast and fears of an invasion grew apace, large areas of the south and east of England were declared 'protected areas'. Orders were issued that every 16- to 60-year-old German or Austrian national found there should be detained, regardless of the categories they had been awarded. My father was one of the first.

He was arrested on 10 May, a year to the day after his escape from Germany and the day on which the German army invaded the Low Countries and Neville Chamberlain resigned as prime minister.

From 16 May, all men and women with Category B status were picked up.[7] When Italy entered the war on 10 June 1940, Winston Churchill famously declared to his Cabinet that the police should 'collar the lot' and 4,000 Italians joined them.[8] Then, from 24 June, some 25,000 16- to 70-year-old males in Category C were detained.

Many accepted their detention patiently, especially as they assumed it would last only a few days. Eric Koch, a law student at Cambridge who had come to England from Germany as a 15-year-old in 1935, was arrested on 12 May as he was preparing for his finals. Years later he wrote:

> Most of us accepted our arrest and internment as a reasonable precaution to be taken by a country threatened with invasion. British newspapers at the time were full of stories of how Hitler's fifth column had undermined Holland's resistance, and there was no reason to assume that England had not been similarly infiltrated. England panicked ... As refugees, we were grateful to England for having given us a haven at a time when other countries were making every effort to keep us out. Besides, we felt it was infinitely better to sit behind British barbed wire than to be exposed to mortal danger in Nazi Europe.[9]

But while most were resigned to their internment – and often impressed by the courtesy of the police officers who arrested them – some could not endure it. Koch cites the example of a family friend who, having been tortured in a Nazi concentration camp, could not face the prospect of further imprisonment and took poison.[10]

My father and Uncle Vernon, who had been arrested in Durham on 12 May, were initially interned on the Isle of Man, which had rapidly become a vast detention centre. My father was held at Onchan, Uncle Vernon at the Central Promenade Camp in Douglas.[11] Other camps were established for male detainees at Ramsey and Peel and, for women and children, at Port St Mary and Port Erin. Proprietors were turned out of hotels and boarding houses, which were promptly surrounded by barbed wire and filled with internees.

As the weeks dragged on, for those like my father who had volunteered to join the British forces, internment became the source of particular disappointment and frustration. Others were bewildered or resentful. But, though their loss of freedom and uncertain future weighed heavily, the conditions in which they were living were not unduly oppressive.

The camps were centres of extraordinary intellectual and artistic activity. Distinguished academics gave well-attended lectures on all manner of subjects, from philosophy and physics to theology and literature. More practical lessons in English and handicrafts were arranged, schools were set up for the children, concerts and plays were performed. Internee administration committees were elected, camp newspapers produced and religious services conducted.

By the spring of 1941, as the threat of imminent invasion diminished after the Battle of Britain, reason had belatedly prevailed and most of the refugee internees had been released. But for some, the administrative obduracy that had earlier cast Jewish refugees as potential fifth columnists had already entered a new and most unwelcome phase.

As the detention camps in the UK quickly began to overflow, the decision was taken to ship some 6,000 detainees to Canada and another 6,000 to Australia. The government's intention had been to transport those it believed to pose the highest security risk. But the number of Category A internees turned out to be so small that, to make room in the camps for further Category C arrests, it felt obliged to fill the ships it had commandeered with Category B and C prisoners. The candidates were chosen more or less at random but they included my father and uncle.[12]

Even at the time, this folly was apparent to the critics of mass internment. In 1940, as the plan was being implemented, François Lafitte, the pioneering social policy analyst, published an uncompromising report on *The Internment of Aliens*, which concluded that 'the War Office, the Home Office and Mr Chamberlain between them made a complete mess of the job of selecting people for deportation ... The plain fact is that thousands of innocent refugees have been treated like cattle in the name of national security.'[13]

Most of the victims of this short-sighted pen-pushing paid the price in years of unjust and humiliating imprisonment. A significant number lost their lives because of it.

When, on 3 July 1940, my father and uncle sailed from Liverpool for Canada on the MV *Ettrick*, they and their fellow passengers were aware that, just twenty-four hours earlier, a converted cruise ship, the *Arandora Star*, also en route to Canada, had been sunk north-west of the Hebrides by a single torpedo from the U-47. Of the 1,673 men on board 734 were Italian; 479 were German Category A prisoners, including both Nazis and refugees, along with 86 POWs; and there were 374 seamen and guards. A total of 805 lives, Italian, German and British, were lost.

The *Arandora Star* had been a sitting duck. Despite the very obvious dangers, the transports crossed the Atlantic without naval escort. As Rachel Pistol noted in her survey of internment, 'none of the transport ships were marked as carrying POWs. Instead they set sail unaccompanied, equipped with anti-submarine guns, and employed a zigzag pattern in their movements, making the ships obvious targets for German U-boats.'[14]

She also describes the shocking conditions on some of them. The *Dunera* was designed to carry 1,600 passengers and crew but sailed for

Australia with twice that number, including 300 who, just a week earlier, had survived the wreck of the *Arandora Star*. To make matters worse, the prisoners were ill-treated by their British guards who 'pilfered everything of value from their passengers including 1,200 watches and hundreds of gold wedding rings'.[15]

Internees on the *Ettrick* did not suffer in the same way but, as my uncle described, conditions on board were both squalid and intimidating: 'The Ettrick was hopelessly overcrowded; worst of all the sanitary facilities were insufficient. The deck was subdivided with barbed wire. On the other side were Nazi prisoners of war straight from the battlefields; they soon realised who we were and shouted across anti-Semitic insults.'[16]

The *Ettrick* sailed with 2,594 passengers, of whom 1,307 were Category B and C internees, mostly Jewish but also political refugees. Of the remainder, 880 were German POWs, including committed Nazis, and 407 were Italians, among them Fascist sympathisers but also many innocent restaurant owners and waiters who had lived peaceably in the UK for several decades.

Sea sickness and dysentery took hold almost as the ship set sail and conditions were made infinitely worse because the toilets, inadequate as they were, were off-limits for much of the day. Eric Koch, who was also aboard, recalled: 'A few slept in the galley, in puddles of grease. There was a penetrating smell of oil throughout the entire area; a single electric fan provided the only ventilation in the hold. We had no boat drill, and none of us would have had a chance to survive had we been shipwrecked or torpedoed.'[17]

Despite the indignity of internment and the ordeal of the crossing, some were glad to be putting distance between themselves and the all-conquering Nazis. On the other hand, they had not been told where they were heading. According to Koch: 'Some said we were on our way to Germany to be exchanged for the British prisoners taken at Dunkirk; others claimed to have heard we were bound to Scotland to build roads or fortifications there. Perhaps we were headed for British Guiana, or Madagascar? The most gruesome rumour was that the German officers were plotting to take over command of the ship.'[18]

The *Ettrick* docked in Quebec on 13 July. The prisoners were sent to Camp L at Cove Fields on the Plains of Abraham in Quebec City, and to Camp Q at Monteith, Ontario. My father, along with some 800 others, was destined for Camp L.

The Canadians and Australians had been led to expect thousands of the most dangerous Nazi POWs, spies and fifth columnists, and red-faced British bureaucrats did little to disabuse them. The Canadian authorities' reception of the internees was uncompromising and conditions in many of the camps, especially at the beginning, were primitive. As my uncle noted, 'in Canada we were informed that they had no "internees"; in their camps they had only "criminals" and "prisoners of war"; so we became "prisoners of war" and had to wear blue denim uniforms with a red circle on the back'. The camp commandant told his new prisoners, 'most of you are Jews; that is alright; but you have to keep clean!'

Not all Canadians saw the internees as a threat. Charles Ritchie, a diplomat at the High Commission in London, noted in his diary on 16 July 1940, just a few days after my father and uncle had arrived in Quebec: 'I now hear that the ferocious internees whom the British Government begged us on bended knees to take to Canada to save this country from their nefarious activities are mostly entirely inoffensive anti-Nazi refugees who have been shovelled out to Canada at a moment's notice where they may have a disagreeable time, as our authorities have no files about them and will not know whom or what to believe.'[19]

According to Eric Koch, 'the Canadian Army treated everybody alike. There was not a trace of anti-Semitism in their behavior. To them we were all dangerous Nazis.' Indeed, though Jewish and political refugees argued passionately that they should be separated from German POWs and Nazis, the Canadian authorities had the greatest difficulty in understanding why such a distinction was either appropriate or necessary.

When Colonel A.M. Campbell left one of the camps after three months as Commandant, he told its internee leaders that he considered them traitors to their own country and that Nazis who were 'at least clear-cut enemies' were preferable to refugees who were 'neither fish nor fowl, nor good red herring'.[20]

However, conditions at Camp L were tolerable. Despite the disapproval of the Director of Internment Operations, who criticised him for fraternising with his prisoners, the Commandant, Major L.C.W. Wiggs, popularly known as Piggy-Wiggy, was easy-going and humane.

As my father wrote: 'Life in the Canadian internment camp was not disagreeable, though no-one really wants to sit behind barbed wire, especially when detention can't be justifed. But we were treated well, we had the chance to work and earn a little money which we could spend in the canteen. Intellectual life was stimulating and we had film shows. We were a good cross-section of German society, from Friedrich Georg, Prince of Prussia and uncle of the Kaiser to Hans Kahle, a commander of the International Brigade in the Spanish civil war.'[21]

My uncle also remembered Hans Kahle who, even as he languished in Canada, was achieving a celebrity he could not have anticipated. As my father wrote in a letter to my mother shortly after the war: 'Reading "For Whom the Bell Tolls". I was very surprised and thrilled to find Hans Kahle mentioned. He was Commander of an International Brigade and Werner and I knew him well from Canada. In the book only his Christian name is given but it's him alright. He is a very nice chap.'[22]

My father also recalled sharing a bunk with Klaus Fuchs, the theoretical physicist who subsequently worked on the development of the first atomic bomb at Los Alamos and in 1950, at the height of the Cold War, was arrested and imprisoned in the UK as a Soviet spy.[23]

After only three months at Cove Fields, the internees were transferred to Camp N, known as Sherbrooke. A former railway repair depot in Newington, Quebec, it was covered in soot and oil, with broken windows and leaking roofs and entirely inadequate sanitary equipment. For good measure, the beds intended for the 736 inmates had been sent to Montreal while the mattresses intended for the camp at Farnham had been delivered to Sherbrooke.

The space allowed for each inmate was significantly less than the minimum provided in British jails and, just one day after their arrival on 15 October, the internees went on strike, demanding a transfer to habitable accommodation. The protest was defused by a mixture of threats and promises, which were in the end fulfilled, albeit very gradually.

But the Camp Commandant, Major W.J.H. Ellwood, was no Piggy-Wiggy and perhaps rather more representative of the Canadian military. In a 1941 entry in his official war diary, he damned his prisoners both as Jews and as Germans: 'In spite of the fact that a certain percentage may be heartily Anti-Nazi, it cannot be forgotten that they are German-born Jews. Jews still retain much of the same instincts they had 1940 years ago and these in particular are very apt to try and take advantage of privileges which if once given result in demands for more. The combination of this insidious instinct and the well-known characteristics of the German habit of breaking every pledge ever made, is not particularly easy to handle except by maintaining strict discipline and rigid enforcement of Camp rules and regulations.'[24]

Despite Ellwood's prejudices and the pilfering and petty persecutions of the NCOs and guards, many of whom were openly anti-Semitic, there was work for volunteers in the making of furniture, kitbags and socks, which would have relieved the tedium as well as providing at least some modest income.

Moreover, as on the Isle of Man, the camps were full of academics, teachers, artists and musicians. They quickly formed a 'Popular University' and schools for the many young prisoners whose education had been disrupted. The European Relief Fund and the YMCA provided books and equipment and several Camp Commandants supported their efforts. One such was Major E.D.P. Kippen of Farnham Camp. According to William Hecksher, a teacher who did much to establish the school there at which students were able to sit and pass matriculation exams, Kippen, was 'silent, military, human and gentlemanly': he did all he could to provide for the intellectual and physical education of refugees, whom he was required officially to treat as prisoners of war.[25]

Sherbrooke had a School of Engineering with a staff of eight professors and graduate students. My uncle lectured in architecture there and designed the camp hospital and shop. Camp L had a Director of Entertainment Operations and major theatrical productions were mounted in several camps, complete with sets, costumes and music. Several productions featured the young Anton Diffring, who went on to star in countless films and on TV, ironically often as a German officer.

According to Eric Koch, Camp B at Little River in New Brunswick had 19 pianists for whom the Canadian Red Cross and YMCA provided both instruments and sheet music. Sherbrooke held the virtuoso violinists Gerhard Kander and Hans Kaufman and the pianists John Newmark and Helmut Blume. 'Many of us,' records Eric Koch, 'had a richer musical life behind barbed wire than we had before or after internment.'[26]

But internees' experience of incarceration varied greatly. Some benefited from the educational and cultural experiences they could enjoy. Some, after the persecution they had endured in Germany, found the camps a place of comparative security. But internment could never be a happy experience. Eric Koch wrote of Sherbrooke:

The lack of privacy, the overcrowding, the sight of the two ugly railway sheds, the feeling of confinement, the constant rumours, and above all, the absence of any real hope for release, had taken their toll. We pursued our various activities, but suffered increasingly from a new disease we called 'internitis', the symptoms of which were a combination of despondency, touchiness, and worst of all self-absorption and self-pity. From the point of view of the Canadian officers we were a sorry lot – bitching and proclaiming ad nauseam, 'there has been some mistake, we are refugees, we are loyal to Britain and – we want to get out of here!'[27]

For those who burned with the ambition to join the army and fight the Nazis, the prolonged and pointless internment was a particularly bitter experience. Their cause was valiantly championed by a small number in both the UK and Canada who thought their position both absurd and inequitable. In Britain, the Labour MP Colonel Josiah Wedgwood was a particularly committed campaigner.[28] He spoke in a debate on internment in the House of Commons on 22 August 1940, which wrought a heavily qualified admission of error from the Home Secretary, Sir John Anderson:

> I am not here to deny for a moment that most regrettable and deplorable things have happened in the execution of the internment policy. They have nothing to do with the merits of the policy. They have been due partly to the inevitable haste with which the policy of internment, once decided upon, had to be carried out. They have been due in some cases to the mistakes of individuals and to stupidity and muddle. These matters all relate to the past. So far as we can remedy mistakes we shall remedy them. As far as we can improve conditions for the future – great improvements are now being made rapidly – we shall make those improvements.[29]

Wedgwood was not appeased. He argued not only that the conditions in which the internees found themselves were inhumane but also that the policy of internment was indefensible in principle, a concession that Anderson had studiously withheld. Wedgwood's cogent and often passionate speech would have been deeply appreciated among the internees and their supporters.

First, he addressed the injustice internment had done to the victims of Nazi oppression:

> They had been chased out of Germany. They had come out of concentration camps in Germany; they had fled from Vienna to Italy; they had been chased out of Italy without being able to find a resting place for themselves; they had been robbed of the last of their goods; they were driven to France, and finally driven out of France to this country; and at the end, when they get to the very country which is fighting for freedom, fighting for them, fighting for their cause, they are treated not as friends but as enemies, treated exactly on a par with German enemy aliens, not distin-

guished in any way either by title or in their treatment by the people in charge of the camps … The Jews, the first victims of Hitlerism, are now more than ever before despairing men and women even in the land of the free.

He went on to argue that the policy had been based on a fundamental misconception of the nature of the war Britain was fighting, that it was not 'a war of nations' but one of principles: 'It is out of date to talk of enemy aliens. It is out of date to talk of aliens at all. The only aliens are the people who believe in the Nazi form of religion. It is not the country in which they were born, but the school of thought to which they belong which divides mankind.'

Next, he ridiculed the logic and utility of internment, likening the detention of 30,000 Jewish refugees in the unlikely event that one might be a Nazi agent to the incarceration of the entire population of Kettering on the grounds that one could be a potential murderer.[30]

Finally, he made a point about reasoned and moral leadership that has as much force today as it had then: 'Right through our history the majorities have always been active. If we had followed the wishes of the majority we should never be where we are to-day. Civilised people, with the culture and the traditions which we enjoy in this country, where we naturally put justice before the will of the majority. Therefore, the argument in favour of universal internment based on the wish of the majority of the people of this country, as shown by the Press or by opinion in this House or by our letter-bags, is no justification to any responsible statesman …'

As early as July 1940, even while the internment camps were filling, the British government had published a White Paper identifying 18 categories of 'friendly aliens' who could be released. By April 1941, though 15,000 remained in detention, some 12,600 releases had been authorised.

But while attitudes were beginning to change in the UK, in Canada they were harder to shift. Charles Raphael, sent to Canada by the Jewish Refugees Committee in the vain hope of negotiating the entry into the

US of internees with the requisite visas, recalled the Canadian position. Its resonance with the attitude of the British bureaucrats who had shipped the internees in the first place is uncanny: 'At first they had been highly suspicious. They had agreed to receive some dangerous enemy aliens ... Then they were told "they're really rather nice people. Would you mind releasing them." They resented this. They felt they'd constructed camps and these camps ought to be filled with dangerous people, and if they weren't, well they'd better stay there until they were dangerous.'[31]

However, in July 1941, the symbolically important decision was made to amend the status of most detainees in Canada from prisoner of war to 'friendly aliens' and to redesignate Sherbrooke, Farnham and Île aux Noix as internment camps.

Conditions improved incrementally. The camps were still run along military lines but internees were no longer required to wear red circles on their jackets and stripes on their trousers. Daily wages for those who volunteered for work increased from 20 to 30 cents, though many internees regarded this reform as duplicitous, suspecting that even if they were no longer considered a threat to security, their productivity had made them too valuable an asset for the Canadian government to forgo.

The internees continued to campaign passionately for the segregation of the Nazis among them. But with the authorities more concerned about Jewish communists than German Nazis, their objections fell on unsympathetic ears.

The desire to be freed from an unjust and unnecessary imprisonment remained the greatest cause for the internees. But, having so strongly resisted Jewish immigration before the war, the Canadian government was now afraid that released refugees would want to stay. Koch quotes the summary of a discussion between the camp leaders at Farnham and Colonel R.W.S. Fordham, the newly appointed Commissioner of Refugee Camps: 'It has been ascertained by the authorities that we are not dangerous. However, the Immigration Laws of this country are an obstacle to our release. Upon enquiry why it is necessary to keep us under severe military guard, in view of our not being dangerous,

Colonel Fordham replied that this is done for our protection. The Canadian soldiers and population hate everything German and do not know the difference between Nazis and us.'[32]

Once again, on another continent, Jews were being held in 'protective custody'. Once again, in another century, the rights of Jews were being suppressed expressly in order to save them from ignorance and prejudice.

Finally, the Canadian government agreed to consider applications for release on an individual basis, so long as internees could find a sponsor and a prospective employer or were young people continuing their education. Farnham was closed in January 1942 and Sherbrooke decommissioned in November. By December, some 800 'friendly aliens' had been released in Canada, and 1,300 returned to Britain.

My father's release was authorised on 1 May 1942. On 9 May, almost two years to the day after his arrest as an 'enemy alien', he boarded the SS *Banfora* at Halifax and sailed back across the Atlantic to his country of refuge.[33]

The *Banfora* docked at Greenock on 26 May. A fortnight later, on 8 June, my father was at last allowed to join the army, first the Pioneer Corps, then, after a spell as a ski instructor with a Scottish mountain infantry battalion, the West Yorkshire (The Prince of Wales's Own) Regiment and finally, in India, the 2nd Battalion, the Duke of Wellington's Regiment.

In training, warned by the army of the consequences of being captured by the Germans, he changed his name. Up against a deadline, he dived into a Glasgow telephone box to consult the directory. Preserving his initials, he emerged, not as superman, but as Fred Bradley.[34]

On leave in London on 13 April 1944, he dropped into the International Youth Centre in Chelsea's Pont Street, a popular haunt for Jewish refugees and left-leaning intellectuals. There he was reintroduced to Trude Zunz whom he had first met when they were members of the BDJJ in Frankfurt, though at the time, as he later rather ungallantly disclosed in a letter from India, she had not made a good impression.[35]

13. My parents, Fred and Trudie Bradley,
newly engaged in August 1944.

He quickly overcame his indifference for they kissed at the cinema while, presciently, watching the *Way Ahead* and, on 19 August, after just 10 dates, they were engaged (under 'that Tree' in Epping Forest). They were married on 26 November 1944, first at Hampstead register office and then at a religious ceremony conducted by the former Rabbi of Bamberg, Max Katten.[36]

Two weeks later, in Glasgow, Fred boarded a troopship to India.

Part Five

RESETTLEMENT
IN THE EAST

*'Now I have to tell you that we will be going away tomorrow
and it will therefore be a while before
you hear from us again.'*

Sally Brandes to his son Fritz,
letter of 26 November 1941

12

THE TURNING OF
THE SCREW

The privations my father endured had been nothing compared to those of his parents. By the time of his internment, they had been evicted from their home and Sally compelled to sweep the streets of his home-town. Since Sally and Bertha had lost their business, they had had to live on their meagre savings. In March 1939, they handed over anything of gold or silver they still owned to the official Bamberg city pawnbro-ker. Their possessions were worth 1,807.60 RM, but were valued at 897.90 RM of which, after the deduction of administrative costs, 873.55 RM was remitted to Berlin.[1] So reduced were their circum-stances that Sally had had to sell my father's stamp collection to the husband of a former employee.

The last letter my father received from his parents reached him at his Canadian internment camp, stained by what he believed to be their tears. It read: '*Wir sitzen auf den Terrasse und es beginnt zu regnen*' ('We're sitting on the terrace and it's beginning to rain').[2]

On 30 April 1939, the Law Concerning Jewish Tenants enabled German landlords to cancel the leases of their Jewish tenants. The *Bamberger Volksblatt* newspaper announced: 'The results will be clear: Jews will have to leave the predominantly Aryan neighbourhoods in the near future. If it should become apparent that not enough apartments are available, the remaining propertied Jewish families will have to open their residences ... to their race comrades.'[3]

Within months, Judenhäuser (Jew houses) were taking in Jews who had been evicted from their own homes. There were 11 in Bamberg. On 29 July 1939, Sally wrote to my father: 'Now to the main cause of misery: yesterday we lost our flat. At first, they said that we could stay and that they would never terminate the lease, and now? That is what a word is worth nowadays. If only we could come out there, so that we wouldn't have to look for another flat. But that is impossible.'[4]

On 13 September 1939, 10 days after Britain had declared war on Germany, Sally and Bertha moved from their home at Friedrichstraße 17 to the Villa Dessauer at Hainstraße 4a. Sally's sister Meta joined them the following April.

The grand townhouse had been built in 1884 by the hop merchant Carl Dessauer to celebrate his commercial success and consolidate his social standing. It certainly had the desired effect: 'You should see the dining room,' exclaimed Sally in a letter to his son. 'We have christened it "Knight's hall". Every room is a hall!'[5] But, as opulent as it might have been, Villa Dessauer was now a Judenhaus. For all its new residents, and for Dessauer's descendants Max and Lily Pretzfelder whose home it was, Hainstraße 4a was to be their last given address.[6]

Sally and Bertha tried with an ever-increasing sense of urgency to emigrate, desperately hoping that friends and relatives who had managed to get away would be able to act as guarantors and sponsors.[7] Their regular letters to their son, carefully crafted for the eyes of the censor, catalogue not only their own attempts but also those of their friends and acquaintances.

Some were successful: 'I want to ask you now if there is a possibility of getting a room with two beds in your house for the middle of July. It is for Mr Welt and his wife. Please let us know in your next letter, but don't forget. The following left for London this morning: Mrs Steinberger, the mother of Mrs Simon, Ernst Silbermann and Lothar Wachtel. Tonight, the two Tietz-Fleischmann girls go with the Kindertransport also to London. So it goes, one after another.'[8]

Others were thwarted. Bertha describes the cruelly dashed hopes of those who had booked passage on the SS *Orinoco*, believing that they had secured their escape to Cuba: 'You can consider yourself lucky to be in England. Ludwig Naumann, his sister and her husband probably can't go to Cuba. They would have sailed on the steamship *Orinoco*, for which you had a ticket, on 27 May. Martin Schönthal, who is in Bamberg at the moment, planned to travel to Cuba in July but, now that the regulations have been tightened, that's not going to be possible. Kurt Klestadt is also waiting for his Affidavit to America. The guarantee alone is not enough.'[9]

A few days later, the *St Louis* was turned back from Cuba: 'First Ludwig Naumann and Friedel Naumann, now Mrs Prager and her husband and child were turned away after they'd already reached Hamburg and now they're back here again. Isn't that terribly bad luck? We also don't know if Wiesenfelder has been allowed to land.'[10]

In fact, Martin Wiesenfelder was one of the many of the *St Louis*'s passengers returned to Europe and captured by the Nazis when they overran France and the Low Countries. He died in Auschwitz.

By now, German Jews were all but stateless. The embrace of the Christian faith no longer offered protection to those who fell foul of the Nuremberg race laws. Sally recounted the experience of his and Bertha's former lodger Artur Heßlein, a 'non-aryan Christian' whose boyhood conversion and deep attachment to Catholicism now counted for nothing. He only managed to escape Germany with the help of the Archbishop of Bamberg, who secured refuge for him in a monastery in São Paulo in Brazil. Sally wrote: 'We had a very interesting travel report from Mr Heßlein. He had a really tough time (draining the goblet of suffering to the last drop). He departed from Hamburg and, when the ship docked again in Bremen, he wanted to use the few hours of the layover to visit the city. "You have a J in your passport. Jews are no longer allowed to step onto German soil." So he was sent back.'[11]

Sometimes Sally and Bertha are hopeful about their own prospects: 'Yesterday, Mr Bechhöfer wrote from New York and asked if we already have an affidavit. He wants to get us one. Is that not true friendship?'[12]

Often they are anxious: 'Regarding our emigration: dear Lutz will give us a relative's affidavit but that alone will not be enough. Mr Karl Bechhöfer (formerly from Nuremberg) firmly promised us a good guarantee but he hasn't written since October. Please, write to him.'[13]

Always they are beset by the obstacles placed in their way by the countries they hoped would provide sanctuary. In June 1939, Sally writes: 'Tomorrow, we will receive the health certificates from Dr Bauchwitz and on Tuesday our passport photos. Then we have everything together to send off. The only things missing are a decent guarantor and a corresponding Affidavit.'[14]

In August, he writes again: 'Regarding Woburn House, we are enclosing the last letter, which we received together with yours. It's good that we had an answer so quickly but we still don't have the main thing and that is the guarantor! It wouldn't be long until we were with you if we could find one.'[15]

But even if they had been able to fulfil the bureaucratic requirements, it is doubtful that they could have afforded to emigrate. As Sally wrote to his son, now interned in Canada, in May 1941: 'The day before yesterday, we received a very nice letter from Uncle Gustav … They are putting in a lot of effort to help us emigrate soon. We also had a nice letter on the same day from Lutz. He said that he wants to provide us with a relative's affidavit. But then there's the small matter of the cost of travel. I don't think that Bechhöfer is in a position to help. Is there no chance of emigrating to Canada? Do you think you can find out?'[16]

Then their letters become increasingly desperate: 'Bechhöfer back-pedalled in so far that he no longer wants to acknowledge his previous promises. How about getting in touch with your cousin Kurt Brandes … and ask him to find you a job so that you can join him and then send for us. It's incredibly difficult for us now to come to the USA, seeing that Bechhöfer has failed us. Where are we supposed to get a good additional guarantor? Lutz is prepared to give us an affidavit but it will probably be limited and who knows when you will be able to help.'[17]

At last they are dejected: 'Uncle Gustav wrote that Lutz has gone back on his promise to provide us with an affidavit. What do you say to that? Bechhöfer did the same as we've already told you. Two fine citizens! Now we have to start our search all over again. Sometimes it is enough to drive us to despair.'[18]

Finally, by August 1941, they are resigned: 'Last week, we had news again from Bechhöfer that we can definitely count on him. It's just a shame that Lutz didn't keep his word even though it's practically worthless now since it's practically impossible to get out. All the American consulates are closed.'[19]

Even as the Nazis turned the screw, Sally and Bertha – partly in order to reassure their son but largely no doubt to satisfy the censor – were writing that they were in good health and in good spirits: 'Your father and I are making a good life for ourselves. Today, for instance, we sat on a bench in the Hain, despite the chill. Apart from the "usual complaints", we're both content.'[20]

Soon it would be illegal for Jews to sit on park benches.

For Sally and Bertha, their son's letters were their only contact with the outside world, their chief solace and, as they constantly reminded him, their greatest joy. Despite their own difficulties, they are unfailingly concerned about his future. Sally offers advice on how he might build a career; Bertha worries about his personal hygiene. Shortly after he had reached England, she wrote: 'Dear Fritz; get your shirt and socks washed. You've been there for more than 14 days and only have 2 shirts. It would have been good if I had sent you off with another shirt and your slippers. As soon as we have your address, I'll send you the Bamberg newspaper, if it's allowed.'[21]

Official records show that from May 1940 to the time of his deportation in November 1941, Sally was 'employed' by the city of Bamberg's civil engineering office.[22] A departmental memorandum of 25 October 1940 states: 'The Jew worker Sally Israel Brandes, living at Hainstraße 4a, is engaged by this department in digging works on am Sendelbach and urgently requires three woollen shirts. It's not known whether he has his own.'

I walked the two miles from the former Judenhaus at Hainstraße 4a to am Sendelbach on a pleasant afternoon in early April, pausing halfway for a cup of coffee at the Kiosk Kunni by the toddlers' playground. For a tourist, it's a lovely riverside stroll.

Am Sendelbach is beyond the waterworks, beyond Bamberg's built-up area. It's a narrow lane in open country, running between a series of waterways, sports fields and allotments. In high summer there would have been little shade; in deep winter, no shelter from the rain and wind or from the driving snow.

I sat down on a grass verge, my back against the pole of a road sign. A few cars passed and one or two bicycles, and my mind drifted in the early evening sunshine. I wondered what thoughts occupied Sally's as he wielded his shovel through the long day and as he trudged to and from his place of work each morning and each evening.

After twenty minutes or so, I brushed myself down, made my way up to Mohnstraße and caught the bus back into town.

Just how precarious life had become for Bamberg's Jewish community is evidenced by a letter of 4 September 1939 written by Dr Ludwig Israel Oster on behalf of the Administration of the Jewish Community of Bamberg, which was by then under curfew:

> To all members of our community
>
> In spite of repeated strong warnings to show utmost restraint during these grave days, it came to our attention that some of our members do not seem to comprehend the demands of our times.
>
> Again, we emphatically demand adherence to the following rules: no unnecessary lingering in the streets – except for necessary purchases or similarly urgent business – particularly no idle loitering, or worse, the congregating of two or more people for conversations in the open streets or squares of the city. (This includes sitting on benches.)
>
> At all times avoid pushing and loud behaviour while shopping or dealing with official bureaus. To the contrary, show in all cases the utmost restraint and a calm and dignified demeanour. No one single individual dares jeopardise our entire community by unseemly and objectionable behaviour. Each and every one is doubly responsible to all of us ...[23]

Martin Morgenroth's death in October 1939 required elections to the chair of the Bamberg Jewish community. Dr Bauchwitz, now stripped of his doctorate and reduced to the rank of 'Jewish medical attendant', succeeded him. Sally was appointed first vice-chairman and Josef Hessberg second.

Their task was in so many ways unenviable. They were subject to the same depredations as their friends and neighbours. But, as well as doing what they could to administer what was left of the community's resources and, somehow, maintain morale, they had also to deal on its behalf with the Gestapo and other official organs of their own oppression.

From 20 September 1939, Jews were prohibited from listening to broadcasts in their own homes and were required to surrender their radio sets on pain of 'severe punishment'. Without access to news, and particularly news from beyond the reach of Nazi propaganda, the Jewish community was prey to rumour. On 16 March 1941, the executive committee issued a bulletin: 'We are compelled to make the following statement: recently renewed rumours circulated which caused apprehension in our community. Again we emphasise that there is no substance to these rumours. We call on members of our community to maintain strict discipline and not allow irresponsible rumour-mongers to cause unnecessary anxiety.'[24]

In all likelihood the use of 'compelled' is not purely figurative. While the committee may have hoped against hope to calm the community's fears, it is probable that the Gestapo had had a hand in drafting this bulletin – and unthinkable that it would have been issued without its authorisation.

Many of the rumours were well founded, particularly those about deportations. As early as October 1939, Jews from Vienna had been transported to Poland, ostensibly to help in the newly occupied country's 'reconstruction'. On the night of 12–13 February 1940, the entire Jewish population of Stettin (now Szczecin in Poland but then on German territory) was rounded up, dispatched by train to Poland and force-marched some 15 miles through deep snow and in freezing temperatures to Lublin where they were abandoned in the Old Town Square; seventy died of exhaustion and hypothermia.

That deportation was widely reported and even Joseph Goebbels was obliged to confirm that it had taken place, conceding that 'the foreign press claims that 1,000 Jews were transported to the Generalgouvernement. This report is true but must be treated with greatest confidence.'[25]

Word of these early deportations may have reached Bamberg. But the community must certainly have known and been severely shaken by the fate of the Jews of nearby Baden and the Pfalz/Saar.

I have often wondered how Great Uncle Ernst Herzstein, Bertha's brother, came to be in the Vichy French concentration camps at Gurs and then Drancy before the life of this principled, decorated war veteran was extinguished in Auschwitz. Now I know.

Ernst was a remarkable man. Born in 1881, he practised as a civil engineer before serving as an officer on the front line in the First World War. Though he was wounded and awarded the Iron Cross, he was a pacifist who managed to avoid firing a single shot in anger. After the war, he refused to draw his disability pension on the grounds that others were in greater need.

Wartime photographs reveal a weary but intelligent face. A much later photo catches him unawares as he's fastening his collar: he looks kindly and quizzical, if a little reserved.

After Kristallnacht, though he was exempt as chairman of the Jewish Frontline Soldiers League, he volunteered to accompany other local Jews to Dachau. There he met his brother-in-law Sally. Two years later, he was one of 7,000 Jews who, on 22 October 1940, were rounded up in Mannheim and other towns in Baden and the Pfalz/Saar.

The operation was known as the Wagner-Bürckel-Aktion after its architects, Robert Wagner and Joseph Bürckel, the local Gauleiters. It was meticulously planned with lists of Jews secretly prepared in advance to facilitate their speedy identification and arrest. Each household was allowed to take with them 100 RM and given half an hour to pack no more than 50 kilograms of luggage. Whatever the deportees could not carry was expropriated.

14. Ernst Herzstein, pacifist holder of the Iron Cross
and victim of Auschwitz.

The frightened Jews were herded to their local railway stations and
onto seven special trains. As the locomotives pulled out, Wagner
proudly boasted that his area had become the first in Germany to be
'Judenrein', cleared of Jews.

Hitler watched closely to gauge the public reaction to this first
deportation of German Jews. It took place in broad daylight and,
according to Géraldine Schwarz, whose non-Jewish grandparents lived
in Mannheim, 'right before the eyes of apathetic citizens who were
incapable of exercising their humanity'.[26] The Führer would have been
delighted.

After a journey of two days and nights, the deportees arrived at Gurs
near Pau in the foothills of the Pyrenees. The camp there had been
constructed a few years earlier as a reception centre for refugees from

Franco's Spain. It comprised a complex of 382 cabins made from wooden planks covered by a tarred fabric that provided little protection from the cold and rain. Each windowless cabin housed sixty malnourished inmates, sleeping on the floor. There was neither running water nor sanitation. Disease, including typhus and dysentery, was rife. Some 800 prisoners died in 1940–1.

Mistele cites an account of conditions there that appeared in the *Badische Presse* of 14 February 1941 in what he believes to be 'the only instance of a semi-official report on the fate of deported Jews in the German press': 'The conditions in this camp are so severe, according to one account, that those who have not seen or experienced them would not believe it possible. In the camp at Vernet men, once strong, but now weakened by hunger and cold, have lost all resemblance to human beings ... in the camp at Gurs an average of 45 people die every week. We lie on the bare floor without mattresses or straw and with only two thin blankets while the temperature drops to minus 10C.'[27]

The *Badische Presse* did not intend its report to be sympathetic. Its headline was 'Fugitive Traitors Living in Luxury in France – Life in the Gurs Emigration Camp'. The resonance with headlines of today is unmistakable.

News of the deportation – the only one westwards from Nazi Germany – would have been deeply unsettling to the Jewish communities of Bamberg and elsewhere. The captives at Gurs were allowed, perhaps encouraged, to write to their families, though it is clear that the censor guided their pens. Certainly, Sally and Bertha were aware that Ernst had been deported. Their letters to my father make frequent though cryptic reference to his welfare without mention of the fate that had befallen him. In June 1941, Sally wrote that 'the day before yesterday, we received a message from Uncle Ernst in which he let us know that he is healthy and in good spirits'.[28]

Some detainees were released from Gurs and some, including Hannah Arendt, who had been interned in 1940 after the Germans occupied France, escaped. But between August 1942 and March 1943, the Vichy administration delivered almost 4,000 of its Jewish prisoners to the Germans. Most were dispatched to the transit camp at Drancy outside Paris from which they were deported to the death camps in Poland. Ernst was one of the first of the 65,000 Jews who passed through Drancy.[29] Only 2,000 escaped the gas chambers. Ernst was not among them. He arrived at Auschwitz on 14 August 1942.

Meanwhile, Sally's and Bertha's own suffering continued to intensify, for the war effort had by no means diverted the Nazis from their persecution of Jews. From January 1940, they were denied ration cards for clothing and, from June 1941, access to shaving soap. Both ordinances were designed not only to humiliate but also to force Jews into a resemblance of the unkempt and threadbare criminals Nazi propaganda made them out to be.

In September 1941, the Police Ordinance on the Identification of Jews required every Jew to wear the yellow star in public. Later that month, Jews were prohibited from using either public or private means of transport and from leaving town. Only those in possession of a certificate permitting them to travel to their place of forced labour were exempt from an otherwise total ban on free movement. On 23 October, all Jewish emigration was suspended 'for the duration of the war'.

In October 1942, the Nazis' district headquarters in Bayreuth issued instructions on food rationing which specified that 'Jews will not be supplied with meat, eggs, wheat products, whole milk, skimmed milk and any other food distributed locally or under special rationing (especially fruit, vegetables and fish).'[30] But by then, Sally and Bertha were long gone.

13

THE ROAD TO RIGA

Jews endured few torments under the Nazis that their forefathers had not suffered from others. There was nothing new in the way they were demonised in official propaganda, in the humiliation for which they were marked by the symbols they were forced to wear, in the punitive taxes they bore and the expropriation of their homes and property. There was nothing new in their exclusion from education, the professions and cultural life, in the rights and liberties they were denied, in the burning of their books and the destruction of their scriptures and synagogues. There was nothing new in their separation and isolation in squalid, defenceless ghettos, in their expulsion from their homelands, in the violence and slaughter they suffered at the hands of riotous mobs or calm men in immaculate uniforms.

In the twentieth century, there were two principal differences. The first was one of scale. The Nazis had both the maniacal ambition to eliminate European Jewry in its entirety and the technology and talent for organisation through which to attempt it.

The second was that for the Jews there was no way out. In previous centuries some at least could hope to escape persecution by converting to Christianity. But for the Nazis, the Jew was eternal, der ewige Jude. The issue was no longer one of deniable faith but of unalterable race and blood: only when the last drop had been drained would the Jewish problem finally have been solved.

* * *

The Nazis had been seeking a radical, irreversible answer to the Jewish question from their earliest days. The Wannsee Conference, held on 20 January 1942 in an elegant lakeside villa to the south of Berlin, concluded that it lay in the industrialised extermination of the entire Jewish population of Europe.

But the gas chambers of Auschwitz, Belzec and Treblinka were only the 'final' component of a 'solution' already being implemented. From the summer of 1941, even while the Nazis were still considering their options, hundreds of thousands of Jews had been butchered as the German army advanced into the Soviet Union.

The mass killing, at least in its earlier stages, had run in parallel with other disposal plans. There was a scheme, for example, to create a great 'Jew reservation' in the Lublin district of Poland into which Jews from all over the continent would be decanted once the Soviets had been defeated. At the same time, Adolf Eichmann, who was to coordinate the logistics for so much of the Final Solution, was promoting a long cherished but wildly impractical plan to ship Europe's Jews to the French colony of Madagascar.[1] As late as 4 February 1942, a fortnight after Wannsee, Reinhard Heydrich, the conference's convener and one of the Holocaust's principal architects, declared that the Arctic would be 'an ideal homeland for the 11 million Jews from Europe'.[2] If he was serious, it was probably only because he doubted that they could survive conditions there.

Though it had become clear long before Wannsee that neither the Polish nor Madagascan option was achievable, the Nazis were determined to make Germany, Austria and Czechoslovakia Judenrein as quickly as possible. It was decided that, in the first instance, all remaining Jews were to be deported 'to the east', to Riga in Latvia and Minsk in White Russia (now Belarus).

In October 1941, the Chief of Security Police, Kurt Daluege, signed orders for the 'evacuation' of 50,000 Jews from Germany and some of its occupied territories. In Franconia, on instructions from the regional head of the Gestapo, Dr Benno Martin, SS Sturmbannführer (Major) Dr Theodor Grafenberger of the Nuremberg-Fürth Gestapo issued the order that Bamberg's Jews and those from other local towns would be deported from Nuremberg on 29 November.[3]

That was the day on which the invitations to the Wannsee Conference were issued and the fate of Europe's Jews sealed.

The Bamberg community's administrative committee was charged with the agonising task of selecting and informing the 118 Jews who were to make up its quota.[4] Of the adults, most of the 60 women and 46 men were in their late fifties or older; 10 were under 20. Perhaps, given Sally's position, he could have avoided this first draft; perhaps he volunteered. In any event, he and Bertha were on the list.

While the fateful letters Dr Bauchwitz must have circulated as chairman of the committee have not survived, Karl Mistele quotes the text of what must have been a very similar notice, issued on 19 November by his counterpart in Stuttgart:

> By the order of the Secret State Police Stuttgart Directorate, we hereby notify you that you and your above mentioned children have been assigned to an evacuation transport to the East. At the same time we advise you that you and your children assigned to the above mentioned transport must be ready at your present place of residence, starting Wednesday 26 November 1941. You are prohibited from leaving the premises, even for a short period of time, without a special permit from the authorities. Forced labour assignments, even in essential industries, do not give exemption from this evacuation order.
>
> Attempts to resist or evade evacuation are useless and will only lead to grave consequences for those concerned.
>
> The enclosed declaration of assets, filled out carefully and separately for each family member, including children, must be turned in to the local police authorities within three days.
>
> Also enclosed is a list of the most essential articles needed for the trip ...
>
> From the time you receive this letter, you are not allowed access to your assets, as per strict orders of the authorities. You can no longer sell, give away, lend, charge against or make any other use of your assets ...

The amount of 57.65 RM for each person must be submitted immediately … Before departure, you must turn in your food ration cards …[5]

Nothing had been overlooked by the Gestapo. The declaration of assets was a 16-page form. Among the items deportees were advised to bring with them, 'of utmost importance are spades, shovels and other construction tools'.

Perhaps this instruction provided a glimmer of hope about what lay in store for the Jews of Bamberg; perhaps it gave them some confidence that they were to build a new life for themselves, albeit in exile somewhere in the east. In any event there is a pathetic poignancy in the letter's closing paragraph: 'Finally, we ask you not to despair. The achievements of our members at their diverse work assignments justify the hope that they will also master those new and difficult tasks.'

The 57.65 RM that each Jew was required to pay was the cost of the rail ticket to their unknown destination. Later, as Daniel Mendelsohn observes in his account of the quest for his own lost family, deported Jews were often required to pay for the bullets that killed them.[6]

On 21 November, Dr Bauchwitz, who was to remain in Bamberg until he was deported with the last remnants of the community 10 months later, wrote only: 'By order of the authorities, all members of the community must remain at their places of residence on Saturday, until noon.'[7]

On the following day, he issued further instructions for the coming days but also appealed for help: 'Not a single delivery of warm woollen garments and good footwear has reached us. We now must turn to those not on the list of deportees and ask them to bring to the office of the community, all day Sunday, woollen articles (underwear and outer garments for men as well as women) and footwear that are in good condition. This is the least we can do for our departing brothers and sisters. We expect everyone to fulfil his obligation to the best of his ability.'[8]

*　*　*

The transport east was scheduled to leave Nuremberg on 29 November. Those on the quotas from Bamberg and outlying towns and villages, including Bayreuth, would first have to travel there. On 27 November, with chilling detachment, the Secretary of the Criminal Police in Forchheim reported to the Mayor the efficient expulsion of the town's Jews: 'They were transported today at 9.00 am by truck to Bamberg. From there, they will travel by rail to Nuremberg, to leave on 29 November by freight train for Riga ... A considerable number of local residents witnessed the deportation with great interest and expressed their immense satisfaction ... It is absolutely certain that by Christmas 1941 Forchheim will be free of Jews.'[9]

After the war, German bureaucrats involved in these operations routinely denied that they had known the ultimate fate of the 'evacuees'. Charged with assisting the deportation of Jews from Franconia and the confiscation of their property, Benno Martin argued that he had sought to protect them wherever possible, that he had been unaware what awaited them and that, had he not cooperated in their deportation, his own safety would have been in jeopardy. The court acquitted him.[10]

Wolfgang Scheffler dismisses this defence:

In actual fact, a great many people in the authorities were aware of the deportation of the German Jews, and the councils were heavily involved. The process was treated as a bureaucratic act by the employment exchanges, industrial firms, tax offices and welfare authorities right through to the courts. The banks issued precise guidelines on how to circumvent the orders given by the Reich Ministry of Finance. The NSGWP [Nazi Party] and their organisations, predominantly the NS Public Welfare Organisation, auctioned and distributed the possessions of the deported as soon as the tax offices and other authorities had helped themselves to personal effects for their own purposes.[11]

Indeed, these appropriations were explicitly and officially sanctioned. A particularly cynical amendment to the German Citizenship Law made plain that the assets of deported Jews 'with a permanent residence abroad' legally became the property of the Reich and 'shall serve as support of all needs for solving the "Jewish question"'.[12]

My grandparents had already been forced to sell their business at a knock-down price. The household and personal property they had to abandon when they were deported from Bamberg was never recovered. Some of their solid German furniture perhaps survives somewhere, adorning someone else's home. If so, those who sit at their table are probably unaware of how they came to own it and of the family that had sat there before them.

On 26 November, the day before the deportation, Sally wrote to his son for the last time: 'Now I have to tell you that we will be going away tomorrow and it will therefore be a while before you hear from us again. We will be together with our family from Bayreuth. You can imagine that we are glad to be with them. Now take care and keep well. Hopefully, the same will go for us.'

In the early hours of Thursday 27 November, Gestapo officers rapped on the doors of the Bamberg Jews assigned to them with instructions to use 'the force, precision and correctness required' to execute their duties.[13] They were to inspect the Jews' homes and, before leaving, ensure that all fires had been extinguished, that arrangements had been made for the collection of foodstuffs and pets and that any valuables had been confiscated and accounted for. Finally, 'every Jew must wear a sign around his neck with his name, date of birth and ID number'.[14]

The Jews were escorted to the assembly point at the Weiße Taube where their luggage was inspected and they were subjected to body searches. Then they were marched to the station and the waiting train.

In Bayreuth, the forty-six Jews on the list, among them Bertha's brothers Julius and Karl with his wife Emma, and her sister Rosel with her husband Hugo Rosenthal, were ordered in the small hours of the morning to the Rotmainhalle on General Hindenberg Straße. There they were loaded onto a truck and driven down the Autobahn to Nuremberg where they arrived at 10.00 a.m.

The experience of the Jews of Bamberg and Bayreuth as they were corralled, processed and paraded through the city's streets will have mirrored that of those they were shortly to join. Bernhard Kolb, a leading member of the Nuremberg community, described the treatment of his friends and neighbours: 'Depending on the conception of duties this process was carried out more or less in a degrading fashion and involved physical abuse. Likewise, the reaction of the public varied considerably. Whilst some bid a tearful and emotional farewell in an unguarded moment passers-by in the street engaged in vile abuse and insults.'[15]

When I visited Bamberg in April 2019, I sought out the places my grandparents would have known: the apartment buildings, the shops, the site of the synagogue opposite which they had lived, the park in which they had strolled on a Sunday, the Jewish cemetery in which they are remembered, though they do not rest there.

I couldn't find the Weiße Taube. Zinkenwörth 17–19 has disappeared under indifferent post-war redevelopment. In the end, Franz Fichtl, curator of Bamberg's Jewish history, guided me to a simple plaque on a white plastered wall outside an antique shop. It commemorates the old synagogue that had served the community for 250 years before making way for the grand new monument to Jewish pride and pre-war confidence on Herzog-Max Straße. When the great synagogue was torched on Kristallnacht, the Weiße Taube was all the community had left. Now there's just a little sign on the wall.

So here they gathered in the freezing first light of 27 November, the once prosperous and the workaday, the proud and the unassuming, the pious and the agnostic, the social democrat and the conservative, united in their Jewishness and their misery.

They cannot have greeted each other with much more than a nod of recognition. Their faces must have been grey with fatigue and worry. Some may have been clinging to the hope that the Nazi bureaucrats had fostered, that they were going to build a new life in some distant corner of the German Reich. Perhaps one day, when they had made a success and things had calmed down, they might return. After all, that's what Jews do: they prosper, they endure, they wait for better times.

Others would not have shared such optimism. This surely was a journey to an unnamed, unimagined destination. All they could know was that the people who were sending them there did not mean them well.

Here at the assembly point, the despondent, disoriented Jews were roughly searched as they would be again and again; with every search, something more that was precious to them would be lost.

Then they were ordered to move off, 100 Jews mostly in their fifties and sixties. Their children who had seen what was coming, who had the skills or the brawn that a few countries were prepared to exploit and the energy, resourcefulness and good fortune to negotiate the necessary paperwork, had left long ago. The older folk remained, but soon they would be gone too.

The Jews of Bamberg would have filed past the old synagogue, emerging from Generalgaße onto Lange Straße within touching distance of the shop where Sally's business had prospered before the boycotts, the crippling taxes, the dwindling customers, the laid-off staff and, finally, the Aryanisation of his and Bertha's life work had destroyed it.

They would have dragged their luggage, all they were allowed, all they could carry, all they had left in the world, up Sophienstraße where Willy Lessing had lived and where he was beaten to death, and on to Luitpoldstraße, the wide long road to the station, across the bridge over the Regnitz where the chill wind would have cut them.

They would have trudged past many of the apartment buildings in which they themselves had lived before being forced into the Judenhäuser. Today each is marked by the Stolpersteine that punctuate the streets – little brass commemorations on Sophienstraße for Alice and Edith Wassermann, Emma Hellmann, Willy Lessing, Albert and Frieda Sulbacher, Elise Kupfer, Heinz, Hans and Hildegard Löwenherz; little plaques on Luitpoldstraße for Luise and Benno Kohn, the Catholic anti-Nazi Hans Wölfel, Babette Bernet, Albert, Lilly and Helga Walter, Karolina Löbl, Samuel and Emilie Palm, Albert, Berta and Willy Aron, Greta Bing who could not bear to live after Kristallnacht, Maria Bickart,

Rosa, Hugo, Emma and Max Rossheimer, Rosa, Irma and two-year-old Sally Walter, Sally and Bertha's friends Rosa and Ignaz Kohn, Hermann Dorn.

As they passed the home of Willy Aron, the Nazis' first Jewish victim in Bamberg, did any think back to that terrible shock in 1933 when his body came back from Dachau in a sealed coffin, and wonder why they did not see that this was the first step on the road they were now taking?

Ordinary Bambergers would have been about their early morning business. Some, tipped off that something was afoot, might have made a detour to Luitpoldstraße to gawp at the wretched procession. Some may have looked on in silent sympathy, most with indifference: this was just one more routine humiliation of the Jews.

Some would have jeered at the doctors who had treated them, the lawyers who had arranged their affairs, the shopkeepers who had sold them their daily necessities or, like Sally, the fabrics of the clothes they were wearing.

When the Jews of Bamberg reached the station, did they wonder when they would see their city again?

At 12.48, goods train 6842 bore the Jews away to Nuremberg where, in freezing, blacked-out barracks on the Nazi rally grounds, they awaited their 'resettlement in the east'.

The pattern was repeated all over occupied Europe: first the disbelief, then the deportation. Even three years later, when the Germans invaded Hungary on 19 March 1944, the country's Jews, though they knew of the expulsions from Slovakia to the north and the massacres in Serbia to the south, clung to the desperate delusion that somehow they would be spared. Reska Weiss recalled in her post-war memoir: 'Hitler had bellowed over the radio that all Jews would be exterminated, but we Hungarian Jews had closed our ears and our hearts, convinced that it couldn't happen to us. And so we sat in our homes – huddled together, anxiously speculating on the news from broadcasts.'[16]

In the end, the truth dawned in Ungvar, the small northern Hungarian town in which Reska lived. Some 14,000 Jews who had for generations lived 'in amity' among the 20,000 Gentiles were rounded up and marched to a makeshift ghetto in the local brickworks. From there they were transported, along with 440,000 other Hungarian Jews, to Auschwitz and, in Reska's extraordinary case, thence to Riga: 'It is customary in small towns for the sympathetic populace to crowd into the streets for a funeral or other sad event. This time, however, the crowds showed no compassion. On the contrary, they seemed to get a spiteful enjoyment out of our misery. Only our Jewish neighbours, pale and terrified, came near us. They realised that our fate would soon be theirs.'[17]

The Bamberg Jews arrived at Nuremberg-Langwasser at 3.39 p.m., joining around 1,000 others, half from Nuremberg, in a temporary holding camp at the vast Nazi Party Rally grounds. There they were again body-searched and any cash and jewellery that had eluded earlier inspections was confiscated, leaving them, if they were lucky, with only a watch and a wedding ring. Their identity cards were stamped 'evacuated'.

They were confined in what Grafenberger referred to as a 'ghetto barracks'. For three days, they were not allowed to leave the blocks, many of which were daubed with anti-Semitic slogans, and no lights were allowed after nightfall. Commissioned by the Nazi Party, cinema-owner Richard Nickel filmed the deportees' misery for the Gestapo's entertainment.[18]

On the Friday, permission to hold a Sabbath service was negotiated. Berhard Kolb recalled: 'People streamed out of the barracks and stood in deep devotion, many holding small prayer books, listening to the old melodies of Friday evening worship. Ludwig Willner, the cantor, sang out across the field, and Lecho Dodi was sung quietly by the congregation. Even the policemen standing along the camp fence seemed moved.'[19]

On Saturday 29 November, in an operation of military precision and utmost secrecy, 1,000 Jews were marched to the freight yard at Nuremberg's Märzfeld station.[20] Bernhard Kolb described the procession:

The train station was located about one kilometer from the camp. Elderly and sick people were allowed to be taken on a truck. The others had to march with their hand luggage and in rows of ten. Luckily the weather was good. Along the streets SS guards stood laughing, and the 'Exodus of the Jews' was captured on camera for posterity ... The area was closed to civilians for several kilometers ... The deportees were counted in front of each car and were arranged according to their numbers in front of the car doors. The signal for boarding was given – the concentration camp methods were starting already. There was no ramp. Women and children and elderly persons had to be lifted onto the train and anyone who did not disappear fast enough into a compartment was violently abused.

The train – Sonderzug Da 32 – pulled out at 3.00 p.m. with eighteen SS guards and two Gestapo officials aboard. A goods wagon, loaded with the tools, building materials and stoves the Jews had brought with them, had been uncoupled.

The exhausted, bewildered, frightened Jews were crowded into third-class carriages, already crammed with luggage. Families were separated; because heating was powered by steam from the locomotive, those in the front few carriages sweated while those to the rear froze; there were no provisions other than those the deportees had brought with them; water was distributed twice throughout the three-day journey to their unknown destination.

Julius Ceslanski, a Nuremberg Jew and one of the few survivors of the transport, recalled after the war: 'At the beginning many rushed to the windows because everyone wanted to know which route we were taking. The train passed the Jewish cemetery which was for all of us, even if no one spoke it out loud, a bad omen of what was to come.'[21]

In February 1942, my father received a letter from his uncle Siegfried Strauß: 'On 25 November, at your father's request, I wrote you a letter which must have been wrongly addressed because it came back. Your parents departed for Riga on 27 November. Meta has stayed behind. Unfortunately, I don't currently have an address as they haven't yet written. Hans, Gretel and Margit likewise went to Riga on 11 December. I imagine they've met up. Hans will be busy as a metal-worker. We're OK. Please Fritz, write to us regularly. I'll let you know as soon as I have your parents' address.'[22] Siegfried and his wife Else were deported to Theresienstadt (Terezín) six months later, on 25 July 1942. Siegfried died the next day. Else was killed in Auschwitz on 23 January 1943. Hans died at Salaspils near Riga, Gretel and Margit at Stutthof in Poland.

As I have explained, my sole and simple aim had been to establish the path of Da 32 as it bore my grandparents and my great uncles and aunts to their exile in the east. In this I failed. The Reichsbahn must have plotted it but no certain record has been found. In any event, it's unlikely that the Sonderzug would have followed its predetermined route. Almost every other train on the long and complex network between Nuremberg and Riga would have taken precedence over it. Every troop transport or supply train hurrying to and from the Russian front would have required it to shunt into a siding and wait perhaps for several hours for permission to resume its miserable journey.

Scholars have tried by an exclusion of improbabilities to establish the transport's likeliest course and that, more or less, is what I tried to follow. But in the end, I had to concede that the idea of tracing my grandparents' route had always been an illusion. Eighty years have passed. Langwasser is no longer a camping ground for the Nazi faithful, nor a detention centre for deported Jews, but a fashionable Nuremberg suburb. The now derelict Märzfeld station, from which their journey began, was closed in 1987. The route of Da 32 has been obscured by time and change.

I knew my journey could in no way replicate Sally's and Bertha's. I knew I could gain no special insight simply by sitting on a train head-ing vaguely towards their destination. I could not imagine their thoughts nor feel their fears. Everything was a compromise: the route I took, which skirted the Russian enclave of Kaliningrad, then Königsberg, with its difficult access and complicated visa requirements; and the mode of transport, because limited railway infrastructure meant that from eastern Poland to Riga I had to travel by bus. On the assumption that the path I followed was at least approximate to theirs, I could only stare out of the window and see what they might have glimpsed when the turmoil within and around them allowed.

So I boarded my train at Nuremberg's main station, heading north through Hof, Chemnitz and Elsterwerda to Berlin. There I spent the night, not in a cold and crowded third-class compartment crammed with disconsolate exiles, but in an unremarkable but comfortable suburban hotel. Next morning, I took the train over the Polish border to Kostrzyn and then on to Krzyz and, via Pila, to Chojnice and Tczew. We rode through endless scrawny fields on the flat, sandy plain, through forests of Scots pine with their slender red trunks under scrubby canopies, past drab, unremarkable towns and villages with every other little house flying a red-and-white Polish flag. We stopped briefly at semi-derelict railway stations which, when my grandparents passed through, had perhaps been buildings of some local distinction.

On we went through the featureless landscape to a second overnight stop at Elblag (then Elbing). There the rails ran out and next morning the bus wound its way for six hours through countless little villages in gently undulating country, through the garrison town of Kętrzyn (then Rastenburg) near which lie the ruins of Hitler's command bunker, the Wolf's Lair. There, within its two-metre-thick concrete walls through which no light and little air could penetrate, he conceived his plans for the extermination of the Jews. Then on to Suwalki, a few miles from Poland's eastern border, into Lithuania and another overnight stop in Kaunas.

Here, on 25 and 29 November 1941, the first mass shootings of German Jews took place. The two transports that arrived in Lithuania's second city (then Kovno) had originally been destined for Riga, but the German administrators in Latvia were not ready for them. First 2,934 Jews from Berlin, Frankfurt and Munich and then a further 2,000 from Vienna and Breslau were unloaded from the trains. They were taken to Fort IX and mown down by the Stormtroopers of Einsatzkommando 3 and their Lithuanian collaborators. Among the victims were Leopold and Cäcilie Zuntz and their 16-year-old son Hermann.

The tourist leaflet I picked up at the hotel reception did not attempt to gloss over the fate of Kaunas's own 30,000 Jews. In the hour I had before boarding my final bus to Riga, I tried but failed to find the memorial for one of the most appalling atrocities I had read about.

The Germans had not had time to establish their command structures when it occurred on 25 June 1941, the day after they had entered the city. The Lithuanians who perpetrated it were so satisfied with their work that they left a detailed, illustrated record of it. One photograph shows a muscular young man standing centre ground on a garage forecourt, staring dispassionately into the camera lens.[23] A huge club of wood or iron rests in his hand. At his feet lie the bodies of a dozen dead or dying Jews. In the background, armed civilians are preparing more of their Jewish fellow citizens for slaughter. According to witnesses, mothers hoisted young children onto their shoulders for a better view and the crowd applauded every blow the resolute young man rained upon the heads of his defenceless victims.

When he and his comrades from the Lithuanian Activist Front had battered fifty Jews to death, he climbed onto the mound of their bodies and played the Lithuanian national anthem on an accordion.[24] He became known as 'the death dealer of Kovno'.

Why do I retell this dismal story? It is because of what Julius Norwilla, a native of Kaunas, wrote about a ceremony that marked the seventy-fourth anniversary of the massacre: 'It is obvious that the Lietūkis Garage massacre is the blackest page in the entire history of my native city and country as well. But where are the discussions about its significance? ... There were no official representatives of the Lithuanian government ... Not one Lithuanian citizen speaker noted who the perpetrators of the massacre were. No moral judgment. No expressions of national regret. No human, humane or humanitarian statement.'[25]

As I was leaving the Hotel Metropolis, I noticed a plaque on the street façade that celebrates the Japanese diplomat Chiune Sugihara who, during his stay there between 28 August and 4 September 1940, 'continued to issue Visas for Life'. He, and the Dutch consul Jan Szwartendijk, saved thousands of lives. The plaque does not mention that they were Jews.

The bus from Kaunas made short work of the 170 miles to Riga on a fast smooth highway across another invisible border and through pleasant flat lands to the sprawling industrial suburbs of the Latvian capital. And suddenly I was there, in the place where Sally's and Bertha's journey ended.

14

THE CLEANSING
OF LATVIA

On 2 December 1941, after a journey of 1,000 miles over three days and nights, the starving, frozen, frightened Jews of Upper Franconia arrived at the Šķirotava freight yard, some six miles south-east of Riga. There, SS men under the command of Obersturmführer (Lieutenant) Kurt Krause, Commandant of the Riga ghetto, welcomed the deportees with random beatings.[1] A former Berlin detective, the murderous Krause was known in the ghetto as 'the man-eater'.

Julius Ceslanski recalled the violence and the humiliation: 'We had to leave the wagons in a big rush. SS beat us randomly with rubber truncheons. While the men were unloading the heavy freight, which had been taken for "relocation purposes", the women had to clean the compartments. There were no brooms, so they used their hands, at best with quickly collected cartons. The Germans especially liked to beat the women on their behind. Everything had to be done in haste.'[2]

Krause summoned the 'King of the Jews', the representative of the transport, and promptly struck him over the head with a dog whip. A dentist from Nuremberg was shot dead on the spot.[3]

Despite all they had already endured, the violence came as a shock to the deportees. Herbert Mai, another of the few survivors of Sonderzug Da 32, then a young boy from Würzburg, had believed they were simply being resettled. The illusion was now difficult to sustain: 'All of a sudden we've seen a lot of uniformed with guns, which we never realised before and they told us and they screamed already, you know, "everybody out of the trains" and then they beat already people up and that was also something new to us, which we never came across ... it was again another screwed a little more of a turn, and everybody was frightened and women were screaming ...'[4]

By the time the transport from Nuremberg had reached Šķirotava, Latvia was already awash with blood.

The slaughter had begun almost the moment the Germans broke their non-aggression pact with the Soviets and marched into Latvia on 22 June 1941.[5] The first massacre of Latvian Jews took place in Grobina the following day. It is estimated that the four SS death squads, the Einsatzgruppen, as they followed the army into Russia in 1941–2, murdered up to 1.5 million Jews, along with partisans, Soviet officials, gypsies and others who offended Nazi ideology. Brigadeführer Franz Walter Stahlecker boasted that, under his command, Einsatzgruppe A had by the close of 1941 accounted for 249,420 Jews, predominantly in the Baltic region.[6]

Between July and November, the fate of Latvia's Jews, at least in the short term, had been the cause of considerable friction between the civilian administration and the security services. Hinrich Lohse, Reichskommisar Ostland, head of the civil administration in the eastern territories, was determined to preserve those who were fit for work, at least for as long as they could be used to support the war effort.[7] At the end of July he ordered that ghettos be established in the major towns and cities and that the Jews be confined there as an accessible source of skills and labour.

By the end of October, Riga's Maskavas Forštate (Moscow Suburb) had been converted into a ghetto. Frida Michelson, one of the few to survive it, described the run-down neighbourhood in the east of the city: 'This area was a desolate and neglected one, where the poorest population lived. Before it was designated as a ghetto, a few poor Jewish families lived here, but for the most part it was settled by Russian workers and craftsmen. The housing conditions in this area were far inferior to other parts of Riga. Many of the houses lacked plumbing, electricity, toilet facilities, gas or central heating systems. There were many one-storey wooden houses, old and dilapidated.'[8]

The 12,000 Latvians living there were evicted, and 33,000 Riga Jews were forced into sixteen chronically overcrowded, ramshackle blocks, surrounded by a high fence topped with barbed wire and patrolled by up to 144 Latvian auxiliaries under the command of German police.[9] At the entrance a sign warned that 'anyone entering the ghetto without permission risks being shot dead without warning'. At 500-metre intervals around the perimeter, similar notices threatened that 'persons who climb over the fence or attempt to make contact with ghetto inhabitants through the fence shall be shot without warning'.

The Latvian Jews did not live long in the ghetto. Most Jews who had lived outside the capital were already dead.

Stahlecker had been clear from the outset that, whatever the value of slave labour, the answer to the Jewish question must be annihilation. In a memorandum of 6 August 1941, issued from Einsatzgruppe A's headquarters in Novoselsk, he responded to Lohse's Guidelines on Treatment of Jews in Ostland, arguing that they were not required for work given the number of Latvians available, that Bolshevik Jews offered a constant threat of disorder, sabotage and terror, and that there was a pressing need to prevent Jews from increasing their own numbers and, in particular, from 'spreading Jewish blood through miscegenation'.

In the most dispassionate of terms, he stated that 'the projected measures concerning the settling of the Jewish problem are not in harmony with those orders concerning Jews in the Ostland given to Einsatzgruppe A of the Security Police and the SD. Nor does the project take into consideration the new possibilities of cleaning up the Jewish question in the Eastern regions.'[10]

Stahlecker won the argument, as the 'attritionalists' generally did against the 'productionists' throughout the Reich and its conquered territories.[11] In the course of July and August 1941, the first two months of the German occupation, the Einsatzgruppen and their Latvian collaborators massacred some 30,000 Jews in the provinces outside Riga.[12] In town after town and village after village, they were rounded up and shot.

So brutal, indiscriminate and public were the killings of men, women and children, that Reichskommisar Lohse sought to restrain the worst excesses, though he was hardly motivated by compassion. On 15

November he wrote, 'naturally, the cleansing of Ostland is an urgent task; its solution, however, must be brought into harmony with the necessities of the wartime economy'.[13]

But by then it was too late. On the same day, Dr Otto Bräutigam, a senior official at the Reich Ministry for the Occupied Eastern Territories, instructed Lohse that 'when solving the problem, economic considerations are to be ignored. You are asked, furthermore, to settle any future question with the HSSPF leader.'[14]

Moreover, a few weeks earlier, Heinrich Himmler had replaced Hans-Adolf Prützmann with SS General Friedrich Jeckeln as Higher SS and Police Leader (HSSPF) for Latvia.[15] Fresh from the slaughter of 33,000 Jews at Babyn Yar in the Ukrainian capital Kiev (now Kyiv), Jeckeln was undoubtedly the man for the job.[16] According to Jeckeln's own testimony after the war, Himmler had told him on 10 or 11 November that 'all Jews in the Ostland had to be destroyed to the last man'. He added, 'you tell Lohse, that is my order, which is also the Führer's wish'.

By 25 October when the gates to the Riga ghetto were slammed shut behind its captives, there were few Jews left alive outside the capital. Just a month later the ghetto itself was liquidated. The concentration of the victims in so confined an area made the slaughter all the easier to accomplish.

As elsewhere throughout Europe, Latvia's Jews, despite their routine experience of prejudice and discrimination, had not foreseen the worst. Max Michelson, 17 years old when the Nazis invaded Latvia, described the false sense of security that had dissuaded many members of his community from emigrating while they had the chance: 'we lived in a society which took anti-Semitism for granted but discounted its potential for large-scale violence and mayhem. Even the dramatic rise of Hitler and his explicitly anti-Semitic rantings did not warn us of the imminent catastrophe.'[17]

As we shall see, the extent and virulence of Latvian anti-Semitism before the Nazi occupation is hotly contested. But there had been pogroms within living memory. Frida Michelson recalled: 'We still remembered the atrocities of 1919 after the occupation of Varakļāni when the Latvian soldiers were given thirty minutes to do as they pleased. Murder, rape and robbery reigned for those thirty unforgetta-ble minutes. Many widows, fingers chopped off for the golden wedding rings, and many bastards with blond hair and blue eyes were left as living memorials.'[18]

Certainly, in the years after the First World War and the civil war that followed, the constitution of the newly independent republic guar-anteed Jews equality under the law and equal rights to education and employment. Jewish businesses flourished and Jewish representatives sat in the Latvian Parliament, the Saeima. But from 1934, after the coup in which Kārlis Ulmanis seized power under the banner 'Latvia for Latvians', old restrictive and discriminatory practices returned. Later, when the Soviets occupied Latvia in June 1940, they closed Jewish religious and educational institutions and detained Jewish polit-ical activists.

While Jews retained their constitutional rights under the autocratic Ulmanis, for the most part they also lived separate lives. Almost all historical accounts and memoirs refer to 'Latvians' and 'Jews'; very few make mention of 'Latvian Jews', much less 'Jewish Latvians'. In this, Latvia was by no means exceptional: the trains that arrived daily at Šķirotava in the first few weeks of December 1941 brought neither German Jews nor Jewish Germans, just stateless, 'alien' Jews.

As Ulmanis strove to create a distinctively Latvian national identity, the country's minorities were for the most part second-class citizens, frequently denied access to the higher echelons of the military, the universities or the civil service. Bernhard Press, a Latvian Jew who survived the Holocaust, wrote of the 'glass wall' that, throughout his childhood, separated Jews from Latvians. He also recalled that princi-pally 'non-aggressive' anti-Semitism took on an altogether different form with the rise of the Nazis:

In the 1930s, this dormant anti-Semitism was heated up by the rabid anti-Semitism spreading from Germany ... When Hitler's armies marched into the Baltic states in the course of their attack on the USSR in the summer of 1941, the final transformation of anti-Semitism took place. What formerly had been hatred and contempt changed into pogroms and massacres of us Jews, who had become fair game.

A large part of the population was immediately willing to collaborate with the German execution squads, while those Latvians who did not participate in the murder of their Latvian compatriots watched indifferently or with exultation as their friends and neighbours were driven to their graves.[19]

Max Michelson recalled that, on 1 July 1941, the day the German army secured its occupation of Riga: 'The local radio station broadcast an appeal for all patriotic Latvians to join the battle against the internal enemy, namely the Jews. According to the anti-Semitic propaganda, all Jews were communists, and all Soviet functionaries were Jews. Jews were to blame for the Soviet occupation of Latvia, particularly for the Soviet-era victimisation and deportation of Latvians. In fact, ethnic Latvian communists had supplied many of the Soviet cadres for the government of Latvia. Having failed to resist the Soviet occupation, the Latvians needed little encouragement to become convinced that they had been betrayed by the Jews.'[20]

That same day, Viktors Arājs, a recent law graduate and former provincial police officer, volunteered his services to Stahlecker. He readily agreed that Arājs should recruit Latvians into his own Sonderkommando, or special unit, and made clear that his task was to unleash apparently spontaneous, locally inspired pogroms against the Jews.[21]

Latvian complicity in and, wherever possible, instigation and leadership of the persecution of Jews was a central plank of Stahlecker's strategy. In a report to his superiors in October 1941, he confirmed that the use of local fascists and anti-Semites would not only relieve Germans of the burden of committing mass murder but also provide a degree of cover for their involvement in it:

Considering that the population of the Baltic countries had suffered very heavily under the government of Bolshevism and Jewry while they were incorporated in the USSR, it was to be expected that after the liberation from that foreign government, they would render harmless most of the enemies left behind after the retreat of the Red Army. It was the duty of the Security Police to set in motion these self-cleansing movements, and to direct them into the correct channels in order to accomplish the purpose of the cleansing operations as quickly as possible. It was no less important, in view of the future, to establish the unshakeable and provable fact that the liberated populations themselves took the most severe measures against the Bolshevist and Jewish enemy quite on their own, so that the direction by German authorities could not be found out.[22]

Almost from the moment of Arājs' meeting with Stahlecker, local volunteers were armed, issued with armbands in Latvian red and white and proceeded to arrest, beat, rape and murder Jews at will.

Within a fortnight, 2,400 of Riga's Jews had been rounded up and incarcerated in the city's Centralka and Terminka prisons and at the headquarters of the police and the fascist movement Pērkonkrusts, Thunder Cross.[23] Few survived. According to Frida Michelson: 'Special attention was given leaders of Jewish societies – the scientists, physicians, engineers, lawyers, architects, businessmen, manufacturers. When recognised, they were removed from the crowd of Jews in detention and shot on the spot. Their Latvian professional colleagues were instrumental in making identification and most of them were pleased with the turn of events.'[24]

On 3 July, 5,000 men and women, 4,000 of them Jews, were shot in the Bikernieki forest, to the east of Riga, the first of many massacres there.[25]

On 4 July, the Latvian daily newspaper, *Tevija*, called for more recruits: 'All nationally-thinking Latvians – members of Pērkonkrusts, students, officers, Aizsargi, and others who wish to take an active part in the cleansing of our country from harmful elements, can register themselves at the Headquarters of the Security Kommando at Valdemāra iela 19, from 9–11 and from 17–19.'[26]

Within the month some 2,800 volunteers had joined up.

On the same day, 300 Jews were forced into Riga's Great Choral Synagogue on Gogol Iela. Frida Michelson recounts eyewitness accounts of what happened there: 'One day the Pērkonkrusts and other Latvian hangers-on surrounded the synagogue and jammed everybody inside. They piled wood and straw on all sides and set it on fire. My Latvian friends who witnessed this told me that the inhuman cries, shrieks and screams of terror were indescribable. People who tried to break out of the windows were mowed down with automatic weapons and pistols while the onlookers howled and rolled with laughter.'[27]

There were no survivors. Similar outrages followed at the city's other places of Jewish worship. Only the Pietavas synagogue survived, because adjoining buildings were occupied by Latvians.

The open-air reconstruction of the Riga ghetto is a worthy monument but it's not actually on the site of that doleful place. As I studied the information boards and toured the exhibits, I could not help feeling that I was visiting a museum – which, in fairness, is how it describes itself – rather than the inhospitable streets in which first Latvian, then German Jews had struggled to stay alive.

It's only a ten-minute walk from there to what remains of the Great Choral Synagogue on Gogol Iela. There the stones speak louder and more insistently.

The destruction of the beautiful synagogue and the 300 people inside it by Latvian militiamen, just three days after the Germans had occupied Riga, was not the first outrage against the country's Jewish community. But, in the heart of the capital city, it was perhaps the most emblematic.

As I stood before the narrow-arched entrance to what had once been a focal point of Jewish life, the awful significance of that event pressed itself upon me: this had been a moment when ordinary Latvians could have publicly or even secretly revolted against the slaughter of their

Jewish neighbours, or at least against their own complicity in it. But on that day, when it became clear that the Nazis meant to destroy the Jews of Latvia, a small but significant minority of local citizens decided to help; and many more, with notable exceptions, resolved to do nothing to prevent them.

Within four days of the Nazi occupation, new laws forbade Jews any social contact with Gentiles and barred them from shopping in their stores or markets, walking on their pavements or visiting their places of culture, leisure or entertainment. In addition they had to wear a yellow patch, later a yellow star, on their clothing. The penalty for any infringement was death.

Even then, many Rigan Jews clung to the hope that they could survive and that the pogroms that had already accounted for so many of their friends and family, particularly outside the capital, were an aberration for which a limited number of rogue Latvian fascists were responsible. According to Max Michelson: 'We not only hoped, we actually expected that once installed, the German civil authorities would suppress what we naively concluded were spontaneous, unauthorised attacks. It was assumed that conditions imposed on us would be harsh, but we nevertheless expected some measure of order and stability. It was inconceivable that the Germans, even the nazi (*sic*) regime, would systematically pursue a policy aimed at annihilating the entire Jewish population ... Germany was a bastion of Western civilisation and culture.'[28]

But Bernhard Press is very clear about the enthusiasm with which his fellow citizens attacked their Jewish neighbours, even as the Red Army was retreating:

An unchecked, unchained slaughter now began, and it lasted for years. Armed men forced their way, by day and by night, into Jewish homes. On the streets and in the shops, factories, and workshops, they hunted us down. They startled Jews out of their sleep and shot them in their beds. Men and women, children and old people were herded into the little groves on the outskirts of large and small towns, forced to dig mass graves or stand at the edge of graves already dug, and shot by the hundreds or thousands. Those who were not shot on the spot were brought to jail and killed there. Newborn babies and infants had their skulls smashed against walls or were thrown into the air and shot at like clay pigeons or spiked on bayonets ... Synagogues were plundered and set afire, and Jews were thrown alive into the flames.[29]

On 7 July, Arājs' recruits, many drawn from the Pērkonkrusts and Aizsargi and from student fraternities, slaughtered some 400 of their Jewish compatriots in what Stahlecker referred to as a 'self-cleansing' operation.

As escape from Latvia was no longer possible, the country's Jews looked for protection to non-Jewish Latvians who had for years been friends, neighbours or workmates. But the propaganda in the daily press and elsewhere warned most of them off: those shopkeepers and others who traded or fraternised with Jews were named and endangered. The *Daugavpils Latviešu Avīze* of 8 July 1941 urged: 'Several people have notified the editorial office that in spite of the need of the German army and the Christian people, the sellers of produce continue to supply the Jews ... The time has come to end all service to the Jews, to end every selling of oneself to the Jews! ... one must remember that it was the Jews who greeted the Red Army in July 1940, and enslaved, tortured, and killed Latvians during Communist rule ... softheartedness towards Jews is useless.'[30]

The Nazis sought not only to exploit latent anti-Semitism but also to appeal to the basic instincts of avarice and greed. Frida Michelson describes the use of this simple tactic in Varakļāni, where the pogrom of 1919 had been unleashed, but where she now sought refuge with her aunt's family. The entire population of the town and the surrounding countryside had been summoned to the marketplace to be addressed by their new masters: 'Achtung! Achtung! Der Herr Oberkommandant of this area is here to convey greetings from our Führer Adolf Hitler, to our Latvian Aryan brothers. After we have distributed presents to you in an act of friendship, Der Herr Oberkommandant himself will speak to you. You are free to enter the Jewish homes and help yourself to what was plundered from you for years by the Jews. It is yours!'[31]

Packs of cigarettes and matches, coffee, watches and spools of thread were tossed into the crowd and, in the mêlée that ensued, the platform on which the German officers were standing was toppled. It was rumoured that over 100 people were injured, trampled underfoot by their neighbours. Shots were fired to quell the mob, and once the riot had subsided the town's Jews were forced to clear the wreckage.

Certainly some Latvians did their best to aid or protect their Jewish neighbours.[32] They were indeed heroic, for the penalty for harbouring Jews was death, not only for the perpetrators but in all probability also for their families. Not infrequently whole villages were razed to the ground when fugitive Jews were discovered there. In her three-year flight from the Nazis and their collaborators, Frida Michelson was on countless occasions turned away and sometimes informed upon by the Latvians from whom she sought help. But throughout that time she was also sheltered, fed, nursed and comforted by courageous Latvians, for the most part Seventh Day Adventists, who risked their lives for her and regarded the opportunity to do so as a blessing.

But, according to Press, they were among the few:

A bloody frenzy had overcome the country, and those who did not raise their hands to commit murder tried at least to harass us … It was not only a sea of hatred that surrounded us; it was also a sea of silence. Tens of thousands and hundreds of thousands were witnesses of the most horrible crime in human history and remained silent about it. None of the churches … tried to stop the killing … no judge let his warning voice be heard. The politicians remained silent … Most of the intelligentsia, together with the majority of the Latvian people, were entirely in favour of the 'elimination' of the Jews and not only encouraged the mob to shed blood but also actively participated themselves.[33]

Throughout July, August and September, the Arājs Kommando toured the countryside in commandeered blue buses to dispatch Jews who had been herded together in the small towns and villages by the Einsatzkommando 2 and local Latvian police.

In Riga, they rounded up first Jewish men of military age, then older men, women and children, detaining them at the Centralka Prison and then, at dawn when there were few on the streets to witness, transporting them by truck and bus to Biķernieki forest. There, groups of between 200 and 1,000 would be lined up, ten at a time, at the edge of pits dug by Soviet prisoners of war, and shot. Those who did not collapse into the pits were kicked into them, dead or alive. At the end of the operation – or in the course of the more extensive ones – the shooters were given vodka to steady their nerves and reward their productivity.

By mid-October 1941, Stahlecker had reported to Berlin that 30,025 Jews and 1,843 Communists had been executed. A third of Latvia's Jewish population had been slaughtered since June. According to the historian Richards Plavnieks, by late November 'for all intents and purposes, every Jew in Latvia was either imprisoned in the large ghettos in Riga, Dagavpils and Liepāja or dead – many at the hands of Arājs' men'.[34]

In October 1941, Nazi administrators in Riga had been panicked by the news from Berlin that 25,000 German Jews were imminently to be dispatched there.[35] Indeed, such was their lack of preparedness that the first five transports had to be diverted to Kaunas, where the deportees were immediately murdered.

In Latvia, Hinrich Lohse's political adviser, Karl Friedrich Trampedach, worried that the civil administration had nowhere to accommodate the deportees and, anxious to protect the labour force corralled in the Riga ghetto, urged the Ostministerium in Berlin to cancel the Riga-bound transports. He was met by a chilling response from Dr Georg Leibbrandt, who told him that he should not concern himself about the Jews as they would in any case be sent 'farther east'.[36] His meaning was clear. Trampedach offered no further resistance.

Ten transports from all over Germany, each carrying around 1,000 deportees, were scheduled to arrive at Riga between 30 November and 18 December. The camps the Germans had hurriedly started to build around Riga had nothing like the capacity required. Room for the Reichsjuden had to be found elsewhere.

On 27 November, as the Jews of Bamberg were gathering outside the Weiße Taube, the Jewish occupants of selected streets in the Riga ghetto were told that they were to be relocated. Around 4,500 men of working age were separated from their tearful families and confined to a cordoned-off section that became known as 'the Small Ghetto'. On 30 November, Riga's Bloody Sunday, the women, children and the old and infirm were driven from their homes by SS men and Latvian auxiliaries and ordered to line up outside their houses. Babies were thrown from windows. In the chaos, around 1,000 were shot in the streets.

Frida Michelson described the scene:

I went to the window to see what was going on. It was already beginning to get light. An unending column of people, guarded by armed policemen, was passing by. Young women, women with infants in their arms, old women, handicapped, helped by their neighbours, young boys and girls – all marching, marching. Suddenly in front of our window an SS man started firing with an automatic gun point blank into the crowd. People were mowed down by the shots, and fell on the cobblestones. There was confusion in the column. People were trampling over those who had fallen, they were pushing forward, away from the wildly shooting SS man. Some were throwing away their packs so they could run faster. The Latvian policemen were shouting 'Faster! Faster!' and lashing whips over the heads of the crowd ...

Within a few hours the streets were cleaned up by the men from the small ghetto under the direction of the German and Latvian masters. Stories filtered back. There were over 700 corpses. They were buried in a common grave in the Old Jewish Cemetery, next to the ghetto.[37]

Some 15,000 Jews, in columns of 1,000, were marched six miles into the Rumbula forest. The night before, the first transport of 1,053 German Jews, from Berlin, had been taken there straight from Šķirotava and shot. Now the Latvian Jews were herded towards the mass graves. They were funnelled through a gauntlet of German and Latvian SD men, forced to give up their last remaining possessions, lined up in the freezing cold and ordered to strip. Then they were made to enter the pits, lie face-down on the bodies of earlier victims, some still living, and shot in the back of the head by crossfire from above. This efficient method of disposal, designed to reduce the size and number of the pits that had to be dug, was the inspired contrivance of SS General Jeckeln. In Ukraine, he had blithely observed to a colleague, 'today we'll stack them like sardines'.[38]

A force of 500 German police and SS men along with 500 Latvian police auxiliaries had rounded up their victims, escorted them to the forest, guarded the route, surrounded the killing ground to cut off all avenues of escape and keep out inquisitive intruders, and formed a funnel to the graves.[39] Now a dozen marksmen lined each of three pits, emptying a magazine of fifty bullets into their victims before retiring to reload, clambering over the bodies of the dead to dispatch the dying.[40]

Jeckeln observed the killing from the embankment above the pits with SS, SD and police commanders and senior civilian administrators whom he had summoned from all over Latvia. The guests were offered schnapps to keep out the cold.

On 8 December the exercise was repeated and another 12,000 Latvian Jews were marched from the ghetto to Rumbula. This time, Frida Michelson was in the endless column marching five abreast to the pits:

As we came near the forest, we heard shooting again. This was a horrible portent of our future. If I had any doubts about the intentions of our tormentors, they were all gone now. All I could see was a mad dog snarling at me with curled lips, showing vicious fangs. How dear life becomes regardless how hard it is to live.

The situation was hopeless. We were guarded on both sides by policemen and SS men. The little forest was in turn also surrounded by a ring of SS men. Nobody had a doubt as to what awaited us. We were all numb with terror and followed orders mechanically. We were incapable of thinking and were submitting to everything like a docile herd of cattle.[41]

In the forest, the Jews were ordered to drop their last remaining valuables into a large box, then to take off their coats, then to strip, then to line up along the edge of the pit. Frida took advantage of a distraction as a policeman was thrusting her towards the guns and threw herself face-down in the snow, feigning death. Soon she was covered by layer upon layer of the shoes of the Jews who were marching barefoot to their grave. For several hours, she lay motionless in a pool of freezing water until the shrieking and the shooting had subsided, the last scavengers had left with their trophies and darkness fell. Then she dug herself out of the mountain of footwear and began her three years of flight, concealment, torment and miraculous good fortune until finally she was liberated by the Red Army.

I walk past the forest's eyes –
its lashes brush my shoulder.
Under my feet, a mound of earth sighs.
These are the only sounds,
and I stop
to stop all sound.
No longer can I hold the dam
that my sight broke down:
the wood is filled with screams
and shudders cleave to the pines, to the craggy bark that
    remembers.
The dirt that covers those interred alive
quivers until dawn.

Ojārs Vācietis, *Rumbula*[42]

I walk the three miles the Berliners who arrived on that first transport would have trudged from Šķirotava to Rumbula.

After half an hour or so, the lorry parks and used car lots abruptly end, and the trees begin. Opposite a petrol station ablaze with neon, a road leads into the forest. Here is the place where 30,000 people lie. A series of raised, rectangular, grass-topped beds, each with a great stone obelisk implanted in it, mark the mass graves. At their centre a Menorah stands among jagged stones, some inscribed by relatives in remembrance of their dead.

No-one else is here. There is bird song. Large black ants hurry about their business. The air is full of floating dandelion spores. It's possible my grandfather lies here.

In his end-of-year report, Einsatzkommando A SS Obersturmbannführer (Lieutenant Colonel) Fritz Dietrich concluded with breezy satisfaction:

Our aim at Commando #2, as envisaged from the very beginning, is a radical solution to the 'Jewish question' by executing all Jews. This led us to wide-ranging mop-up operations in the entire area, implemented by special commandos with the help of hand-picked forces of the Latvian Auxiliary Police (mostly relatives of exiled or murdered Latvians). At the beginning of October, the approximate number of Jews executed in our zone of activity was 30,000. In addition, a few thousand Jews were eliminated by the [Latvian] Self Defence Units, on their own initiative, after the usual pep-talk.

The complete liquidation of all Jews in Latvia was not possible due to economic circumstances, especially the requirements of the army ... However, by the end of October the countryside of Latvia is completely purged ...

At the beginning of November, only some 30,000 Jews were left in the ghetto of Riga, 4,300 in Libau and 7,000 in Dünaburg. After that time, 4,000–5,000 Jews were executed in connection with criminal prosecutions, such as failing to wear the Jewish star, black market activity, fraud etc. In addition, Jews in the ghettos who were not fully able to work or were of no other use were eliminated in the course of several extended actions. Thus on 9 November 1941, 11,034 were executed at Dünaburg; at the beginning of December, during an extensive operation ordered by a high official of the SS and Police, 27,800 in Riga; and in the middle of December 1941, 2,350 Jews in Libau at the request of the Reichskommissar. The remaining Jews (2,500 in Riga, 950 in Dünaburg and 300 in Libau) were spared because they were highly skilled workers.[43]

After the events of 30 November and 8 December, of the 65–70,000 Jews trapped in Latvia by the Nazi invasion five months earlier, only around five to 6,000 were still alive.[44]

The massacre of Latvia's Jews was by no means a secret. Indeed, shortly after Bloody Sunday in Riga, long queues of local Latvians formed outside the ghetto in the hope of acquiring, at bargain prices, the furniture, clothing and other effects of the victims.

In his report of 23 December 1941, SS Brigadeführer and Major General of Police Walther Schröder noted: 'In Riga, the mass shooting of the Jews housed up to now in the ghetto is discussed in general. The greater part of the population of Riga speaks of it with gratification and hopes for a complete elimination of the Jews and thus the freeing up of the ghetto for residential purposes.'[45]

The empty, echoing ghetto was, however, to be used for other purposes.

For decades after the war, the fate of Latvia's Jews, despite, or perhaps because of, the scale of the calamity and how it had come about, remained virtually unacknowledged.

The Soviets' Extraordinary Commission for the Investigation of National Socialist Crimes began its work shortly after the Red Army recaptured Riga in 1944. But while, in Latvia as elsewhere, the Soviets were keen to highlight Nazi atrocities, they downplayed the targeting of Jews and did little to mark, much less to commemorate, the sites where they had been massacred.

According to Didzis Bērziņš and Paula Oppermann, after the Commission left, 'the forest was neglected; human remains could be discovered as they lay only barely covered by soil. Apart from individual survivors who came to Rumbula occasionally, the only people interested in the place seemed to have been Latvians searching the forest for property of the murdered.'[46]

On the few monuments to the massacred in Latvia, no explicit mention was made of the Jewish victims. In 1962, under the less repressive, post-Stalin regime of Nikita Khrushchev, Riga City Council organised ceremonies in the forest at Biķernieki, though, as Bērziņš and Opperman observe, this was largely to commemorate the Latvian partisans and Russian POWs who had been murdered there.

Nonetheless, these events emboldened a group of Latvian Jews to erect a temporary sign at Rumbula which recorded in Yiddish that 'Here, 38,000 of Riga's Jews died 30 XI 1941–8/9 XII 1941'. It was the only memorial to the Jewish victims of Nazism in the Soviet Union. It remained there until 1964 when it was replaced by a permanent monument 'to the victims of fascism 1941–1944', adorned by the Hammer and Sickle. Again, its inscription made no mention of the Jewish victims, simply declaring that 'in the years 1941–1945 here in Rumbula's forest 50,000 Soviet citizens, political prisoners, prisoners of war, and other victims of Fascism were brutally executed and shot'.[47]

A memorial was opened at the Salaspils camp in 1967, the entrance to which bears the inscription '*Aiz šiem vārtien vaid zeme*' ('Behind these gates the earth groans'). But the murder of the Jews who built the camp and were imprisoned there was overlooked until more recently a permanent exhibition was established at the site.

Only in 1990, in the twilight of the Soviet Union, did the Latvian government pass a resolution 'on the impermissibility and condemnation of genocide and anti-Semitism in Latvia', which declared: 'Since 1940, when the state of Latvia was liquidated, waves of genocide have rolled over the Republic. All peoples living in the Republic have been its victims, but especially the Jews … It must be noted with especially deep regret that among those who helped to carry out the terror started by the occupiers were citizens of Latvia. There is not, and cannot be any justification, nor can there be statutes of limitation for the sanguinary genocide against the Jews as a crime against humanity.'[48]

In 2001 and 2002, memorials were dedicated in Biķernieki forest and at Rumbula, fully acknowledging the Jews who died there.[49] It was, however, another thirteen years before a senior Latvian politician made an official visit to the sites. In 2015, the President, Raimonds Vējonis, acknowledged both the depth of the tragedy and the role Latvians played in it: 'We are acutely aware of this here at Rumbula, the site of a monstrous crime. We are in a place where people were betrayed and slaughtered. This was an act instigated by occupying powers. Our state had been destroyed. Regrettably, there were those amongst us who turned to evil. What they did is deplorable and must be condemned.'[50]

While Vējonis acknowledged the 'monstrous crime', his words were carefully chosen. Though he could hardly conceal the complicity of many Latvians, he was anxious to mitigate their guilt. As he submitted, echoing the resolution twenty-five years earlier, the state had been destroyed and the genocide was instigated by others.

Perhaps that is why, earlier that year, UNESCO had been obliged to cancel the opening of an exhibition commemorating the child victims of Salaspils at its offices in Paris. Latvian officials, exercising their power of veto, had objected that it risked damaging Latvia's image during its presidency of the European Union.[51]

There is little doubt or debate about the extent of Latvian participation in the persecution of Jews during the Nazi occupation. As the historian Aivars Stranga concludes in a paper to the state-sponsored Symposium of the Commission of the Historians of Latvia, a minority of Latvians murdered Jews and another minority tried to save them.[52] Most Latvians were bystanders. But almost all were to one extent or another implicated in or beneficiaries of the crime:

The local residents took part in the extermination of Jews and in the related activities in different ways: the first in the line, of course, were the direct murderers; their responsibility and crime is indisputable. Close to them in this regard stand those who did not shoot themselves, but who guarded the doomed Jews and conducted them to the site of murder. Their guilt is almost as great. Others were involved in the registration of Jews only. Others – often under compulsion – dug graves and covered them after the massacre or guarded the victims' belongings. Still others registered the belongings of the executed ones (who in rather many cases had been their neighbours with whom the perpetrators had lived side by side for many decades), distributed and appropriated it: these people belonged to the largest group of the population, the immorality and greed of which was shocking. While the number of direct murderers constituted a few hundred in 1941, almost anyone who had the chance took part in the appropriation of the victims' belongings, without the slightest sense of shame or moderation.[53]

How is a young nation to live with such a legacy?

Latvia's relationship with its history is complicated. Its people were the victims of three brutal, totalitarian occupations, by the Soviets, the Nazis and then the Soviets again, which spanned fifty of the hundred years since the country won its independence in 1920. These traumas inevitably colour Latvians' attitudes both to the barbarities of those harrowing times and to the level of responsibility their countrymen must assume for them.

Some Latvian historians have come to terms with the past. Others have sought to relieve their country's present of at least some of its heavy burden. The task they set themselves, it seems, is to provide an endurable context for terrible events. The facts of the atrocities and the identity of their perpetrators are not in question. The issue for the historians, as for the politicians, is the attribution of guilt. A considerable number want to argue that Latvians may have been the instruments but were not the instigators of the crimes in which they participated. For them, motive, or lack of it, is key.

Stranga asserts that Latvians bore no deep-running animosity towards the Jews. Indeed, the spontaneous pogroms the Nazis had anticipated never materialised as Stahlecker had hoped and the 'extermination of Jews ... was carried out on their instructions and inspiration'.[54]

Andrew Ezergailis argues that it was not race hate that drove Latvians to murder Jews, but revenge for the Soviets' destruction of their country during the *Baigais Gads*, the 'Terrible Year' of 1940–1. The diabolical skill of Nazi propaganda had been to associate Jews with the hated Bolsheviks and, in particular, with the persecution of Latvians by the Cheka security service, which, it falsely claimed, was dominated by Jews.[55]

In his analysis of the six forces he identifies behind the motivation of the Arājs Kommando's recruits, Richards Plavnieks ranks the success of Nazi propaganda at the top with 'scant indigenous Latvian anti-Semitism' at the bottom.[56] He suggests that 'they seem to have become anti-Semitic because in particularly traumatic historical circumstances they were virulently anti-Communist and allied to the virulently anti-Communist *and* anti-Semitic Nazis'.[57]

There can be little doubt that many Latvians welcomed the Germans as liberators from Soviet oppression and were perhaps too readily duped into associating Jews with Bolshevism. But the suggestion that they should have turned on their Jewish neighbours so quickly and with such merciless violence without at least a latent disposition to anti-Semitism is difficult to credit.

The Nazis clearly thought that they were sowing seeds in fertile soil. In his official report, Hauptmann Paul Salitter, the police captain in charge of the transport that brought 1,000 Jews from Dusseldorf to Riga in mid-December 1941 – among them my father's cousin Gretel Goldschmidt, her husband Hans and their daughter Margit – remarked on the appetite of Latvians for revenge against the Bolsheviks, but also observed: 'The Latvians hate the Jews with a vengeance and for this reason, ever since their liberation, have taken a great part in the extermination of these parasites. As I could ascertain by talking to the Latvian railroad personnel, they cannot understand why the Germans bring Jews to Latvia instead of exterminating them in their own country.'[58]

Indeed, calls for anti-Bolshevik volunteers were steeped in the language of anti-Semitism. The daily newspaper *Nacionālā Zemgale* declaimed just a week after the Germans occupied Riga: 'This nation was driven to its knees by the bands of Jews and Asiatics who, like highway robbers, killed everybody who did not lick their boots. The hired hands of the red Jewry, masking as defenders of the people, forged devilish plans and invented the most inhuman tortures, so to drive the fear of the slave into Latvians, and destroy this otherwise flourishing people on the shores of the Baltic.'[59]

Some went still further. The historian Gertrude Schneider, a survivor of the Riga ghetto, cites an article in *Tevija* which demanded that 'because the Jews had sought to destroy the Latvian nation, they could not be permitted to survive as a national cultural entity; therefore, all the Jews would have to die'.[60]

Nevertheless, Latvian historians who believe that Latvians have been unfairly indicted can also explain why other scholars think differently. They argue that misconceptions about the extent of Latvian anti-Semitism, collaboration with the Germans and complicity in the murder of Jews were deliberately seeded by both Nazi and Soviet propagandists.

Discussing the 'Nazi public relations line', Ezergailis suggests that 'the basic stratagem ... was to distance the Germans from the crime and accuse Eastern Europeans of killing their neighbors'.[61] Elsewhere he argues that 'a string of tangential contingencies that had an appearance of plausibility', as distinct from hard evidence, has misled not only Holocaust historians but 'unfortunately also many Holocaust survivors'.[62]

He goes further in questioning the personal testimony of Jewish survivors, claiming that they themselves had been seduced by Nazi propaganda into believing what they thought they had seen with their own eyes:

The genesis of the survivors' version of the Holocaust history is still a mystery and needs deeper investigation. It could have emerged only under conditions of fear and within a vacuum of information, an environment where people had no better source of information than one's traumatized neighbor's tale who in turn could have heard it from another terrified Jew on the job site …

The survivors value, rank, rate 'seeing eyes' over all other evidence – archival, documentary, structural, and rational … None of the survivors realized that what the Jews saw on the streets of Riga was a theatre staged by the occupying power. The Latvians that they saw on the streets scurrying and molesting Jews were pawns acting on an invisible chess board designed by Hitler's planners of the Holocaust … the Jews had no other option than, at least in part, to see the Holocaust through the glasses that the Nazis provided for them. Killing the Jews was one side of the Nazi policy, poisoning their mind was another one.[63]

Provocative though these arguments may be, if the evidence supports them, historians are of course right to challenge conventional wisdom. It is right too to acknowledge that Latvians have had only thirty years of independence in which to begin the task of distinguishing the facts of their recent history from the propaganda of totalitarian occupiers. Of course that process should continue, so long as its methodology is objective. But in Poland in 2018 we have seen the enactment of legislation that, in outlawing reference to Polish complicity in the Holocaust, seeks to serve a national interest not necessarily compatible with the truth. This creation of national mythologies, while limited to neither Latvia nor Poland, is as dangerous in nominally democratic countries as it is in dictatorships.

After the war, of course, as Plavnieks notes, 'the Latvians could always tell themselves that the Germans were making them do it, designating the targets, providing the logistics, and giving the orders. For their part, the Germans could make themselves believe that it was really the Latvians who were the inhuman (perhaps the subhuman?) killers, while they distanced themselves both physically and via this psychological abstraction.'[64]

Wherever the balance lies between those who planned and those who executed, and whatever the complex make-up of their motives, by the time the Arājs Kommando had completed its 'anti-Bolshevik' mission, it had accounted for around half the Jews of Latvia and many thousands from Germany, Austria, Czechoslovakia and elsewhere.[65] In the forests of Rumbula and Biķernieki there are pits filled with bones.

15

THE END GAME

As my grandparents disembarked from Sonderzug Da 32 on 2 December, they would have been confronted by the snow-covered mountain of luggage abandoned three days earlier by the 1,000 Jews from Berlin as they were marched from their train straight to the pits of Rumbula.[1] They would not yet have understood what they saw.

The Jews from the Nuremberg transport would be allowed to live a little longer. But as the Riga ghetto had by now only been half-cleared, they were to be held at Jungfernhof, a ramshackle farmstead that was rapidly being converted into a camp but was almost entirely unprepared to receive them.[2] They were formed up in 200 columns of five in the sub-zero temperatures of the coldest Latvian winter in living memory.

The march to Jungfernhof, though only a mile, must have seemed an ordeal without end for the deportees, frozen by frost and fear, and now suddenly witnesses to and victims of a brutality that would have chilled them still further. Herbert Mai recalled: 'some people, older people which fell down, and then the guards just killed them right there on the road, and again the screw was tightened a little bit more, all of a sudden we've seen killings, which we've never seen before'.[3]

When they reached Jungfernhof, they found a scattering of dilapidated cowsheds and stables. Trude Schloss, a 16-year-old who reached Škirotava with the Stuttgart transport two days later, recalled her first impressions: 'It was bitter cold and we were made to walk about five kilometers, prodded by Latvian SS in a most brutal fashion, until we reached what must have been an estate at one time and was then a collection of barns and wooden shacks ... Men and women were separated and housed in the stalls used for cattle and horses ... Three days later, there were three more transports. One was from Vienna and the other from Hamburg ... There were now four thousand Jews in a space that could not even hold four hundred.'[4]

Fanny Dominitz, another 16-year-old separated from her family, arrived at Šķirotava with the Hamburg transport on 9 December. She wrote in later life:

> We walked and walked – only fields. I didn't know it was fields, I thought that I was no longer in this world but somewhere else. The whole atmosphere so cut off from the world; no tree, no bird-chirping, no human being, no house, one could see nothing. And then suddenly in the distance a small camp could be seen. As we came closer we saw that it was fenced in by barbed wire and temporary gates made of wood and barbed wire opened up in front of us. Soldiers stood there but not German soldiers, they were Latvian soldiers. We were pushed in as if into a cage and the doors were closed. It seemed: I was trapped in a cage ...
>
> And this is how our day went. Early in the morning standing in line. We were counted because so many died. There was an outbreak of dysentery. One could not bury the people there. The bodies piled up into a huge mountain. And the mind could not grasp what the eyes saw.[5]

Conditions in the camp were appalling. Snow fell through the gaping roof of the men's barrack, no heating had been provided and there was no kitchen until the prisoners had built one.

Erich Wassermann was 20 when he and his family were deported from Würzburg. He was the only survivor. In evidence he submitted to war crimes investigators in 1946 he recalled: '10–20 Jews died daily of starvation and the immense cold. In one of the barracks (no 5), several men were found every morning covered with snow, frozen to death during the night. Until the end of February c 500 Jews died this way, and not having been buried, froze into one big heap.'[6]

As harsh as these conditions were, the SS, under the command of SS Oberscharführer (Company Sergeant Major) Rudolph Seck, were determined to make them worse. Survivors Susanne Rieger and Gerhard Jochem recalled their reception at the camp: 'From the beginning he made his intentions absolutely clear to us. He made it known that he had already killed thousands of Jews and to kill more would make no difference to him. His first victim was a youth from Fürth who was shot dead by Seck because he did not march fast enough on the way to Jungfernhof.'[7]

Erich Wassermann was witness to the same macabre bravado. In his deposition against Seck he wrote:

Lashes of whips drove us into the camp (Jungfernhof). At the station, several were shot by the SS. All orders came from the commander of the camp, R Seck. He sent more than 4,000 Jews to their death in this camp. While I was present he shot four old men after getting them out of the barracks with these words: 'We don't need any lazy people here and they're not good for anything else.' Almost every day he beat men and women. One day, the whole camp had to fall in. One man by the name of Adler was thrashed by Seck personally. He got 25 lashes on his naked buttocks. Afterwards, Seck boasted: 'It doesn't matter to me to finish one more or less of you. I killed not only hundreds but also thousands of you.'[8]

After the war, Seck was charged with eight specimen counts of murder, seven of which were committed at Jungfernhof. Witnesses told the court of his gratuitous and unquenchable sadism: 'One day in January 1942 the accused ordered the prisoners out of the blocks and to assemble in front of block 5. The accused instructed a prisoner who arrived late to turn round. The accused then pulled his pistol and shot the prisoner in the back of the neck ... On another occasion in January 1942 the accused was in the yard when a Jew crossed the yard holding his trousers up with his hands as he had no braces. This provoked the accused. He pulled his pistol and shot the prisoner from a distance of one metre.'[9]

Josef Katz, who spent 14 days in Jungfernhof before being transferred to the Salaspils camp, records:

> I am told that yesterday the newly-named commandant went for a walk through the camp with his staff. He had ten old Jews dragged from the barracks and shot, one after the other. He did not want them to suffer, he said … People are dying every day. They are carried out on stretchers and buried in a mass grave near a potato patch. It is said that in the very short time we've been here, 200 Jews have been buried there already. Sometimes when I return from work at night, I see the Chief Rabbi, leaning on his cane, walking slowly behind a corpse.[10]

Seck was convicted in 1951 and sentenced to life imprisonment for crimes against humanity.

The cavernous local train from Riga's main station rattled for no more than fifteen minutes before shuddering to a stop at Šķirotava. The imposing red-brick station building was there when my grandparents arrived on the other track 78 years before me. There's nothing else to see other than marshalling yards and freight cars at rest – except a monument of rusted iron.

Nearby, three large plaques, in Latvian, Russian and English, explain that on 14 June 1941, on 25 March 1949 and throughout the Soviet occupation, a total of 60,000 Latvians were deported from this station to the Gulags where many of them perished. It exhorts, 'let us commemorate these events and never allow the destruction of the Latvian State and its citizens'.

There is no reference to the transports that brought German, Austrian, Czech and Hungarian Jews to Šķirotava. There is no mention of their fate on Latvian soil nor the need to commemorate it.

The road my grandparents trudged from Šķirotava station leads down past a secondary school and a group of high-rise flats, then across the busy Maskavas road with the garish Zoom shopping centre at its junction, before it dissolves into a dirt track. A lone jogger and a couple of women arm in arm and deep in conversation pass in the opposite direction. A wagtail darts across my path. It takes me twenty-five minutes to walk the mile that seemed so much further to the terrified Jews who slipped and stumbled through the snow at the end of machine gun barrels and rifle butts.

At what little remains of Jungfernhof, there is a wide pool and beyond it two ruined stone buildings. A notice pinned to a tree warns that archaeological excavations are under way and unauthorised access is prohibited.

Further on, a large information board sets out the long history of the site, dedicating just a couple of dispassionate lines to its use between 1941 and 1943. Beyond, the broad Daugava River flows calmly towards Riga and the Baltic. There are benches. Some face the pond, others the river. There is a promenade along the riverbank. This must be a popular spot in summer. I can hear only the light breeze in the silver birches.

Here Sally said farewell to Bertha and Hugo to Rosel, for within days of their arrival at Jungfernhof they were marched on through the freezing snow to build a new prison for themselves at Salaspils. They must have hoped their parting would be brief. Perhaps they knew it would not be.

This is the last place Bertha Brandes lived – and Karl and Emma Herzstein and Julius Herzstein and Rosel Rosenthal. I place a stone in the rubble. Jews leave stones for remembrance for, unlike flowers, they do not die. On the only wall left standing, a sign prohibits entry: 'Apdraud dzīvību' ('Danger to life').

Just hours after the last Latvians of the Riga ghetto had been marched away to Rumbula, deportees arriving from Germany were moved into their deserted homes. There was blood everywhere; half-eaten meals were frozen to the tables.

By 18 December, when the transports had been suspended so that the trains could ferry German troops home on Christmas leave, there were 5,073 German Jews in the ghetto. In the new year, a further 10 transports brought the total up to 15,074.

The remaining Latvian Jewish men were confined to their own Small Ghetto, segregated by barbed wire along Ludzas Iela from what became known as the Reichsghetto. Some 500 Latvian Jewish women, most employed as seamstresses, occupied a Women's Ghetto on Ludzas Iela. Many of these survivors bitterly resented their displacement by the German Jews. Some believed that their families and friends would have survived, at least a little longer, had their homes not been required for the incomers.

In fact, the Nazis had originally planned to execute the Reich Jews as they arrived in Riga, as they had those on the first Berlin transport. But even Stahlecker conceded that 'a total elimination of the Jews cannot be carried out, at least not at the present time, because in Lithuania and Latvia most of the skilled crafts are in Jewish hands ... and it would be impossible to replace the Jewish workers with Lithuanians and Latvians'.[11]

So the deportees were kept alive so long as their labour was required and they were fit to work, and the ghetto had value because it was larger and closer to the factories and workshops than either Jungfernhof or the camp under construction at Salaspils. But conditions were dire.

Gertrude Schneider, who as a 13-year-old had been deported with her family from Vienna, described her first impressions when she arrived there fully three months after its original inhabitants had been marched away:

> It was the most decrepit place you can imagine. Those houses, the stench, the snow on the street ... no water in the houses ... We walked into a room that had been a kitchen ... and food was actually on the table in a frozen state. Because the cold was very bad and they were killed between November and December when it was very cold also, so the food didn't spoil. We could thaw it out and eat it ... There were slippers under the bed ... There were teeth in a glass next to the bed ... false teeth in a glass, frozen into the glass.[12]

They found a frozen baby in the toilet and blood on the stairs. Even now, many of the new arrivals could not accept that fellow human beings could be capable of such deliberate depravity. They did their best to believe that the Latvian inhabitants had been perhaps roughly relocated to another camp. As Gertrude Schneider said, 'the shock was great, but yet, the human mind refuses to acknowledge that you are going to be killed'.

In retrospect, she believed that a few did clearly see what the Nazis had planned for them and, if they could, took control of their own destinies. The couple who found the baby swallowed Veronal that night and died four days later. Elsewhere, she recalled the fate chosen by one man, his wife and three children: 'He took his children and his wife and they all sat down in the courtyard ... And he took the little one in the middle between his wife and he. And so they said, "and now we'll sleep outside". Now he was a mountain climber so he knew what snow does, that you get tired, at first you're cold but then you're tired. And so in the morning they were found sitting together, holding each other, frozen.'[13]

Around 800 prisoners died in Jungfernhof in the winter of 1941–2 from hunger, cold and disease. Bodies were piled up in a shed because graves could not be dug for them in the frozen earth. In January 1942, Seck had the ground dynamited so that 500 dead could be buried.[14]

But this rate of attrition was not sufficient for the Nazis. Rudolf Lange, commander of the Riga Sicherheitsdienst and Sicherheitspolizei, the intelligence and security police, a relatively junior officer but a killer of such ruthless efficiency that he had been invited by Reinhard Heydrich to attend the Wannsee Conference, returned with renewed enthusiasm for his part in the Final Solution.[15] A concerted start was to be made on Jews who were of no value to the war effort. Those who were unable to work, through illness, frailty or age, began to disappear.

Gertrude Schneider recalled that when her transport arrived at Škirotava on 10 February, it was met by Lange and his deputy SS Untersturmführer (Second Lieutenant) Gerhard Maywald:[16]

Even though he was somewhat smaller and darker than the blond, blue-eyed Maywald, he looked very handsome in his fur-collared uniform coat and seemed every inch an officer and a gentleman. It never occurred to the newcomers to suspect such a man of being a murderer.

He greeted the transport commander Alois Brunner warmly and then addressed these latest arrivals, telling them that those who were unwilling or unable to walk the seven kilometres to the ghetto could make the trip on the buses and vans that had been especially reserved for them. 'In this way,' he said, 'those of you who ride can prepare a place for those who walk.' It was an extremely cold day – 42 degrees below zero to be exact – and so the majority of the hapless, unsuspecting Jews from Vienna took his advice and lined up to board the buses and vans. They did not realise that one of those vans was a 'gas' van.[17]

Gertrude's younger sister Rita pleaded to be allowed to board a bus. When her exasperated father slapped her, Lange 'turned round, gave her a stern look and told her that children should always listen to their parents'. Only 300 walked; the other 700 disappeared, some into the gas van, most into the forests where they were shot.

Deception and murder went hand in hand. As SS Obersturmbannführer Dietrich reported:

Since December 1941, transports from the Reich arrive in quick succession. Until now a total of 19,000 Jews were deported to Riga … The mortality figure of the evacuated Jews is steadily on the rise. Evidently, the old and feeble Jews are not able to survive the extremely harsh winter months. To prevent outbreaks of epidemics in the ghetto and at both camps, individual Jews infected by dysentery and diphtheria were isolated and executed. To conceal these measures from the local Jews and those in the Reich, the removal of the sick was disguised as a transfer to a Jewish old-age home or hospital. Mentally ill Jews were accorded the same treatment.[18]

In the first weeks, perhaps months, the stratagem worked. Karl Mistele quotes the testimony of an unnamed survivor of Jungfernhof: 'Beginning in February 1942, the so-called transports started. First the mentally ill were removed. We had no inkling that they were to be killed. The rumour was that they were transferred to hospitals in Riga. This was followed by more transports, mostly of sick, old and feeble people. Even those transports did not arouse suspicion.'[19]

But still the Jews were not dying fast enough.

In early February, the 10 streets of the Riga ghetto, named for the cities of their inmates' origin, were each required to submit a list of 60 to 120 people for resettlement; Jews from Berlin were allocated 600 places. They were told that they were to be relocated to work in the fish canneries at Dünamünde, known to Latvians as Daugavgrīva. This would become known as the Dünamünde Aktion (Operation Dünamünde).

The prospect of easier work and better living conditions generated such enthusiasm that 400 who were not on the quota volunteered and were accepted. Gertrude Schneider described the sense of excitement: 'The people who were to leave busied themselves with packing the few belongings they still owned. Valuables, such as watches and other jewelry that they had kept in defiance of orders to turn these items over to the Germans, were sewn into their clothing. Staple foods ... were transformed into baked goods so that they could be transported more easily. There was an air of real excitement in the ghetto. It seemed that everyone remained up half the night from Saturday to Sunday, either getting ready to leave or helping those who had been "chosen" to go.'[20]

On Sunday 15 March some 1,900 Jews assembled in the ghetto, lining up for the buses which, they believed, would take them to a better life, or at least a less harsh one. But there were no canneries. Dünamünde had been unoccupied for decades. It was a ghost town.

Bernhard Press describes how the awful reality of the Dünamünde Aktion gradually dawned:

Old men and women had to approach in rows of ten and were taken away in trucks that supposedly drove back and forth between the ghetto and Daugavgrīva. While some of the people were loaded onto the trucks, the others patiently waited their turn. The SS people even set up chairs for the very frail ones so that the waiting would not be overly strenuous for them. Initially Krause's unfortunate victims still believed in the fairy tale of the food cannery, but when the empty trucks returned after only twenty minutes to take away a new group of old people, these unfortunate people and their relatives understood what the 'cannery' was all about. Loud lamenting and weeping broke out. The old and sick people tried to resist being taken away, and their relatives tried to pull them out of the Gestapo's clutches. The whole situation was a convenient excuse for the SS people to show their true faces. With blows of their truncheons and clubs, with kicks and punches, they brutally and mercilessly forced their victims into the trucks and, since now there was nothing left to hide, robbed them of their blankets, bags, bundles and food as well.[21]

They were driven to Biķernieki forest. There they were made to strip and line the mass graves that had been dug for them.[22] Then they were shot. A few days later, their clothes were sent back to the ghetto to be sorted. For those who remained, there could be no doubting their fate.

In retrospect, it does not seem credible that the deportees who had already suffered and witnessed so much did not recognise the full extent of what was happening. But it is surely not surprising that these, for the most part, middle-class, relatively sheltered people still could not comprehend the depths to which their Nazi tormentors and their Latvian collaborators were willing to sink. Nor could they live without hope. As Gertrude Schneider recounts: 'Their preoccupation with survival, their will and hope to live, left little room for such doubts. The grim reality was unacceptable. People lived one day at a time and rationalised that if they could keep on doing that, they would be able to hold out. They took such comfort as there was from the thought that there was nothing they could have done to help those who had been taken away, and from the fact that, following Operation Dünamünde, things soon returned to normal in the ghetto.'[23]

But eleven days later, on Thursday 26 March, 1,700 prisoners at Jungfernhof fell to the same deception. Seck had complained that over-crowding was preventing him from transforming the camp into the model farm he had been instructed to create. Lange authorised him to clear it of all who were surplus to his requirements. Seck selected 440 of the fittest prisoners and those with specialist skills. The men were locked in block 5 and the women in the sewing room. The very young, the old and the ill were loaded onto buses. Their luggage was abandoned.

Karl Mistele quotes the deposition of a woman from Nuremberg who survived her deportation: 'Rumours had it that the transport was intended for the canning plants at Dünamünde. Believing this, nobody objected to the transport. As a matter of fact, some were quite cheerful, hoping for a better life at the canneries, especially as far as food was concerned … The transport of 26 March emptied our camp. Only about 450 people remained, mostly able-bodied workers. It took three to four weeks after the transport for the real story to reach us, namely that all deportees were killed on the same day in a forest near Riga.'[24]

My grandmother Bertha, her sister Rosel, her brothers Julius and Karl and Karl's wife Emma had climbed aboard those blue buses.

Andrew Ezergailis described the system of slaughter the German SD and their Latvian collaborators adopted throughout Latvia:

> Depending on the number of people to be killed, the action was usually performed by a gang of twenty men. The victims were brought up to the pit in groups of ten. Each person was shot by two men. Ten of the killers knelt and aimed at the back, and ten, standing up, at the neck of the victims. On each end of the pit was a man with a machine gun looking out for potential escapees … The victims who were not killed by the salvos were delivered 'mercy shots', either by the examiners or the commanding officers at the pits …

At the end of the operation, and sometimes during it, schnapps and zakuski were delivered. The members doing the shooting were always rewarded with alcohol in Biķernieki, but those standing watch or in the gauntlet had to wait until they returned to headquarters.[25]

A Latvian auxiliary policeman, Peteris Iklaws, testified after the war:

When we arrived in the ghetto, which was located in Jumprawmujzha (Jumpravmuiza, Jungfernhof), a group of Jews who were to be shot was already standing there ready ... Then we drove on to the Biķernieki woods ... The shooting site was about 100 metres from the place where we unloaded. The victims went to the pit between a cordon of two rows [of men] from the Arājs Commando ... In the course of the day, I made no fewer than 4–5 trips. The shooting of the Jews lasted from morning to evening. On this day around 2,000 Jews were murdered.

After the Jews had been unloaded from the truck they were ordered in German to strip ... The Jews grasped what would happen to them. For that reason, out of panic, several of them did not undress. The policemen from the Arājs Commando violently tore their clothes off them, and they were stripped down to their undergarments. After I, together with other policemen, had taken the Jews to the shooting site, I left the truck several times and [went] over to the pit several times because I was interested in seeing what was actually happening ... I saw Arājs, Lange, and other German officers walking back and forth next to the pit and shooting into the pit with pistols.[26]

Arnis Upmalis volunteered at 19 for the Arājs Kommando in January 1942 and was very soon involved in one such mass execution. He told a court in Hamburg in 1975:

Around my third day of duty with the Arājs Commando, when I was relieved from guard duty, I had to report to Building 19 on Waldemar St on orders from company leader Kjurbis. They issued us with guns with live ammunition. A bus blue in colour drove up. Then those who had been serving in the commando longer than me said: 'We are going to Bickerniecki (*sic*) again.'

... We pressed deeper into the forest on the path and came to a large freshly dug pit, which was 300–400 metres from the country road. The pit was about 30–40 metres long, about 5 metres wide and 2 metres deep. One end of the pit was sloping so that one could go down inside it. It was said that prisoners of war had had to dig the pit ...

The shooting lasted from about 10 am until 7 pm, until dusk fell. All day long, victims were brought to the shooting site ... The attendant circumstances of this shooting operation have remained ingrained upon me my entire life. I went through a great deal on this day.[27]

The killings in the Biķernieki forest continued throughout the spring and summer. Isaak Kleiman, a Latvian Jew, whose family had been among those murdered at Rumbula but who survived the war, helplessly watched the daily convoy of victims from the place of his forced labour:

... that whole spring and summer of 1942 we were witnesses to the systematic destruction of foreign Jews. Every day we saw the large blue buses bringing these hapless deportees from the Skiritova (*sic*) Railroad Station directly to the forest. The scenario was always the same: Each bus slowed down on Stirnu and then made a wide turn into the forest; shortly thereafter, we could clearly hear the ra-ta-ta-ta of repeater rifles and later a few single shots. Soon after that, each bus left, only to return again and again. We counted at least fifteen and often as many as twenty-five buses a day just for Bikernicku Forest (*sic*). Other Kommandos told of such buses, also carrying foreign Jews, going to Salaspils.

At times they were seen driving into the Rumbula Forest, where the Latvian Jews had been murdered.[28]

Another witness, Malwine Stabulnik, told Soviet investigators in 1944: 'Among the many graves we saw ... an open grave filled with the corpses who had been shot. The corpses lay in disorder only lightly dressed or in underclothes. They were the corpses of women and children. The corpses showed signs of having been brutally abused and tormented before being shot. Many had scratches to the face, swellings on their heads, some with their hands severed, their eyes gouged out or bellies split open. Beside the grave there were pools of blood, hair, severed fingers, brains, cranial bones, the shoes of children and other personal belongings ...'[29]

There were killing grounds like this throughout Latvia. Reska Weiss was sent out from Daugavpils with a work detail of 30:

> After tramping for some miles, we reached a forest clearing. Here there was a lorry on which there was a barrel of slaked lime. We were ordered to form a line from this barrel to a patch of ground covered by branches, about twenty yards distant. An order was then given to pour the lime on this patch, adjoining which some squares of turf had been cut out. We filled our buckets with the lime and covered the patch, finishing the task fairly quickly. We were next ordered to lay the squares of turf next to each other so as to completely cover the branches and the lime. As our feet sank into the soft earth we paid no attention to what lay underneath.[30]

The following day, several hundred women were sent out with 20 SS guards: 'About four miles from our starting point we halted at a sun-parched clearing surrounded by a wood planted with saplings ... The guards marked out a large area and those of us with spades began to cut out squares of turf, heaping them into a large pile at the side. The others were told to break off small branches and twigs which had to be stacked elsewhere. Then we were ordered to dig out the soil in the marked area. "What a big air-raid shelter this is going to be," we told each other, as we shoveled out the soft earth.'[31]

When, towards evening, the SS men appeared satisfied with the size of the pit, the exhausted women prepared to return to camp:

> An order was rapped out: thirty prisoners were told to stand in one row facing the forest: then another thirty – and another thirty. Again and again the command was repeated, with an SS guard positioned at the end of each row. We gazed at each other terrified. We had never had to line up like this before …
>
> Suddenly terrible screams, accompanied by the crackle of rifle fire, rent the air …
>
> The moment came. The last row of prisoners in my line turned and dragged themselves towards the pit. There was a stampede to the right and to the left. But the women could not run far. A few steps and they were riddled with bullets. I stood in front of the pit quaking. For a fleeting moment, through glazed eyes, I saw my companions in the pit. Some of them were still moving compulsively. I heard a loud rifle volley, then silence and darkness …[32]

Miraculously, Reska and one other woman survived uninjured. They crawled out of the pit and hid in the undergrowth. Now Reska understood what she had been doing two days earlier. When a work detail appeared the following morning to perform a similar task, the two women attached themselves to it and returned to the camp and to the further, almost unimaginable ordeals Reska endured before she was finally liberated.

Biķernieki has an impressive memorial. But it has more than that. At least 36,000 were murdered under these trees, perhaps many more, Jews, Latvians, Soviet prisoners of war, mostly Jews.[33] There were so many that the Germans could disinter and incinerate only a third of what remained before the Red Army overwhelmed them in 1944.

There are fifty-five burial sites spread throughout the woods like some haphazard, sprawling village. As at Rumbula, flat mounds are topped with coarse grass and retained behind low moss-covered concrete walls. These are the pits in which the victims were lined up and shot down. Here lie Bertha Brandes, her sister Rosel Rosenthal and her brothers Julius and Karl Herzstein and his wife Emma.

This is a very quiet place. You can hear a woodpecker at work, birds singing out from the trees. When you press into the forest among the graves, the breeze shuts out the hum of the traffic on the highway which bisects it.

At the centre of the memorial stands a large black granite altar. Inscribed on each of its four sides, in Latvian, Russian, Hebrew and German, is a verse from the book of Job: 'O earth cover not my blood and let my cry find no resting place'.

Radiating out from the centre are cemeteries of jagged stones, upright and urgent, in little communities formed by the avenues which pass between them. Each group is identified by a slab bearing the name of a town from which the Jews of Biķernieki were deported. I place the smooth little stones I have brought from my garden in Shropshire on the slabs for Bamberg and Bayreuth which face each other across a narrow path. They are my bond.[34]

I walk back to the road along the track the victims trudged into the forest and towards the pits. I can almost imagine that they are making way and allowing me to go.

15. One of the mass graves at Biķernieki.

16

NOW WE ARE FREE

After the deportation of 27 November 1941, 126 Jews remained in Bamberg, among them Sally's sister Meta.

The decrees kept coming: from 12 December 1941, Jews were barred from access to public telephones; from 14 February 1942, no cakes could be sold to them. The following day, Jews were prohibited from owning pets and two days later from subscribing to or buying newspapers. From 16 March they could no longer purchase flowers.

On 25 April 1942, SS Sturmbannführer Grafenberger was happy to report in a telegram to his headquarters that, at 3.20 p.m., a train had pulled out of Würzburg with 852 Jews on board, halting at Bamberg to 'evacuate' another 103. Having collected 47,750 RM in fares from its 'passengers', it proceeded to the Izbica ghetto, a staging post for the Belzec and Sobibor death camps.[1]

In all there were five transports from Bamberg.[2] In September 1942, Dr Bauchwitz, the chairman of the Jewish community, wrote to the few Jews left in the city: 'As an addendum to our last bulletin concerning emigration note the following details which we ask you to convey to all the other members of the community: 1. Evacuation from Bamberg takes place from the White Dove. Exact time is still unknown but is expected to be in the first week of September. Destination is Theresienstadt.'[3]

Instructions follow about permissible luggage, the surrender of assets and the fees payable for the 'stay' at Theresienstadt ('for each month up to the age of 85, RM 150 – 5 years minimum'). The references to 'emigration' and 'evacuation' and the arrangements for fees suggested that deportees, most of whom were now elderly, were heading for an old folks' home.

Indeed, this was the fiction the Nazis sought to pass off on an unsuspecting – or, perhaps, unenquiring – world. When, as late as June 1944, a Red Cross delegation was invited to visit the 'resettlement centre', gardens were planted, houses painted and cultural events staged. Once the honoured guests had departed, deportations from Theresienstadt to Auschwitz, Majdanek and Treblinka resumed. Of the 140,000 Jews who entered Theresienstadt, 33,000 died there and 90,000 were forwarded to the death camps.

On 1 September, Meta was obliged to agree to her removal to an unspecified 'Jewish home for the elderly and infirm', which would provide 'board and lodging for life', along with laundry and medical care. Though destitute, she was required to pay a non-refundable 165 RM for the privilege. The authorities, however, reserved the right to 'terminate the contract for "important reasons"'.[4]

Meta was among the elderly Bamberg Jews who assembled on 9 September 1942 at the Weiße Taube for the journey to Nuremberg and onwards to Czechoslovakia. Dr Bauchwitz, with no community left to administer, travelled with her.

Meta's sister Paula had arrived at Theresienstadt on a transport which had left Dortmund on 29 July. For the two weeks before she was sent on to Treblinka on 23 September, the sisters were in the same camp, though it is doubtful that they would have known. Meta died in Theresienstadt on 13 May 1943, my father's twenty-eighth birthday. The record shows that she was cremated in coffin number 16586 on 15 May. Paula died at Treblinka.

Karl Mistele notes that as the final transport left Bamberg, Karl Bezold, head of the local Gestapo, wrote to an antique dealer friend serving on the Russian front: 'I fulfilled my previously made promises and accumulated quite a lot of old but beautiful objects. I wish you would return soon, so I can get rid of the lot. I don't have the space. Today, 10 September 1942, I evacuated the last 125 Jews. Now we are free!'[5]

16. Meta and Paula Brandes at their shop in Rengsdorf with my father in his Lederhosen, now in my possession.

There was nothing left of the Jewish community. By 1944, even its cemetery had been expropriated. The land was leased to the Bosch conglomerate which used the funeral hall as an armaments dump. The iron chains around the graves were stripped away and made over to the Nazi war effort.

At Börneplatz in the centre of Frankfurt, standing out from the wall which wraps around the old Jewish cemetery and the site of the grand synagogue, burned to the ground on Kristallnacht, there are 11,957 little ledges. Each bears the name of a victim of the Holocaust and the years of their life and the place of their death, nothing more. On many there are stones, left by relatives or passers-by, for remembrance.

It seems that the long, grey wall goes on forever. Then it ends. But, around the corner, it begins again, and then again; so many ledges, so many names and dates and places.

A group of Italian schoolchildren lounge on the steps of the Ghetto Museum, drinking coke, staring into their mobile phones, chatting excitedly, laughing.

17. Wilhelm Albert Zunz's memorial, one of 11,957 at
Börneplatz in Frankfurt.

Among the names on the endless wall, my mother's cousins
Alexander and Margarete Loeb, their daughter Ottilie and Margarete's
mother Karoline Busek, all murdered in the Łódź ghetto.[6] There are
many Zuntzes too.

Here is my mother's uncle Albert Zunz, the mechanical engineer, the
cheerful war veteran, the open-hearted socialist, the only Zunz left in
Nazi Germany.

He had been baptised and married Ida Stoll, a Protestant. But
according to the Nuremberg Laws, he remained a 'full Jew' and, because
he and Ida were childless, one 'without privileges'. From 1936 he was
barred from practising as an engineer; in 1940 the Gestapo raided his
and Ida's apartment on Linnéstraße, confiscating jewellery, silverware
and clothing. The following year, they were given 24 hours' notice to
leave their home.

Albert was arrested on 14 April 1943. On 4 May he was taken from
his police cell to Frankfurt's Preungesheim Prison where he was held in
solitary confinement for 4½ months before enduring an eight-day train
journey to Auschwitz. Two weeks later, according to the testimony of a

survivor, Hermann Kugelmann, he was transferred with others, clad only in their underclothes, to Birkenau where he perished in the gas chambers.

Ida, who had been allowed to see him only very briefly before he was sent to Auschwitz, tried everything to save him. She petitioned high officials and even wrote to Heinrich Himmler. She received only an official notice dated '8 November 1943, Auschwitz' which confirmed that the 'evangelical former Jew', the engineer Albert Israel Zunz, died at 10.40 a.m. on 30 October 1943 at Kasernenstrasse, Auschwitz. A death certificate, signed by the SS doctor Werner Rohde and lodged in the Auschwitz registry, records the cause of death as 'Altersschwäche', the weakness of old age. Ida lived on for another forty-two years, never reconciled to the loss of her beloved husband.[7]

I leave a stone on each of the little memorials for the Loebs, for Karoline Busek and for Albert. After the rain, the Spring sun is shining. Why should the young Italians not enjoy it?

17

SEARCHING FOR SALLY

At the war's end, my father twice sought transfer from India to the British Army of the Rhine so that he could search for his parents, or at least establish their fate. His first application for a compassionate posting was turned down by GHQ in India as 'not strong enough'. At his second attempt, applying for a posting as an interpreter, for which he was eminently qualified, he wrote:

> The question of my parents' fate weighs increasingly on my mind and I find it more and more difficult to concentrate on my work. I have been in suspense for the last four years and feel that the only means to end it is to try to take matters up myself – I am the only child and there is nobody else who could do it for me. As a former inmate of Buchenwald Concentration Camp (Nov 38 – Apr 39) I am under no illusions about the treatment my parents had to suffer at the hands of the Nazis and I can find no peace until the question whether they are dead or alive is answered.[1]

His application was rejected.

In the months to come he would learn from survivors that Bertha, his mother, was dead; that Uncle Julius, Uncle Karl and Aunt Emma were dead; that Aunt Rosel and Uncle Hugo were dead. Perhaps by then he knew that Uncle Ernst and Aunt Meta and Aunt Paula were dead too.

But what of his father; what of Sally?

Friedel Reinauer and her daughter Hanneliese, and Günther and Elisabeth Kosterlitz were the only ones of the forty-six Jews deported from Bayreuth who returned. After the war, and when they had recovered sufficient strength, Friedel and Günther and Alice Meyer, from Würzburg, all of whom had been on the same transport as Sally and Bertha, wrote letters which eventually found their way to my father.

Written in plain terms, they outline the fate of the Brandes and Herzstein families and many of their friends and neighbours – and Günther Kosterlitz's letter provided a glimmer of hope that Sally may not have perished in Riga.

Friedel and Leopold Reinauer ran a textile business in Bayreuth. In the town's tight-knit Jewish community, they would have known the Herzstein family and, in all likelihood, through business if not socially, Sally and Bertha Brandes in Bamberg.

In January 1947, Friedel wrote to Thesi Ehm, Karl and Emma Herzstein's daughter and Bertha's niece, who had survived Theresienstadt and was now the only member of the Herzstein family left alive in Germany.[2]

Bayreuth. 6 January 1947[3]

I imagine that you have now received my letter which crossed with yours. I was so happy to know that you are still alive. I would like to give you a more detailed account of what happened to us today.

We came to an abandoned farmstead near Riga which had been converted into a so-called refugee camp. We were soon joined by 3,000 people from Vienna, Hamburg and Würtemburg. It was a dreadful place, especially for the men who were housed in a barracks with only half a roof. On the first night, Mr Oppenheimer, from Wolfsgaße, froze to death in front of the barracks.[4]

A few days after our arrival, 400 men were sent to a terrible extermination camp.[5] Hugo Rosenthal (your uncle), Brandes (uncle), Max and my husband were all there. Huge numbers died there and Hugo was one of the first.

We did not have much work to do. Your father had to cut wood, but was quite good at it, Julius (uncle) was in an awful state. He thought he couldn't go on. I must say Rosel had enough on her plate; the whole family clung to Rosel (sister of my father-in-law).

By March '42 our camp had shrunk to 2,200 people. Many had died, among them the sick and elderly. Then there were only 500; 1,700 people were taken away, apparently to another camp.

Hanneliese and I were almost tempted to volunteer (for one of the transports). We did not think of murder at the time. There were several people from Bayreuth on this transport including your parents, Julius already on a stretcher and near death, Bertl Brandes (aunt), Rosl, Frau Kohl, Frau Strauss whose husband had died in the first days, Frau Dr Steinberger, Frau Wolf, the Wannbachers.[6]

Only Dr Steinberger, our doctor, we four, Herr Wolf and De Jongs remained.[7] A few days later, we learned that the whole transport had been driven into the forest and machine-gunned. Max (our son) was among those who had to unload the clothes they'd been ordered to strip off and he found in the pockets the identity cards of people we knew.

In July '42 we were moved into the Riga ghetto. There I met Herr Wolf and Brandes (uncle), and was reunited with my husband. Steinberger was also there.

In 1943 we were transferred to a newly built concentration camp [Kaiserwald]. Since then, I heard no more of Brandes. At the end of the year, my husband and Dr Steinberger were sent to Auschwitz. Wolf died in '44 and my poor boy, who as a car welder had it a lot better than some, was killed in October in an air raid on Libau.[8] It was only in Berlin that I heard the news from one of his comrades. That was the bitterest thing for me.

Meanwhile, Hanneliese (my daughter) has married and we have built up a business again and are quite content. You just have to put everything behind you. It was a miracle that Hanneliese and I came through it all. We worked in an AEG factory, repairing cables essential to the war effort.[9] So we were left alone.

After our liberation by the Russians, I came to a Russian field hospital with 80 pfennigs in my pocket. They did not think I'd pull through. In August '45 we arrived back here. I'm still pretty frail, even though I spent six months in that hospital in Bromberg. Now I am well recovered.

Friedel and Hanneliese had endured Jungfernhof, the Riga ghetto, Kaiserwald concentration camp, evacuation to Poland and the death march from Thorn (now Torun) to Bromberg (now Bydgoszcz) which ended on 26 January 1945 when the SS guards fled the approaching Soviet forces. They had lost Friedel's husband and son, Hanneliese's father and brother. It is hard to imagine the desperation of Friedel's condition which had left her 'pretty frail' even after six months in hospital. But when she reached the Russian hospital, she weighed just 45 pounds.

Mother and daughter finally reached Bayreuth on 14 August 1945.[10]

Alice Meyer was deported to Riga along with her sister Johanna, a victim of the Dünamünde Aktion. After the war, she wrote from her home in Würzburg to Margot Pretzfelder who had emigrated to London with her husband Paul and was in touch with my father. Paul's parents, Max and Lily Pretzfelder, the owners of Villa Dessauer, Sally's and Bertha's last address, were also murdered at Dünamünde.

After the war, Alice wrote in a mix of English and German which I have faithfully reproduced, with translation where necessary.

Würzburg. 23 October 1945.

It is right, I came at the end of November 41 from here to Jungfernhof near Riga and with our transport were all the people together which you called from Bamberg. Excuse my bad English, but I dont know, if I write in German, if it is right, We were gathered in Nuernberg, till we were thousand people, the people were from Bamberg, Nuernberg, Fuerth, Bayreuth, Erlangen and

Coburg. I know all ladies, they were all in my Barracke, then I was *Barrackenleiterin* [head of the barrack].

I am sorry, I must bring to you only *Hiobsbotachaften* [bad news, literally Job's messages]. February 1942 was an action [mass execution] and March 42 again. Your parents-in-law and Mrs. Anna Fischel, Mrs. Morgenroth, Heyman, Mrs. Rehbock, Mr and Mrs Silbermann, Mr. Klestadt, two family Kohn, are all dead.[11] My sister was with the same transport and she never came back. 1700 men, women and children *verlud man* [were loaded] in buses (closed) *fuhr* [driven] into the forrest from Riga and *legte die Menschen mit Maschinengewehren um* [and were machine-gunned]. First they must *sich auskleiden, grauenhaft* [they had to undress, it's terrible]. Miss Anna Kohn remain with me till February 45 and she is living.[12] But she was seriously ill, she got *sehr starke Erfrierungen* [very bad frostbite] at the feet. After our *Befreiung* [liberation] in Bromberg (Polen) she must go in an hospital there and was operated, her toes must *abgenommen warden* [be amputated]. I leave Bromberg in April, but I heard now, she came back to Germany, but till now, I have no connection with her. If I know anything, I will give you news, as soon as possible. She is a poor thing, a very good character and was always *hilfsbereit* [ready to help] for everybody. Mrs. Kuhn came also in this transport for death, but her husband was till 1943 in Riga, also Fleischmann and wife, but till now nobody came back. Schoenthal, Fein, Sacki, Hahn, Brandes I remember so well, lay buried in the forrest of Riga.[13] Julius Schapiro came 44 to Stutthof near Danzig [now Gdansk], wo die *Gaskammern waren* [where the gas chambers were]. His wife and daughter with an action 44 from Riga Ghetto *aus* in the death.[14] Where you look and ask, nobody has returned. But the next days, I write to the Jewish community in Bamberg, who is coming back now and then I will tell you …

Please dont be sad, believe me, it was very heavy for me, to give you such a news. Dont despair, you have your husband and perhaps children but my husband is dead and it can be a very long time, till I have the opportunity to come to my sister and brother in U.S.A.[15] I am quite alone in Germany, all my relations are killed or died in the concentration camps ...

In December 1946, having survived Latvia, Stutthof and the death marches, Alice was able to join her family in Milwaukee. She was a witness at the Nazi war trials and died in 1991 at the age of 90.

Günther Kosterlitz and his wife Elisabeth had been deported from Bayreuth on the Nuremberg transport.

As the Red Army advanced into Latvia, they were evacuated from Libau, where Günther had been badly injured in an air raid in December 1944. They were shipped to Germany and spent time in the Fuhlsbüttel prison in Hamburg before being force-marched 50 miles to the Hassee camp near Kiel.

Remarkably, Günther and Elisabeth were among the 169 Jewish prisoners released into the care of the Swedish Red Cross following the encounter in the small hours of 21 April 1945 between Heinrich Himmler and Norbert Masur of the World Jewish Congress. They had been brought together by Himmler's Swedish osteopath Felix Kersten and Count Folke Bernadotte, the head of the Swedish Red Cross, an initiative which led Hitler, in his Last Will and Testament, to 'expel the former Reichsführer-SS and Minister of the Interior, Heinrich Himmler, from the party and from all offices of State'.[16]

Günther wrote to my mother who had been in touch with the Red Cross which no doubt prompted Günter's letter.

Solliden, Korsnäs, Sweden. 3 December 1945[17]

We arrived together at Jungfernhof outside Riga on 1 December 1941.[18] After a few days, Sally and I were moved to the concentration camp at Salaspils while, because only men went to Salaspils, Bertl and my wife remained at Jungfernhof.

Hugo Rosenthal and his wife Rosel from Bayreuth, Bertl's sister, were also with us. Hugo came to Salaspils and Rosel likewise remained in Jungfernhof ... Bertl Brandes and Rosel

Rosenthal were involved in the Dünamünde Aktion in March 1942. We heard nothing more of them and had to assume when the Aktion had been completed that there was little hope that they would still be alive.

Sadly, Hugo Rosenthal died in Salaspils. His bed was next to Sally's and I was in the same barrack block. Sally did all he could for Hugo but he could not save him.[19]

In August 1942, Sally and I had the good fortune to leave the hell of Salaspils for the Riga ghetto where sadly he could not find Bertl and learned that she had been taken to Dünamünde. My wife was in the ghetto.

We spent a lot of time with Sally. He was healthy and was on a forced labour squad on the Latvian railway until August 1943 when he was moved to the Kaiserwald concentration camp and we weren't able to speak any more. In November 1943, when the ghetto was closed down, we were imprisoned elsewhere.

Where Sally went then is difficult to say, possibly to Stutthof concentration camp near Danzig. It's possible that he's still alive for, though it's hard to believe, some were able to save themselves. It's possible that he fell ill and was executed. Should I hear anything more about Sally, I shall let you know as soon as possible.

My wife and I were transferred from Riga to the camp at Libau and from there by ship to the Gestapo prison in Hamburg. From there we were marched to the concentration camp at Lübeck where, on 1 May 1945, we were rescued by the Swedish Red Cross.

Three weeks after the date of the letter, on 28 December, Günther and Elizabeth Kosterlitz sailed from Göteborg on the SS *Stockholm*, arriving in New York on 6 January 1949. They settled in Denver, Colarado and later that year became US citizens.

How had Sally survived Jungfernhof, Salaspils and the Riga ghetto, and what became of him after Günther Kosterlitz had lost sight of him at Kaiserwald?

* * *

Towards the end of July 1941, months before the decision to deport German Jews to Latvia, Stahlecker applied to Berlin for permission to build a camp capable of holding, assessing, interrogating and processing all the Jews and other detainees of Riga. In September, Rudolph Lange, then head of Einsatzgruppe A's Gestapo department, with a chilling reference to the transitory nature of the Riga ghetto, added his enthusiastic support:

> An additional aspect that speaks for the establishment of a [concentration camp] near Riga is the fact that there are about 23,000 Jews in Riga. The crowding of the Jews into a ghetto can only be a temporary solution. Soon the need will arise to clear the housing space occupied by the Jews for other purposes. Furthermore [we] must also strive to put to work as close to 100 per cent as possible of the male as well as the female Jews, who up to now have only partially been drawn on for work by Wehrmacht offices etc ... It can already be said that the space envisioned offers so many possibilities that all the remaining Jews in Riga, and in Latvia, could be concentrated there. In the process, Jews must be accommodated separately from Jewesses in order to prevent further reproduction.[20]

Work on the construction of the camp at Salaspils was slow. Some of the ground had been prepared in October 1941 by Soviet PoWs, but when the transports from the Reich began to arrive at Šķirotava a month later, little progress had been made. From early December, all able-bodied men at Jungfernhof between the ages of 16 and 50, and in due course those arriving on fresh transports, were sent to build the new camp. By early 1942, 1,000 Jews were working there.

Sally Brandes, Hugo Rosenthal and Günther Kosterlitz may have been among the fifty or so men from the Nuremberg transport who, on 4 or 5 December, were the first to be marched the eight miles through thick snow to Salaspils.[21] When they arrived, there was neither food nor shelter: aching with hunger and numbed by the cold, they would have had to sleep in the open, if sleep could come.

Josef Katz describes how a fortnight later, on 18 December 1941, he was among thirty Jews who followed them from Jungfernhof. After two miles, the Latvian SS guards halted the column and, at gunpoint, stripped their prisoners of any valuables they still had: 'We are glad when we get to the new camp, Salaspils. It lies in the midst of a pine forest, far from the view of other people. We new arrivals find a half-finished barrack, roofless and windowless … There is nothing in sight but snow, trees and sky … The roof is hastily finished that same day in the dark and the windows are boarded up. There is no light. We stumble and step on each other trying to find a place.'[22]

Murderous though conditions had been at Jungfernhof, at Salapils they were significantly worse. The camp was freezing in winter and lice-infested in summer. There was just one rusty water pump and, when food was available, it was limited to some 300 to 400 grams of bread and a watery soup garnished by rhubarb leaves or fish heads and occasionally supplemented by a helping of rotten potatoes or sauerkraut.[23]

On these meagre rations, the inmates had to clear the forest to make way for forty-five barrack blocks along with watchtowers and fences. They could only survive by bartering for food with the local Latvians they encountered at work. If they were caught, they risked summary execution. Those who tried to escape were shot or hanged.[24] As early as 30 December 1941, two teenagers from Hanover, Erich Hanau and Kurt Hirschkowitz, absconded in a desperate attempt to reach their families in the ghetto. Three days later, they were brought back to Salaspils and shot in front of the assembled prisoners. Rudolph Lange, who had given the order, warned that for every one who attempted escape, ten more inmates would be executed.

By the middle of February 1942, the half-built Salaspils held around 1,500 prisoners. In May they were joined by 300 more from the ghetto. Josef Katz described the living conditions:

The barracks measures approximately 200 by 33 feet and houses 600 men. The bunks, arranged in six tiers, are near the walls to the left and right, with a third row in the centre. On each side there is an aisle about five feet wide, in which the men crowd each other when they get up in the morning and again when they make coffee at night. Since there is no chance to eat our sumptuous dinner sitting down or even standing up, we all lie on the bunks with our cup of coffee and dry bread. Each bunk is about five feet wide. At night, when all five bunk occupants are present, we can lie only on one side, because there is no room for any other position. Most of the Jews have diarrhea due to the lack of solid food. The latrine is about ten yards away from the barracks. The men can't hold their bowels for that long. They soil their bunks. A sickening stench develops from the dirty blankets, dirty underwear and the dead who are found in their bunks in the morning.[25]

By April, the Germans realised that their slave labourers at Salaspils were so physically debilitated and replacements so hard to find that they had no option but to restore them to some kind of health. Some 400 were sent back to the Riga ghetto to recuperate. Only half survived the next few months.

Gerda Gottschalk, who had been deported from Leipzig, was shocked by their condition as they reached the ghetto: 'In April 1942, an ambulance finally arrived from Salaspils. A truck stopped in front of the Commandant's office. The streets were cordoned off. A Jewish ghetto policeman stepped up on the vehicle, he brought a human figure down, others did the same. They stood there, human beings, but it was impossible to recognize whether a child or an elderly person, whether a woman or a man. Then the names were read out. Their relatives rushed to them and began to see them. It took weeks until these sick persons found their balance again.'[26]

The rest of the Jewish inmates were sent back to the Riga ghetto in July and August 1942.[27] By then well over 1,000, including Hugo Rosenthal and Hans Goldschmidt, Margarete Brandes' husband, were dead. Somehow, Sally survived.

In all, it's estimated that some 23,000 prisoners passed through Salaspils. 3,000 of them died there.[28] From December 1943, its remaining prisoners were progressively decanted to camps in Poland and

Germany. In September 1944, the camp was set on fire, partly to deny the approaching Red Army the use of it, partly to destroy the evidence of its terrible existence.

Salaspils is about a mile off the Maskavas road, through the forest. Nothing is left of the camp my grandfather helped build in the bitter winter of 1941–2. But there is a huge monument erected by the Soviets. A group of monolithic statues stands in an open field, symbolising the socialist virtues of motherhood, sacrifice and solidarity and celebrating the heroic resistance of the Latvian people against the Nazis. When they were installed, no reference was made to the Jews who suffered and died there though today an exhibition, opened as recently as 2018, makes redress.

I visited Salaspils on 8 May. Though I did not know it, this is the day Latvia marks the German surrender and commemorates the victims of the Second World War. I found myself in the midst of a procession of foreign diplomats, Latvian dignitaries and local schoolchildren who, four by four, were laying flowers on a great concrete altar beneath which beats the great metronomic heartbeat of the dead. I placed a stone among the carnations and tulips for Hugo Rosenthal who died here. The Foreign Minister and another VIP made short, respectful speeches, the military band played and I, discreetly, slipped away.

We know that Sally was one of the last Jewish prisoners dispatched from Salaspils to the Reichsghetto in August 1942. There, as Günther Kosterlitz recounts, he searched in vain for Bertha and learned that he would not see her again.

Conditions in the ghetto were not as brutal as they had been in Salaspils. But they were harsh enough. When Lilly Pancis arrived there with a transport from Bielefeld eight months earlier, she could not take in what confronted her: 'We did not immediately grasp the things that our eyes saw, our ears heard. Hundreds of people, old and young, looking hungry and ragged, some with the yellow star sewn on their breast and back, others with stars saying "Jude" in front, were on the streets, rags wrapped around their feet, bundled up against the bitter cold, thirty degrees below zero Celsius. And guards with dogs and guns everywhere.'[29]

Everyone was hungry. As Gertrude Schneider recalled, 'each person still received 220 grams of bread per day, one portion of somewhat tainted fish per week, an occasional serving of turnips, sour cabbage or frozen potatoes and, from time to time, one portion of horsemeat. The few small children who were still around received one litre of fat-free milk per week.'[30]

Despite the risks, the starving Jews would exchange whatever they still had with Latvians at work or through the wire for bread, butter or eggs. As the spring thaw set in, they cultivated vegetables, nourished by the overflowing cesspits, on the scrubland between buildings. In the summer they bartered their winter clothes, doubting that they would need them when the cold returned.

Nonetheless, the Jews of the ghetto did their best not only to survive, but also to approximate some sense of normality. A Jewish council, the Judenrat, under the strict control of the Nazis, coordinated a bureaucracy of Jewish administrators and police. Frida Michelson saw clearly the dilemma the Council members faced and, ultimately, the futility of their efforts: 'Some members of the Judenrat occasionally tried to intercede to ease the burden of the terrorised Jews, to no avail. It became clear that the Judenrat was a fiction, created to help the Nazis organise the annihilation of the Jewish population.'[31]

The Germans expected from the Judenrat efficiency in maintaining order and organising the slave labour. But whatever its members' involuntary role in facilitating their designs, they also strove to make life as tolerable as possible for the ghetto's inmates for as long as they survived.

There was a small, ill-equipped hospital staffed by Jewish physicians. A secret theatre performed abortions for, as sexual relations were strictly forbidden, women risked dire punishment, including sterilisation, if they were found to be pregnant; babies born in the ghetto were routinely killed by lethal injection.

Schools for 4- to 15-year-olds sprang up, staffed by former teachers. Young people were taught skills which might make them useful to the

Germans and, it was hoped, equip them for life after the war. University professors gave lectures. Religious and cultural groups met secretly to try to sustain a Jewish way of life.

The arts flourished. An enterprising inmate came upon a gramophone at his place of work, dismantled it piece by piece and reassembled it in the ghetto to play records stolen by the Jewish women who cleaned the houses of army and SS officers.

Plays were performed and cabarets organised. Musicians who had somehow managed to hang on to their instruments or acquire new ones gave concerts of both popular and classical music. Commandant Krause even procured a cello for the ghetto orchestra and was the frequent and appreciative occupant of a front-row seat at its performances.

But these escapes from harsh reality were fleeting. More often, Krause stalked the ghetto's streets, ordering the summary execution of those he judged guilty of the smallest misdemeanour. Men were publicly hanged in Blechplatz (Tin Square) and left swinging in the breeze as a warning to others. Women, he personally took to the wall of the old Jewish cemetery where he shot them.

One of them was Meta Baum. Hilde Sherman-Zander told her story in evidence to a war crimes tribunal in Hamburg in 1953: 'Upon her return from a day on her forced labour commando, Baum was stopped at the ghetto gate by Tuchel and Neumann and accused of stealing the soup found in her canteen. Baum, a Rhineland woman known to all due to her red hair, had seven children in the ghetto and needed every additional scrap of food she could find. The two German policemen nevertheless dragged her away and took her to Commandant Krause. Krause ordered her to the cemetery immediately and shot her there although the children pleaded for the life of their mother the entire way.'[32]

Rudolph Lange required no pretext for his brutality. He simply shot Jews where and when they displeased him. Eduard Roschmann, who took over as ghetto commander in early 1943 when Krause was transferred to Salaspils, was a killer of a less spontaneous character, preferring to send his victims to the Centralka Prison from which they rarely emerged alive.[33]

There were incidents of defiance and, at least on one occasion, an uprising. In October 1942, in an attempt to link up with local partisans, a group of nine Latvian Jews managed to break out of the ghetto in a commandeered truck. But they were betrayed and ambushed. Three members of the Gestapo and all but two of the Jews were killed.[34]

Under torture, one revealed the existence of an arsenal of weapons which had been smuggled into the ghetto by a labour detail employed at an army storage depot. All 41 members of the Jewish police in the Latvian part of the ghetto were arrested. On 31 October, they were marched to Blechplatz and shot. According to Gertrude Schneider, 'the blood-soaked soil where the Jewish policemen died was later scooped up by several of the murdered men's girlfriends, who placed the soil into small bags that they tied around their necks'.[35]

The occupants of the ghetto existed only as slave labourers. Every morning between 6.00 and 7.00 a.m., some 8,500 of them would be marched out to over 200 places of work.[36] In winter they would be employed clearing snow from the city's streets and debris from the frozen Daugava; throughout the year they would mend roads and railways, sort and store the looted property and the blood-stained clothes of murdered Jews, load and unload ships and goods trains, dig graves in the forests for the mass shootings, and in any number of ways support the Wehrmacht's war effort.

After the annihilation of their families in the Rumbula forest, the surviving Jews in the sealed-off Latvian quarter had few illusions and fewer expectations about the fate that awaited them. But still many in the Reichsghetto clung to the hope that they, as Germans, would be spared. Even after Dünamünde, many rationalised that only those unfit for labour had perished and that so long as they worked hard and kept order, their lives retained value.

As Gertrude Schneider acknowledges, despite its horrible privations, dangers and deaths, life in the ghetto was not as unremittingly harsh as elsewhere. She found among other survivors she interviewed in later years that: 'While they remembered the cold, the hunger, and other physical discomforts, they also point with pride to the institutions they had been able to establish in the ghetto, the schools, the theatres, the concerts and the sports events. They proudly recall that they had succeeded in establishing, even in the ghetto, a society where ethical standards were scrupulously observed ... When discussing their apparent inability to perceive the reality of the "Final Solution", survivors mention that the ghetto had seemed to them like home.'[37]

The liquidation of the ghetto brought this fantasy to an end. In the spring of 1943, Himmler decreed that the ghettos must be extinguished: they offered too much mutual support and too much hope to Jews who, despite their privations, were still not dying quickly enough. Ominously, he ordered that 'inhabitants of the Jewish ghettos who are not needed are to be evacuated to the East'. The greater part of the Riga ghetto was cleared in the summer and autumn of 1943.

On 2 November, the security police supported by the SS searched it. They arrested all those who had not been allocated work for that day and emptied the hospital. Those who could walk were assembled on Blechplatz where Roschmann, Krause and his driver Max Gymnich selected 2,000 young, old and sick Jews who were then herded onto trains and deported to Auschwitz. When they arrived on 5 November, around 120 men and 30 women were dispatched as slave labourers to Birkenau. The rest were sent straight to the gas chambers. Three survived.

When the work details returned to the ghetto in the evening they found it empty other than for 120 men and 30 women. The loved ones they had left that morning were gone. A commando of 40 women and 20 men was instructed to remove all traces of the ghetto and repatriate any valuables they found to Germany. By July 1944, the task had been completed.

According to Günther Kosterlitz, Sally Brandes was transferred from the ghetto to the new Kaiserwald concentration camp in or after August 1943. In a memoir written immediately after the war, Max Kaufmann remembered a place which had once been an upmarket residential district: 'The name Mežaparks, or Kaiserwald, is familiar to every inhabitant of Riga. At one time it was for us the embodiment of the best and most beautiful things, for all of us had spent wonderful times there. Today Kaiserwald will remain in the memory of not just the Riga

Jews but also many other European Jews who were taken there. For us, Kaiserwald is a large cemetery, a cemetery without graves …'[38]

The camp had been built by 450 non-Jewish political prisoners and career criminals who had been transported from Sachsenhausen concentration camp near Berlin in March 1943. Under the command of Sturmbannführer (SS Major) Albert Sauer, it was principally a holding camp with a capacity of around 2,000.[39] By the end of August, 7,874 Jews had been registered there and 1,950 were living in the camp.[40] Over the next year 18,000 prisoners passed through, either to Kaiserwald's many satellite work camps, the Aussenlager, or directly to their execution.

Surrounded by electrified barbed wire and overlooked by four watchtowers, Kaiserwald was divided into segregated quarters for women and men. In the former, some 250 women and children occupied each of four wooden barracks. When the satellite camps were closed in the spring and summer of 1944, the numbers increased to 500–800 per block. In the men's quarters, up to 500 were crammed into each of the four barracks. None was adequately heated. There was scant sanitary provision. Contact between men and women was forbidden. The punishment for any infraction was severe.[41]

Bernhard Press describes the awful ritual which Sally and others had to endure as they entered the camp:

> Many of the large work gangs of Jews travelled the long distance from the ghetto to Kaiserwald on foot.[42] Most of the inmates carried small bundles. Larger sacks containing their last remaining belongings followed on trucks and wagons. At the entrance to the camp, the bundles and sacks had to be thrown into a shed. Their owners never saw them again. Moreover, these unfortunate people were even robbed of their very last pieces of clothing and belongings. Immediately after passing through the camp gate they were ordered into shower rooms and ordered to undress within seconds. Then ice-cold or boiling hot water streamed down on them, after which the new arrivals, who were still wet – there was of course no soap or towels – were thrown rags which they were supposed to put on.

The men received dirty and patched old jackets and trousers that were too large or too small or torn, blood-smeared Soviet uniforms full of bullet holes. The women got skirts and blouses in similar condition, in some cases ball gowns with deep décolleté and high heeled shoes ... An X was painted on everyone's chest with white or yellow paint and a stripe was painted down their sides and trouser legs ... Within a short time, some people deteriorated to the point where they no longer had the strength to wash themselves. Everyone slept in his or her dirty rags. The barracks were full of vermin, and all the inmates had lice. The food was nothing but starvation rations, and the work was hard. If anyone was caught trying to bring food into the concentration camp, he was punished with truncheon blows. Smuggling in written notes from other camps was punished by death.[43]

Each day, Kaiserwald's inmates would be marched out in columns to their places of work at army stores, depots and workshops and several German firms, among them the electricals giant AEG where Friedel and Hanneliese Reinauer worked. At regular intervals those who were no longer considered fit for work would be picked out and shot.

Josef Katz, who arrived at the camp in November, observed:

The Kaiserwald concentration camp is a very small place: it has only three men's and three women's barracks, a joint sick ward, one clothing chamber and the workshops situated beyond the fence. The clothing chamber has a tailor shop attached to it. There is a carpenter shop, a smithy, a small workroom for the radio mechanics, and then there are the roofers whom I will join the next day. And beyond the fence there is a place where electrical appliances are disassembled for the Wehrmacht. Most of the workers there are women, who break down batteries or radio instruments into their original components for future re-use. The women's camp contains a laundry and the kitchen. This is all of Camp Kaiserwald, in which there are about 5,000 Jews.[44]

The prisoners were malnourished, lice-ridden and viciously preyed upon by SS men and the convicts who had built the camp and were now placed in authority over them. Josef Katz described some of the career criminals who served as Kapos, including Xaver Appel, a Berlin gangster and convicted killer known simply as X:

> Mr X, formerly the Kolonnenführer of an Aussenkommando, is now in charge of the 'interior service'.[45] Several interesting rumours are being spread about him. At the camp he is registered as a dangerous criminal; he has to wear a black triangle. It is said that he was a professional car thief who already spent six years in concentration camps. He came to Riga via Buchenwald and Dachau, and was made Kolonnenführer because of his outstanding achievements in killing Jews … Besides X, the camp senior is also in a position of power. He cannot possibly have been as well off when he was free as he is now in the concentration camp … With his arms crossed behind his back, his boots polished to a brilliant shine, his cheeks smoothly shaven, he struts about in his kingdom like a little emperor. The care of his physical well-being is in the hands of a servant who also does the heavy cleaning in the camp senior's room. He himself has no other occupation than to parade his powerful figure in the camp. Every now and then he socks somebody in the face, as a kind of morning exercise.[46]

The daily routine at Kaiserwald was unrelenting. Max Kaufmann recalls:

> We were awakened at four in the morning. A whistle from the block elder meant 'wake up'. Totally exhausted, lacking the sleep we needed, bitten by lice that had tormented us all night, we had only a few minutes to get dressed …
>
> The zebras came and roughly pulled out the prisoners who had to bring the coffee for the men's and women's camps from the kitchen.[47] Those who refused were beaten with truncheons …

People ran to wash themselves in the small washroom, but not everybody did so. Many people whom one remembered as well-groomed and elegant men in the good old days had already deteriorated to such an extent that they no longer found it necessary to wash, and even slept in their dirty work clothes. Others avoided the washroom because they wanted to stay out of the truncheons' way.

The coffee arrived! Each person received it in a bowl that was often none too clean. A few minutes later a bell rang, which meant 'Assemble for the morning roll call!'

We ran through the narrow barracks door and lined up in front of our block, always in rows of five. Everyone had to come out, even the small children. Those who had fallen ill during the night and were unable to walk to the infirmary were carried out and laid on the ground …

The block elder was already looking over his block before the SS people came. 'Eyes right, eyes left, and move! Caps off, caps on!' At this we had to click our heels together. Everything had to be done flawlessly, and woe to him who did it wrong. The truncheon was then put to use and blood would flow …

The work crews left the concentration camp. 'Caps off, caps on!' We had to count off; a new group of guards joined the old one and the column would disappear behind the barbed wire, marching toward its work place …

Twelve o'clock: a bell signaled noontime!

We ran out of all the workshops into the barracks, where the food was distributed … We lined up in long columns with our bowls in our hands to receive our 'meal'. In my time, at the end of 1943, the rations were very bad. At noon we received a ladleful of turnip or cabbage soup that was always full of sand …

Even as we ate, the bell was already ringing one o'clock: 'Back to work!'

… A bell rang: six o'clock! Assemble for the evening roll call! The same procedure as in the morning, except that now there was not so much hurry. Sometimes it lasted hours, and it didn't matter to the guards whether we were standing in the rain or the cold of winter.

... People died like flies, but even this bothered nobody. Every day it was the same ...

Now everyone ran and rushed into the barracks to 'eat' and 'rest' ... The ration for the whole day was 200 to 250 grams of bread with a bit of margarine or soft cheese. Once a week, on Sundays and holidays, we received a spoonful of sugar or syrup. Everything was washed down with hot black coffee, which was sometimes sweetened. Of course on such rations we could barely stand upright, much less work.

Those who had pilfered or traded something during their work now started to trade with it. In most cases it was only a couple of potatoes, bread, or other small items. Even bone marrow and similar waste products brought back by the slaughterhouse work crew were very much in demand. Everything was spread on bread. Others bought items of clothing to trade at their work stations the next day.

But finally we had to go to sleep ... Each one of us would have been happy to fall asleep forever. The women were no better off.

That is what a day in Kaiserwald was like.[48]

As Kaufmann suggests, women faced a similar ordeal. Lilly Pancis recalled: 'We now found out what real hunger meant. Thin soup was given out once a day in the evening, after work. There were beatings, killings, and the guards were like mad animals. We were pushed into the barracks, four or five women on a narrow bunk bed. For lack of space, I was squeezed against the edge of the wooden frame. The wood rubbed through my thin clothing and my back became infected; I still have the scar.'[49]

In March 1942, Himmler had established Sonderkommando (Sk) 1005 under SS Standartenführer (Colonel) Paul Blobel.[50] Its task was to destroy evidence of Nazi war crimes throughout the occupied territories. In January 1944, Blobel arrived in Riga. Now groups of 10, known as Kommando Nr 1189 or the Stützpunkt, were sent out from Kaiserwald to Rumbula and Biķernieki to exhume the bodies of the dead, incinerate them and rebury what remained.[51]

The men worked in chains. According to historians Angrick and Klein, 'they were expected to dig up the pits with shovels, to stack the extremely decomposed bodies over prepared layers of wood by using hooks, to sift the remnants for gold teeth and jewelry, to use a ball mill to crush the bones that did not burn, and to scatter the ashes near the gravesite'.[52]

After a fortnight of this gruesome work, they would themselves be shot, cremated and interred in the forest. Then a new squad would be sent out to do the same work and meet the same fate.

During the winter, transports brought Jews from other parts of Latvia, from the ghettos in Vilnius and Kaunas in Lithuania and from Łódź in Poland. By March 1944, Kaiserwald and its satellites held around 12,000 prisoners, including all the Jews in Latvia who were not in hiding and 5,000 Romanian, Slovakian and Hungarian Jewish women who had been transferred from Auschwitz.

The satellite camps included the Reichsbahn, based at the freight station on Hanzas Iela, from which some 850 inmates worked. We know from Günther Kosterlitz that Sally was working on the railways, at least until August 1943. Though the work, unloading freight wagons or laying tracks, was hard, the living conditions, according to Max Kaufmann, were better than in most of the satellite camps. But, on the slightest pretext, prisoners were moved back to Kaiserwald or to the Stützpunkt, from which no one returned alive.

On 28 April 1944, all the remaining children were removed from Kaiserwald and its satellites. Many had been subjected to medical experiments by the notorious camp doctor Eduard Krebsbach and his assistant Heinz Wisner.[53] Accounts differ as to precisely how the children were murdered. Some believe that they were killed in a gassing van, others that they were locked in a cattle car, shunted to a siding and left there until, after three days, the screaming stopped.

The selections continued throughout the summer. In one, to which the surviving prisoners subsequently referred as Operation Krebsbach, the doctor and his assistant spent the greater part of 28 July strolling idly between the ranks of the assembled Jews and, with nods and gestures, marked out those, mostly under 15 or over 50, who were to die in the Biķernieki woods.

According to Marģers Vestermanis, a survivor of Kaiserwald and founder of the Jews in Latvia Museum, at least 70 per cent of the camp's inmates had died before it was abandoned in October 1944. Between August and October, with the Soviet army approaching, the Germans transported the remaining 6,000 inmates to Stutthof in Poland. Those who were unfit for work were executed.

By this time, it was considered an urgent priority to evacuate the Sk 1005 men who had directed the Stützpunkt operations, lest they fall into the hands of Soviet interrogators. Before they boarded ship in late September, they undertook one final assignment. They drove some 400 Jews, for the most part Hungarian women and children, to a killing site near Kaiserwald. There they were made to form up. The first column was ordered to lie face-down on a pile of logs; they were then shot in the back of the neck. The second column was forced to lie on top of the victims. They too were shot, and then the next column and the next until all were dead. Then the Sk 1005 men set the logs alight and retreated in orderly fashion to the harbour.

On 10 October 1944, the Germans burned all Kaiserwald's incriminating paperwork and the following day the few remaining prisoners were moved out. The Red Army entered the camp two days later and converted it into a prison for German PoWs.

Today there is no sign of Kaiserwald. Where that baleful place once stood is now a tidy but unlovely Soviet-era housing estate of three-storey barrack-like blocks, bounded on one side by a police station and a children's playground and on the other by a broad expanse of railway tracks.

At the entrance to the estate, there's a little yellow clapperboard Orthodox church. Inside, people are praying. On a wooden bench by the open door sits an elderly woman dressed in black. On her lap she's gently rocking, backwards and forwards, a shapeless figure swaddled in winter clothing, though the day is mild. It's hard to tell, but perhaps this is her grown-up daughter. It's not really my business.

Opposite stands a memorial to those who suffered in this place. On one side, someone has left flowers, which are wilting now. Someone else has defaced the Star of David and, next to it, scrawled a large swastika.

Günther Kosterlitz speculated that Sally could have been one of the last surviving Jews evacuated from Latvia to the death camp at Stutthoff (now Sztutowo) in Poland. Could this be possible?

Between 29 June and 14 October 1944, 26 transports brought 47,109 Jews from camps throughout the Baltic States to Stutthof. The camp had been built by slave labour on the site of an old people's home some twenty miles east of the then German city of Danzig.[54]

Three of the transports came from Riga. The first, a converted cargo ship, the SS *Bremerhaven*, left the Latvian capital on 6 August 1944 with its cargo crowded below decks without food, water or sanitation. According to Gertrude Schneider, there were 'almost two thousand of us – eleven hundred men and nine hundred women. There were also over three thousand of the Hungarian Jewish women, who had arrived in Riga only three months earlier from Auschwitz. In addition, there were almost three thousand Russian prisoners of war.'[55]

The *Bremerhaven* docked in Danzig two days later and the prisoners were crammed into the holds of filthy coal barges and freighted down a branch of the Vistula River to Stutthof. It is likely that my father's cousin Gretel Goldschmidt and her 13-year-old daughter Margit were on the transport that followed on 25 September. Two days after the last left on 11 October, the Germans evacuated Riga as the Red Army entered the city.

After the harrowing journey from Riga, the first glimpse of Stutthof was reassuring. According to Gertrude Schneider, 'the long, low-slung white buildings had green shutters, there were beautiful flowers all around these buildings, and the grass was lush and green'.[56]

But the reality was very different. Above the gates that formed a second entrance hung a large, foreboding sign, 'Du lebst nicht um zu arbeiten, Du arbeitest um zu leben' ('You do not live to work, you work to live'). On arrival, prisoners over forty were selected and shot.

Though Stutthof had been used by the Danzig police as a labour camp, first for political prisoners and then for criminals and Russian POWs, Himmler, on a visit on 23 November 1941, conferred on it the status of a 'concentration camp'. The following year, an attractive villa for the Kommandant and an SS administration and accommodation block were added. In 1943 it was further enlarged to provide 30 barracks, 20 for prisoners and 10 as armament workshops.[57] By 1944, 70 per cent of the prisoners were Jews and 20 per cent Russians.[58]

For the survivors from Latvia, there was little relief. As Josef Katz wrote: 'The whole camp has Polish leaders for the inmates. These Poles are bastards. They are extremely anti-Semitic; most of them are hardened criminals serving time for serious crimes. They suddenly realise that there are human beings living among them, namely, the Jews. We are considered fair game. Anybody here can beat or torture a Jew with impunity.'[59]

Finally, with the addition of a gas chamber and crematorium, Stutthof became an extermination camp.[60] From the summer of 1944, when the Commandant SS Obersturmbannführer Paul-Werner Hoppe was ordered to apply the 'final solution' to all his Jewish prisoners, the death rate rose to such an extent that the crematorium could not deal with the dead.[61]

Gertrude Schneider recalled: 'Although the gas chamber was a small one, as gas chambers go, it could nevertheless "dispatch" between fifty and sixty Jews every thirty minutes. Since it did work around the clock, with the victims standing right beside it awaiting their end, there were just too many bodies to be burned, even with the new crematorium. To remedy this untenable situation, prisoners dug several large ditches right next to the Jewish camp, and these ditches were used for burning the overflow of corpses. The stench of this on-going operation was evident long before the camp came into view.'[62]

Every night, 1,000 bodies were stacked and incinerated on the bonfires. Josef Katz watched as one consignment was fed into the gas chamber: 'Around eleven o'clock in the morning, some strange vehicles pass through the camp on the road to the crematorium. The four-wheeled carts are crammed with women who are barely alive. They are pulled by several of their campmates; other women, wrapped in shawls, follow on foot. Two female SS guards drive them on with long whips. It is said that these women will be gassed and then cremated.'[63]

The gas chamber had initially been disguised as a disinfection room. When its real function became widely known, those being forced toward its doors began to resist. The SS then deployed an elaborate and cynical deception. A freight car was modified to make it air-tight and positioned alongside another and, sometimes, a locomotive. An SS man disguised as a railway official ushered groups of unsuspecting Jews into the first wagon, which was then sealed. Another SS man emptied a Zyklon B canister down a chute.

Even with this rate of slaughter, such was the overcrowding and the lack of the capacity of the gas chamber and crematorium that many new arrivals were transported further, to concentration camps in Germany, or to death camps in Poland and Czechoslovakia. On 13 August, just a few days after they had arrived at Stutthof, most of the men from Riga were dispatched to Buchenwald, Mühldorf or Kaufering.

It is estimated that 100,000 prisoners, non-Jews as well as Jews, passed through Stutthof and that 60,000 died there from exhaustion, starvation, disease – typhus, diphtheria and dysentery in particular were rampant – or by murder, whether by lethal injection, in the gas chamber, by bullet, or even savaged by specially trained German Shepherds.

Reska Weiss describes the heart-breaking reunion she witnessed in one of Stutthof's satellite camps when the woman standing next to her at roll-call suddenly spotted her daughter in the adjoining section of the camp:

When the assembly had finished and the guards had disappeared, Irma ran to the wire fence and called: 'Annie, Annie, my little daughter, my child,' and she ran forward with outstretched arms. On the other side of the fence the assembly was also over, and hearing Irma's cry a young girl over there called out: 'Annie dear your Mummy's here.' Mother and daughter rushed towards each other, but stopped stock-still in front of the wire fence, through which ran a high-tension current. Their hands touched, but they also touched the wire, and only for a brief second were they permitted to gaze into each other's eyes. Then both of them fell dead.[64]

The fact that Germany was by now losing the war on both fronts seemed in no way to diminish the delight the SS guards took in the cruelty they inflicted on their prisoners. Reska Weiss described one such torment:

In the mornings we saw a score of SS guards standing just behind twenty to thirty Jewish prisoners in striped clothing, looking from a distance like zebras. At first they had to stand rigidly to attention, then the SS guards shouted the command: 'Jump!' We could see the prisoners squatting on their heels, their hands behind them, between their legs, in order to grasp their ankles. Then they had to jump like frogs, while the guards guffawed: 'Jump, Jew, jump!'

After two or three jumps many lay exhausted on the ground. Some managed to perform six or seven times, and the guards ordered them to keep on jumping. The whip came down on their thin bodies and they were left lying on the ground.

The dead were later removed by their fellow prisoners. For many SS guards this was the daily entertainment.[65]

The sadism and cynicism knew no bounds. Later, when Reska had to clean the sick bay latrine, she asked a guard for soap. The following morning he threw a small bar at her feet and grinned as he told her, 'Here's your soap. Wash yourself with your mother.' It was stamped with the letters RJF. They stood for Reines Juden Fett, Pure Jewish Fat.[66]

* * *

It might be anticipated that, with defeat inevitable and imminent, the Nazis' bloodlust would dissipate. This was not the case. As the eastern front grew closer in January 1945, 50,000 mostly Jewish prisoners were evacuated from Stutthof. It is believed that 25,000d died in the three months between 25 January 1945 when these infamous death marches began and 9 May when the Red Army entered the camp.[67]

Around 5,000 were marched north to the Baltic, forced into the sea and machine-gunned. Others were sent out in columns of a 1,000 in deep snow and freezing temperatures and virtually without provisions along roads clogged by retreating German troops. Those who fell behind were shot. When they and their German guards were cut off by the advancing Soviets, they were forced back into Stutthof.

In testimony recorded in 1990, Rochelle Blackman Slivka recalled how, aged 23, she and her sister marched for six weeks through the Polish winter:

> We used to start out about six o'clock to walk, in the morning, six o'clock in the morning to walk, with a piece of bread and the black coffee and walk a whole day until we find a, uh, place at night where to stay. Either a barn somewhere, or a church … wherever they could find a place for us. Then they used to give us again a piece of bread and coffee and we used to go to sleep. We walked like that for six weeks. We weren't allowed to … to bend over to take some snow to wet our lips. Those who did bend over to take, they were shot by the guards. Those who helped each other to walk were shot. We weren't allowed to do that either. We walked like that for six weeks.[68]

By now, millions of Jews from all over Europe had been murdered. But the suffering of the survivors, so close to liberation, continued relentlessly. Josef Katz described the condition to which he and his comrades had been reduced as they lay in the infirmary at the Rieben labour camp in Eastern Pomerania (now northern Poland) during a pause in their death march: 'The men lying here are members of the human race only in outward appearance. They have lost all civilization or humanity.

Here everyone fights everybody else for a place near the stove, for a piece of potato peel, or for the last possessions of a comrade who has just died. The pockets of the dead man are quickly searched, the lunch bag is snatched from under his head and ransacked, and the blanket is torn from his body. It no longer matters how one lives so long as one survives.'[69]

Reska Weiss describes the 'two types' among her fellow prisoners:

There were those so bowed by humiliation, by loss of self-respect, by deprivation of former status, that they became completely lethargic and perished, bereft of all will to live; and there were others who overcame the first shock, the despair and the stupefaction, and accepted the state of affairs, apathetically it is true, but fighting with an animal passion for daily requirements, for a better place to lie, for a crust of bread …

Culture, breeding ancestry, played very little part in all this. They built a hard, protective crust around themselves and became immune to the sufferings of their fellow prisoners. Why worry about another's pain, when one was preoccupied with one's own?

… Camp life reduced us to imbecility. We lost all hope in a life that might ever be different. And in this soul-destroying process animal instincts gained the upper hand.[70]

But she is clear that without 'what had once been controlled or suppressed', few would live to see freedom: 'no one who has not been in a concentration camp dare pass judgment on others, for no one who has not experienced this agony knows what it means to "live" and to "survive"'.[71]

Elsewhere she writes that 'it is quite impossible to convey adequately what life was like under the conditions we endured. How can warm and well-fed people project themselves through empathy into the agonies of the starved and the frozen?'[72]

Lilly Pancis, who survived the ghetto, Kaiserwald, Stutthof and the death marches, recalled her moment of liberation. She spent the last few weeks of her captivity in a barn, which her German guards feared to enter because typhoid was raging inside: 'Then, on March 10, 1945, the barn doors opened wide and Russian soldiers came in. They clasped their hands, their faces showed disbelief, and they stood there like monuments. Women who were lying close to them kissed their boots and held onto their legs. They told us that we were free and that the Germans had disappeared. Of the 1,000 women, only 300 were left.'[73]

By the end of April, Stutthof was surrounded by Soviet troops with only an outlet to the sea. Some 5,000 prisoners were loaded onto ramshackle barges, making for concentration camps around Hamburg. Some sank; one, flying a yellow flag indicating that people with contagious diseases were aboard, was turned away at every port and, drifting for 11 days, was twice bombed by Allied aircraft before a third attack set it alight. According to one witness, only 33 of the 2,000 Jewish women on board survived.[74] A few, however, found themselves in small boats under the control of the Swedish Red Cross and were evacuated to Malmö.

More died in Soviet bombing raids on Stutthof itself. At the end of April 1945, the remaining inmates who were strong enough to walk were evacuated. The guards blew up the crematorium and set the buildings on fire. A group of women too weak to move were burned alive in them. When the Red Army liberated the camp, they found only 100 survivors.

The war, if not the suffering, was over. Just 52 of 1,008 Jews who had been deported from Nuremberg to Riga on 29 November 1941 had survived. Where was Sally?

None of the principal databases that record the known fate of the victims of the Holocaust can provide a place or time or a manner of death for Sally Brandes. The International Tracing Service at Bad Arolsen reproduces only the card index, which notes that 'Brandes, Sally, prisoner number 21463', was released from Dachau on 10 December 1938. The Memorial Book of the German Bundesarchiv confirms that he was deported to Riga on 29 November 1941 and, under the heading 'destiny', simply that he was 'officially declared dead'. The Shoah Names Database at Yad Vashem states the same. The UN's Central Tracing Bureau, predecessor to the ITS, closed its file on Sally Brandes on 22 July 1946 with the speculation, '"repatriation"? probably extermination'.

Those who were with Sally in Riga and survived to bear witness provide clues about his fate but no certainty. Friedel Reinauer tells how she and Hanneliese met him in the Riga ghetto some time after they came there in July 1942. But when they were transferred to Kaiserwald in August 1943, she writes, 'I heard no more of Brandes'.

Günther Kosterlitz confirms that he and Sally were transferred from Salaspils to the Riga ghetto in August 1942 and that Sally 'was healthy and was on a forced labour squad on the Latvian railway until August 1943'. Then 'he was moved to the Kaiserwald concentration camp and we weren't able to speak any more'.

From Günther Kosterlitz's testimony, it's likely that Sally was working on the Reichsbahn commando for much of the year he spent in the ghetto. But what happened to him after he entered Kaiserwald?

It was perhaps a long shot but, before I travelled to Riga, I contacted the Latvian State Archive to ask whether it held any information about my grandfather. Two days later, Rita Bogdanova emailed to tell me that she had found a single document from September 1943, a list of peat bog workers. Sally Brandes' name was on it.[75]

He was still alive at least one month after the last sighting of which my father had been aware!

Sally's assignment to the peat bogs was perhaps inevitable. The previous year, largely because of labour shortages, capacity at Latvia's 17 peat-cutting fields had plummeted to an unsustainable average of 37 per cent. On 14 April 1943, Rudolph Lange wrote to remind the Wehrmacht Territorial Commander Ostland that peat production was essential to the war effort: 'Over the next few days, the county commissar – labour administration – in Riga in cooperation with the Regional Commander of the Security Police and SD will extract the Jewish workers suitable for peat work from the contingents made available to you up to now and deploy them for peat work until autumn 1943 ... Objections cannot be taken into consideration.'[76]

Some 1,300 Jews were deployed to the peat bogs.

Three weeks later, I was sitting at a desk in the reading room of the Archive on Slokas Iela, before me the document Rita Bogdanova had found. In a memorandum of 15 September 1943, the director of the peat factory at Priedaine, G. Paeglis, informed Kūdra-Torfindustrie, the German-run trust that oversaw the Latvian peat industry, that as of 6 September it had employed a Jewish labour force, which had been transferred from a factory in Smārde.[77] It listed thirty men and twenty women. 'Brandess, Sally' (*sic*) was one of them.

Searching through the fat file for 1943, I found two more documents, hand-written on squared paper, probably copies of typed originals. In the first, undated but doubtless issued in early October, Paeglis confirmed that the Jews who were at Predaine on 6 September had been joined on 2 October by an additional 18 men and 12 women. In the other, dated 28 October, he informed the Commandant of the Riga ghetto that 48 men, including 'Brandess Sally', and 31 women, no doubt at the close of the peat-cutting season, had been returned to his care.[78]

I felt an eerie exhilaration at seeing Sally's name on those lists, knowing that his existence had caused someone to inscribe it, discovering that he had been alive at least two months longer than we had known.

But it was fleeting. I knew that the work in the soaking, freezing peat bogs was among the hardest and cruellest the starved, exhausted Jews had had to endure. I knew too that Sally was now two months closer to the end.

Günther Kosterlitz had written that, after Sally had been transferred to Kaiserwald, they had lost touch: 'where Sally went then is difficult to say, possibly to Stutthof concentration camp'. I had harboured the hope that he had survived at least that long. But what kind of hope was this, and for whom? The transport to the camp was an unspeakable horror; life, and death, in the camp were worse.

Alice Meyer had reported in her letter that 'Schoenthal, Fein, Sacki, Hahn, Brandes I remember so well, lay buried in the forrest (*sic*) of Riga'. Was she referring to the wives, or the husbands, or both?

There is little prospect of finding further evidence. The Germans destroyed most of their records as they fled Latvia. The State Archives in Riga hold very little information about the German Jews who lived and died there.

There is no record of Sally in the Stutthof archives. It is possible that he died, as many did, during the terrible journey there. He could have been one of the 10,000–20,000 who, unregistered, were executed on arrival. But I doubt that he made it that far.

He would have been returned from the peat bogs to the Riga ghetto just as it was being cleared for the last time. By now, he was 61 years old. To have survived so long, when from the moment he set foot in Latvia, the old, the sick, the weak, those in any way unfit for work, were routinely being selected for execution, is remarkable. After all he had endured, he must have been a man of extraordinary strength, in mind and in body.

Perhaps he was part of the squad that laboured until the next summer to remove the traces of the ghetto's existence. Perhaps he was on the transport that carried 2,000 of its last occupants to Auschwitz on 2 November 1943. There is no record of his having been there. But the large majority of the Jews from Riga were taken straight to the gas chambers. Neither their arrival nor their deaths were registered. Only three survived.

It's possible that he was transferred back to Kaiserwald and that, in early 1944, he was assigned to the Stützpunkt, in which case he would not have lived much longer – or wanted to.

Or, perhaps, crushed by hunger, and fatigue, he had at last fallen ill and been dispatched by a bullet or lethal injection.

At any time, he may have been loaded onto a truck or a bus and driven out into the beautiful, dark forest at Rumbula or Biķernieki. There he may still lie under the cool, indifferent pines. I left stones at all these places.

18

RAYS OF LIGHT

My father grew up a target for the vilest prejudice. His formative years were blighted by discrimination that denied him the opportunities that were his by right. He endured the unspeakable brutality of the concentration camp. He was parted from the friends he cherished. He was exiled from the city he loved. He had lost his inheritance and his prospects. His family and all else he held dear were annihilated. In his adopted country he was humiliated and imprisoned. Though, eventually and against all odds, he made a life for himself and his family there, he was never able to realise his rich potential. But, whatever the traumas, the grief and the disappointment he endured, he never complained.

How did he cope?

A brief, unpublished memoir written by my mother's cousin Paul Nickelsberg many years later as he recalled his first few months in the US perhaps provides a clue.[1] Like my father, Paul was a fundamentally decent man. Like my father, he was a man of reason.

With this beginning of a new life in a new land that would soon become 'our country', a heavy curtain came down over our past which no force, no time could raise again. I left them behind that curtain, good and bad; even my hatred I left behind.

Memories can be so heavy that it is impossible to bear them any longer, impossible to carry their burden into a new life.

There is no nostalgia for the refugee. It was like drinking a cup of Lethe's waters.[2] I did not hate all Germans nor the whole

271

18. Fred Bradley.

German nation. I just did not belong with them any more. The Nazis – they were not worth hating. I despised them.

Paul goes on to reflect on the first and the last of the visits he and Tilde made to Germany after the war. Though in 1956 the country was gradually emerging from its ruins, he was especially saddened by 'the invisible wreckage in the souls of people': 'I could meet them, talk with them, strangers as well as such I knew, without bitterness but I felt I was not of their kind any more. Meeting with old friends, however, was happiness; it was a great joy to see them again.'

Paul had clearly developed a defence against the pain of cruel memories, consciously perhaps though surely aided by the passage of time and the living of a new life. But his humanity is evident too: he does not dwell on the past and he does not hold 'the tired, dispirited' people he meets in 1956 responsible for the enormities of the past, still less the new generation he encounters in 1975 in 'a different, a better Germany'.

I believe my father shared both Paul's 'coping strategy' and his capacity – perhaps need – to forgive, at least to the extent that he could. He knew what lay behind him, but he did not want his own innocent childhood, nor even the thwarted promise of his youth, to be withheld from him altogether.

So, though he doubtless remembered all too painfully the evil done to his family and himself, my father chose to speak of the good.

He records in his history that even after Hitler had come to power, they had been spared the trauma of their friends turning against them. The Zunzes were not so fortunate. As the Nazis tightened their grip, even my uncle's godmother Frau Werner, after whom he had been named, ostracised them.

My uncle recalls that Jews were the target for vicious and almost routine anti-Semitism even before the time of the Nazis. The principal of his school, Dr Gaede, a convinced socialist, did his best to instil in his students a proper understanding of the horrors of war. But many of his teachers were army veterans with the kind of chauvinistic contempt for the fledgling German democracy that foreshadowed the rise of the

Nazis. He recalls too the words of one of his classmates, who told him, 'never mind that you don't observe the Jewish religion, you are a Jew all the same and we should really beat you up'.

Some of my father's cousins had similar experiences. Lutz recalled in a letter to him: 'Your letter about Rotenburg really brought back so many memories of a time when we were still together, thinking of a period when we always had our house full with our closest family, meaning our uncles and aunts and cousins. During the summer vacation time our house was never empty. Looking back we were always happy there. But this is a long time ago and I was a witness of our last remaining days there. I feel only hatred and a strong aversion towards people who used to be our friends.'[3]

My father's experience was different. Though from 1933 he was barred from several of the clubs and societies to which he had belonged – stamp collecting, swimming, kayaking – he had fond memories of his school and his treatment there. He wrote to the Principal in 1990: 'In stark contrast to the experience of students at other schools who, at the most impressionable time of life, were very much the victims of anti-Semitic animosity, I could count the number of anti-Semitic remarks directed at me during the two years of Nazi rule I attended the school on the fingers of one hand. The New Gymnasium was a bulwark against National Socialism.'[4]

When, as the last Jew to graduate, he was awarded his School Leaving Certificate in 1935, he was, to the shock of the audience gathered in the hall, the only student not to hoist the Nazi salute. He sensed a particular warmth in the Principal's handshake and that not all of those present disapproved of his defiance.

My father was anxious to acknowledge the risks several non-Jewish friends took to sustain their relationships with the Brandes family and made a point of recording some of the acts of loyalty and friendship that meant so much to his parents and himself.

In a brief memoir, *Lichtblicke in der Finsternis* ('Rays of Light in the Darkness'), he wrote: 'The horrors of the years 1933–45 cannot be forgotten. But nor can the steadfast friendship and the compassion that we also experienced in those years … As the Nazi terror took hold, many Germans either remained indifferent or went along with it. But others did what they could to keep their relationships with Jewish friends alive. They were spied upon and in the end had to submit to intolerable pressure. Many of these friendships silently survived the Nazis and were rekindled after the war – in many cases lasting a lifetime.'

In his note, he recalls instances of friendship, compassion and solidarity that stayed with him always.

Two months after Hitler came to power on 30 January 1933, the Nazis carried out the first act of organised, nationally coordinated discrimination against German Jews. On 1 April, Aryan citizens were encouraged to boycott Jewish-run businesses, including Sally's shop. It is hard to imagine how traumatic those events must have been for Sally, for Bertha, for Fritz – how isolated and intimated they must have felt.

On that day, my father's classmate Annemarie Schuebel approached him in the school yard and silently pressed his hand. That simple generous, courageous gesture meant everything to him. They remained friends for the rest of their lives.

Franz Merlet, a fellow Oddfellow, was Sally's best friend. The families regularly went walking together in the countryside around Bamberg. When it was no longer safe to do so, to avoid trouble they began to travel to their destination in different train carriages, then by different trains. One day they were pelted with stones by people they recognised and who plainly knew them. That was their last excursion together. Even then, Herr Merlet did not give up their friendship, visiting Sally surreptitiously late at night, until those visits too had to stop.

In some cases, even committed Nazis stood by their Jewish friends. Alfred Duethorn joined the Hitler Jugend. But because he refused to disown my father he was denied promotion. In the end, they could only go for walks together in the woods under cover of darkness. After the war, my father sent him food parcels.[5] Half a century later, in a letter to Herbert Loebl, he wrote, 'my school friends kept faith with me to the end, so I keep faith with them now'.[6]

Perhaps my father was too ready, too anxious, to seek out the rays of light. An encounter with Lorenz Zahneisen, the Nazi mayor of

Bamberg, made a deep impression on him. He repeated in multiple letters his account of what he took to be an act of kindness: 'The Brandes family lived for a time in a house at 16/II Herzog-Max Straße owned by the Council opposite the synagogue. At one point Mayor Zahneisen lived on the first floor. One day he summoned my father to his office. My father was very apprehensive about this appointment but Zahneisen warned him that within three months, all Jews living in Council accommodation would have their leases cancelled. "I'm telling you," he said, "so that you can avoid getting into difficulties." If news of this compassionate act had leaked out, it could have spelled the end of the mayor's career.'

My father was unduly generous. Zahneisen was a committed Nazi and a thorough-going anti-Semite. He was also a self-seeking opportunist who, when the Kahn family was evicted from their home on HainStraße, happily eased himself into their elegant villa. Above all, it was Zahneisen who coordinated and launched the terrifying attack on Bamberg's Jewish community on Kristallnacht. This was not a compassionate man.

When my father related his story to Herbert Loebl, Loebl admonished him, I think rightly: 'I would remind you that he was the editor of *Die Flamme*, the local Nazi rag since 1925, which was virulently anti-Semitic and helped to subvert the Bamberg public to such an extent that the majority voted for the Nazis ...'[7]

But, for my father, it was important to cling to the best, sometimes in the worst of people. Even in Buchenwald, he found glimmers of generosity, for example in the guards who, when they could, distributed extra rations. As he observed, the risks were high: an SS officer considered to have treated prisoners with too much respect was likely to find himself among them.

Right up to the end, some non-Jews in Bamberg strove to retain and express their humanity, though they knew the risks of being informed against were very serious. On his release from Buchenwald, my father recalls being silently embraced on Adolf Hitler Straße (now, once again, Lange Straße) by an old schoolteacher, Alexander Siebenlist. On another occasion, his father's schoolmate Dr Feser, the local vet, stopped in the street to shake his hand. Herr Suenkel, an official at A.E. Wassermann Bank, took care of priceless family documents and photo albums throughout the war.[8] Thanks to him, I am now their custodian.

My father was most insistent on this point. In a letter many years later he wrote: 'To restore the balance, there should now be a book written about acts of kindness shown towards German Jews, often at personal risk ... Why should I forget these instances while remembering all the atrocities? Every nation has its dregs of criminals, except that in Germany they came to power!'[9]

He then puts 'a question that is difficult to answer and I have not heard asked very often: if Hitler had persecuted only Gypsies, how many of us would have stuck our necks out to show kindness to them?' That question haunts me.

Paul Nickelsberg closes his note with memories of the mountains of the Black Forest and, in particular, of one he had climbed in the midsummer of 1932.

He had reached the summit in the late afternoon: 'the sun high in the blue sky, the whispers of the woods all around, the view to the horizon serene and beautiful'.

The nearest village was two hours' walk away. He could make the inn and its promise of food and comfort by nightfall. 'But why should I leave this enchanted spot so soon? ... I decided to spend the night on the mountain. I watched a wonderful sunset. Birds sang their evening tunes. The voices of the night were mysterious and entrancing.'

A tourist trip in 1975 to the Belchen, one of the highest peaks in the Black Forest, had triggered this remembrance. Standing on the summit, more than forty years since he had last climbed it a few months before the Nazis swept to power, he was struck by the same powerful beauty: 'As I stood on top of the Belchen, I got lost in dear memories of long ago. There may have been a different Germany and a different generation and I may no longer belong with them. All this may be so. But the mountains are still the same.'

For my father and, I believe, for Paul, there was something greater than history, to which they had a right and in which they had a share.

For Paul, in that instance, it was the Belchen. For my father it was Bamberg. For both, it was the sense of a common humanity in which, despite everything they had endured, they continued to place their faith.

AFTERWORDS

'I don't think any thought process is possible without personal experience. That is, every thought is an afterthought, a reflection on some matter or event.'[1]

Hannah Arendt

I dare to think that what I have learned, others should know. Because what happened to my family is more than a private affair. Because I opened my father's trunk and now concealing what I found would be a betrayal not only of my grandparents and the sacrifices they made – or became – but also of those that others are being forced to make now, and still others will make unless we prevent them.

I flew home from Riga on 10 May 2019: the day in 1933 on which Heine's books were burned; the day on which my father had escaped Nazi Germany in 1939; the day in 1940 on which he was arrested and interned by the British; the day on which he died, a British citizen, in 2004.

I had seen what I had needed to see. I had discovered as much of the 'what?' and 'where?' of my family history as I was ever likely to learn. But the why? I felt that I had not yet completed my journey.

A fair portion of what I have written is taken up by my attempt to understand the origins and endurance of popular prejudice against Jewish people. But how, in living memory, could it become so overwhelmingly powerful a force as to induce so many to put aside so much of what made them human – the ability to reason, to conceive moral systems, to frame just laws – and set about the destruction of their neighbours? What kind of men and women were they? What kind of circumstances triggered so extreme a reaction in them? Are they replicable? How do we recognise them? How do we protect each other against them?

I

THE SHAMEFUL SECRET

Should we be astonished that within a few months of the end of the war, and as the ghastly evidence of the death camps was filling cinema newsreels, my parents were writing to each other about popular anti-Jewish protests in industrial Birmingham and well-heeled Hampstead?

And seventy-five years on, with everything we now know about the Holocaust, should we be shocked that so many on the political right and the political left, so many Christians and Muslims, so many apolitical agnostics still appear to regard Jews with distaste or distrust or, often enough, with ill will?

Dismayed no doubt, but perhaps not surprised. The Holocaust suppressed anti-Semitism but it did not destroy it. It has been too necessary for too many for too long – and so it remains.

Anti-Semitism may be neither as pervasive nor as poisonous in Britain as it has been elsewhere but, though we may not care to admit it, it runs deep in our culture. As I have sought to illustrate, superstitions about and hostility to Jews have been embedded in almost all the great religious and political movements that have shaped our thought and values. Each generation has inherited a predisposition that is too rarely examined. But anti-Semitism is there – sometimes greater, sometimes smaller but never entirely absent – in our literature, in our religion, in our politics.

A century after England had expelled its Jews, the character of the Christ-killing 'false Jews' in Langland's *Piers Plowman* and the story of ritual murder in Chaucer's 'Prioress's Tale', set in a far-off city for lack of 'cursed Jewes' closer to home, would have been readily understood by their audiences. When Marlowe wrote *The Jew of Malta* and Shakespeare *The Merchant of Venice* at the end of the sixteenth century, Jews had been banished for three centuries. On which Jews of their acquaintance, or rather on what long-established travesty, did these great playwrights base their vengeful, iconic money-lenders?

Shakespeare was too great an artist to allow his work to serve simply as cruel caricature and there is ambivalence in his portrayal of Shylock. Nor does he shrink from exposing the moral weaknesses of his principal Christian characters. Nevertheless, in the end, the Christians all prosper and the Jew alone is humiliated and defeated; his life is preserved only through Christian charity and, of course, on condition that he ceases to be a Jew.

So, while this hugely influential drama raises ethical questions on all sides, it scarcely disputes that the Christian's dominion over the Jew remains the natural relationship between them. Judaism has nothing to offer Christianity, other than its surrender. The Jew is to be treated, if not with contempt, then with condescension, as his Christian betters dispose.

Two centuries later, 'Shylock!' was the taunt Benjamin Disraeli had to endure, though nominally an Anglican from the age of 13, right from his first election campaign to the end of his long political career. It is often claimed, with some satisfaction, that Britain elected a Jewish prime minister long before Jews were enfranchised elsewhere. But it was only his father's foresight in having his son baptised – so that, as Hannah Arendt put it, he could enjoy 'the opportunities of ordinary mortals' – that allowed Disraeli to enter the House of Commons in 1837, the year in which Dickens' Fagin first impregnated the popular imagination.[1]

In truth, Disraeli, architect of modern Conservatism, upholder of the monarchy, the aristocracy and the Empire, was never entirely accepted in polite political circles. In 1859, when he was for the second time chancellor of the exchequer, the prime minister, Lord Derby, was happy to read aloud to party colleagues a letter from a fellow Tory about 'that nasty, oily, slimy Jew'.[2] Disraeli the Christian Conservative was still, so far as Christian Conservatives were concerned, a Jew, and an unwholesome one at that.

Indeed, so obdurate was Parliament's resistance that the first practising Jew, Lionel Rothschild, was only admitted to the Commons in 1858, eleven years after he had first been elected. A decade later, Queen Victoria vetoed Gladstone's proposal that Rothschild be ennobled because of the 'feeling of which she cannot divest herself, against making a person of the Jewish religion, a Peer'.[3] She relented, but only sixteen years later.

In the mid-twentieth century, George Orwell could still observe that, among the English upper classes, a Jew could never be regarded as an equal:

> ... thirty years ago it was accepted more or less as a law of nature that a Jew was a figure of fun and – though superior in intelligence – slightly deficient in 'character'. In theory a Jew suffered from no legal disabilities, but in effect he was debarred from certain professions. He would probably not have been accepted as an officer in the navy, for instance, nor in what is called a 'smart' regiment in the army. A Jewish boy at a public school almost invariably had a bad time ... Wealthy Jews tended to disguise themselves under aristocratic English or Scottish names, and to the average person it seemed quite natural that they should do this, just as it seems natural for a criminal to change his identity if possible.[4]

Sir Horace Rumbold, Britain's ambassador to Germany between 1928 and 1933, deplored the increasing violence of the anti-Semitism he witnessed on the streets of Berlin. But he evidently felt no embarrassment in observing that 'I am appalled by the number of Jews in this place. One cannot get away from them. I am thinking of having a ham-bone amulet made "to keep off the evil nose", but I am afraid that even that would not be a deterrent.'[5]

In similar terms, the writer and politician Harold Nicolson commented that 'although I loathe anti-Semitism, I do dislike Jews', the exemplification of a singular upper-class English capacity simultaneously to deprecate and indulge in vulgar prejudice.[6] Such cornerstones of the British establishment might not care to see Jews assaulted in public places; but nor would they wish to encounter them at embassy receptions or on country house weekends.

That languid anti-Semitism may go some way to explaining why, as Adolf Hitler pointedly observed, the British establishment remained for the most part unmoved by the Nazis' persecution of the Jews. Politicians and civil servants knew about the concentration camps from the mid-1930s onwards. They were certainly aware of what was happening in them when, two years into the war, the government called on the press to help dispel public complacency. A Ministry of Information memorandum of 25 July 1941 cautioned editors that, in reporting 'concentration camp torture stories', 'a certain amount of horror is needed but it must be used very sparingly and must deal always with the treatment of indisputably innocent people'. Then, for clarity's sake, the author added, 'and not with Jews'.[7]

Eighteen months later, by December 1942, the US, the Soviet Union and Britain knew that genocide was under way in the death camps.[8] But saving Jewish lives was never an Allied war aim. As late as 1944, when Auschwitz was within range of the bombers, destroying the gas ovens or disrupting the rail routes into the camp were not made a military priority.

Even just after the war, when the gruesome details of the death camps were in plain sight, sympathy for the survivors was often limited and conditional. According to Jean-Paul Sartre, as the French set aside their differences in a national celebration of the Allied victory, the fate of the 70,000 Jews who had been deported from France was considered an embarrassment: 'Now all France rejoices and fraternises in the streets; social conflict seems temporarily forgotten; the newspapers devote whole columns to stories of prisoners of war and deportees. Do we say anything about the Jews? Do we give a thought to those who died in the gas chambers at Lublin? Not a word … Well-meaning journalists will tell you "in the interest of the Jews themselves, it would not do to talk too much about them just now".'[9]

It wasn't just that France did not want to contemplate the Vichy government's complicity in the murder of French Jews. It also turned its back on the 2,500 who returned from the camps. Among them was Simone Veil, a survivor of Auschwitz and Belsen. In later life, she held high office in the French government and as President of the European Parliament. But, when she died in 2017, Andreas Whittam Smith recalled that she wrote of her return to France that, 'people looked straight past us as though we were invisible ... We felt around us a kind of general and nameless ostracism ... We were nothing but shameful victims, tattooed animals.'[10]

In February 2019, at the height of the populist 'gilets jaunes' demonstrations in France, postboxes in Paris displaying commemorative portraits of Simone Veil were defaced by swastikas.

Orwell observed that in Britain the war had actually generated an increase in anti-Semitism, even among 'humane and enlightened people'. 'In the eyes of many ordinary people', he wrote, '... the Jews are one people of whom it can be said with complete certainty that they will benefit by an Allied victory.'

Indeed, in early August 1947, against the background of persistent rumour-mongering about Jewish black marketeering, the murder by the Irgun of two British servicemen in Mandate Palestine sparked attacks on Jews and their property in several English towns and cities.[11] In Manchester, a 700-strong mob smashed the windows of Jewish-owned shops; synagogues were desecrated in Hendon and Plymouth.[12]

On 6 August, the *Morecambe & Heysham Visitor* warned in an editorial that 'Britain is in the grip of the Jews', denounced them as 'a plague' and threatened that 'violence may be the only way to bring them to the sense of their responsibility to the country in which they live'. The editor and author of the article, James Caunt, was prosecuted for seditious libel but, to the acclaim of the public gallery, unanimously acquitted after the jury had deliberated for just thirteen minutes.[13]

These prejudices were by no means limited to 'ordinary people'. Three years after the end of the war, Christopher Mayhew, then a junior Foreign Office minister, was so struck by the open anti-Semitism of his boss, the Foreign Secretary Ernest Bevin, that he recorded in his diary that 'there is no doubt, to my mind, that Ernest detests Jews'. He went on to list some of Bevin's choicest prejudices against the 'Chosen People', before observing that 'I allow him only one point – that in giving voice to his irrational and indefensible prejudices he is speaking for millions of British people.'[14]

Orwell noted that such anti-Jewish sentiments were rarely explicit. While the British claimed to be offended by the bad behaviour of Jews, for example in food queues, in reality 'these accusations merely rationalise some deep-rooted prejudice'. In an observation with particular resonance today, he suggested that 'to attempt to counter them with facts and statistics is useless, and may sometimes be worse than useless'.

Elsewhere in post-war Europe Jews were treated far worse. On 4 July 1946, little more than a year after the end of the war, a mob attacked Jews in the Polish city of Kielce. The pogrom had been sparked by the claims of a local man that his eight-year-old son had been abducted by Jews and held in a cellar in which he had seen the bodies of fifteen ritually murdered Christian children. The police raided a Jewish community building that had no basement but that was providing temporary refuge for some 150 Jews who had returned to their hometown from the camps.

In the violence that followed, forty-two Jews were bludgeoned, bayoneted or stoned to death and forty more were injured. An editorial in *The Jewish Chronicle* recorded with despairing resignation that 'the old wickedness still persists, waiting to be called into action by the same foul and hoary old fable – and Europe is still the old Europe ...'[15]

The pogrom led to a mass exodus of what remained of the Polish Jewish community though many had nowhere to go other than a Displaced Persons camp somewhere in Germany. There they, and others from all over Europe, were often forced to live in abject conditions, partly through lack of preparation and the sheer pressure of numbers, but also by design. The Allies had no wish to alienate the defeated Germans further by offering generous support to stateless Jews.

They also calculated that harsh conditions would encourage refugees to 'go home' rather than continue to drain the resources of the fledgling United Nations or, worse still, consider applying for visas. Indeed, in the first two post-war years, the US maintained its pre-war quota system and Britain continued to restrict entry to Palestine.

Naked prejudice also played its part. Though it seems unthinkable in the circumstances, General George Patton, US commander in southern Germany, where most of the DP camps were located, felt able to offer the opinion that 'the Jewish type of Displaced Person … [is] a sub-human species without any of the cultural or social refinements of our time'.[16]

German Jews returning from Latvia and elsewhere found that their 'Aryan' neighbours 'expressed more regret for their own fate than for the victims of the crimes committed in the faraway east'.[17] Shockingly, according to Angrick and Klein, almost 40 per cent of the 500 Jewish cemeteries in occupied West Germany were desecrated between 1945 and 1950. It appeared that 'the deep-seated anti-Semitism of broad parts of the population had merely been given a democratic whitewash'.[18]

Conditions in Soviet Russia were worse still. Under Joseph Stalin, the Soviets did their best to marginalise the suffering of the Jews and to cloak their own anti-Semitism in an ideological objection to Zionism – this despite their influential support for the creation of the state of Israel.

In 1948, in an official campaign against 'rootless cosmopolitans', Jewish academics were dismissed from the universities and Jewish writers and artists jailed or executed. Five years later, in 1953, Jewish doctors were accused of a conspiracy to assassinate Stalin. Even after his death, throughout the Cold War, Jews behind the Iron Curtain were cast as bourgeois capitalists and collaborators with the imperialists, in short, as enemies of the state; in retribution, their rights of emigration to Israel were suppressed.

How could it be that, in western as in eastern Europe, in the capitalist and communist worlds alike, the horror of the Holocaust had not administered a shock powerful enough to disable anti-Semitism in all its ugly, age-old guises?

Primo Levi suggests that even in the moment of his liberation from Auschwitz he could see in the eyes of the Red Army soldiers not only an enormous emotional difficulty in dealing with what they saw before them, but also, simply as human beings, an intuitive revulsion against their complicity in it: 'They did not greet us, nor did they smile; they seemed oppressed not only by compassion but by a confused restraint, which sealed their lips and bound their eyes to the funereal scene. It was that shame we knew so well ... that the just man experiences at another man's crime; the feeling of guilt that such a crime should exist, that it should have been introduced irrevocably into the world of things that exist, and that his will for good should have proved too weak or null, and should not have availed in defence.'[19] Was the suffering of the Jews too great to grasp? Is this what Sartre had observed and Simone Veil had experienced in France?

Was the feeling of complicity in what happened, or guilt in failing to prevent it, too hard to bear? And from those instinctive responses, is it possible that there grew a sneaking resentment that the Holocaust had conferred on the Jews an entitlement they would not otherwise have had, and on the Gentile world a debt it might have to discharge?

Is modern Britain an inherently anti-Semitic society? I don't believe so. But are British people free of a prejudice that has been a feature of their culture for 1,000 years? No, they are not. Anti-Semitism is like pornography. Most denounce it; few admit to indulging in it; but many, privately and once in a while, struggle to resist its unsettling allure. It is their shameful secret. Orwell's observation in 1945 holds true: 'This feeling that antisemitism is something sinful and disgraceful, something that a civilised person does not suffer from, is unfavourable to a scientific approach, and indeed many people will admit that they are frightened of probing too deeply into the subject. They are frightened, that is to say, of discovering not only that antisemitism is spreading, but that they themselves are infected by it.'

As his earlier writings reveal, Orwell was himself infected.[20] But he was also sufficiently self-aware to admit to and seek to overcome the symptoms. As he argued, 'the starting point for any investigation of antisemitism should not be "Why does this obviously irrational belief appeal to other people?" but "Why does antisemitism appeal to me?"'

The notion of 'infection' is important. In my view, there are today two principal kinds of political anti-Semite. As we have seen, there are those on the right who trace all the ills of the world to the door of the Jews. They are generally unashamed of their anti-Semitism.

But, as we have also seen, even the great apostles of the Enlightenment, for Eric Hobsbawm the 'most admirable of all human movements', were susceptible to anti-Semitism.[21] In our own time, those who consider themselves in the progressive vanguard are often among the last to ask Orwell's searching question. As he wrote of his contemporaries: 'What vitiates nearly all that is written about antisemitism is the assumption in the writer's mind that he himself is immune to it. "Since I know that antisemitism is irrational," he argues, "it follows that I do not share it." He thus fails to start his investigation in the one place where he could get hold of some reliable evidence – that is, in his own mind.'[22]

Indeed, there are many on the left who believe that their commitment to anti-racism inoculates them against anti-Semitism, and perhaps in many cases it does. Yet the beliefs some espouse, the causes they adopt and the rhetoric they use in promoting them raise legitimate doubts about a small but noisy minority.

There are those, for example, whose opposition to Zionism and Israel is so obsessive and so strident that it calls into question their attitude to Jews. That is not to suggest that any critique of Zionism or Israel or support for the Palestinians is somehow suspect. But, when the language and imagery of protest gives rise to the reasonable suspicion that 'Zionist' is being substituted for 'Jew' as an object of opprobrium, or when the lone Jewish state is held to standards applied in no other circumstances and to no other country, it is right to interrogate meanings and motives.

The left did not always have an ideological problem with Israel. For the first twenty years of its existence, it was celebrated as a beacon of socialism in action. That sympathy began to fray after the Six Day War of 1967 and unravel in 1973 when Israel decisively repulsed the attacks of her Arab neighbours.

Irrespective of what was at stake for Israelis, their military victory and, above all, occupation and subsequent settlement of further Palestinian land was unacceptable, particularly to the anti-imperialists of the Marxist left for whom Israel had become, as Anthony Julius has put it, 'the Jew among nations'. Israel had ceased to be a land of kibbutzim and blooming deserts and become instead a military power and, worse still in their view, a regional surrogate for the US. Or, in the words of Yvonne Ridley, a leader of the now-defunct Respect Party, 'that disgusting little watchdog of America that is festering in the Middle East'.[23]

As Dave Rich observed in his analysis of *The Left's Jewish Problem*: 'If Israel's creation was the result of a Western colonial plan, then Holocaust survivors were imperialist pawns rather than refugees and their migration to Palestine is neither a tragic accident of history nor an authentic Jewish yearning for national self-determination, but simply part of the West's ongoing colonial instinct to dominate the world.'[24]

Surrounded and hugely outnumbered by intractable enemies and abandoned by former friends, Israel has increasingly adopted a siege mentality, swung in its own politics from left to right, from optimism to grim self-reliance, from valiant defence to oppressive occupation. By degrees, the left's understanding has evaporated and its opposition intensified. So much so, that the fiercest anti-Zionists have no energy left to condemn the repressive Arab autocracies and the intolerant Islamic theocracies that are their enemy's enemies.

Though aggressive anti-Zionism has only recently re-emerged as an article of faith in some parts of the Labour Party, it is by no means a new phenomenon. In the mid-1980s, I wrote about the way in which the growing influence of left-wing factions was making the position of many Jewish members increasingly uncomfortable. I cited a leading politician who, in promoting his particularly strident brand of anti-Zionism, called into question the loyalty of Jewish party members, asserted that Jewish representative bodies were dominated by neo-fascists, identified Israel's leaders with the architects of the Final

Solution and claimed that the Jews had exploited the Holocaust in their campaign for a Jewish homeland.

I also drew attention to others in positions of authority in the party who were openly expressing more traditionally anti-Semitic sentiments. I cited one senior local politician who, in casting aspersions on the Jewish Home Secretary of the day, suggested that there were too many Jewish MPs in Parliament, on both the Conservative and Labour benches.

The common theme between these two positions, it seemed to me, was that Jews appeared no longer to know their place: some on the Labour right expressed outrage that Jews should occupy positions of authority over 'real' Britons; some on the left argued that while Palestinians deserved a homeland, Jews did not and, what's more, had cynically and ruthlessly conspired to get one and to keep it.

I could have written that article in 2020. Indeed, more than thirty years after it was published, with Labour – or at least, parts of it – once again at war with large sections of the Jewish community, I wrote a sequel in which I begged radical anti-Zionists to reflect on why they feel so much more strongly about Israel/Palestine than any other conflict in the world; why they question Israel's right to exist; why they equate the Jewish national liberation movement with racism and the Palestinian equivalent with freedom and justice; why they think it appropriate to compare Israelis to Nazis; why they hold British Jews accountable for the actions of the Israeli government; and why they believe that Jewish expressions of concern about anti-Semitism are fabricated and 'weaponised' in a conspiracy against themselves.[25]

The answers are hard to find. But it is difficult to overlook Sartre's observation that, 'if the anti-Semite is impervious to reason and to experience it is not because his conviction is strong, rather his conviction is strong because he has chosen first of all to be impervious'.

The number of overt anti-Semites on the left is small. But there are many among the more extreme anti-Zionists who are carriers of the infection. They may be 'accidental' anti-Semites, but, particularly through the amplifier of social media, they are spreading a contagion and causing real alarm and offence to Jews.

Every day on online platforms, often on the slightest pretext, users link, confuse or conflate Jews, Zionists and the state of Israel – some carelessly, others deliberately. A neutral mention of Jews or Judaism rarely escapes condemnation of injustices done to Palestinians; references to Zionism often induce comparisons to Nazism; comments about Israel routinely provoke allegations about its shadowy influence on global affairs. Almost invariably, the effect, by design or omission, is to signify that Jews are guilty by association.

So well established are the terms of these debates that this effect can be achieved even without direct reference to Jews, Zionists or Israel. Consider the message tweeted by Kerry-Anne Mendoza, editor of *The Canary*, when the International Day of Solidarity with the Palestinian People coincided with the UK's Jewish Labour Movement conference on 29 November 2020. Just a month after the Equalities and Human Rights Commission had found that the Labour Party had unlawfully discriminated against Jewish members, she observed: 'Imagine if during a day of international solidarity with the oppressed of Apartheid South Africa, the Labour leadership opted instead to spend the day with white supremacists. That's what Keir Starmer and Angela Rayner are doing today.'[26]

In just thirty-seven words, she had conflated Israel with apartheid South Africa, identified Jews with white supremacists and questioned the integrity and independence of the Labour leadership for associating with a Jewish socialist society affiliated to their party since 1920.

It is impossible to see into the souls of such polemicists and that is often their chief defence against the charge that their anti-Zionism too closely resembles something else. As they insist, their ideology is proof that they do not have a racist bone in their bodies.

But when those on the left point the finger at the apparently all-powerful Israeli lobby or the Jewish influence in banking, business and media, it is difficult not to hear echoes of more explicit right-wing rhetoric about Jewish conspiracies, Jewish supremacism and Jewish lies about the Holocaust. It's as if, for their very different political purposes, while the revisionists of the right seek to deny the facts of recent history, those of the left are intent on diminishing their significance.

In these circumstances, it is legitimate to ask, with Orwell, whether they might be inadvertently rationalising some deep-rooted prejudice, something they may be too frightened to examine for fear of what they might find.

In 2013, the then back-bench MP and now former Labour leader Jeremy Corbyn observed about a group of Jewish Zionists that 'having lived in this country for a very long time, probably all their lives, they don't understand English irony'.[27] Though precisely what he meant is contested, the implication was that these Jews were in some way 'other': that there was a distinction between being English and Jewish, a distinction that politicians of other parties and in other times had not infrequently made.

More prosaic, but revealing nonetheless, was the response of some of former Labour MP Luciana Berger's constituents when she resigned from the party in 2019 over what she described as the hard left's 'culture of bullying, closed mindedness and bigotry', including anti-Semitism.[28] The *Guardian* cited a Labour-voting pensioner's somewhat qualified sympathy: '"She didn't deserve to be treated that way," he said, adding as an unthinking afterthought, "even though she is Jewish."'[29]

Now as then, on the left as on the right, and sometimes in the centre, to some at least, the Jew remains the 'other' – and as a placard at an anti-Trump rally in London in 2019 proclaimed, 'They all work for Rothschild'.[30] Another, at an anti-Israel demonstration two years later, reached still further into the ancient iconography: casting the Palestinians in the image of Christ shouldering his cross to Calvary, the banner declaimed, 'Do not let them do the same thing today again.'[31]

In one important sense, ideological objections to Zionism provide its strongest justification. Marxists believe that the 'Jewish question' will be settled only when Jews are fully assimilated into an egalitarian, non-discriminating socialist society, and that the Jewish aspiration for self-determination is by definition reactionary. But this belief in the benign forces of history denies the Jewish experience of history itself. The ideologues of the left insist that Jews abandon Zionism as their principal defence against persecution and place their faith instead in the good intentions of the anti-Zionists. That betrays an extraordinarily unreflective arrogance.

As I have suggested, my fear is that these carriers of infection, without ever being conscious that they are its hosts, will spread a contagion. And never has it been easier to broadcast the corruption of ideas. The internet has made 'facts' more accessible than ever to a general public. But it has also helped to promote a huge volume of fantasies, delusions and downright lies. The truth is out there, but sometimes a great deal harder to find than the less complex, more appealing disinformation that obscures it.

There is nothing new about deception in politics. In the past, however, lies were routinely concealed; now they're brazen. In the past, untruths could be exposed by those we trusted; now cynical manipulators ensure that no one is to be believed and that the truth can be whatever we – or they – want it to be. What's worse, many consumers of this distorted reality don't care that they are being manipulated by opportunists. They are complicit: they want to be free of the encumbrance of reason to believe what they choose. Thus, those Sartre described as the 'inadequate', for whom anti-Semitism holds a particular appeal, can, by making an enemy of the 'other', feel that they have become at last 'an elite of the ordinary'.[32] This is the fertile soil in which conspiracy theories flourish.

It is no coincidence that the supporters of populist movements are significantly more likely than others to subscribe to such fantasies – whether they're about immigration, climate change, vaccines or aliens from other galaxies. Recent research suggests that as many as 60 per cent of Britons – and 71 per cent of Brexiteers – believe in at least one conspiracy about the way they are governed or the information they receive from public authorities and the media.[33] And, as we know only too well, it can be a short step from conspiracy theory to violent political action. As recently as 6 January 2021, followers of QAnon were in the vanguard of the storming of the US Capitol and the deeply disquieting assault on American democracy that has by no means receded since.[34]

And where there are conspiracy theories, there are generally anti-Semites. Perhaps the most poisonous myth of recent times, *The Protocols of the Elders of Zion* (the notorious forgery purporting to describe a Jewish plan for global domination) is still widely circulated, particularly on the internet.[35] Many of those who believe that the Jews are bent on world domination find the perfect Hebrew in George Soros, the billionaire financial speculator turned global philanthropist. His imagined power and allegedly malign purposes render him the supreme puppet-master for conspiracists from Russia to the Gulf and a useful bogeyman for populist politicians from the Hungarian prime minister to the former American President.

Another set of recent findings provides a timely warning. In November 2018, CNN published a survey of opinion about Jews in seven European countries.[36] Across the sample, roughly a third believe that Jews are too influential in political affairs, while 40 per cent of respondents in Poland and Hungary, a third of Austrians and a quarter of Germans and French said that Jews have too much influence in business and finance. One in five Austrians, Germans and French believe that they have too much influence in the media and one in four too much influence on wars and conflicts.

At the same time, 40 per cent of Austrians admitted to knowing 'just a little' about the Holocaust while 20 per cent of French 18- to 34-year-olds had never heard of it. A third believes that Jews in general and Israel in particular exploit it to promote their own interests.[37] What's more, while 40 per cent believe that anti-Semitic violence is on the increase, 28 per cent suggest that Israel and 18 per cent that Jews themselves are to blame for it, recalling Roald Dahl's remark that 'even a stinker like Hitler didn't just pick on them for no reason'.[38]

The familiar language, imagery and mythology still hang in the air. The Holocaust has inhibited but not eliminated anti-Semitism. That is why the anti-Semites of both right and left work so hard to disarm the lessons we have learned.

It would be a mistake to allow the Holocaust to define anti-Semitism; it was simply its most lethal expression. It has a much longer history; it has also, regrettably, a present and a future.

I am not suggesting that anti-Semitism is once more becoming an irresistible threat. But, in its various guises, it is seeping towards the centre from the political fringes. We would be foolish not to recognise the potential, in the convergence of ill-starred circumstances, for bad things to happen.

II

CHOICES

'*Wir sind kleine Leute*' ('We are little people'). That's what, in the early 1950s, 10 former and for the most part unrepentant Nazis told Milton Mayer, an American journalist who strove, by knowing them, to understand the ideology they had followed.[1]

Sartre would have recognised them all as 'mediocre men'. Nine of them had been born into mediocrity. The tenth made himself mediocre because to be anything else would have unsettled his conscience and threatened his status, his career and, perhaps, his security.

In the 1930s, Mayer had tried without success to interview Adolf Hitler. But after the war, he came to realise that the best guide to the heart of Nazism would be the little people who in their millions had made a reality of their leaders' delusions.

The Reich, Mayer concluded, had the structure of a pyramid. At the apex stood a tiny elite – Hitler, Goering, Goebbels, Himmler – and, immediately below them, a few hundred more decision-makers such as Reinhard Heydrich, the architect of the Final Solution.

They gave their orders to a few thousand indispensable technocrats, among them Adolf Eichmann, who engineered the Nazi machine. They in turn supervised several thousand more anonymous civil servants and compliant lawyers, teachers, journalists and others who lubricated the mechanism at every level and in every location.

Below them, Mayer estimated, were a million 'riffraff', the doers of the dirty work from the smashing of windows to the breaking of bones, from the burning of synagogues to the murder of Jews and Gypsies. At the base were the rest, the 68–69 million 'little' Germans who 'had only to go on as they were and keep out of trouble'.[2]

As Mayer understood, Nazism was not simply a tyranny of the few over the many. It was a mass movement: 'it was what most Germans wanted – or, under pressure of combined reality and illusion, came to want. They wanted it; they got it; and they liked it.'[3]

But how could 70 million people come to want a political programme that suppressed all dissent, imprisoned its political opponents, slaughtered the defenceless and precipitated a world war that ended in their country's destruction and division? How could they, individually and collectively, surrender their free will to the state without foreseeing, or perhaps even caring, where blind faith might lead?

Through the eyes of the 10 little men Mayer came to befriend in the small Hessian town of Marburg, he helps us see the Germany of the 1920s and 1930s, not as we are used to seeing it, from the outside and with hindsight, but from within and as it was lived – and not as a monstrous drama but in the humdrum ordinariness of everyday life.[4]

The 10 were for the most part veterans of the First World War, disillusioned and embittered by defeat, impoverished by unemployment and hyper-inflation and frightened by the threat of Bolshevism. For them, democratic politics had proved a sham and a failure: they were alienated by the factional infighting and the shabby compromises of the Weimar Republic and contemptuous of the corruption and excess of cosmopolitan elites. They saw themselves as the forgotten, the ignored, the left behind.

This is how Mayer, writing in the mid-1950s, described Nazism's populist appeal:

National Socialism was a revulsion by my friends against parliamentary politics, parliamentary debate, parliamentary government – against all the higgling and the haggling of the parties and the splinter parties, their coalitions, their confusions, and their conniving. It was the final fruit of the common man's repudiation of the 'the rascals'. Its motif was, 'Throw them all out' ... My friends wanted Germany purified. They wanted it purified of the politicians, of all the politicians. They wanted a representative leader in place of unrepresentative representatives. And Hitler, the pure man, the antipolitician, was the man, untainted by 'politics', which was only a cloak for corruption.[5]

The Nazi Party offered a simple explanation for Germany's degradation. It promised to deal decisively with those who had stabbed it in the back in war and were now betraying it again in peace. It promised to drain the swamp and make Germany and its people great again: 'Deutschland über Alles' ('Germany First!').

And, so far as the 10 little men and millions like them were concerned, the party fulfilled its promises. Almost all of them told Mayer in the 1950s that life had never been – and probably never would be – as good as it had been in the 1930s. They had jobs and job security; they had order; the Nazi Party guaranteed their welfare and provided excellent public services; national pride had been restored. All the state required in return was unquestioning loyalty. For the vast majority, that was not too much to ask. As one of the little men told Mayer, things started to go wrong not with the persecution of the Jews, but with the outbreak of war, for it was the war that brought about the defeat of Germany and the end of Nazism.

The millions of Germans living through Nazism day by day could not see how one small step would lead to another or where the path might ultimately take them. Besides, they had no yardstick against which to measure the health or normality of their society. They had little contact beyond their own social circles and less still with the outside world. Under the Nazis, there was no debate, no independent press and no access to foreign media; there was instead relentless propaganda on behalf of the state and against its enemies. There was almost no way for ordinary Germans to see Nazism as non-Nazis saw it; unless they fell foul of the Gestapo, they just felt their own lives gradually but steadily improving. This was totalitarianism by popular consent.

As the historian Florian Huber has observed, even though the Nazi leadership had been explicit about its intentions from the outset: 'the desire for security and stability was so great that the Germans preferred to turn a blind eye to certain aspects of this new reality, as long as they weren't personally affected. They didn't probe too deeply. They didn't stop to ask what the changes meant, what was going to happen next. Life went on.'[6]

It was this incrementalism and the detachment it fostered – in Hannah Arendt's famous phrase, this 'banality of evil' – that made Nazism's progress towards its ultimate goals so difficult to apprehend and so much harder to oppose. There were some who did plainly see the road they had taken; the German Lutheran pastor Martin Niemöller was famously one of them.[7] But Mayer's philologist friend, an academic who regarded himself as a 'big man', was more typical:

> To live in this process is absolutely not to be able to notice it – please try to believe me – unless one has a much greater degree of political awareness, acuity, than most of us had ever had occasion to develop. Each step was so small, so inconsequential, so well explained or, on occasion, 'regretted,' that, unless one were detached from the whole process from the beginning, unless one understood what the whole thing was in principle, what all these 'little measures' that no 'patriotic German' could resent must some day lead to, one no more saw it developing from day to day than a farmer in his field sees the corn growing. One day it is over his head.[8]

This rationalisation cannot be easily dismissed: is it not an account of how most of us lead our lives, finding greater comfort in conformity than in questioning, too absorbed in the everyday to worry about what does not harm us? Paul Nickelsberg's faithful, anti-Nazi Aryan friend 'closed his eyes to the disgraceful things which were happening to Jews all over the country. These things seemed very, very remote … He refused to believe that such things might happen to his close friend.'

All the same, the philologist's narrative is pitifully self-serving. We know with what diligent care the good farmer tends his crop, calibrates its growth and carefully uproots the weeds that threaten it. It is impossible to imagine that the corn could grow over his head unnoticed.

In truth, the philologist, his university colleagues and his middle-class friends, in common with the millions of little men, chose not to know what was happening in their names. The one of the 10 in Marburg who had chosen mediocrity, a school teacher, did so, like so many others, because, had he allowed his better self to prevail, he could not have taken advantage of what Nazism offered him: professional advancement, social security, standing in the community, a uniform – and an age-old enemy to hate and a national destiny to fulfil.

Besides, according to the 10 little men, they were too removed from power to know about the Nazis' excesses and then their atrocities. They dismissed the rumours they heard as enemy propaganda. The bigger men chose not to know – and if they did not know, what could they do?

Yet, at the beginning especially, had sufficient numbers of Germans actually read the copy of *Mein Kampf* they ostentatiously displayed on their sideboards, had they listened attentively to the Führer's speeches and to Goebbels' radio broadcasts, had they more than glanced at the copy of *Der Stürmer* they bought each week, they would have known where Nazism was taking them and they could have stopped it, or at least tried before it was too late.

But they had not wanted to know where they were going and, even after the war, many refused to acknowledge where they had been. When Julius Posener, who had fled Berlin in 1933, returned with the British army to work on the rebuilding of democratic institutions in western Germany, he was shocked by the apparent lack of remorse and the self-pity he encountered. He concluded that 'a lot of Germans knew something. They'd hear something, from some cousin or other, and suddenly a curtain would be drawn back before them – but because they didn't really believe it, the curtain would fall shut again. Who, after all, would probe into a truth as awful as that?'[9]

Others had seen the truth with their own eyes but, by a deliberate effort of will, prevented it from troubling their consciences or obstructing the fulfilment of Germany's, and their own, destiny. Melita Maschmann, a Hitler Youth leader whose commitment to Nazism survived long after the war, wrote years later of her instinctive but momentary revulsion at the destruction wrought by Kristallnacht on the streets of Berlin: 'For a second, I felt clearly that something awful had happened. Something frightfully brutal. But almost in the same instant I abandoned my misgivings and switched to accepting what had happened as a fait accompli.' She goes on to describe how she developed this knack of 'switching off quickly' for 'I knew that any serious doubts would have swept away the foundations of my life.'[10]

As Primo Levi observed:

> ... most Germans didn't know because they didn't want to know. Because, indeed, they wanted not to know. It is certainly true that State terrorism is a very strong weapon, very difficult to resist. But it is also true that the German people, as a whole, did not even try to resist. In Hitler's Germany a particular code was widespread: those who knew did not talk; those who did not know did not ask questions; those who did ask questions received no answers. In this way the typical German citizen won and defended his ignorance, which seemed to him sufficient justification of his adherence to Nazism. Shutting his mouth, his eyes and ears, he built for himself the illusion of not knowing, hence not being an accomplice to the things taking place in front of his very door.[11]

And of course, the Nazis were eager to consolidate this 'illusion of not knowing'. As early as 1933, the Bavarian Culture Minister Hans Schemm advised a meeting of professors that 'from now on it is not up to you to decide whether something is true, but whether it is in the interests of the National Socialist Revolution'.[12]

This is how the philologist and the teacher silenced their consciences. They disabled the capacity for moral judgement that would normally govern their choices and disarmed the faculty for reason that they applied to their studies. In their place, they substituted the primacy of the state and their obedience to it: if the Führer decreed that abnormal, even abhorrent, measures were necessary, who were they to object? The absolute conviction that it was a citizen's duty to observe the law absolved him first of responsibility and then of guilt. In time, it also supplied the alibi for those who argued that the precedence of military discipline over moral scruple provided the legal authority to kill the innocent in the service of the state.

As Mayer put it: 'It was this, I think – they had their own troubles – that in the end explained my friends' failure to "do something" or even to know something. A man can carry only so much responsibility. If he tries to carry more, he collapses; so, to save himself from collapse, he rejects the responsibility that exceeds his capacity ... They were unaccustomed to assume public responsibility.'[13]

Yet inevitably, by what they did not do as well as by what they did, the little people have to accept their share of responsibility. The historian Peter Hayes suggests that the Nazis came only gradually to the realisation that they could and should annihilate the Jews. Between their rise to power in 1933 and the annexation of Austria in 1938, he argues, 'the so-called Third Reich learned what it could do, namely persecute the German Jews without encountering serious resistance from Germany's other inhabitants or from other countries'.[14]

Certainly there was opposition, but acts of public defiance were isolated and without sustained impact and, as the historian Detlev Peukert observed, 'the divided labour movement [could not] even come close to agreeing to set aside its philosophical and tactical differences for the sake of a common defence against the fascist threat'.[15] Whatever disabilities and risks the left faced, this is a damning indictment.

The excuse – that the state had emasculated the citizen, that national destiny had obliterated individual free will, that everyone was taking orders from the man who, in the end, escaped his responsibility by suicide in a Berlin bunker – cannot hold. Moreover, little people were complicit by their little actions as well as by their little omissions. Writing about the trial of Adolf Eichmann, the ultimate amoral instrument, Hannah Arendt justly convicted them: 'In its judgment the court naturally conceded that such a crime could be committed only by a giant bureaucracy using the resources of government. But insofar as it remains a crime – and that is of course the premise for a trial – all the cogs in the machinery, no matter how insignificant, are in court forthwith transformed back into perpetrators, that is to say, into human beings.'[16]

She goes on to argue that, if it were otherwise, a common felon could simply point to crime statistics and claim that he had no choice but to commit his offence 'since after all somebody had to do it'. To a dismaying extent, such arguments were too often accepted in West German war crimes trials. The prosecution had to prove 'premeditation'; the defence often successfully argued 'necessity' – that is, that an individual who committed murder had done so under orders. In the case of Arno Besekow, the leader of a detachment of Einsatzkommando 2 that had been involved in the mass killings at Biķernieki, a court in Hamburg found in 1975 that, though he had committed crimes, his personal guilt had been minimal. It judged that he had found it difficult to 'distinguish between right and wrong according to today's standards' and that 'the state itself was in this case the lawbreaker'.[17]

Arendt was vehemently but unjustly condemned by those who read her accounts of the Eichmann trial as the defence of a mass murderer. As she observed, 'the sad truth is that most evil is done by people who never make up their minds to be good or evil'.[18] The shabby bureaucrat she saw in the dock was incapable of moral judgement: he did not have the capacity to differentiate good from evil. He was a man with a function but without stature. He simply did what was expected: he accepted no moral responsibility and therefore felt no guilt. As he himself admitted, 'a life predicated on being obedient and taking orders is a very comfortable life indeed. Living in such a way reduces to a minimum one's own need to think.'[19] When asked by Benjamin Halevi, one of the three judges at his trial, whether in the performance of one's duty conscience should be abandoned, Eichmann responded, 'you could say that'.

But Eichmann's failure to take responsibility did not absolve him of his crimes. Rather it condemned him and millions of others who sacrificed reason to strong leadership and substituted law and bureaucracy for values and conscience. Without them, evil on any scale could not have been committed: it may have been the vision of the few, but it was the achievement of the many. We want to see Eichmann as demonically, almost heroically, evil, as someone exceptional. But he was not. As Arendt put it, 'the trouble with Eichmann was precisely that so many were like him, and that the many were neither perverted nor sadistic, that they were, and still are, terribly and terrifyingly normal'.[20] Eichmann was, after all, one of us. Ordinary people were murdered by ordinary people.

Mayer believed that the Germans were a particular people with a distinctive, destructive national culture that predisposed them to Nazism. But the insights he gained from his pioneering research convinced him that they were not unique. In certain circumstances, he feared, other societies, unless they were more vigilant and resistant, might succumb to the appeal of something similar. He returned from Germany to a democracy agonised by Senator McCarthy's purges of communists and homosexuals and to a land of liberty in which racial segregation was routinely enforceable by law:

> I came back home a little afraid for my country, afraid of what it might want, and get, and like, under combined pressure of reality and illusion. I felt – and feel – that it was not German Man that I had met, but Man. He might be here, under certain conditions. He might, under certain conditions, be I …
>
> … For there is no harm that anyone else can do to a man that he cannot do to himself, no good that he cannot do if he will. And what was said long ago is true: Nations are made not of oak and rock but of men, and, as the men are, so will the nations be.[21]

In this last sentiment lies the possibility of redemption.

*   *   *

In resisting the Nazis' attempts to implicate them in the Final Solution, Finland, Bulgaria and Denmark, in their different ways and to different extents, provide proof that nations, and the men and women who define them, can be free to decide what they will be and do.

As co-belligerents, as distinct from allies, Finland and Germany cooperated in the war against the Soviets. Extraordinarily, Jews in the Finnish army actually fought alongside the Wehrmacht. But when Himmler pressed the Helsinki government to deport its Jews, he was told that Finland had no Jewish question to answer. When it was discovered that eight Austrian Jewish refugees had been secretly handed over to the Gestapo by the police, the public outcry was intense. The only other Jews to perish during the war years died on the battlefield.[22]

Bulgaria did not have a spotless record. As an Axis ally since 1941, it enacted rafts of anti-Jewish legislation and handed over to the Germans 11,000 Jews captured in Thrace and Macedonia, territories it occupied after the Germans had overcome Greece and Yugoslavia. Almost all of them died in Treblinka.

Tsar Boris and his government initially acceded to German demands to deport the 50,000 Jews living in Bulgaria itself. But even as arrangements were in hand, public demonstrations and protests from opposition politicians, trade unionists, intellectuals and, influentially, the Bulgarian Orthodox Church led to a change of heart. According to legend, in Plovdiv, Bulgaria's second city, Bishop Metropolitan Kiril stood in the path of the train that was to carry the city's Jews to the death camps. Around 8,500 Jews who had been rounded up were released the same day and the transports were cancelled. Sofia's 20,000 Jews were exiled to the countryside and their property expropriated while the able-bodied men among them were interned in labour camps. But Bulgaria's Jewish community was not exterminated.

When so many Germans, French, Poles, Latvians and others were willingly giving up their Jews to the Nazis, what made the Bulgarians different?

First, as a German ally, Bulgaria was not occupied, and its government retained a degree of autonomy. But importantly too, for the 500 years that Bulgaria had been part of the Muslim Ottoman Empire,

Christians and Jews had shared a common cause and lived for the most part harmoniously. Anti-Semitism was not (is not) absent from Bulgarian society, but in the 1940s enough ordinary people and political and religious leaders had the principle and courage to defend Bulgarian Jews. They stopped the trains.

Denmark offers the only example of an outright rejection of the role a country under Nazi dominion was expected to play in the Final Solution. Though it was occupied by the Germans from 1940 until 1945, its Jewish community remained almost untouched by the Holocaust.

When it became known, in September 1943, that the Nazis were planning to deport Danish Jews to the camps, their fellow citizens responded spontaneously. First they hid them. Then, over a period of two months, some 300 vessels, sailing from twenty-six embarkation points on the island of Zealand, spirited them away across the Öresund to neutral Sweden. Among the fugitives were the 17-year-old Peter Zuntz and his mother Olga, who, after Kristallnacht, had married a Danish cousin and escaped to Copenhagen.[23]

Of Denmark's 7,500 Jews, only 464 were arrested and deported to Theresienstadt. Even then, the Danish government and the Danish Red Cross assiduously attended to their wellbeing, winning for them protection and privileges that no other prisoners enjoyed in the camp. Only 53 perished there, most of old age or illness. Around 7,000 Danish Jews survived the war in Sweden.

What made Denmark different?

It is important to acknowledge the external factors that made the protection of Denmark's Jews less of a challenge than it was elsewhere. It is also important to recognise that, on their own, they would have saved few lives.

First, the Germans treated Denmark differently to most of the countries they occupied. They sent in a relatively small contingent of military and civil administrators and left the country's institutions – its king, government and parliament – more or less intact. This was something of an experiment: the Germans wanted to demonstrate to the world that they could govern with a light touch as well as with an iron fist. Of greater strategic importance, they did not want to deploy to Denmark the military and other resources they so urgently needed on the Eastern front. They also believed, mistakenly, that the Danes would acknowledge an Aryan kinship and willingly acquiesce in the occupation.

Of greater importance still, the Reich was dependent on imports of Danish agricultural produce and keen to avoid civil unrest that might disrupt supplies. They therefore followed a highly pragmatic course. As Cecil von Renthe-Fink, Germany's ambassador to Denmark, reported shortly after the occupation began on 9 April 1940, 'if we were to go any further than strictly necessary (for instance in the matter of persecuting the Jews in Denmark) it would have a paralysing effect and cause disturbances'.[24] That remained the German approach at least until the breakdown of relations with the Danish government and King Christian X in August 1943.

Second, the protection and rescue of the Jewish community presented significantly less of a logistical challenge in Denmark than elsewhere. The community was small and concentrated on the capital. Sweden, which had explicitly confirmed that it would accept the refugees, was at its closest as little as seven miles away across a narrow body of water.

Third, the German occupiers appeared uncharacteristically reluctant to follow Berlin's instructions to deport Denmark's Jews. SS Obergruppenführer Werner Best, the Reichsbevollmächtigter (plenipotentiary) who had succeeded Renthe-Fink in November 1942, had served murderously in Poland and France, but seemed less than committed to his task in Denmark.[25] Whether or not he personally authorised or simply acquiesced in the initiative, it was a German diplomat, Georg Duckwitz, who first negotiated a safe haven for Denmark's Jews with the Swedish government and subsequently tipped off the Danish Social Democrats that they were about to be arrested.[26]

The Wehrmacht, under the command of General Hermann von Hannaken, carried out its orders at best half-heartedly. Remarkably, police and soldiers who were sent to arrest Jews often simply turned on their heels if the door they knocked on was not opened to them.

Meanwhile, the German naval commander sent his patrol boats for probably unnecessary servicing just a few days before they would have been needed to intercept the flotilla spiriting Danish Jews to safety.

But, crucially, none of this would have made a difference had Danish institutions, Danish politicians, journalists and intellectuals and, above all, the Danish people not determined to save their Jewish neighbours.

There were home-grown Nazis and collaborators in Denmark as elsewhere. There were those who sought to profit from Jewish misfortunes. It is true too that the Danish government had actively discouraged Jewish immigration throughout the 1930s. But Danish anti-Semitism was not deeply rooted. Perhaps uniquely in Europe, Danes did not discriminate between Christians, Jews and others: Danish citizens, brought up in the culture of a robust civil society and the ethos of a well-established welfare state, were Danish citizens; a threat to one was a threat to all.

The Danish government, though it pragmatically cooperated with the Nazi authorities, resisted pressure to discriminate against the Jews and clamped down on anti-Semitic propaganda. Jewish lives carried on almost as normal: Jewish schools remained open, the synagogues too. For three years the Danish policy of arms-length collaboration kept the Germans at bay: the Danish police kept order, the Danish courts administered justice, the Danish armed forces remained intact.

But as the war turned, popular resistance to the occupation grew. In August 1943, strikes and demonstrations broke out in a number of Danish towns; on 29 August, the Germans imposed martial law and the Danish government resigned. The Danish navy sailed some of its ships into Swedish ports and scuttled thirty-two others; the Germans interned Danish soldiers.

At the end of September, Best received orders to round up the Jews and two freighters were dispatched to Copenhagen to pick them up. But at the moment when Denmark's Jews were at greatest risk, Danish animosity against the Nazis was at its most intense.

When, on 28 September, Duckwitz warned the Social Democrat politician Hans Hedtoft that an operation against the Jews was imminent, word was immediately spread throughout the Jewish community.[27] A relay of messengers, many of them party members, went from house to house, warning Jews to pack and leave immediately. Some 2,000 were hidden in Copenhagen's hospitals, and 5,000 with non-Jewish friends and acquaintances. When the Germans came to arrest them on 1 October, they found only 280 still in their homes, mostly elderly people who had either not heard or not heeded the warning. Another 190 were captured trying to escape, 80 of them discovered hiding in a church in Gilleleje.

The resistance movement was at that time relatively fragmented, so much depended on the readiness of ordinary Danes to come to the aid of their countrymen. Herbert Pundik, then a Jewish teenager in Copenhagen, estimates that tens of thousands stepped forward to play their part. His own family was helped, over the four days it took them to reach the coast, by twenty people who sheltered, fed and transported them, found them a boat and sailed them over to Sweden. This was not the resistance of a secret underground but of a people in indignant revolt.

Looking back on his experiences, Pundik wrote:

The thousands and thousands who helped us reach safety behaved in a way that is hard to define in words. Solidarity, humane behavior, love of one's fellows. These are such big words that they lose credibility. They are so bombastic, and that was just what it was not. The rescue operation was anonymous; it went on quietly and unspectacularly. There were no generals or privates. People did what was needed ... People were torn out of their everyday existence, and after the job was done, most of them returned to wherever they had come from. They received no medals or parades. Most remained unsung heroes ... Many Jews did not know whom to thank for their lives when they returned from Sweden.[28]

And so I return to my father's question: 'if Hitler had persecuted only Gypsies, how many of us would have stuck our necks out to show kindness to them?'

Viktor Frankl, the Austrian neurologist and psychiatrist who survived Auschwitz, wrote just after his liberation that 'there are two races of men in this world, but only these two – the "race" of the decent man and the "race" of the indecent man'.[29] He believed that it is within our power to choose which we are to be: 'A human being is not one thing among others; things determine each other, but man is ultimately self-determining. What he becomes – within the limits of endowment and environment – he has made out of himself. In the concentration camps, for example, in this living laboratory and on this testing ground, we watched and witnessed some of our comrades behave like swine while others behaved like saints. Man has both potentialities within himself; which one is actualised depends on decisions but not on conditions.'[30]

Just as the Germans – or the large majority of them – chose to close their eyes at first to the petty injustices and eventually to the mass murder committed in their name, so the Danes chose to uphold the values of a common humanity and to act to protect their fellow citizens, even if that exposed them to grave risks. The saving of Denmark's Jews provides the proof that, as Pundik put it, 'people can accomplish something – even fighting against a superior power – if only they dare make a choice'.[31]

At Eichmann's trial, judge Halevi asked him, 'if there had been more civil courage, things could have been different?' Eichmann agreed, 'Yes, absolutely.' 'So this was not destiny. It was not inevitable. It was a question of human behaviour.' Yes, Eichmann conceded, 'a question of human behaviour'.

When populist politicians denounce the truth as 'fake news' and offer us 'alternative facts' that better suit our prejudices and their agendas; when we are encouraged to disregard the experts and overthrow the elites; when national newspapers denounce independent judges as 'enemies of the people';[32] when we are tempted to abandon reason for gut instinct and to abominate those with whom we disagree without

313

first engaging with them; when we are persuaded that there is no other cause greater or more pressing than our own and that our rights justifiably outweigh our responsibilities; when we are told that our national destiny is best pursued in isolation rather than in cooperation with others; when we refuse to play a part in resolving fatal conflicts and turn our backs on the refugees they create; when we are invited to reconsider whether democracy truly meets our needs – then, I suggest, we need urgently to take stock of where we are, how and why we arrived there and, above all, where we are heading. Then we need to reset our compass and take a different path, even if it is not the easier way.

III

THE LAST WORD

'When you throw a stone into a lake, first you have large ripples, then the ripples getter smaller and smaller still. Then the surface is calm. But the stone is still at the bottom.'

Ruth Frade Foster[1]

I did not set out to write this book, or any other. Indeed, I'm deeply conscious that I cannot add significantly to what's already been written by historians or survivors or witnesses with far greater authority than I.

So how did I come to write it?

I had started with the insistent need to know the answers to two apparently straightforward questions: what route did Sonderzug Da 32 take as it bore my grandparents into exile; and what, in the end, happened to my grandfather? Five years later, I have little certainty about the first and less about the second. To that extent, my project ended in failure.

But this search for simple historical fact led to so many more questions, and ultimately to two that were inescapable and irreducible. The first, about why my grandparents were made to make that journey, became clear and compelling early in the process. The second, about why I felt the need to follow it, formed gradually.

I am by no means the first to set out on this quest for knowledge and meaning. Others before me have felt the need to round off and smooth the jagged, interrupted lives of their lost ones. A quiet, irresistible resolve grew inside them, as in me, that these lost should be found; that they should not forever lie cold and unclaimed in unmarked graves; that they should again be something more than the anonymous victims of careless slaughter.

Philip Kuhn, a near contemporary, whose grandfather Philipp kept a kosher butcher's shop in Bamberg's Luitpoldstraße, and, with his wife Helene, accompanied Sally and Bertha into exile, has struggled with a similar, ill-defined but pressing need: 'a thing which has not been understood inevitably reappears; like an unlaid ghost, it cannot rest until the mystery has been solved and the spell broken'.[2] In his case: 'This project of a family history exists therefore not only as a piece of historical reclamation but also as an offering of funereal rites over my grandparents' un-marked graves … The writing of my grandparents' history becomes the Kaddish also told so that they might at last "enjoy" that "state of authenticity" of which they have been deprived for so long.'[3]

Yet I knew from the outset that I could not make any meaningful difference in this or any other world. I cannot say Kaddish. Without religious faith, I do not believe that I have brought peace to unhappy souls. I knew that there would be no reparation, no restoration, no resolution for those whose lives were unfinished.

Others have come to a similar realisation. Towards the end of his epic search for the six lost members of his family, Daniel Mendelsohn asks: 'For whose benefit, exactly, is the wholeness that I want so desperately? The dead need no stories: that is the fantasy of the living who unlike the dead feel guilt … It is we, the living, who need the details, the stories, because what the dead no longer care about, mere fragments, a picture that will never be whole, will drive the living mad.'[4]

Philip Kuhn reaches a similar understanding, for he recognises that 'I define my self (*sic*), therefore, not only as the author of this story but also as a character in its narrative.'[5] And that is what I have become. I am the ghost in my grandfather's shop, at my grandmother's table, on the street outside their apartment, beside their unknown graves. It is their benediction I seek.

* * *

My father loved his adopted country. He loved it for the sanctuary it afforded him, albeit belatedly and without great enthusiasm, and for the opportunity it gave him to build a new life, in peace and freedom. Not uncritically, for he was always on the side of the underdog, he loved its broadly generous values, its solid commitment to democratic principle, its calm reasonableness.

But he was never a nationalist. As he explained to me more than once, it cannot be proper to take pride in anything other than personal achievement. Men and women may congratulate themselves on the good fortune of being born in a free society, but they cannot – or should not – take pride, as do Sartre's mediocre men, in a simple accident of birth. Nor should they take their good fortune for granted.

I inherited my politics from him, though my enduring disregard for the establishment is infinitely greater than his. Even so, for most of my life, I have harboured the belief that the British are somehow 'special': that when other nations are excitable and unpredictable, we are steady and consistent; that when others are rash and intemperate, we are rational and deliberate; that when they are shallow in their democratic convictions, we are steadfast in ours. I consoled myself that, if our innate conservatism is an obstacle to progress, it is also a brake on backsliding.

But British society has changed and I am less confident in its strengths and virtues than once I was. In 2007, I wrote an essay that, in distilling the experience of my twenty years in frontline politics, sought to sound an alarm about the crisis to which I felt we were driving ourselves.[6]

I wrote that 'over the last three decades, each of the many steps we have taken towards personal self-sufficiency has led us further from the sense of community ... We are less deferential but also less trusting, less dependent but also less tolerant, more mobile but more insular, wealthier and healthier but not happier. We look like a successful society but we do not feel like one.'[7] I worried too about our diminishing capacity for common cause and our loss of faith in the political process. Though I was not without hope that we could choose a different path, I voiced a fear that today seems prescient. I worried that 'contemporary Britain may seem robust and resilient. But the outer show of material wellbeing masks deep-seated grievances and divisions. Prolonged economic turbulence or some other perhaps unexpected challenge to our current stability could expose an altogether more brittle society.'[8]

I had reached the conclusion that whatever might have been inherently 'special' about Britain had already diminished to the extent that it could no longer be relied upon to withstand the pressure of radical external change. This was a troubling realisation for one who wanted to believe that British society could be immune to the catastrophes to which other societies had succumbed.

But, over the last 10 years and more, it is a conviction that has been reinforced, not only by our accelerating decline since the financial dislocations of 2008 and the soul-numbing debate about our place in the world that has followed, but also by the conclusions I have reached in researching and writing this book.

For, in seeking to understand why my grandparents were forced to take that eastbound train in November 1941, I have formed the view that the differences between the British, the Germans and the Latvians are largely superficial and circumstantial.

The Holocaust did not happen because the Nazis wanted above all to extinguish the Jewish race. As I have sought to show, anti-Semitism may have been deeply embedded in German culture, but it was never sufficiently dominant to bring forth the Nazis and their ideology. They emerged from the calamitous circumstances in which Germany found itself after its defeat in the Great War, from which, it seemed, only Adolf Hitler's simple solutions could deliver it. Bloodlust did not bring the Nazis to government. It was unleashed only when they had secured and consolidated their absolute power.

Similarly, as Ilya Lenskis, director of the Jews in Latvia Museum, explained to me in Riga, even if there had been discrimination against the Jews under the Ulmanis dictatorship, there had been little violence: there would have been no Holocaust in Latvia without the Nazis. The fact was that Latvian society was unstable, the foundations of its democratic institutions shallow and the value it placed on human life insubstantial. In short, it was ill-equipped to resist either Nazi propaganda or the temptation to profit from collaboration. Latvian complicity in genocide was, in his view, driven more by opportunism than anti-Semitism.

What if Hitler had heeded his generals' advice against the invasion of Soviet Russia? What if the Nazis had focused their resources entirely on the western front? What if they had invaded Britain? To what extent and for how long would we have resisted their occupation? Longer than the Latvians? More thoroughly than the French? Would we have hidden and protected our Jews like the Danes? Or rounded them up and handed them over?[9]

The Holocaust could not have occurred without anti-Semitism. But it did not happen because of it. Anti-Semitism did not give birth to Nazism. It was the obsession of a few ideologues. But they knew how to conjure it from deep cultural recesses and how to normalise and harness it. In Germany and the territories it occupied, opportunities flowed for those who collaborated, especially for those who embraced the ideology; summary punishment followed for those who defied it.

I believe that an occupied Britain would have resolutely resisted Nazism. But I am not confident that its resistance would have endured indefinitely.

It's my conviction that men and women have an infinite capacity for good. But we know that they (we) also have a limitless capacity for evil. We are good enough to frame the laws we need to contain the worst excesses of our human nature. But we are bad enough to need them. Democracy, with its infinitely complex systems and processes and its finely balanced rights and responsibilities, represents the most sophisticated and effective means we have yet devised to regulate human behaviour within a free society.

But we have seen that enlightened cultural values and the rule of law cannot invariably withstand major economic or other extraordinary shocks. When a society's faith in democracy is insecure or undermined, as it was in Weimar Germany, when its political institutions are weak, as they were in Latvia, when unprincipled populists drown out the voice of reason, when systems of personal and public morality succumb to the instincts of the mob, anything becomes possible.

What happened to the members of my family was not an aberration and Jews are not the only victims of genocide. Prejudices contaminate many cultures and they are often lethal. But though we may not be able to eradicate them, we can, if we choose, control and contain them.

As Primo Levi wrote in the postscript to his iconic account of his experiences at Auschwitz: 'The camps were not an accident, an unforeseen historical happening … In every part of the world, wherever you begin by denying the fundamental liberties of mankind, and equality among people, you move towards the concentration camp system, and it is a road which it is difficult to halt.'[10]

It is difficult. But it should not be impossible. It is why we need strong democratic institutions, sustained and constantly reinvigorated, by citizens as well as politicians. That is why we need more, not less understanding and equality between the disparate sectors of our societies, and more, not less cooperation between nations. That is why we need to celebrate and practise our freedoms and rediscover our common ground. That is how we will restore our immunity to demagoguery, dictatorship and destruction.

That is why we need to remember not just the Holocaust, which destroyed six million European Jews, but also – though we swore we would never let it happen again – all the other genocides that have taken place since, in Cambodia, Rwanda, Bosnia, Darfur and elsewhere in Asia, in Africa, in the Americas, in Europe. This is not only a matter of Jews and Gentiles.

And so I return once more to my father's unavoidable question: 'if Hitler had persecuted only Gypsies, how many of us would have stuck our necks out to show kindness to them?' We cannot say, because we do not know.

That is why, while it is right to judge those who commit unspeakable crimes against their fellow human beings, it is important also to understand the circumstances in which they felt free to do so. We need to know not just what happened when the train reached Riga, but how it came to set out.

It is also one of the many reasons why we cannot hold subsequent generations responsible for the crimes of their grandparents. As raw as his experiences must have been immediately after the war, Levi wrote that he bore no hatred for the Germans, for 'I believe in reason and discussion as supreme instruments of progress, and therefore I repress hatred even within myself: I prefer justice'.[11]

It is why we need to understand what, in certain circumstances, we ourselves might be capable of doing. History is not simply determined by forces beyond our control. It is also shaped by the individual and collective decisions of men and women. It is our duty to recognise those certain circumstances, not as they recede but as they approach, and, by an act of will, take all necessary steps to avoid them.

For we are never at the end of human history – or at least not quite yet. When we speak of the past, we inevitably envisage what has gone before and has now ended, as if there were a moment when it stops and the present begins. But that moment is always now. It is the present that never really begins. We are always in the midst of history, our own and everyone else's.

The Holocaust and its legacy are a history we are still living. In the events of our own times, we are all perpetrators, or bystanders, or victims or resisters, or perhaps more than one at once. The question is: which of those roles do we choose for ourselves? This is a choice we have to make.

In writing this book, I wanted to pay some kind of homage to the ordinary lives my grandfather and my grandmother had lived before they were brought short by their extraordinary deaths. I wanted somehow to make those lives more significant, to reclaim for Sally and Bertha their individuality and the humanity that had been stolen from them. I wanted them, through me, to have the last word.

From beneath the indifferent pines of Latvia, my grandfather and my grandmother and all those buried with them cry out: choose reason, choose justice, choose humanity.

19. Bertha and Sally Brandes, lost in the east. My father took this photograph and kept it on his bedside table for the rest of his life.

IN MEMORIAM

What follows can only provide an approximate and incomplete list of those members of my grandparents' families who were lost in the east. In my best attempt at accuracy, I have cross-referenced the most authoritative databases, those of Yad Vashem in Israel, the Bundesarchiv and the Arolsen Archives, formerly the International Tracing Service, in Germany and the Holocaust Memorial Museum in the US. Sometimes they complement each other; sometimes there are gaps or a divergence of detail. Such has been the challenge, after the war and since, of accounting for six million dead.

And where to begin and end? All the Brandes, Herzstein and Loeb family members featured in the book, and who are known to have perished, are listed here. Sadly though, I could find no records for the family of Leo Brandes.

The Zunz/Zuntz family presents greater difficulties. Those mentioned in the book, and who perished, appear here. But I have also included others whose birth and/or residence in Frankfurt suggests kinship. Of course it does not guarantee it, any more than the birth or residence of a Zunz/Zuntz elsewhere denies it. In short, I know little about the lives of these people. But I do know that, whether or not they were relatives of mine, they died in the same places, in the same way and for the same reasons as those who were.

BRANDES

Sally Brandes
Born 4 January 1882, Rotenburg an der Fulda
Resident of Bamberg
Imprisoned 11 November 1938–10 December 1938, Dachau
 concentration camp
Deported from Nuremberg 29 November 1941 to Jungfernhof camp,
 then Salaspils camp, Riga ghetto and Kaiserwald camp, all in Latvia
Murdered: date and place unknown.

Bertha Brandes (wife of Sally)
née Herzstein
Born 21 January 1886, Bayreuth
Resident of Bamberg
Deported from Nuremberg, 29 November 1941 to Riga, Jungfernhof
Murdered: 26 March 1942, Dünamünde.

Meta Brandes (sister of Sally)
Born 23 January 1875, Rotenburg an der Fulda
Resident of Bamberg
Deported from Nuremberg 9 September 1942 to Theresienstadt
 ghetto, Czechoslovakia
Murdered: 13 May 1943, Theresienstadt.

Paula Brandes (sister of Sally and Meta)
Born 21 July 1876, Rotenburg an der Fulda
Resident of Meinerzhagen
Deported from Dortmund, 29 July 1942 to Theresienstadt, then 23
 September 1942 to Treblinka extermination camp, Poland
Murdered: date unknown, Treblinka.

Max Rosenthal (widower of Rosa née Brandes, Sally's sister)
Born 16 December 1881, Meinerzhagen
Imprisoned 11 November 1938, Lüdenscheid prison, then 22
    December 1938, Sachsenhausen concentration camp
Deported from Dortmund 30 April 1942 to Zamość ghetto, Poland,
    then to either Sobibor or Belzec, Poland
Murdered: date and place unknown.

Siegfried Strauß (brother-in-law of Sally's brother Max)
Born 18 July 1875, Burghaun
Resident of Krefeld
Deported from Düsseldorf 25 July 1942 to Theresienstadt
Murdered: 26 July 1942, Theresienstadt.

Else Strauß (wife of Siegfried)
née Baruch
Born 14 April 1889, Werden
Resident of Krefeld
Deported from Düsseldorf 25 July 1942 to Theresienstadt, then to
    Auschwitz
Murdered: 23 January 1943, Auschwitz.

**Margarete (Gretel) Goldschmidt (Sally's niece, daughter of his
brother Max)**
née Brandes
Born 12 September 1905, Rotenburg an der Fulda
Resident of Krefeld
Deported from Düsseldorf 11 December 1941 to Riga ghetto, then 1
    October 1944, Stutthof concentration camp, Poland
Murdered: date and place unknown.

Hans Goldschmidt (husband of Gretel)
Born 26 June 1901, Mülheim an der Ruhr
Resident of Krefeld
Deported from Düsseldorf 11 December 1941 to Riga ghetto, then
  Salaspils
Murdered: date unknown, 1942, Salaspils.

Margit Goldschmidt (daughter of Gretel and Hans)
Born 5 March 1931, Aachen
Resident of Krefeld
Deported from Düsseldorf 11 December 1941 to Riga ghetto, then 1
  October 1944, Stutthof
Murdered: date and place unknown.

Gertrud (Gerda) Levy (niece of Sally)
née Hecht
Born 20 June 1901, Rengsdorf
Resident of Trier and Linz am Rhein
Deported from Berlin 18 March 1943 to Theresienstadt, then 12
  October 1944 to Auschwitz extermination camp
Murdered: 12 October 1944, Auschwitz.

Selma Schwarzschild (sister of Johanna Brandes)
née Brandes
Born 16 December 1873, Peckelsheim
Resident of Frankfurt
Deported from Frankfurt 16 September 1942 to Theresienstadt
Murdered: 14 May 1943, Theresienstadt.

HERZSTEIN

Ernst Herzstein (brother of Bertha)

Born 9 April 1881, Bayreuth

Resident of Mannheim

Imprisoned 11 November 1938–20 December 1938, Dachau
concentration camp

Deported from Mannheim 22 October 1940 to Gurs, then Drancy
collecting detention camp and then, 14 August 1942, Auschwitz
extermination camp

Murdered: date unknown, Auschwitz.

Karl Herzstein (brother of Bertha)

Born 15 February 1876, Bayreuth

Resident of Bayreuth

Deported from Nuremberg 29 November 1941 to Riga, Jungfernhof

Murdered: 26 March 1942, Dünamünde.

Emma Herzstein (wife of Karl)

née Schimmel

Born 2 April 1884, Pappenheim

Resident of Bayreuth

Deported from Nuremberg 29 November 1941 to Riga, Jungfernhof

Murdered: 26 March 1942, Dünamünde.

Julius Herzstein (Bertha's brother)

Born 6 June 1891, Bayreuth

Resident of Bayreuth

Deported from Nuremberg 29 November 1941 to Riga, Jungfernhof

Murdered: 26 March 1942, Dünamünde.

Rosa (Rosel) Rosenthal (sister of Bertha)

née Herzstein

Born 11 March 1884, Bayreuth

Resident of Bayreuth

Deported from Nuremberg 29 November 1941 to Riga, Jungfernhof

Murdered: 26 March 1942, Dünamünde.

Hugo Rosenthal (husband of Rosel)

Born 27 February 1881, Mayen

Resident of Bayreuth

Deported from Nuremberg 29 November 1941 to Riga, Jungfernhof, then Salaspils

Murdered: 31 January 1942, Salaspils.

Jeanne Simon (daughter of Erna Simon née Rosenthal, Rosa and Hugo's granddaughter)

Born 22 November 1933, Brussels

Deported from Drancy Camp, France with Transport 61, 28 October 1943 to Auschwitz

Murdered: date unknown, Auschwitz.

ZUNZ

Wilhelm Albert Zunz

Born 20 October 1874, Frankfurt am Main

Resident of Frankfurt

Imprisoned 14–16 April 1943, Frankfurt police jail, then 20 April–4 May 1943, Frankfurt, then 4 May–20 September 1943 Frankfurt-Preungesheim prison

Deported from Frankfurt 20 September 1943 to Auschwitz

Murdered: 30 October 1943, Auschwitz.

Robert Zunz
Born 31 January 1881, Frankfurt
Resident of Frankfurt
Imprisoned 14 November–23 December 1938, Dachau concentration
    camp
Deported from Frankfurt 11 June 1942 to Majdanek, Poland, or
    Sobibor
Murdered: date and place unknown.

Karl Klonimus Zuntz
Born on 20 May 1897, Frankfurt
Resident of Frankfurt
Deported from Frankfurt 15 September 1942 to Theresienstadt, then
    6 October 1944 to Auschwitz
Murdered: date unknown, Auschwitz.

Ella Zuntz (wife of Karl)
née Joelsohn
Born 4 March 1895, Hamburg
Resident of Frankfurt
Deported from Frankfurt 15 September 1942 to Theresienstadt, then
    6 October 1944 to Auschwitz
Murdered: date unknown, Auschwitz.

Miriam Zuntz (daughter of Karl and Ruth, his first wife)
Born 15 May 1934, Frankfurt
Resident of Frankfurt
Deported from Frankfurt 15 September 1942 to Theresienstadt, then
    6 October 1944 to Auschwitz
Murdered: date unknown, Auschwitz.

Harry Zuntz (son of Karl and Ruth)
Born 14 May 1933, Frankfurt
Resident of Frankfurt
Deported from Frankfurt 15 September 1942 to Theresienstadt, then
    6 October 1944 to Auschwitz
Murdered: date unknown, Auschwitz.

Esther Zuntz (daughter of Karl and Ruth)
Born on 6 March 1928, Frankfurt
Resident of Frankfurt
Emigrated 22 November 1938 to Amsterdam, Netherlands
Imprisoned 11 February–6 July 1943, Westerbork camp
Deported 6 July 1943 to Sobibor
Murdered: 23 July 1943, Sobibor.

Leopold Zuntz
Born 30 January 1884, Frankfurt
Resident of Frankfurt
Deported from Frankfurt 22 November 1941 to Kaunus, Lithuania,
    Fort IX
Murdered: 25 November 1941, Kaunas.

Cäcilie Zuntz (wife of Leopold)
née Hessenberger
Born 28 April 1887, Staden
Resident of Frankfurt
Deported from Frankfurt 22 November 1941 to Kaunas
Murdered: 25 November 1941, Kaunas.

Hermann Zuntz (son of Leopold and Cäcilie)
Born 11 September 1925, Frankfurt
Resident of Frankfurt
Deported from Frankfurt 22 November 1941 to Kaunas
Murdered: 25 November 1941, Kaunas.

Gustav Zuntz
Born 9 November 1891, Frankfurt
Resident of Frankfurt
Deported from Frankfurt 15 September 1942 to Theresienstadt
Murdered: 17 May 1944, Theresienstadt.

Hedwig Zuntz (Gustav's wife)
née Hammel
Born 6 December 1901, Friedberg
Resident of Frankfurt
Deported from Frankfurt 15 September 1942 to Theresienstadt, then
    Auschwitz
Murdered: 9 October 1944, Auschwitz.

Hedwig Löb
née Zunz
Born on 15 August 1874, Frankfurt
Resident of Montabaur and Frankfurt
Deported from Frankfurt 1 September 1942 to Theresienstadt, then
    29 September 1942 to Treblinka
Murdered: date and place unknown.

Alice Roßwald
née Zunz
Born 17 April 1876, Frankfurt
Resident of Frankfurt
Deported from Frankfurt 1 September 1942 to Theresienstadt, then
    29 September 1942 to Treblinka
Murdered: date and place unknown.

Charlotte Gans
née Zuntz
Born 11 May 1881, Frankfurt
Resident of Winterswijk, Netherlands
Deported 1942 to Auschwitz
Murdered: 3 December 1942, Auschwitz.

Emilie Cohn
née Zuntz
Born 31 May 1877, Frankfurt
Resident of Frankfurt
Deported 16 September 1942 to Theresienstadt
Murdered: date and place unknown.

LOEB

Alexander Loeb
Born 4 March 1884, Bad Dürkheim
Resident of Frankfurt
Deported from Frankfurt 20 October 1941 to Łódź ghetto, Poland
Murdered: 28 March 1942, Łódź.

Margarete Loeb (wife of Alexander)
née Buseck
Born 20 July 1894, Frankfurt
Resident of Frankfurt
Deported from Frankfurt 20 October 1941 to Łódź
Murdered: date unknown, Łódź.

Ottilie Loeb (daughter of Alexander and Margarete)
Born 26 November 1925, Frankfurt
Resident of Frankfurt
Deported from Frankfurt 20 October 1941 to Łódź
Murdered: date unknown, Łódź.

Karoline Busek (Margarete's mother)
née Hess
Born 27 July 1870, Offenbach
Resident of Frankfurt
Deported from Frankfurt 20 October 1941 to Łódź
Murdered: date unknown, Łódź.

ILLUSTRATIONS

NOTES

Prologue

1. From an article I wrote to mark Holocaust Memorial Day, 27 January 2005, in the *Newport Advertiser*.

Introduction

1. Address to the *Reichstag* on 'The Jewish Question', 30 January 1939, included in N.H. Baynes (ed.), *The Speeches of Adolf Hitler, April 1922–August 1939*, Volume I, Oxford University Press, London, 1942, pp. 737–41.

PART ONE – ORIGINS

1 Finding My Father

1. F. Bradley, *The Chronicle of the Brandes/Bradley and Herzstein Families* (unpublished). The quotations throughout this section are drawn from this work.
2. Letter of 27 May 1945.
3. The Torah is the Pentateuch, the first five books of the Old Testament, which provide the basis for Jewish law and custom.
4. Letter to Herbert Loebl of 8 August 1996. In the UK Loebl became a successful businessman, philanthropist and diligent memorialist of the Bamberg Jewish community.
5. The Talmud is the accumulated commentary on and interpretation of the teachings and ethics of the Torah.

6. As Anthony Julius has observed, many Jews of recent generations 'have come to … realise themselves as Jews in resistance to anti-Semitism'. *Trials of the Diaspora: A History of Anti-Semitism in England*, Oxford University Press, 2012, p. xxxiv.

2 The Architecture of Anti-Semitism

1. Letter of 11 September 1945. My translation from the German.
2. Letter to my mother of 23 June 1946. Julius Streicher, editor of the virulently anti-Semitic weekly, was convicted at Nuremberg of crimes against humanity and executed on 1 October 1946.
3. It was coined by the German historian Heinrich von Treitschke in his essay *Ein Wort über unser Judenthum* (A Word about Our Jews), published in 1880. Treitschke was, in turn, echoing the teachings of Martin Luther.
4. The cathedral was consecrated in 1237. The original, badly eroded figures were removed to within the cathedral in 1937 and recently replaced by replicas.
5. A third is evidently of the head of Christ wreathed in light.
6. As does the stone carving of the bearded Jew with an animal's body, a long tail and the giveaway pointed hat in the cloisters of the nearby Dominican monastery.
7. Simon Schama, *The Story of the Jews: Finding the Words, 1000 BCE–1492 CE*, Vintage Books, London, 2014, p. 367.
8. See Birgit Wiedl, 'Laughing at the Beast: The *Judensau*: Anti-Jewish Humor and Propaganda From the Middle Ages to the Early Modern Period', in *Laughter in the Middle Ages and Early Modern Times*, ed. Albrecht Classen, Walter de Gruyton, Berlin and New York, 2010.

3 Articles of Faith

1. 1965 edition.
2. See Mark Oppenheimer's article 'Reclaiming "Jew"' in the *New York Times* of 22 April 2017.
3. Gospel According to St John, Chapter 8, Verse 44 (KJV).
4. St Paul, First Epistle to the Thessalonians, Chapter 2, Verses 15–16 (KJV).
5. St Augustine, *Confessions*, Book 12, Chapter 14.17. He lived from 364 to 430.

6. Gregory of Nyssa (331–96) and John Chrysostom (344–407), quoted in Richard L. Rubenstein and John K. Roth, *Approaches to Auschwitz: The Holocaust and Its Legacy*, Westminster John Knox Press, 2003, p. 52.

7. James Parkes, *The Conflict of the Church and the Synagogue: A Study in the Origins of Antisemitism*, Jewish Publication Society, New York, 1934, p. 163.

8. Cited in Schama, p. 212.

9. The *Mishnah* is the first great written account of Jewish oral traditions, composed at the beginning of the third century.

10. Herbert Loebl, Lecture Four in a series of nine, delivered in 1989 in the Department of Religious Studies at the University of Newcastle, collected under the title *The Holocaust: 1800 Years in the Making* and archived by the Leo Baeck Institute, New York, p. 46.

11. John Calvin, *A Response To Questions and Objections of a Certain Jew*.

12. Translated by Martin H. Bertram, *On the Jews and Their Lies, Luther's Works*, Volume 47, Fortress Press, Philadelphia, 1971. *Von den Juden und ihren Lügen* ran to 65,000 words. First published in 1543, it remains in print.

13. It is by Leonhard Gollwitzer.

14. Matthew, Chapter 27, Verse 23 (KJV). On the lower bridge, the *Untere Brücke*, two plaques are displayed on the town hall wall. The first, installed in 1957, commemorates Bamberg's Second World War dead. It was not until 1986 that a second tablet acknowledged the victims of the Nazis.

15. See Maxine Schur, *Voltaire and the Jews*, Continuing Studies, Stanford University, 2009.

16. Voltaire, *Essai sur les mœurs et l'esprit des nations* (*An Essay on Universal History, the Manners, and Spirit of Nations*), 1756, Volume I, p. 186.

17. Ibid., Volume II, p. 83.

18. In his essay *Il faut prendre parti ou le principe d'action* (*We Must Take Sides – Or, the Principle of Action*), 1772.

19. Jean-Jacques Rousseau, *Considerations on the Government of Poland and its Proposed Reformation*, 1772.

20. The *Editto sopra gli ebre* (Edict against the Jews) of 1775. The character of Nathan is said to be modelled on Lessing's friend, the Jewish philosopher Moses Mendelssohn.

21. The Prussian statesman Christian William von Dohm was inspired by Lessing to write *Über die bürgerliche Verbesserung der Juden* (Concerning the Amelioration of the Civil Status of the Jews), published in 1781 as an indictment of Christian persecution and an argument for Jewish emancipation.

22. Quoted in David A. Bell, 'Trapped by History: France and Its Jews', *World Affairs*, Vol. 172, No. 1 (summer 2009), pp. 24–34. The debate took place in 1789.

23. See Rachel Schulkins, 'Burke, His Liberal Rivals and the Jewish Question' *Otherness: Essays and Studies* 3.2, June 2013.

24. *Good Friday or The Murder of Jesus Christ by the Jews* by Wm. Cobbett, MP for Oldham in *Cobbett's Weekly Political Register*, Volume LXXIX, 9 March 1833, p. 613, digitised by Google. Almost exactly a hundred years later, the *Völkisher Beobachter* of 26 June 1933 declared that 'we must build up our state without Jews. They can never be anything but stateless aliens, they can never have any legal or constitutional status.' Cited in Venetia Newell, *The Jew as a Witch Figure*, in the *Witch Figure* (ed. Venetia Newell), Routledge & Kegan Paul, London, 1973, p. 101.

4 A Small City in Germany

1. Adolf Eckstein, *Geschichte der Juden im ehemaligen Fürstbistum Bamberg*, Handels-Druckerei, Bamberg, 1898, pp. 1–2. Eckstein was Bamberg's rabbi between 1888 and 1926. My translation.

2. Quoted in Ruth Gay, *The Jews of Germany: A Historical Portrait*, Yale University Press, New Haven and London, 1992, p. 8.

3. Loebl, Lecture Four, p. 40.

4. Benjamin of Tudela, *The Itinerary of Rabbi Benjamin of Tudela*, translated, edited and published by A. Asher, London and Berlin, 1840, p. 164.

5. The Council was convoked by Pope Innocent III with three principal objectives: to recover the Holy Land, reform the Church and suppress heresy.

6. In England, *Statutes of Jewry* of 1253 and 1275 consolidated these restrictions.

7. This was neither the first nor the last such massacre in England. In 1190, for example, a mob, incited by religious zealots and by members of the gentry seeking to escape their debts, besieged York's Jewish community, which had taken refuge in the royal castle. Some 150 perished either by suicide or murder.

8. The chroniclers of the day estimated 100,000.

9. Schama, p. 367.

10. They were also known as *Armleder*, after the leather arm protectors they wore.

11. Gay, p. 28.

12. Loebl, Lecture Five, pp. 48–51. The Thirty Years' War raged across central Europe between 1618 and 1648.
13. A ritual bath.
14. Simon of Trent was canonised as a Christian martyr in the same year.
15. One less predictable argument in 1656, but now all too familiar, was that the country was already over-populated.

PART TWO – THE FAMILY AS HISTORY

5 Lives on Licence

1. He was known as Pesach von Zons.
2. The houses of the ghetto were often named after animals, plants or fruits.
3. The story of Ogy's suicide is recorded in the *Chronica der Weiberuhmten freyen Reichs-Wahl und Handels-Stadt Franckfurth am Mayn*, published in 1734 by Achill Augusti von Lersner and cited in Marlies Lehmann-Brune, *Der Koffer des Karl Zuntz: Fünf Jahrhunderte Einer Jüdischen Familie* (*The Suitcase of Karl Zuntz: Five Centuries of a Jewish Family*), Droste, 1997, pp. 33–4.
4. In 1502, Aberle was dismissed from his post as *Baumeister*, master builder, a prestigious position in the community. The reasons are unknown.
5. Dr Alexander Dietz, *Stammbuch der Frankfurter Juden 1349–1849* (History of the Frankfurt Jews), J. St. Goar Frankfurt, 1907, p. 339.
6. Dietz, p. 339.
7. There were some thirty Rothschild charities. The Zunz Foundation, founded in 1801, every three years provided a dowry for a young Jewish woman from the interest on a settlement of 3,000 gulden.
8. Her book, drawn upon here, contains much information about the Zunz family and the Frankfurt ghetto.
9. Samson Salomon, ?–1712; Glückel von Hameln, 1646–1724.
10. Dr Abraham Schweizer, *Die israelitische Gemeinde zu Baiersdorf*, translated by my father. Dr Schweizer was rabbi of Weikersheim between 1900 and 1913 and then of Horb am Neckar from 1913 to 1936. He died at Treblinka in 1942.
11. The Sephardi Jews invited to regenerate Hamburg's economy had been exempted.
12. Glückel von Hameln, trans. Beth-Zion Abrahams, *The Life of Glückel von Hameln*, East & West Library, London, 1962, pp. 13–14.

13. Ibid., p. 5.
14. Ibid., p. 45.
15. Ibid., p. 80.
16. Chaim died in 1689.
17. Glückel, p. 138.
18. See Loebl, Lecture Six, p. 62.
19. Glückel, pp. 147–8. In the Book of Esther, Haman is the Babylonian King Xerxes' evil vizier who plots the destruction of the Jews of Persia but is foiled by Queen Esther, herself a Jew. The events are celebrated in the Jewish holiday of *Purim*.
20. Ibid., p. 158.
21. Ibid., p. 150.
22. Ibid., p. 150.
23. Ibid., p. 161.
24. Ibid., p. 166.
25. Gay, p. x.
26. Ibid., p. 68.
27. Quoted in Gay, p. 68, *Bemerkungen eines Reisenden durch Deuatschland, Frankreich, England und Holland*, c. 1795.
28. The ghetto was demolished between 1867 and 1882. Its great Börneplatz Synagogue was destroyed on Kristallnacht on 9/10 November 1938.
29. Quoted in Lehmann-Brune, p. 84. (My translation.)

6 The Age of Reason and Unreason

1. My translation.
2. Leopold Zunz, 1794–1886.
3. Heinrich Heine (1797–1856) is linked to the Herzsteins through the marriage of Samson Herz's daughter and Glückel von Hameln's son.
4. He had, also in 1818, graduated from Göttingen University as a doctor of law. Of the professions, only medicine was open to non-baptised Jews.
5. Cited in Gay, p. 141.
6. Ludwig Börne, seventy-fourth letter in the series *Briefe aus Paris*, written in February 1832. Cited in the chapter on 'The Jews and Society' in Hannah Arendt's *The Origins of Totalitarianism*. At the end of the century, Gustav Mahler, also baptised, declared, 'I have been thrice homeless: as a Bohemian in Austria, as an Austrian in Germany, and as a Jew throughout all the world; everywhere rejected, nowhere welcomed.'

7. Adolf Eckstein, *Die Jsrael. Kultusgemeinde Bamberg von 1803–1853. Festschrift zur Einweihung der neuen Synagoge in Bamberg*, Handels-Druckerei, Bamberg, 1910, p. 5.

8. He went on to patent and manufacture, with his partner Jacob W. Davis, the jeans with which his name is synonymous.

9. Some believe that 'Hep' is an acronym for the Crusaders' cry, '*Hierosolyma est perdita*' or 'Jerusalem is lost'.

10. Cited by Beisbart, Daniel and Duesel, location 1144.

11. They had been obliged to use burial plots first at Zeckendorf, some fifteen miles away, then in Walsdorf, some ten miles distant.

12. However, it was not until the adoption of the Bamberg Constitution on 8 August 1919 that all citizens in Bavaria were granted equal rights irrespective of religion.

13. See Gay, pp. 167 and 180.

14. See Heide Friedrich-Brettinger, *Die Juden in Bamberg*, Hartdruck, Würzburg, 1962.

15. The school closed in 1942. The building now houses another Jewish school, which has become known as The Philanthropin.

16. Moritz was at various times professor of physiology at Bern, Florence and Geneva and, inter alia, contributed greatly to the understanding of the thyroid gland and the cerebral cortex. Hugo was co-founder of both the Italian socialist newspaper *L'Avanti* and the *Gazzetta Chimica Italiana*. He was professor of chemistry at Pisa, Florence and Turin, discovered the eponymous Schiff bases and developed the Schiff test for aldehydes.

17. It is not known whether further volumes were lost, but this one, in his immaculate script, was handed down the generations and is currently held by my sister. In 2014, the Jewish Museum in Frankfurt, to which it had been loaned, mounted a dramatised performance of extracts which I attended with my cousin Walter Koring.

18. All extracts from the diary are my translations of Walter Koring's transcription.

19. The Hippodrome, now the site of the Frankfurt Burse.

20. King Frederick of Denmark had decided to annex the Duchies of Schleswig and Holstein and put down a revolt by Germans in the latter. They appealed to Prussia, which sent troops.

21. Gay, p. 172.

22. Jakob Herz, 1816–71; Julius Herz, 1825–1910.

23. Dr Lewinsky was Rabbi of Hildesheim. His 'Professor Dr Jakob Herz: A Profile' appeared in *Israelitisches Familienblatt*, Number 26, 1903, p. 17 (translated by my father).

24. However, as Gay notes, on p. 184, in the whole of Germany, even by 1909, only twenty-five Jews had attained the rank of full professor, a number that by 1917 had fallen to thirteen.

25. In *Das Denkmal für Jakob Herz in Erlangen: Ein Beispiel für die Uberwindung der Ausgrenzung von Juden im 19. Jahrhundert*, Erlanger Bausteine zur Fränkischen Heimatforschung, Volume 55, 2015, p. 345. The extracts from the *Erlanger Tagblatt* are cited here. (My translations.)

26. It was designed by the celebrated Vienna-based sculptor Caspar von Zumbusch.

27. The Credit Institute for Trade and Commerce had been founded in 1855 by Anselm Salomon Freiherr von Rothschild.

28. *Allgemeine Zeitung des Judenthums*, 2 September 1879, cited in Gay, p. 217.

29. In such tracts as *Der Sieg des Judenthums über das Germanenthums* ('The Victory of Judaism over Germandom'). Marr borrowed the term he coined from the study of the contrasting Aryan and Semitic language types. He is often cited as the father of anti-Semitism though in old age he repudiated the beliefs on which much of his life's work had been founded.

30. Gay, p. 212.

31. Johanna Harris-Brandes, *Megillat Johanna* (ed. Liora Bernstein, trans. Eva M. Edge), Kindle Edition, 2011, p. 41. Jews, like demons and witches, had long been associated in folklore with the 'stench of the Devil'. Oberaula, some twenty-five miles from Rotenburg an der Fulda, was then a village of around 800, of whom about ninety, in twenty-five families, were Jews.

32. Rotenburg was then part of the Kingdom of Westphalia, ruled by Napoleon's brother Jérôme Bonaparte. Geisel's five brothers chose different names, including Sommer, Tannenwald and Nusbaum; two are unknown.

33. Harris-Brandes, p. 54.

34. Ibid., p. 53.

35. She died in Cambridge, Massachusetts, in 1965 at the age of 86.

36. Harris-Brandes, p. 8.

37. Ibid., p. 112.

38. Ibid., p. 76.

39. Ibid., pp. 39–40.

40. Ibid., p. 86.

NOTES

PART THREE – THE LAST GENERATION

1. *Synagogue Poetry of the Middle Ages*, published in 1855 (my translation).

7 Four Families

1. Lueger's exploitation of anti-Semitism was cynical. Many of his friends were Jewish and, when challenged on this, he memorably, but chillingly, retorted: 'I decide who is a Jew!'
2. Theodor Herzl, *The Jewish State*, Penguin Books, London, 2010, p. 2. Dreyfus was a Jewish French army officer falsely accused of spying for the Germans. He was sentenced in 1895 to life on Devil's Island. He was pardoned in 1899 and exonerated in 1906.
3. Herzl, pp. 8–9.
4. According to my father's chronicle.
5. Hirsch lived from 1841 to 1918 and Hannchen from 1842 to 1932.
6. By 1912, its name had changed from *Colonial und Manufacturwaren von Hirsch Brandes* to *Manufaktur – Modewaren H. Brandes*.
7. Sigmund Loeb, 1852–97; Eugenie Feis, 1856–1946.
8. Karl Hermann, 1870–1946; Helene, 1885–1974.
9. And, in England, as Trudie.
10. On the advice of the War Office when he joined the army in 1943, he anglicised his name to Vernon Zunz Newcombe, adapting his wife Ilse Neukampf's surname.
11. He went on to a distinguished career in architecture and town planning, involved in the development of Stevenage new town, building social housing in Malaya, working for the United Nations first in Pakistan and then Jordan and, on returning to the UK, as a lecturer at the University of Edinburgh and finally as Professor of Town Planning at the University of Wales in Cardiff.

8 The End of the Beginning

1. He served in the Ersatz-Bataillon des bayerischen Landwehr-Infanterie-Regiments Nr. 8 and, in 1935, was awarded the NS-Frontkaempferehrenkreuz (Cross of Honour for Frontline Fighters).
2. The equivalent of A levels.
3. Quoted in Beisbart, Daniel and Duesel, location 1257.

4. Research by Impuls eV, the Bamberg historical society, for its project on the 'Aryanisation' of Bamberg.
5. Friedrich Nietzsche, *Ecce Homo*, 'Why I Am So Clever' 4 (trans. Walter Kaufmann), Vintage Books, 1969, p. 245.
6. Cited on the History Place website at https://www.historyplace.com/worldwar2/triumph/tr-bookburn.htm.
7. Heinrich Heine, *(On the History of) Religion and Philosophy in Germany: A Fragment* (trans. John Snodgrass), Beacon Press, Boston, pp. 159–60.
8. Alfred Rosenberg, 'Race & Race History', from the preface of the 1938 edition of *Der Mythus des 20. Jahrhunderts*, in *Alfred Rosenberg Selected Writings*, p. 34.
9. Ibid., p. 36.
10. The Nazis won 43.9 per cent of the vote and initially required the support of the German National People's Party (DNVP) in the Reichstag.
11. Dr Scheidmadl, 'Rück-und Ausblicke' ('Looking Back and Forward'), quoted by Impuls (my translation).
12. In 1967, a plaque was attached to the house in which he had lived at Heuwaagstraße 18 and in 1983 a stone monument was erected, fittingly at the junction of Universitätstraße and Krankenhausstraße (University and Hospital Streets). In 2000, a bronze plate was set in the ground at the spot in Hugenottenplatz where his statue had stood and in 2002, a new road, Jakob Herz Weg, was named after him. A specialist school for sick children also bears his name. In 2009, Friedrich Alexander University Erlangen-Nürnberg established the Jakob Herz Prize for Medical Research, a €10,000 endowment awarded for outstanding scientific achievement in the field of theoretical and clinical medicine.
13. In 1988 it became Jakob Herz Straße.
14. Recalled by Herbet Loebl in Lecture One, p. 7.
15. By the time of the enforced sale of the business in December 1938, it had been further reduced to three.
16. My father's letter to Stephan Link of 27 January 1995. See also *'Bambergs Wirtschaftjudenfrei': Die Verdrängung der jüdischen Geschäftsleute in den Jahren 1933 bis 1939*, Collibri, Bamberg, 1998, to which Link contributed.
17. Loebl, Lecture Two, p. 22. In his first lecture (p. 7) he records the statement of the Archbishop of Bamberg to the *Bamberger Volksblatt* of 10 November 1933, supporting the Nazis' 'necessary moral and economic regeneration of Germany'.

18. Hannah Arendt, *Eichmann in Jerusalem: A Report on the Banality of Evil*, Penguin Classics, 2006, p. 39. Arendt had been arrested in 1933 and left Germany shortly thereafter.

19. Ibid., p. 39.

20. The journal is reproduced in Karl H. Mistele, *Das Ende einer Gemeinde. Juden in Bamberg 1930–1942*, Stadt Bamberg, 1988. Published online in English as *The End of a Community: Jews in Bamberg 1930–1942*, trans. Jacob Feuchtwanger, by the Center for Jewish History and the Leo Baeck Institute, 1995, at https://digipres.cjh.org/delivery/DeliveryManagerServlet?dps_pid=IE8250671.

21. Timothy W. Ryback, *Hitler's First Victims: And One Man's Race for Justice*, Vintage, 2015, pp. 126–35.

22. The BDJJ.

23. Letter of 21 June 1996.

24. The Law Concerning Jewish Tenants enacted on 30 April 1939 enabled private landlords to cancel the leases of their Jewish tenants. Jews evicted from their homes were forced to live together in houses generally owned by Jews.

25. Mistele, p. 14.

26. Ernest Haas, *Neumarkt – Fürth – Riga – USA*, published at http://www.rijo.homepage.t-online.de/pdf/EN_BY_JU_haas.pdf, 2012, p. 4.

27. Quoted in Gloria Deutsch, 'Veterens (*sic*): Crystal clear memories of Kristallnacht', *Jerusalem Post*, 8 November 2012, https://www.jpost.com/magazine/features/veterens-crystal-clear-memories-of-kristallnacht.

28. Claus W. Hirsch, 'German-Jewish Soldiers in World War I', in *Stammbaum*, Issue 10, December 1996, pp, 21–4, corroborated by Heide Friedrich-Brettinger in *Die Juden in Bamberg*, pp. 24–7 and Tim Grady in *German Jewish Soldiers of the First World War*, Liverpool University Press, 2011.

29. Werner M. Loval, *We Were Europeans: A Personal History of a Turbulent Century*, Gefen Publishing House, Jerusalem, 2010. Loval was a cousin of Herbert Loebl.

30. Quoted in Laura Abbate, *Das Leben in Bamberg überschattet vom Nationalsozialismus* ('Life in Bamberg under the Nazi Shadow'), on the Kulturwekstatt Bamberg website, http://www.kulturwerkstatt-bamberg.de/oberfranken/nationalsozialismus/bamberg/index.htm. (My translation.)

31. Cited in Herbert Loebl, *Juden in Bamberg. Die Jahrzehnte vor dem Holocaust*, Fränkischer Tag, Bamberg, 2000, pp. 68–72. (My translation.)

32. Ibid., p. 200. (My translation.)
33. See Antje Yael Deusel, Ortwin Beisbart and Franz Fichtl, *Gedenkbuch der jüdischen Bürger Bambergs* (Memorial Book for Jewish Citizens of Bamberg), Verein zur Förderung der jüdischen Geschichte und Kultur Bambergs e. V., 2010, p. 49 and p. 86 respectively.
34. Quoted on the Stolpersteine Bamberg website, http://www.stolpersteine-bamberg.de/.
35. Eighty-one were from Bamberg and twenty-six from outlying districts.
36. Report of the Bamberg police, dated 11 November 1938, cited in Mistele, p. 35.
37. A simple commemorative sculpture now stands in its place.
38. Loval, pp. 57–8.
39. Ibid., p. 66.
40. Paul Nickelsberg, '1938', Part III of 'The Writings of Paul Nickelsberg' (unpublished), pp. 8–9.
41. (Selig) Siegfried lived at Goethestraße 85. On 9 March 1939 Max and Johanna were able to emigrate to South Africa to join their son Kurt. Their daughter Gretel (Margarete) with her husband Hans Goldschmidt and daughter Margit went to live with Siegfried and his wife Else in Krefeld in 1939 before being deported to Riga. Siegfried and Else were deported to Theresienstadt on 25 July 1942 and did not return.
42. Recorded by Ludwig Brandes in his post-war claim for compensation and featured on the Hassia Judaica website, http://www.hassia-judaica.de/eng_index.html.
43. The letter, dated 18 October 1939, was translated by Heinrich Nuhn and published in the Leo Baeck Institute Yearbook 2015, https://academic-oup-com.eres.qnl.qa/leobaeck/article/60/1/293/2804607. The family reached New York in January 1940.
44. Testimony of 1 December 1946, cited on the Hassia Judaica website.
45. Quoted in *The History of Jews of Baiersdorf*, Leo Baeck Institute Centre for Jewish History. The synagogue has gone but the cemetery, in which so many of the Herz family lie, remains. As the note reports, 'in 1997 the name *Judengasse*, situated in the very centre of Baiersdorf, again bears its old name'.

9 The Beginning of the End

1. Cited by Impuls. from documents held in the Bamberg City Archive. (My translation.)

2. Noted on the Stolpersteine Bamberg website under 'Jüdische Wirtschaft in Bamberg'.
3. Quoted from City Archive material by Impuls. (My translation.)
4. Letter from Ludwig Berger of 26 May 1946 (my translation). The air raid was on 22 February 1945.
5. He also sought 20,000 RM for household furniture, silver, china, clothes and linen that had to be abandoned at HainStraße 4a when Sally and Bertha were deported, 10,000 RM for a life insurance policy that the Nazis forced Sally to sell, the 20,000 RM the family had had to pay as its share of the fine levied on the Jewish community after Kristallnacht and the 1,000 RM he had to surrender to the German Foreign Exchange Office on leaving the country.
6. 'Reference' issued by Schwarzschild Ochs, 10 November 1938. (My translation.) Sally wrote to the company on 8 February 1939 while my father was in Buchenwald, asking that it pay the 246 RM (about £20) in wages due to my father during this notice period. He wrote again on 28 May to its London office after my father had emigrated, appealing, in vain, that it make good its debt.
7. Information provided by the Stiftung Gedenkstätten Buchenwald und Mittelbau-Dora (Buchenwald and Mittelbau-Dora Memorials Foundation).
8. This section is based on '1938', Part III of 'The Writings of Paul Nickelsberg'. Paul and his sister Marta were children of Adolph Zunz's daughter Emma and her husband Emile Nickelsberg.
9. According to records in the Buchenwald Archive, Paul, prisoner number 29323, was, like my father, held in the Pogromsonderlager.
10. 'The Buchenwald Song', words by Fritz Löhner-Beda, who died at Auschwitz after his time in both Dachau and Buchenwald; music by Hermann Leopoldi, who survived both camps.
11. Peter Forster, a member of the Social Democratic Party, and Emil Bargatzky, a criminal, escaped from Buchenwald on 13 May 1938, killing an SS guard. Bargatzky was quickly recaptured and hanged on 4 June. His corpse was left dangling for three days as a warning to others. The gallows remained on the assembly ground for the six months before they could be used on Forster.
12. Letter from my father to Karin Mistele of 5 June 1991, in which he writes that, thanks to a socialist Kapo who had been a prisoner since 1933 and was in charge of the bread ration, his group had a little more to eat than others.

13. Paul Nickelsberg, 'And Everybody Was Happy', in 'The Writings of Paul Nickelsberg' (unpublished).

PART FOUR – RESETTLEMENT IN THE WEST

10 The Emigration Trap

1. The data largely reflect those provided on the German Jewish Refugees 1933–9 page of the United States Holocaust Memorial Museum website, https://encyclopedia.ushmm.org/content/en/article/german-jewish-refugees-1933-1939, though at 40,000 it underestimates the number reaching the UK. In all, around 70,000 of the 500,000 who applied for entry were admitted.
2. Before the Japanese invaded in December 1941, 11 countries oversaw the administration of the International Settlement at Shanghai, which did not require entry visas. Most of the Jews who reached there via the USSR survived the Japanese occupation.
3. Anne Karpf, 'We've been here before', *Guardian*, 8 June 2002, https://www.theguardian.com/uk/2002/jun/08/immigration.immigration andpublicservices.
4. Wesley P. Greear, 'American Immigration Policies and Public Opinion on European Jews from 1933 to 1945', School of Graduate Studies, East Tennessee State University, 2002, https://dc.etsu.edu/cgi/viewcontent.cgi?article=1802&context=etd.
5. Peter Hayes, *Why? Explaining the Holocaust*, W.W. Norton & Co., New York, 2017, pp. 269 and 291.
6. Jack R. Fischel, *The Holocaust*, Greenwood, 1998, pp. 28–9.
7. Cited on the Facing History & Ourselves website, https://www.facinghistory.org/resource-library/text/statements-representatives-evian-conference-july-1938.
8. Canada admitted only 4–5,000 Jewish refugees between 1933 and 1945, Australia 10,000 and South Africa 6,000.
9. Facing History & Ourselves.
10. *Observer*, 31 July 1938, https://www.theguardian.com/uk/2002/jun/08/immigration.immigrationandpublicservices.
11. Louise London, *Whitehall and the Jews, 1933–1948: British Immigration Policy, Jewish Refugees and the Holocaust*, Cambridge, Cambridge University Press, 2001.
12. After the Arab Revolt of 1936–9. British policy was, in any case, to limit the proportion of Jews to a third of the population of Palestine.

13. Kathryn Blaze Carlson, '"None is too many": Memorial for Jews turned away from Canada in 1939', *National Post*, 17 January 2011, https://nationalpost.com/news/none-is-too-many-memorial-for-jews-turned-away-from-canada.

14. Schröder was posthumously honoured as Righteous Among the Nations by the State of Israel in March 1993.

15. Quoted in Wayne S. Cole, *Charles A. Lindbergh and the Battle Against American Intervention in World War II*, Harcourt Brace Jovanovich, 1974, p. 144.

16. Letter of 26 April 1945.

17. Quoted by Karpf, https://www.theguardian.com/uk/2002/jun/08/immigration.immigrationandpublicservices.

18. Letter of 15 October 1945.

19. W.H. Wilkins, *The Alien Invasion*, Methuen and Co., London, 1892, p. 11. Cited by Daniel Renshaw in 'Prejudice and Paranoia: A Comparative Study of Antisemitism and Sinophobia in Turn of the Century Britain', Central Archive, University of Reading, 2016, pp. 5–6.

20. Ibid., p. 14.

21. Louise London, *Whitehall and the Jews, 1933–1948*, Cambridge University Press, 2000, p. 12, quoted in Anne Karpf, https://www.theguardian.com/uk/2002/jun/08/immigration.immigrationandpublicservices.

22. Ibid., p. 13.

23. Ibid.

11 Welcome to Great Britain

1. In answer to a series of questions put to him by Karin Mistele in her letter of 28 February 1991.

2. From Goethe's play *Götz von Berlichingen*. The name came to be shorthand for the phrase itself.

3. Many with valid visas who remained determined to immigrate had to make the hazardous return voyage to Britain and back to America.

4. The closing lines of Emma Lazarus's sonnet *The New Colossus*, inscribed within the Statue of Liberty, run 'Give me your tired, your poor,/Your huddled masses yearning to breathe free … I lift my lamp beside the golden door!'

5. Letter of 10 June 1945.

6. The Tribunal Card for 'Fritz Israel Brandes', dated 4 October 1939, is held in the National Archives.

7. Rachel Pistol, a historian who has specialised in WW2 internment, suggests that it is more likely that my father was arrested in this sweep.
8. 'Collar the lot! Britain's policy of internment during the Second World War', http://blog.nationalarchives.gov.uk/blog/collar-lot-britains-policy-internment-second-world-war/.
9. Eric Koch, *Deemed Suspect: A Wartime Blunder*, Methuen, Toronto, 1980, p. xiv. He became a distinguished broadcaster, lecturer and author and died in Canada in 2018 at the age of 98.
10. Ibid., p. 3.
11. It is likely that my father had first been detained at Kempton Park racecourse and then Huyton on Merseyside before transfer to Onchan after it opened on 29 May.
12. According to Koch, p. 262, the total of 6,675 internees deported to Canada comprised 2,112 in Category A (including 178 refugees), 2,290 in Category B and C, 405 Italians and 1,868 German POWs.
13. Francois Lafitte, *The Internment of Aliens*, Penguin, New York, 1940, pp. 36–7.
14. Rachel Pistol, 'Enemy Alien and Refugee: Conflicting Identities in Great Britain during the Second World War', *University of Sussex Journal of Contemporary History*, Vol. 16, 2015, p. 48.
15. Ibid., p. 47.
16. The *Ettrick*, also a requisitioned liner, was itself torpedoed by U-155 120 miles north-west of Gibraltar on 15 November 1942 and sunk with the loss of 24 lives.
17. Koch, p. 41.
18. Ibid.
19. Ibid., p. 68. Ritchie later served as Canada's Permanent Representative to the United Nations, its ambassador to West Germany, the United States and the North Atlantic Council and its High Commissioner in London.
20. According to Ernest Borneman, quoted in Koch, p. 92.
21. Letter to Karin Mistele of 5 June 1991. Prince Frederick of Prussia, 1911–66, became a British citizen in 1947 under the name Mr Friedrich von Preussen.
22. Letter of 21 March 1946. Hans Kahle, commander of the Eleventh International Brigade, had become a friend of Ernest Hemingway and the model for General Hans in *For Whom the Bell Tolls*, first published in October 1940. After the war, he returned to East Germany and became head of the People's Police and state chairman of the Socialist Unity Party of Germany in Mecklenburg.

23. After the war Fuchs was head of the Theoretical Physics Atomic Energy Research Establishment at Harwell where he was arrested. After nine years in prison, he emigrated to East Germany where he became deputy director of the Institute for Nuclear Research.

24. Quoted in a newspaper article, 'How Jewish "enemy aliens" overcame a "traumatic" stint in Canadian prison camps during the Second World War' by Graeme Hamilton, *National Post*, 7 February 2014.

25. Quoted in Koch, p, 148.

26. Ibid., p. 155.

27. Ibid., p. 143.

28. Josiah Wedgwood, 1st Baron Wedgwood, was a Liberal and, from 1919, a Labour MP for Newcastle-under-Lyme. He served between 1906 and 1942 when Winston Churchill appointed him a Labour peer. He was a decorated veteran of the Boer and First World Wars and joined the Home Guard in 1940.

29. *Hansard*, 22 August 1940, Vol. 364, cc. 1475–1586.

30. The Conservative MP for the University of Cambridge, Kenneth Pickthorn, took a different view: 'I should say it was their [the War Cabinet's] duty to do this at whatever cost to human misery, or at whatever risk to what is called British prestige.'

31. Interview in the Imperial War Museum's Oral History project, quoted by Koch, p. 185.

32. Ibid., p. 218.

33. My uncle Vernon had returned aboard the SS *Thysville*, the first transport home, reaching Britain on 11 January 1941. He was interned on the Isle of Man for another six months before his release was authorised on 15 July as his work as an architect was considered 'of national importance' and a job awaited him at the Durham Water Board.

34. He joined the army as Private Fritz Brandes 13116350 and was demobbed as Sergeant Fred Bradley on 20 November 1946. Both he and my mother were naturalised on 21 July 1947.

35. The premises, at Eschersheimer Landstraße 65, are now occupied by the Basaglia coffee shop. When I visited in March 2019, I casually mentioned that my parents had first met there. I had hoped for a complimentary cup of coffee but was disappointed.

36. He wrote in his chronicle: 'My sole motive was to maintain continuity, a link with my Bamberg past.'

PART FIVE – RESETTLEMENT IN THE EAST

12 The Turning of the Screw

1. My father wrote to the Swiss Embassy in London on 22 November 1997 requesting guidance on how he should 'establish my claim for the gold stolen from my late parents and myself after the Kristallnacht 1938 and presumably transferred to Switzerland by the Nazi Government during World War II'. He received no response.
2. Quoted in a letter from my father to Herbert Loebl, 8 January 1998. His parents' letter is not among those I have seen.
3. Quoted in Mistele, p. 51.
4. Letter of 29 July 1939.
5. Letter of 21 August 1939.
6. Max and Lily Pretzfelder were deported to Riga with Sally and Bertha. After the war, Villa Dessauer became America House, the centre of a US Government re-education programme in democratic values. Since 1987, it has housed Bamberg's Stadtgalerie (City Gallery).
7. Documents held by the Bamberg City Archive reveal that Sally and Bertha had applied in May 1937 for travel passes to the spa at Pystian in Czechoslovakia (now Piešťany, Slovakia) for the relief of Sally's sciatica. Though no objections were made by the police or finance departments, Sally was asked to provide medical evidence of his condition and the application seems to have lapsed.
8. Sally's letter of 26 June 1939. Moritz and Selma Welt emigrated to England in 1939. Margot and Elisabeth Tietz-Fleischmann moved on from the UK to the USA after the war. Their elder sister Inge survived the war, living in Paris on forged papers. Their parents, Ludwig and Irma, were deported to Riga.
9. Bertha's letter of 28 May 1939. Ludwig Naumann, the Pragers, Martin Schönthal and Kurt Klestadt all finally managed to leave Germany. My father never mentioned any plans he might have had to emigrate to Cuba.
10. Bertha's letter of 1 June 1939.
11. Sally's letter of 1 June 1939. Once the owner of a major textile business in Bamberg, Arthur Heßlein emigrated to Brazil in 1939 and died there in reduced circumstances in 1949. From 1945, he sent money and food parcels to Bamberg.
12. Letter of 19 May 1939. Karl Bechhöfer was most likely a business contact. He died in Los Angeles in 1943.

13. Letter of 22 May 1941. Lutz (Ludwig) was Sally's nephew who had emigrated to the USA in 1939.
14. Letter of 18 June 1939.
15. Letter of 13 August 1939. The German Jewish Aid Committee was based at Woburn House.
16. Letter of 29 May 1941.
17. Letter of 13 July 1941. Kurt, Lutz's brother, had emigrated to South Africa.
18. Letter of 26 July 1941. Gustav Herzstein, Bertha's brother, had emigrated to the USA, via Guatemala.
19. Letter of 20 August 1941.
20. Letter of 15 May 1939. The Hain is Bamberg's principal park.
21. Letter of 28 May 1939.
22. See the Stolpersteine Bamberg website, http://www.stolpersteine-bamberg.de/.
23. Quoted by Mistele, p. 57.
24. Ibid., p. 6.
25. Ibid., p. 68. The Generalgouvernement was the Nazi administration of the Lublin region of Poland.
26. Géraldine Schwarz, *Those Who Forget: One Family's Story, A Memoir, a History, a Warning*, Pushkin Press, London, 2021, p. 2.
27. Mistele, p. 69.
28. Letter of 8 June 1941.
29. It is possible that, prior to his arrival at Drancy, he spent some time in a 'hospital camp' for elderly inmates near Toulouse. A letter from the Jewish Refugee Committee of 3 April 1945 informed my father that 'the United Kingdom Search Bureau has just received the information that Ernst Herzstein was transferred on 20 February 1941 to Camp de Noé and that he left this camp for an unknown destination'.
30. Mistele, p. 66.

13 The Road to Riga

1. SS Obersturmbannführer (Lieutenant Colonel) Adolf Eichmann was responsible for much of the logistical planning of the transportation to and the operation of the death camps. Kidnapped by Mossad agents in Buenos Aries in May 1960, he was tried in Israel and hanged on 1 June 1962. Interestingly, in 1903 the British Government had proposed the establishment of a Jewish settlement in East Africa, an invitation the Zionist Congress declined.

2. From a speech in Prague on 4 February 1942, quoted in Andrej Angrick and Peter Klein, *The Final Solution in Riga, Exploitation and Annihilation, 1941–1944*, Berghahn Books, New York, 2009, p. 190. SS Obergruppenführer und General der Polizei Reinhard Heydrich was also chief of the Reich Main Security Office with responsibility for the Gestapo, Kripo (Kriminalpolizei or criminal police), and SD, the Sicherheitsdienst (the SS intelligence service). In 1941, as Reich Protector of Bohemia and Moravia, he was assassinated by partisans in Prague.

3. In 1942, as the Deputy Protector of Bohemia and Moravia, Daluege ordered the atrocities at the villages of Lidice and Ležáky in reprisal for Heydrich's assassination. He was hanged in Czechoslovakia in 1946.

4. The community now numbered 418, approximately a quarter of its size at the turn of the century.

5. Mistele, pp. 72–3.

6. Daniel Mendelsohn, *The Lost: A Search for Six of Six Million*, William Collins, London, 2013.

7. Mistele, p. 73.

8. Ibid., p. 74.

9. Ibid., p. 76.

10. The case was heard in July 1953 at the *Landgericht* (Regional Court) Nürnberg-Fürth.

11. Wolfgang Scheffler, lecture on *The History of the Deportation of Jewish citizens to Riga in 1941/1942*, organised by the Volksbund Deutsche Kriegsgraeberfuersorge e. V. [German War Graves Commission] on 23 May 2000 to celebrate the formation of the Riga-Komitee.

12. Mistele, p. 78.

13. These were the instructions issued in Frankfurt. There is no reason to believe that they varied in Bamberg.

14. Mistele, p. 80.

15. Bernhard Kolb, 'Die Juden in Nürnberg', unpublished, written around 1946, p. 49. The manuscript, held in the Stadtarchiv Nürnberg, is quoted by Ekkehard Hübschmann in his essay 'The Deportation from Nuremberg on 29 November 1941', in Wolfgang Scheffler and Diana Schulle, *Buch der Erinnerung. die ins Baltikum deportierten deutschen, österreichischen und tschechoslowakischen Juden* (*Book of Remembrance: The German, Austrian and Czechoslovakian Jews Deported to the Baltic States*), K.G. Saur, Munich, 2003, Vol. 2, pp. 541–59.

16. Reska Weiss, *Journey Through Hell: A Woman's Account of Her Experiences at the Hands of the Nazis*, Vallentine, Mitchell & Co., London (1961), pp. 9–10.

17. Ibid., p. 16.
18. The film, *Exodus of the Children of Israel from Franconia*, has been lost.
19. Kolb, p. 50.
20. According to Ekkehard Hübschmann, p. 541, the transport carried a total of 'at least' 1,008 Jews, including 118 from Bamberg, 46 from Bayreuth, 25 from Coburg, 4 from Erlangen, 8 from Forcheim, 89 from Fürth, 516 from Nuremberg and 202 from Würzburg. Only 52 survived.
21. Quoted on the Yad Vashem website in 'Transport, Train Da 32 from Nürnberg, Bavaria, Germany to Riga, Vidzeme, Latvia on 29/11/1941', https://deportation.yadvashem.org/index.html?language=en&itemId=9437978&ind=-1.
22. Letter of 8 February 1942.
23. The Rare Historical Photos website features this and other photographs along with a description of the event, https://rarehistoricalphotos.com/kovno-garage-massacre-lithuania-1941/
24. Or harmonica, according to Angrick and Klein, p. 60.
25. Julius Norwilla, 'The June 2015 Memorial for the Lietūkis Garage Massacre in Kaunas, Lithuania', 2 July 2015, https://defendinghistory.com/the-june-2015-memorial-for-the-lietukis-garage-massacre.

14 The Cleansing of Latvia

1. Krause, subsequently commandant of the Salaspils camp, was captured and executed by Soviet partisans on 8 December 1944.
2. Quoted on the Yad Vashem website.
3. Mistele, p. 84.
4. Extract from a video interview with the University of Southern California Shoah Foundation, 2015.
5. The German invasion of the Soviet Union, Operation Barbarossa, brought the Molotov–Ribbentrop Pact to an end.
6. Stahlecker was an SS Brigadier General and commander of the SS security forces for the Reichskommissariat Ostland. He was commander of Einsatzgruppe A from 6 February 1941 until his death at the hands of Soviet partisans on 23 March 1942.
7. Hinrich Lohse, a member of the Reichstag from 1932, was Gauleiter of Schleswig-Holstein and, from July 1941, head of the civil administration in the eastern territories. He played a key role in facilitating the liquidation of Jews and others in the Baltic States and, in 1948, was sentenced to 10 years' imprisonment. He was released on health grounds in 1951.

8. Frida Michelson, *I Survived Rumbuli* (trans. Wolf Goodman), Holocaust Library, New York, 1979, p. 70.

9. Smaller ghettos were also established in Daugavpils and Liepāja (known by the Germans as Dünaburg and Libau).

10. Cited in Andrew Ezergailis, *The Holocaust in Latvia, 1941–1944: The Missing Center*, Historical Institute of Latvia with the United States Holocaust Memorial Museum, Riga and Washington (1996), p. 378.

11. Hayes, *Why? Explaining the Holocaust*, p. 181.

12. See Aivars Stranga in the English summary of *Holocaust in German-occupied Latvia: 1941–1945*, in *Proceedings of the Symposium of the Commission of the Historians of Latvia on the Holocaust Research in Latvia*, Volume 18, published Riga, 2008, p. 28.

13. Cited in Angrick and Klein, p. 270.

14. Cited in Ezergailis, p. 337. HSSPF is the acronym for Höherer SS-und Polizeiführer HSSPF.

15. Jeckeln was HSSPF in Russia South and Russia North in 1941 with overall command of the *Einsatzgruppen*. He was captured near Berlin by the Red Army in May 1945, tried by a Soviet military tribunal and hanged on the site of the Riga ghetto on 3 February 1946.

16. The Babyn Yar massacre took place on 29–30 September 1941.

17. Max Michelson, *City of Life, City of Death: Memories of Riga*, University Press of Colorado, 2004, p. 4. Max was not related to Frida Michelson, née Frida Frid.

18. Frida Michelson, p. 31.

19. Bernhard Press, *The Murder of the Jews in Latvia, 1941–1945*, Northwestern University Press, Evanston, 2000, pp. ix–x.

20. Max Michelson, p. 86.

21. The Arājs Kommando was the name commonly given to the Latvian Auxiliary Security Police, later the Latvian Security Division of Security Police and Security Service. Arājs was rewarded with the rank of SS Sturmbannführer (Major). He was detained as a POW by the British in 1945, and on his release in 1949 assumed a new identity. He was rearrested in Frankfurt in 1975, convicted in Hamburg in 1979 and died in prison in 1988.

22. Acquired and translated in 1946 by the Office of the United States Chief of Counsel for the Prosecution of Axis Criminality and cited at the Nuremberg trials.

23. Pērkonkrusts was a fascist, anti-Semitic movement founded in 1933. As an ultra-nationalist organisation, it was in fact anti-German, not least because of the dominance of Latvia by the Baltic Germans for some 700

years. However, it adopted the swastika as its symbol and members were prominently involved in the persecution of the Jews from the moment of the Nazi occupation.

24. Frida Michelson, p. 49.

25. See Grigorijs Smirins in the English summary of *Jews of Riga in the Period of the Nazi Occupation (1941–1944)* in *Proceedings of the Symposium of the Commission of the Historians of Latvia*, p. 117.

26. Quoted in Richards Plavnieks, *Nazi Collaborators on Trial during the Cold War: Viktors Arājs and the Latvian Auxiliary Security Police*, Palgrave Macmillan, Switzerland, 2018, p. 30. Tevija means 'Fatherland', Aizsargi was an ultra-nationalist paramilitary organisation founded in 1919, and 19 Valdemars Street (or Valderama Iela) – the former home of a Jewish banker – was the Arājs Kommando's headquarters until early 1942.

27. Frida Michelson, p. 61. It is likely that she has substituted Pērkonkrusts for the Arājs Kommando, which no doubt would have included several of its members.

28. Max Michelson, p. 87.

29. Press, p. 45.

30. Cited in Andrew Ezergailis, pp. 90–1.

31. Frida Michelson, p. 37.

32. See, for example, David Silberman's account of *Jan Lipke: An Unusual Man*, in Gertrude Schneider (ed.), *Muted Voices: Jewish Survivors of Latvia Remember*, Philosophical Library, New York, 1987, pp. 87–111.

33. Press, pp. 50–2.

34. Plavnieks, pp. 42–3.

35. Another 25,000 were destined for Minsk.

36. Cited in Ingo Haar and Michael Fahlbusch (eds), *German Scholars and Ethnic Cleansing, 1919–1945*, Berghahn, 2005, p. 67. Leibbrandt was head of the Political Department at the Ostministerium, which he represented at the Wannsee Conference. He was detained between 1945 and 1949 but the charges against him were dismissed in 1950.

37. Frida Michelson, pp. 77–8.

38. See Richard L. Rubenstein and John K. Roth, *Approaches to Auschwitz*, Westminster John Knox Press, Louisville and London, p. 179.

39. Alfred Gottwaldt and Diana Schulle, *Die 'Judendeportationen' aus dem Deutschen Reich 1941–1945*, Marixverlag, 2005, p. 113.

40. See Ezergailis, *The Holocaust in Latvia 1941–1944: The Missing Center*, p. 254.

41. Frida Michelson, p. 88.

42. The opening of the poem *Rumbula* by Ojārs Vācietis in a translation by Charles Fishman and Inta Ezergailis, in *Methodical Materials, Holocaust Commemoration in the Baltic,* journal of the Centre for Judaic Studies at the University of Latvia, Riga, 2016, p. 27.

43. The report, dated 31 December 1941, quoted by Mistele, p. 85. Units under Dietrich's command were responsible for a series of massacres in Libau, though, when he was hanged for war crimes in 1948, it was for the murder of Allied pilots who had bailed out of a disabled aircraft.

44. Andrew Ezergailis in David S. Wyman and Charles H. Rosenzveig (eds), *The World Reacts to the Holocaust,* Johns Hopkins University Press, 1996, p. 367, estimates that of the 94,000 Jews living in Latvia at the time of its 1935 census, probably no more than 1,500 were alive at the end of the war, of whom 'perhaps two hundred Latvian Jews survived by hiding with gentiles'. According to his analysis, 5,000 were deported to Siberia in June 1941 shortly before the Soviets retreated, a further 5,000 emigrated and around 18,000 fled the German advance into the Russian interior. Of the 66,000 trapped in Latvia when the Nazis invaded, around 59,000 were murdered within the first six months of the occupation. A further 5,000 were forced into slave labour and subsequently shipped to Poland and Germany in 1944 and many died at the Stutthof camp or on the death marches of the winter of 1944–5.

45. Quoted in Angrick and Klein, p. 163. Schröder was sentenced after the war to two years nine months' imprisonment and died in 1973.

46. See Didzis Bērziņš and Paula Oppermann, *The Rumbula Memorial: History and Present,* in Methodical Materials, 'Holocaust Commemoration in the Baltics', pp. 22–3, citing Alexander Bergman, *Aufzeichnungen eines Untermenschen. Ein Bericht über das Ghetto in Riga und die Konzentrationslager in Deutschland,* Bremen 2009, p. 48.

47. See Bērziņš and Oppermann, p. 26.

48. Quoted in translation in Ezergailis, *The Holocaust in Latvia 1941–1944: The Missing Center,* p. 380.

49. A memorial to Kaiserwald was erected in 2005.

50. Quoted in Bērziņš and Oppermann, p. 30.

51. 'UNESCO Holocaust exhibit nixed after Latvian protests', *The Times of Israel,* 22 January 2015, https://www.timesofisrael.com/unesco-holocaust-exhibit-nixed-after-latvian-protests/.

52. The Symposium's papers were accessible in 2018 at https://www.president.lv/en/activities/commissions-and-councils/commission-of-historians. The Symposium convened regularly between 2003 and 2011.

53. Aivars Stranga, in the English summary of *Holocaust in German-occupied Latvia: 1941–1945*, in *Proceedings of the Symposium of the Commission of the Historians of Latvia*, Volume 23, published Riga, 2008, p. 29.

54. Stranga, in the English summary of *Problems in the Holocaust Research*, in *Proceedings of the Symposium of the Commission of the Historians of Latvia*, Volume 11, published Riga, 2004, p. 31.

55. In fact, according to *The Latvian Holocaust* on the Holocaust Revealed website, none of the commissars of the Latvian Soviet Republic and only one of the thirty-five members of the Central Committee of the Communist Party of Latvia, elected in December 1940, were Jewish. Moreover, Jews, regarded by the Bolsheviks as bourgeois capitalists, were disproportionately represented among the Latvians exiled to Siberia as the Soviets prepared to abandon Latvia.

56. Plavnieks, p. 49.

57. Ibid., p. 52.

58. Salitter's report of 26 December concerns the transport of 11–17 December. A translation is included as an appendix in Gertrude Schneider's *Journey into Terror: Story of the Riga Ghetto*, Praeger, Westport, Connecticut, London, 2001, p. 152.

59. Article of 9 July 1941, quoted in Ezergailis, *The Holocaust in Latvia 1941–1944: The Missing Center*, p. 87.

60. 'The Jews: the Source of Our Destruction', 11 July 1941, as summarised by Gertrude Schneider, *Journey into Terror*, p. 2.

61. Andrew Ezergailis, *Knowledge of the Holocaust in 1941*, in *Proceedings of the Symposium of the Commission of the Historians of Latvia*, Volume 18, published Riga, 2006, p. 39.

62. Andrew Ezergailis, *Six Versions of the Holocaust in Latvia*, in *Proceedings of the Symposium of the Commission of the Historians of Latvia*, Volume 18, published Riga, 2006, p. 69.

63. Ibid., pp. 75–6.

64. Ibid., pp. 68–9.

65. In *The Holocaust in Latvia 1941–1944: The Missing Center*, p. 188, Andrew Ezergailis estimates that, in all, the Arājs Kommando murdered at least 26,000 Latvian Jews and perhaps the same number again when it was deployed in Belarus and elsewhere. According to his analysis, it killed 5,000 Latvian Jews in Biķernieki Forest between July and September 1941, 8,000 German and other Jews in Biķernieki between January and March 1942, 9,000 Jews from Latvian provincial towns and villages between July and December 1941, and, in addition, 2,000 Latvian communists and 2,000 Gypsies and people with mental disabilities.

15 The End Game

1. Gottwaldt and Schulle, *Die 'Judendeportationen' aus dem Deutschen Reich 1941–1945*, p. 114.
2. Known in Latvian as Jumpramuize.
3. Extract from a video interview with the University of Southern California Shoah Foundation, 2015, available on the Yad Vashem website at https://deportation.yadvashem.org/index.html?language=en&itemId=9437978&ind=-1.
4. Trudy Ullman Schloss, 'A Farm Called Jungfernhof', in *The Unfinished Road: Jewish Survivors of Latvia Look Back*, ed. Gertrude Schneider, Praeger, New York, 1991, pp. 58–9. By 9 December, four transports had arrived from Nuremberg, Stuttgart, Vienna and Hamburg. According to Gottwaldt and Schulle, p. 114, the total of 3,984 deportees included 136 children under 10 years of age and 766 over-60s.
5. Fanny Englard (née Dominitz) survived Jungfernhof, the Riga ghetto, Kaiserwald, Stutthof and the death marches and emigrated to Palestine in May 1947. This extract from her unpublished memoir courtesy of Philip Kuhn.
6. Erich Wassermann's testimony is held in the archives of Yad Vashem, https://documents.yadvashem.org/index.html?language=en&search=global&strSearch=8741416&GridItemId=8741416.
7. Susanne Rieger and Gerhard Jochem, *A Journey to Death: The Deportation of November 1941 from Nuremberg to Riga-Jungfernhof* (trans. Anne E. Herrmann), Rijo Research, p. 11.
8. Wassermann testimony.
9. Cited in Wilhelm Mosel, *Hamburg Deportation to Riga*, Deutshe-jüdische Gesellschaft, Hamburg, 2008.
10. Josef Katz, *One Who Came Back: The Diary of a Jewish Survivor* (trans. Hilda Reach), Herzl Press, New York 1973, p. 29. Joseph Carlebach, Chief Rabbi of Hamburg and Altona, was murdered in the Dünamünde Aktion of 26 March 1941.
11. Quoted by Bernhard Press from G. Hausner, *Die Vernichtung der Jude* (The Extermination of the Jews), Kindler Verlag, Munich, 1979, p. 88.
12. Transcript of an interview with Gertrude Schneider in the Claude Lanzmann Shoah Collection in the Steven Spielberg Film and Video Archive at the US Holocaust Memorial Museum, pp. 19–20.
13. Gertrude Schneider interview, pp. 23–4.
14. According the testimony of Hans Werner Loszynski at Seck's trial, cited by Schneider in *Journey into Terror*, p. 11.

15. Rudolph Lange was at that time head of the Gestapo department within *Einsatzgruppe A*. In December 1941, he became commander of *Einsatzkommando 2* and was promoted to the rank of SS Colonel. He committed suicide in 1945 to avoid capture by the Red Army.

16. Gerhard Maywald went on to supervise the construction of the Salaspils camp and was involved in the Dünamünde Aktion. He was convicted in Hamburg in 1977 and sentenced to four years' imprisonment for complicity in the murder of 320 Jews at Jungfernhof. The judge explained his leniency on the grounds that Maywald was not a Jew-hater and had suffered in the course of a lengthy investigation.

17. Schneider, *Journey into Terror*, p. 24.

18. Quoted by Mistele, p. 85.

19. Mistele, p. 86.

20. Schneider, *Journey into Terror*, pp. 34–5.

21. Press, p. 136.

22. The pits were probably dug by Jews from the ghetto who made up the Krause 1 Kommando. They were told that they were digging fortifications but were subsequently segregated from the ghetto and barracked in a building close to the Centralka Prison. Their own life expectancy was limited.

23. Schneider, *Journey into Terror*, p. 39.

24. Quoted in Mistele, p. 86.

25. Ezergailis, *The Holocaust in Latvia 1941–1944: The Missing Center*, pp. 190–1.

26. Witness statement cited in Angrick and Klein, p. 332.

27. Ibid., p. 220.

28. Isaak Kleiman, 'And the Lord Spoke on My Behalf', in Schneider, *The Unfinished Road: Jewish Survivors of Latvia Look Back*, pp. 103–4. These Kommandos were work details, not to be confused with military or paramilitary formations.

29. Cited in Mosel.

30. Weiss, pp. 72–3.

31. Ibid., p. 73.

32. Ibid., p. 75.

33. Some put the figure as high as 47,000.

34. The Hebrew for pebble is *tz'ror*, which also means 'bond'.

16 Now We Are Free

1. Displayed in 'Von der Weißen Taube zum Bahnhof: Der letzte Weg der Bamberger Juden' ('From the White Dove to the Station: The Final Path of Bamberg's Jews'), the material that accompanied a guided walk organised by Bamberger Bündnis gegen Rechtsextremismus (Bamberg Against Fascism) on 15 November 2009.
2. Though scholars differ, Bamberger Bündnis estimates that at least 223 Jews were deported from Bamberg in five transports: 27 November 1941, 119 people to Riga; 24 March 1942, 22 to Lublin; 25 April 1942, 13 to Lublin; 9 September 1942, 68 to Theresienstadt; 23 September 1942, 2 to Theresienstadt. Ekkehard Hübschmann, in the *Book of Remembrance*, p. 544, lists seven, adding those of 18 June 1943 to Theresienstadt and Auschwitz and of 17 January 1944 to Theresienstadt.
3. Mistele, p. 98.
4. I am indebted to Ekkehard Hübschmann and his research colleague Christian Salomon Lehmann for providing me with a copy of this contract with the Reichsvereinigung der Juden in Deutschland, the Reich Association of Jews in Germany, essentially a Gestapo-run body.
5. Mistele, pp. 101–2.
6. Known to the Germans as Litzmannstadt.
7. Rohde was hanged in October 1946 for his part in the execution by lethal injection of four British women SOE agents at Natzweiler concentration camp.

17 Searching for Sally

1. Letter of 8 October 1945.
2. When Thesi's Gentile husband Herbert refused to divorce her, he was sent to a labour camp. Their daughter Ute, left behind in Zwickau when they were arrested, also survived. She and her family live in Dresden.
3. My translation.
4. Jacob Oppenheimer was 67.
5. This would have been Salaspils.
6. Fanny Kohl, Adelheid Stauss, Franziska Steinberger and Sara Wolf all perished at Dünamünde. Jacob Strauss had died in December 1941. Seven members of the Wannbacher family died in the Holocaust, six in Riga.
7. Moses and Else de Jong from Ahaus were deported from Bielefeld on 13 December and perished in Riga.

8. Leopold's health deteriorated in Salaspils. He was transported to Auschwitz on 2 November and died in the gas chambers on 30 November 1943, according to *Die Hölle von Riga* (*The Hell of Riga*) on the website Gelsenzenrum. Dr Leo Steinberger died at Auschwitz on the same day. Alfred Wolf died at Stutthof in October 1944. The air raid took place on 22 October 1944. Max was 21.

9. These were telephone cables used for military communications. The factory in Riga was relocated to Thorn in East Prussia. Half the workforce was transported there in cattle trucks, the rest shipped to Stutthof. In 1965, following litigation, each of the few survivors received $500 in compensation for their forced labour.

10. Friedel lived there until her death in 1986 at the age of 86. Hanneliese and her husband Felix Wandersmann emigrated to Israel in the 1970s but, after Felix's death, she returned to Bayreuth to be close to their three daughters. I had hoped to meet her, perhaps the last survivor of Da 32. Sadly she was in poor health when I visited Bayreuth in April 2019.

11. Max and Lily Pretzfelder, Anna Fischel, Martha Morgenroth, Martin Morgenroth's widow, Lilly Heymann, Frieda and Ida Rehbock, Friedrich, Alice and Rositta Silbermann, Paul Klestadt, Benno and Luise Kohn, Ignaz and Rosa Kohn and Esther Kohn (unrelated), were all from Bamberg.

12. Daughter of Benno and Luise Kohn who perished in Riga.

13. Helene and Philip Kuhn, two Fleischmann couples from Bamberg, Ludwig and Irma, and Oskar and Paula, Julius and Regina Schönthal, Recha and Max Fein, Gustav and Ida Sacki, Heinrich and Martha Hahn, all from Bamberg. I assume the reference to Brandes is to Bertha.

14. Julius and Eleonora and their daughter Ruth Schapiro were deported from Bamberg to Riga where Eleonora and Ruth perished. Julius survived Riga, Kaiserwald and Stutthof before being transferred to Buchenwald. It is thought that he died of a heart attack in Tröglitz on 26 January 1945. A second daughter, Judith, had emigrated to Palestine in September 1938.

15. Alice's husband Dr Oskar Meyer, a neurologist and psychiatrist, had died in 1941.

16. As part of the agreement they reached, some 7,000 women were also freed from Ravensbrück camp.

17. My translation.

18. In fact the transport arrived on 2 December.

19. Hugo Rosenthal died on 31 January 1942.

20. Memorandum quoted in Angrick and Klein, p. 199.
21. See Wolfgang Scheffler, *The Fate of the German, Austrian and Czechoslovakian Jews Deported to the Baltic States 1941–1945: A Historical Overview*, footnote 61, p. 56 in *The Book of Remembrance*. Sally, 59, and Hugo, 60, were significantly older than the upper age-limit.
22. Katz, p. 31.
23. See Angrick and Klein, p. 249.
24. The commandant was SS *Oberscharführer*, Company Sergeant Major, Richard Nickel, whose deputy, Oberscharführer Otto Teckemeier, was known as 'Stuka' for his sudden and brutal assaults on prisoners. Nickel disappeared after the war. Teckemeier was sentenced to six years' imprisonment for his crimes.
25. Katz, p. 46.
26. Gerda Gottschalk, *Der letzte Weg*, Südverlag, 1991, p. 38, quoted in Angrick and Klein, p. 254.
27. Stahlecker's ambitions for Salaspils were not fulfilled. Only fifteen prison blocks were actually constructed and the camp never served as the key holding centre for Jews, becoming instead a 'labour correction camp' for political prisoners, deserters and 'work-shy' Latvians.
28. Angrick and Klein put the estimate at 12,000, p. 255, and dismiss Soviet claims that as many as 53,000 perished in the camp.
29. Lilly Pancis, 'Deportation to the East', in Gertrude Schneider (ed.), *Muted Voices: Jewish Survivors of Latvia Remember*, p. 42.
30. Schneider, *Journey into Terror*, p. 62.
31. Frida Michelson, p. 65.
32. Angrick and Klein, p. 318. The murderous police corporal Otto Tuchel was sentenced to life imprisonment in 1973 for his crimes at Rumbula and in the ghetto. Remarkably, according to Angrick and Klein, p. 442, he was 'the only member of all the Order Police units and offices of HSSPF Ostland who had to atone for his crimes'.
33. Roschmann, an SS Obersturmführer (first lieutenant) had been involved in the Dünamünde selections and, subsequently, with the operations of Sonderkommando 1005, which oversaw the elimination of evidence of the mass killings in Latvia. In 1948, with the help of Bishop Alois Hudal and the Collegio Teutonico in Rome, he escaped to Argentina where he was tracked down by Simon Wiesenthal. He was characterised in Frederick Forsyth's novel *The Odessa File* and the subsequent film as the 'Butcher of Riga'. Facing attempts to extradite him to Germany, he fled to Paraguay where he died of heart failure in 1977.

34. Other accounts suggest that one of the security forces was wounded but none killed.

35. Schneider, *Journey into Terror*, p. 70.

36. Another 2,000 were 'barracked' outside the ghetto at their places of work and 1,000 were employed at workshops within the ghetto.

37. Cited in the Epilogue, written in 1979, to *Journey into Terror*, pp. 99–100.

38. Max Kaufmann (trans. Lairndota Mazzariuns), *Churbn Lettland: The Destruction of the Jews of Latvia*, Hartung-Gorre, Konstanz, 2010.

39. Sauer served in a series of concentration camps between 1935 and 1944. He died of wounds in Falkensee near Berlin on 3 May 1945.

40. See Scheffler, *The Fate of the German, Austrian and Czechoslovakian Jews Deported to the Baltic States 1941–1945*, p. 75.

41. See Franziska Jahn, *Konzentrationslager Riga-Kaiserwald*, in *Der Ort des Terrors, Geschichte der nationalsozialistischen Konzentrationslager*, Volume 8, Wolfgang Benz and Barbara Distel (eds), CH Beck oHG, Munich, 2008, pp. 15–88.

42. The distance is around five miles.

43. Press, pp. 142–3.

44. Katz, p. 140.

45. Foreman of a work detail employed outside the camp. Bernhard Press identifies Mr X as Xaver Apel of the Berlin *Saß* gang. He was serving a life sentence for a double murder. He was himself killed at Stutthof shortly before it was liberated by the Red Army. See *The Murder of the Jews in Latvia*, p. 144.

46. Katz, pp. 143–4.

47. The non-Jewish prisoners were known as 'zebras' because of the distinctive black and white stripes of their uniforms.

48. Kaufmann, pp. 176–81.

49. Pancis, p. 47.

50. Blobel played a leading role in the Babyn Yar massacre and in the development of the gas chambers. He was hanged at Landsberg Prison on 7 June 1951.

51. The literal meaning of 'Stützpunkt' is 'base'. It was a Sonderkommando or 'special detail'.

52. Angrick and Klein, p. 407.

53. Krebsbach was convicted for the crimes he had committed previously at Sachsenhausen and executed on 27 May 1947. Wisner was sentenced in 1985 to five years on charges of accessory to murder.

54. Andrew Ezergailis estimates that in 1944 there were at least 12,000 Latvian and 'Reich' Jews still alive. Many were killed in the course of the year. Others were transported back to Poland and Germany, many to Stutthof. See Ezergailis, *The Holocaust in Latvia 1941–1944: The Missing Center*, p. 364. They were joined by others from Lithuania, Czechoslovakia, Hungary and Germany.
55. Schneider (ed.), *The Unfinished Road: Jewish Survivors of Latvia Look Back*, p. 3. Different sources suggest various dates for the transports to Stutthof. According to Angrick and Klein, p. 417, 14,395 prisoners arrived there from Riga and Liepāja between 8 August and 1 October 1944.
56. Schneider, *The Unfinished Road*, p. 3.
57. According to Andrew Sparke in *Stutthof: In Search of a Nazi Death Camp*, APS Publications, 2015, pp. 9–10, some 2,000 SS guards, including Norwegian volunteers and Ukrainian auxiliaries, served at Stutthof. At the time of its liquidation in January 1945, there were 1,056 staff and guards.
58. Ibid., p. 12.
59. Katz, p. 214.
60. Sparke, pp. 5–6.
61. Hoppe escaped from Fallingbostel internment camp in 1948 but was recaptured six years later and sentenced in 1957 to nine years in prison. He died in 1974.
62. Schneider, *The Unfinished Road*, p. 2.
63. Katz, p. 216.
64. Weiss, p. 114.
65. Ibid., p. 115.
66. Ibid., pp. 153–4.
67. Angrick and Klein, p. 426.
68. Recorded interview, 1990, US Holocaust Memorial Museum.
69. Katz, p. 245.
70. Weiss, p. 121.
71. Ibid., p. 120.
72. Ibid., p. 176.
73. Pancis, p. 53.
74. Sparke, p. 29.
75. File 5910/3/7.
76. Quoted in Angrick and Klein, pp. 279–80.
77. *Kūdra* is Latvian and *Torf* is German for peat. Predaine is some ten miles north-west of Riga. Smārde is around thirty-five miles west.

78. According to Angrick and Klein, p. 385, Kūdra had hoped to keep 700 Jews on throughout the winter and there were plans to employ the other 600 in sugar-beet processing. But on 27 September, after lengthy negotiations, SS Captain Wilhelm Schitli of the SS Economist Office vetoed these plans and ordered them back to Riga.

18 Rays of Lights

1. Paul Nickelsberg, *No Nostalgia for the Refugee* (unpublished), 1975.
2. In Greek mythology the Lethe flowed around the cave of Hypnos and through the Underworld where all those who drank from its waters experienced complete forgetfulness.
3. Letter of 18 October 1966. In a subsequent letter (2 July 1967), Lutz wrote wistfully that, looking at the pictures my father had sent, 'everything comes to life as it was yesterday … I didn't know any more how attached I still am to this place, and for a moment you forget all the misery.'
4. Letter to Franz Bauer of 18 January 1990 (my translation). Not all the school's Jewish pupils shared his nostalgia.
5. In a letter to Karin Mistele of 4 December 1991, my father recounts that they met again on his first post-war visit to Bamberg, though never again.
6. Letter of 13 January 1998 to Herbert Loebl.
7. Letter of 13 January 1998.
8. The Jewish-owned Wassermann Brothers Bank, founded in 1785 in Wallerstein, became, as A.E. Wassermann, one of Germany's largest private banks after it relocated to Bamberg in 1848.
9. Undated letter to Ilse (possibly Rosenthal) in which he responds to an article written by Horst Brand, editor of *Dissent*.

AFTERWORDS

1. *In Conversation with Günter Gaus*, broadcast by ZDF, 28 October 1964, H. Arendt, Interview, 'Zur Person' (1964, English subtitles), YouTube.

I The Shameful Secret

1. In *The Jews and Society*.
2. Quoted by the historian of the Conservative Party, Lord (Alistair) Lexden, in a letter to *The Times*, 30 September 2016.

3. Cited in Anthony Julius, p. 256.
4. George Orwell, 'Antisemitism in Britain', *Contemporary Jewish Record*, London, April 1945.
5. Cited in Julia Boyd, *Travellers in the Third Reich: The Rise of Fascism Through the Eyes of Everyday People*, Elliott & Thompson, London, 2017, pp. 81–2. Sir Horace was no Nazi sympathiser and warned the Foreign Office of Hitler's military and expansionist ambitions.
6. Quoted in Anthony Julius, p. 419.
7. The memorandum, 'Combating the apathetic outlook of "What have I got to lose even if Germany wins"', is held in the National Archives, INF 1/251.
8. On 17 December, Foreign Secretary Anthony Eden read to the House of Commons the Allies' joint declaration, which acknowledged that 'the German authorities … are now carrying into effect Hitler's oft repeated intention to exterminate the Jewish people in Europe'. *Hansard*, 17 December 1942, columns 2082–7.
9. Jean-Paul Sartre, *Anti-Semite and Jew* (trans. George J. Becker), Schocken Books, New York, 1995, p. 51. It was first published in 1946 in French.
10. Andreas Whittam Smith, 'Anti-Semitism in France: A prejudice that hardened in 1789 and which has come in waves ever since', *Independent*, 14 January 2015.
11. The Irgun was a right-wing Zionist paramilitary organisation violently opposed to British rule in Palestine and active between 1931 and 1948.
12. Report by The Jewish Telegraphic Agency of New York, 6 August 1947.
13. Twitter thread, 1 November 2019 by Dr James Vaughan, https://twitter.com/EquusontheBuses/status/1190244844087762944?s=20.
14. Diary entry of 16 May 1948, cited in Mayhew's autobiography, *Time To Explain*, Hutchinson, 1987, p. 120. Bevin was not unique among Labour leaders. In the year before his election to Parliament, Keir Hardie's *London Labour* newspaper of 19 December 1891 asserted that 'wherever there is trouble in Europe, wherever rumours of war circulate and men's minds are distraught with fear of change and calamity, you may be sure that a hook-nosed Rothschild is at his games somewhere near the region of disturbance'.
15. *The Jewish Chronicle* editorial of 12 July 1946. Half a century later, after the fall of Communism, the son admitted that his disappearance had been fabricated by his father.
16. Hayes, *Why? Explaining the Holocaust*, p. 301.

17. Angrick and Klein, pp. 435–6.
18. Ibid., p. 436.
19. Primo Levi (trans. Stuart Woolf), *The Truce*, Abacus, London, 1987, p. 202.
20. See, for example, *Down and Out in Paris and London*, published in 1933, and https://www.theguardian.com/books/2002/aug/13/biography.highereducation
21. Eric Hobsbawm, *Fractured Times: Culture and Society in the Twentieth Century*, Little, Brown, London, 2013, p. 78.
22. Orwell, *Anti-Semitism in Britain*.
23. Quoted in Anthony Julius, p. 574.
24. Dave Rich, *The Left's Jewish Problem: Jeremy Corbyn, Israel and Anti-Semitism*, Biteback Publishing, London, 2018, p. 105.
25. Peter Bradley, 'A Simple Test', Progress, 11 April 2018.
26. See https://twitter.com/TheMendozaWoman/status/1333021623738363904?s=20, last accessed 21 December 2021. The *Jewish Chronicle* reported on 30 November that the tweet had led to her suspension from the platform, though it quoted a Twitter spokesman as saying 'the account referenced was mistakenly suspended and has now been reinstated'. See https://www.thejc.com/news/uk/canary-editor-mendoza-suspended-from-twitter-after-white-supremacist-jlm-post-1.509193.
27. See https://www.bbc.co.uk/news/av/uk-politics-45300519.
28. Resignation letter of 18 February 2019, addressed to her Liverpool Wavertree constituents.
29. Andrew Anthony, 'Anger, denial and prejudice fester on the streets of Liverpool Wavertree', *Guardian*, 23 February 2019, https://www.theguardian.com/uk-news/2019/feb/23/liverpool-wavertree-labour-constituency-antisemitism-luciana-berger-derek-hatton.
30. https://antisemitism.org/anti-trump-protest-in-london-takes-no-issue-with-placard-claiming-they-all-work-for-rothschild/ 4 June 2019.
31. Reported, inter alia, by *Jewish News*, '"Jews are Christ killers" banner at anti-Israel protest', 22 May 2021.
32. Sartre remarked in the essay that 'if the Jew did not exist, the anti-Semite would invent him'.
33. Cited by John Naughton in 'Populism and the internet – a toxic mix shaping the age of conspiracy theories', *Guardian*, 25 November 2018.
34. QAnon is a principally internet-based US-originated umbrella term for a number of toxic and often anti-Semitic conspiracy theories, central to which is the claim that the world is in the grip of a clique of Satan-worshipping paedophiles.

35. First published in Russia in 1903 in instalments in the newspaper *Znamya* (The Banner).

36. CNN, 'Anti-Semitism in Europe Poll 2018', https://edition.cnn.com/interactive/2018/11/europe/antisemitism-poll-2018-intl/.

37. CCN also reported that 54 per cent of respondents said Israel 'has the right to exist as a Jewish state'. It called this a 'solid majority of Europeans'.

38. In an interview with the *New Statesman* in 1983, https://www.newstatesman.com/culture/books/2021/10/roald-dahls-anti-semitism-was-grotesque-i-should-know-i-saw-it-first-hand.

II Choices

1. Milton Mayer, *They Thought They Were Free*, University of Chicago Press, 2017, p. 44.

2. Ibid., p. 82.

3. Ibid., p. x.

4. Mayer disguises Marburg as 'Kronenberg'.

5. Ibid., pp. 101–2.

6. Florian Huber (trans. Imogen Taylor), *Promise Me You'll Shoot Yourself: The Downfall of Ordinary Germans in 1945*, Penguin Books, 2020, p. 159.

7. Niemöller at first welcomed the Nazis' rise to power but came to write the oft-quoted (and misquoted): 'First they came for the socialists, and I did not speak out – Because I was not a socialist … Then they came for me – and there was no one left to speak for me.'

8. Mayer, p. 168.

9. Julius Posener, *In Deutschland 1945 bis 1946*, Berlin, 2001, p. 25, cited in Florian Huber, p. 246.

10. Melita Maschmann, *Fazit: Kein Rechtfertigungsversuch*, Deutsche Verlags-Anstalt, 1963, p. 58, quoted in English in Florian Huber, p. 199.

11. Levi, p. 428.

12. Hayes, *Why? Explaining the Holocaust*, p. 95.

13. Mayer, pp. 75–6.

14. Hayes, *Why? Explaining the Holocaust*, p. 74.

15. Detlev Peukert, *Inside Nazi Germany: Conformity, Opposition and Racism in Everyday Life* (trans. Richard Deveson), Yale University Press, New Haven, 1987, p. 27.

16. Arendt, p. 289.

17. Quoted in Angrick and Klein, p. 447.
18. In her unfinished *The Life of the Mind*, Harcourt Brace Jovanovich, 1977–8.
19. An extract from Eichmann's memoir discovered in the Centre for Research on Nazi Crimes in Ludwigsburg and published by *Die Welt*, 13 August 1999. He wrote that, after the war, 'I found myself completely incapable of living as my own person and fell into a deep depression.'
20. Arendt, *Eichmann in Jerusalem*, p. 276.
21. Mayer, pp. ix–x.
22. See Tapani Harviainen, 'The Jews in Finland and World War II', in *NordiskJudaistik Scandinavian Jewish Studies*, Vol. 21, No. I–2, 2000, pp. 157–66.
23. Olga's first husband, Hans Zuntz, had died in 1927.
24. Quoted in Herbert Pundik, *In Denmark It Could Not Happen: The Flight of the Jews to Sweden in 1943*, Gefen Publishing House, Jerusalem, 1998, p. 142.
25. Best was sentenced to death by a Danish court in 1948 but his sentence was reduced to twelve years and he was released in 1951. In 1958 he was fined 70,000 marks by a Berlin de-Nazification court and, in March 1969, again detained. Though he was charged with further war crimes in February 1972, he was released as medically unfit for trial. He died on 23 June 1989.
26. Duckwitz subsequently became West Germany's Foreign Secretary under Willi Brandt and in 1971 was recognised by the Israeli Government as one of the Righteous Among Nations.
27. He served twice as Danish prime minister after the war.
28. Pundik, p. 167.
29. Viktor E. Frankl, *Man's Search for Meaning*, Rider, 2004, p. 94.
30. Frankl, p. 135.
31. Pundik, p. 170.
32. 'Enemies of the people: Fury over "out of touch" judges who have "declared war on democracy" …', https://www.dailymail.co.uk/news/article-3903436/Enemies-people-Fury-touch-judges-defied-17-4m-Brexit-voters-trigger-constitutional-crisis.html.

III The Last Word

1. Ruth Foster, survivor of the Riga ghetto and Stutthof, in a taped interview with the Imperial War Museum, 1999, https://www.iwm.org.uk/collections/item/object/80018238.
2. Philip Kuhn, *Phantoms in the Family History*, Part 1 in *Second Generation Voices*, London, May 1998, Number 8, p. 9.
3. Ibid., Part 2, September 1998, Number 9, p. 22.
4. Mendelsohn, p. 523.
5. Kuhn, Part 1, p. 11.
6. Peter Bradley, 'AntiSocial Britain and the challenge of citizenship', The Social Market Foundation, London, 2007, https://www.smf.co.uk/wp-content/uploads/2007/06/Publication-AntiSocial-Britain-and-the-challenge-of-citizenship.pdf.
7. Ibid., p. 4.
8. Ibid., p. 7.
9. Bernard Levin was not sanguine. He wrote in the *New Statesman* of 12 November 1965: 'If anyone doubts that it would have been possible to staff British concentration camps, he can have my postbag after my next outrage.' Cited in Newell, p. 96.
10. Primo Levi, *Postscript: The Author's Answers to His Readers' Questions*, published with *If This Is a Man* and *the Truce*, Abacus, London, 1987, p. 435.
11. Ibid., p. 423.

SOURCES

Academic and Commentary

Andrej Angrick and Peter Klein, *The Final Solution in Riga: Exploitation and Annihilation, 1941–1944*, Berghahn Books, New York (2009)

Hannah Arendt, *Eichmann in Jerusalem: A Report on the Banality of Evil*, Penguin Classics (2006)

David Baddiel, *Jews Don't Count*, TLS Books, London (2021)

David A. Bell, *Trapped by History: France and Its Jews, World Affairs*, Vol. 172, No. 1 (Summer 2009)

Didzis Bērziņš and Paula Oppermann, *The Rumbula Memorial: History and Present*, in Methodical Materials 'Holocaust Commemoration in the Baltics', Centre for Judaic Studies at the University of Latvia, Riga (2016)

Ortwin Beisbart, Rudolph Daniel and Antje Yael Deusel, *Jewish Bamberg: A Walking Tour Through the Town*, Weiss, Bamberg (2013)

Andrew Ezergailis, *The Holocaust in Latvia, 1941–1944: The Missing Center*, Historical Institute of Latvia with the United States Holocaust Memorial Museum, Riga and Washington (1996)

Ruth Gay, *The Jews of Germany: A Historical Portrait*, New Haven and London, Yale University Press (1992)

Tim Grady, *German Jewish Soldiers of the First World War*, Liverpool University Press (2011)

Peter Hayes, *Why? Explaining the Holocaust*, W.W. Norton & Co., New York (2017)

Florian Huber (trans. Imogen Taylor), *Promise Me You'll Shoot Yourself: The Downfall of Ordinary Germans in 1945*, Penguin Books (2020)

Anthony Julius, *Trials of the Diaspora: A History of Anti-Semitism in England*, Oxford University Press (2012)

Milton Mayer, *They Thought They Were Free*, University of Chicago Press (2017)

Karl H. Mistele, *The End of a Community: Jews in Bamberg 1930–1942* (trans. Jacob Feuchtwanger), Center for Jewish History and the Leo Baeck Institute, New York (1995)

George Orwell, 'Antisemitism in Britain', *Contemporary Jewish Record*, London, April 1945

Detlev Peukert, *Inside Nazi Germany: Conformity, Opposition and Racism in Everyday Life* (trans. Richard Deveson), Yale University Press, New Haven (1987)

Rachel Pistol, 'Enemy Alien and Refugee: Conflicting Identities in Great Britain during the Second World War', University of Sussex, *Journal of Contemporary History* 16, 2015

Richards Plavnieks, *Nazi Collaborators on Trial during the Cold War: Viktors Arājs and the Latvian Auxiliary Security Police*, Palgrave Macmillan, Cham, Switzerland (2018)

Daniel Renshaw, 'Prejudice and Paranoia: A Comparative Study of Antisemitism and Sinophobia in Turn of the century Britain', Central Archive, University of Reading (2016)

Dave Rich, *The Left's Jewish Problem: Jeremy Corbyn, Israel and Anti-Semitism*, Biteback Publishing, London (2018)

Nina Rowe, *The Jew, the Cathedral and the Medieval City: Synagoga and Ecclesia in the Thirteenth Century*, Cambridge University Press, Cambridge (2011)

John L. Rubinstein and John K. Roth, *Approaches to Auschwitz: The Holocaust and its Legacy*, Westminster John Knox Press, Louisville and London (2003)

Jean-Paul Sartre, *Anti-Semite and Jew* (trans. George J. Becker), Schocken Books, New York (1995)

Peter Schaapman, *The Rescue of the Danish Jews in the Latter Half of 1943: Myths and Facts*, Amsterdam, July 2012

SOURCES

Simon Schama, *The Story of the Jews: Finding the Words, 1000 BCE–1492 CE*, Vintage Books, London (2014)

Simon Schama, *The Story of the Jews: Belonging, 1492–1900*, Vintage Books, London (2018)

Wolfgang Scheffler and Diana Schulle, *Book of Remembrance: The German, Austrian and Czechoslovakian Jews Deported to the Baltic States (Buch der Erinnerung: die ins Baltikum deportierten deutschen, österreichischen und tschechoslowakischen Juden)*, K.G. Saur, Munich (2003)

Rachel Schulkins, 'Burke, His Liberal Rivals and the Jewish Question', *Otherness: Essays and Studies* 3.2 (June 2013)

Maxine Schur, *Voltaire and the Jews*, Continuing Studies, Stanford University (2009)

Anthony Sparke, *Stutthof: In Search of a Nazi Death Camp*, APS Publications, Stourbridge (2015)

Alfred Wiener, *The Fatherland and the Jews*, Granta Books, London (2021)

David S. Wyman and Charles H. Rosenzveig (eds), *The World Reacts to the Holocaust*, Johns Hopkins University Press, Baltimore and London (1996)

Proceedings of the Symposium of the Commission of the Historians of Latvia on the Holocaust Research in Latvia, volumes 12–27, published Riga, 2004–11.

Other

Glückel von Hameln, trans. Beth-Zion Abrahams, *The Life of Glückel von Hameln*, East & West Library, London (1962)

Theodor Herzl, *The Jewish State*, Penguin Books, London (2010)

Eyewitness accounts

Julia Boyd, *Travellers in the Third Reich: The Rise of Fascism Through the Eyes of Everyday People*, Elliott & Thompson, London (2017)

Viktor E. Frankl, *Man's Search for Meaning*, Rider, London (2004)

Johanna Harris-Brandes, *Megillat Johanna* (ed. Liora Bernstein, trans. Eva M. Edge), Kindle Edition (2011)

Stanislav Jaskolski, *Come With Me and Visit Hell* (trans. Jim Przedzienkowski), ebook (2011)

Josef Katz, *One Who Came Back: The Diary of a Jewish Survivor* (trans. Hilda Reach), Herzl Press, New York (1973)

Max Kaufmann, *Churbn Lettland: The Destruction of the Jews of Latvia* (trans. Laimdota Mazzarins), Hartung-Gorre, Konstanz (2010)

Eric Koch, *Deemed Suspect: A Wartime Blunder*, Methuen, Toronto (1980)

Philip Kuhn, *No Stone Unturned: Letters from Bamberg 1938–1941*, Itinerant Publications, Buckfastleigh (2005)

Philip Kuhn, *Phantoms in the Family History*, Second Generation Voices, London: Part 1, May 1998, Number 8, pp. 9–13/Part 2, September 1998, Number 9, pp. 19–22

Primo Levi (trans. Stuart Woolf), *If This Is a Man* and *The Truce*, Abacus, London (1987)

Werner M. Loval, *We Were Europeans: A Personal History of a Turbulent Century*, Gefen Publishing House, Jerusalem (2010)

Frida Michelson, *I Survived Rumbuli* (trans. Wolf Goodman), Holocaust Library, New York (1979)

Max Michelson, *City of Life and Death: Memories of Riga*, University Press of Colorado, Boulder (2001)

Bernhard Press, *The Murder of the Jews in Latvia, 1941–1945*, Northwestern University Press, Evanston (2000)

Herbert Pundik, *In Denmark It Could Not Happen: The Flight of the Jews to Sweden in 1943*, Gefen Publishing House, Jerusalem (1998)

Tilly Rehbock Wiesenfelder Auerbach, *Tilly: An Oral History* (as interviewed by Ellen Robinson Epstein), L. Brenwasser, L. Wiesenfelder and F. Queller, Bamberg and Scarsdale (1995)

Nathan Shapow (with Bob Harris), *The Boxer's Story: Fighting for My Life in the Nazi Death Camps*, Biteback Publishing, London (2019)

Gertrude Schneider, *Journey into Terror: Story of the Riga Ghetto*, Praeger, New York (2001)

Gertrude Schneider, *Muted Voices: Jewish Survivors of Latvia Remember*, Philosophical Library (1987)

Gertrude Schneider (ed.), *The Unfinished Road: Jewish Survivors of Latvia Look Back*, Praeger, New York (1991)

Reska Weiss, *Journey Through Hell: A Woman's Account of Her Experiences at the Hands of the Nazis*, Vallentine, Mitchell & Co., London (1961)

Eli Wiesel, *Night* (trans. Marion Wiesel), Penguin Books, London (2008)

We Remember our Relatives and Friends, Holocaust Memorial Foundation of Illinois (1991), videocassette (55 mins)

Family quests

Jeremy Dronfield, *The Boy Who Followed His Father Into Auschwitz*, Penguin Random House UK, London (2019)

Bart van Es, *The Cut Out Girl*, Penguin Random House UK, London (2018)

Esther Safran Foer, *I Want You to Know We're Still Here: My Family, the Holocaust and My Search for Truth*, HarperCollins, London (2021)

Hadley Freeman, *House of Glass: The Story and Secrets of a Twentieth-Century Jewish Family*, 4th Estate, London (2020)

Daniel Mendelsohn, *The Lost: A Search for Six of Six Million*, William Collins, London (2013)

Ariana Neumann, *When Time Stopped: A Memoir of My Father's War and What Remains*, Scribner, London (2020)

Philippe Sands, *East West Street*, Weidenfeld & Nicolson, London (2017)

Géraldine Schwarz, *Those Who Forget: One Family's Story, A Memoir, a History, a Warning*, Pushkin Press, London (2021).

German language

Antje Yael Deusel, Ortwin Beisbart und Franz Fichtl, *Gedenkbuch der jüdischen Bürger Bambergs* (Memorial Book for Jewish Citizens of Bamberg), Verein zur Förderung der jüdischen Geschichte und Kultur Bambergs e. V. (2010)

Adolf Eckstein, *Geschichte der Juden im ehemaligen Fürstbistum Bamberg*, Handels-Druckerei, Bamberg (1898)

Adolf Eckstein, *Die Israel. Kultusgemeinde Bamberg von 1803–1853. Festschrift zur Einweihung der neuen Synagoge in Bamberg*, Handels-Druckerei, Bamberg (1910)

Heide Friedrich-Brettinger, *Die Juden in Bamberg*, Hartdruck, Würzburg (1962)

Franz Fichtl, Stephan Link, Herbert May and Sylvia Schaible, *»Bambergs Wirtschaftjudenfrei«. Die Verdrängung der jüdischen Geschäftsleute in den Jahren 1933 bis 1939*, Collibri, Bamberg (1998)

Alfred Gottwaldt and Diana Schulle, *Die »Judendeportationen« aus dem Deutschen Reich 1941–1945 Eine kommentierte Chronologie.* Marixverlag, Wiesbaden (2005)

Ekkehard Hübschmann, 'Die Deportation aus Nuremberg am 29. November 1941', in Scheffler, Wolfgang and Diana Schulle, *Buch der Erinnerung. Die ins Baltikum deportierten deutschen, österreichischen und tschechoslowakischen Juden*, Munich, 2003, pp. 533–67

Ekkehard Hübschmann, *Die Deportationen von Juden aus Franken nach Riga*, In: Frankenland 56, 2004, H.5, pp. 344–69

Ekkehard Hübschmann, *Physische und behördliche Gewalt. Die „Reichskristallnacht' und die Verfolgung der Juden in Bayreuth*, Bumerang, Bayreuth (2000)

Franziska Jahn, *Konzentrationslager Riga-Kaiserwald* in *Der Ort des Terrors, Geschichte der nationalsozialistischen Konzentrationslager*, Volume 8, Wolfgang Benz and Barbara Distel (eds), CH Beck oHG, Munich (2008)

Marlies Lehmann-Brune, *Der Koffer des Karl Zuntz: Fünf Jahrhunderte Einer Jüdischen Familie*, Droste, Düsseldorf (1997)

Albrecht Liess, *Wege in die Vernichtung: Die Deportationen der Juden aus Mainfranken 1941–1943*, Generaldirektion der staatlichen Archive Bayerns (2003)

Herbert Loebl, *Juden in Bamberg. Die Jahrzehnte vor dem Holocaust*, Fränkischer Tag, Bamberg (2000)

Herbert Schultheis, *Buch der Erinnerung; Die ins Baltikum deportierten deutschen, österreichischen und tschechoslowakischen Juden*, K.G. Saur, Munich (2003)

Websites

Arolsen Archives (International Tracing Service) – https://arolsen-archives.org/en/search-explore/search-online-archive/

Memorial Book of the German Federal Archives (Gedenkbuch of the Bundesarchiv) – https://www.bundesarchiv.de/gedenkbuch/directory

Centre for Jewish History – http://www.cjh.org

Leo Baeck Institute, London – http://www.leobaeck.co.uk/

Leo Baeck Institute, New York – https://www.lbi.org

US Holocaust Memorial Museum – https://www.ushmm.org

Wiener Library – http://wienerlibrary.co.uk

Yad Vashem – https://www.yadvashem.org

INDEX

ACKNOWLEDGEMENTS

My wife, Annie, for her forbearance in the long gestation of this work.

Elise Bath and Christine Schmidt of the Wiener Library for their early encouragement and guidance.

Christine Bartholomäus of the Bayreuth City Archive for her generous and fruitful search for Herzstein family documents.

Liora Bernstein, granddaughter of Johanna Harris-Brandes, for allowing me to quote from *Megillat Johanna*, which she edited.

My sister Anne Bradley and friends Leonie Bennett, Christine Jenkins, John Reading and Jayne Shor for their constructive criticism of drafts of my manuscript at various stages.

Rita Bogdanova and Gunta Minde of the Latvian State Archives for identifying and translating documents relating to Sally Brandes.

Christiane Clegg for the translation of my grandparents' letters to my father on which my versions are based.

Stefanie Dellemann of the Buchenwald Memorial Archives who provided the prisoner records of my father and Paul Nickelsberg and information about Peter Forster's and Emil Bargatzky's ill-fated escape.

Alfred Eckert for his generosity in sharing his extensive knowledge of the deportees of Sonderzug Da 32.

Franz Fichtl for sharing his knowledge of Bamberg's Jewish community and its history, and for guiding me around Bamberg's Jewish landmarks.

Elaine Gentile for generously allowing me to quote from her father Paul Nickelsberg's memoirs.

Irene Gill for her introduction to *Der Koffer des Karl Zuntz*.

Colin Holmes, Emeritus Professor of History at the University of Sheffield, for his expert insights and advice.

Ekkehard Hübschmann for his patience and resourcefulness in sharing his knowledge of the Jewish community of Upper Franconia, and the Herzsteins in particular, and for guiding me around Bayreuth.

My cousin Walter Koring for his account of his and his mother's wartime experiences.

Philip Kuhn, whose father was also a refugee from Bamberg and whose grandparents perished in Latvia, for sharing his thoughts and sources.

Ilya Lenskis of the Jews in Latvia Museum for his invaluable knowledge, help and guidance in Riga.

My cousin David Newcombe for allowing me to quote from his father's unpublished Zunz family history.

Heinrich Nuhn, creator and curator of the Jewish Museum in Rotenburg an der Fulda and the Hassia Judaica website, for sharing his detailed knowledge of the Jewish community of Rotenburg, and in particular of the Brandes family, and for guiding me around the town – and to him and his wife Inge for their generous hospitality.

Paula Oppermann of the University of Glasgow for sharing her knowledge of the Holocaust in Latvia and for her encouraging review of an early draft of my manuscript.

Dr Rachel Pistol of King's College, London, for her invaluable advice on Britain's internment of 'enemy aliens' during the Second World War.

Andreas Ullman of the University of Bamberg for his invaluable help and advice.

Jonathan de Peyer, my editor, for his help, support and expertise throughout the publication process and all of the team at HarperNorth for their care and attention.

Doug Young, my agent, of PEW Literary for his knowledge, insights and calm, resourceful guidance.

20. Leaving Biķernieki.

**Harper
North**

BOOK CREDITS

HarperNorth would like to thank the following staff
and contributors for their involvement in making
this book a reality:

Laura Amos
Hannah Avery
Fionnuala Barrett
Claire Boal
Caroline Bovey
Charlotte Brown
Sarah Burke
Alan Cracknell
Jonathan de Peyer
Anna Derkacz
Tom Dunstan
Kate Elton
Mick Fawcett
Nick Fawcett
Simon Gerratt
Monica Green
Tara Hiatt
Graham Holmes

Ben Hurd
Patricia Hymans
Megan Jones
Jean-Marie Kelly
Oliver Malcolm
Alice Murphy-Pyle
Adam Murray
Genevieve Pegg
Agnes Rigou
Emma Rogers
James Ryan
Florence Shepherd
Zoe Shine
Eleanor Slater
Emma Sullivan
Katrina Troy
Phillipa Walker
Kelly Webster

For more unmissable reads,
sign up to the HarperNorth newsletter at
www.harpernorth.co.uk

or find us on Twitter at
@HarperNorthUK

**Harper
North**